A NEVER-ENDING CONFLICT

A NEVER-ENDING CONFLICT

A GUIDE TO ISRAELI MILITARY HISTORY

EDITED BY

MORDECHAI BAR-ON

Praeger Series on Jewish and Israeli Studies

Leslie Stein, Series Editor

Westport, Connecticut
London

Library of Congress Cataloging-in-Publication Data

A never-ending conflict : a guide to Israeli military history / edited by Mordechai Bar-On.
    p. cm.—(Praeger series on Jewish and Israeli studies, ISSN 1550-1159)
    Includes index.
    ISBN 0-275-98158-4 (alk. paper)
    1. Arab-Israeli conflict. I. Bar-On, Mordechai, 1928– II. Series.
    DS126.9.N48   2004
    956.9405—dc22   2004050865

British Library Cataloguing in Publication Data is available.

Library of Congress Catalog Card Number: 2004050865
ISBN: 0-275-98158-4
ISSN: 1550-1159

First published in 2004

Praeger Publishers, 88 Post Road West, Westport, CT 06881
An imprint of Greenwood Publishing Group, Inc.
www.praeger.com

Printed in the United States of America

The paper used in this book complies with the
Permanent Paper Standard issued by the National
Information Standards Organization (Z39.48-1984).

10 9 8 7 6 5 4 3 2 1

Contents

Foreword

Ever since the State of Israel saw the light of day in May 1948, it has faced constant attempts to eliminate it. In the process, it has had to engage in a series of conventional wars and ward off ongoing guerilla skirmishes and sheer acts of terrorism initiated by the Palestine Liberation Organization and its allies, such as Hamas. All this has exacted a heavy toll in terms of loss of life and economic and social dislocation.

This book serves to provide some perspective of the nature and impact of each of Israel's many military campaigns. Its editor, Mordechai Bar-On, is uniquely placed in being able to determine who among Israel's academic community is eminently suitable to analyze specific episodes in Israel's efforts to defend itself. Like Bar-On, all of the writers are essentially men of peace who bear no intrinsic malice against their country's adversaries. Their judgments are well balanced and insightful, affording the reader a rare opportunity to begin to understand the true complexities of the issues at hand. Furthermore, some of the obfuscations, deliberate and otherwise, relating to Israel's defense forces have effectively been dispelled.

Leslie Stein

General Editor, Praeger Series
on Jewish and Israeli Studies

Introduction

Mordechai Bar-On

For three generations, a violent conflict has ensued between the indigenous Arab population of Palestine and the Jews, who sought to establish an independent state in the land they considered their ancient home and the cradle of their unique culture. Sporadic cases of violence began soon after the first Zionist colonies were established in the 1880s.[1] Rudimentary national consciousness appeared among the Palestinian Arabs at the beginning of the twentieth century.[2] However, Palestinian resistance to the Zionist endeavor assumed organized and concerted political and military measures only during the 1920s. Resistance arose in response to the pledge Great Britain gave to the Zionist movement to help the Jews to establish a "National Homeland" in Palestine. That pledge, which was manifested in the November 2, 1917 Balfour Declaration, was adopted in 1922 by the League of Nations and included in the charter of the British mandate for Palestine.[3] The increased rate of Jewish immigration that soon followed alarmed the Arabs and galvanized them to start organizing their own national efforts to stem the Zionist tide.[4]

In 1920 and 1921 some nationally motivated Arab violence erupted in a few mixed communities and against a number of Zionist colonies but was quickly suppressed by the British garrison stationed in the country in the wake of the Great War. After eight years of quiet, larger-scale violence erupted for a few days in 1929 in which some 200 Jews were killed and some Jewish communities, notably in the town of Hebron, were totally destroyed. The fast-growing Jewish community of Palestine had in 1920 begun to establish its own paramilitary organization, the Haganah, which in 1929 was ill-equipped and poorly organized. It required some reinforcement of the British troops from neighboring countries to end this wave of violence. By 1936 the Palestinian leadership managed to launch a full-scale "revolt" that lasted for three years and included many frontal military confrontations between Jews and Arabs and exacted hundreds of casualties from both sides.

Ever since then, with a few brief intermissions, the Palestinian-Israeli conflict, with its political, economic, and cultural ramifications, assumed continuous and growing measures of military violence. In fact, there has barely been a year in which no cases of nationally motivated violent clashes have been recorded. The never-ending conflict has experienced ups and downs. During some years, one may have observed only low-level violence, yet during others, more intensive and occasionally highly dramatic conflagrations have taken place. Twelve such major eruptions may be cited, ranging from the first "Arab Revolt" in 1936–1939 to the current "al Aqsa Intifada" that began in the fall of 2000 and is still raging as these lines are being typed.

Hundreds of books and thousands of articles have surveyed these conflicts. Moreover, the events have been subjected to bitter historiographical and ideological controversies, not only between Israeli and Palestinian supporters but no less among Israeli historians and publicists. Unfortunately, not every lay reader has access to this wealth of information. In response, some writers attempted to meet the need for a concise narrative, the most recent of which are the summaries presented by Benny Morris and Avi Shlaim.[5] In this volume we adopt a different approach. Twelve Israeli historians, fully conversant with these conflicts,[6] were asked to revisit them and present to the reader some of their reflections and an updated analysis, based on their own specific points of view and historical assessments.

It should be recognized from the outset that while not necessarily representing Israeli apologists, all of the chapters have been written from an Israeli perspective. Most reflect, in one measure or another, recent trends of critical approaches to Israeli history or at least try to deal with these trends and confront them honestly. The editor consciously refrained from interfering with the specific points of view of the contributors and of the content and method they chose to present. It is hoped that this method will enable the reader to obtain a richer and more interesting insight to the intricate and convoluted ways in which the Arab-Israeli conflict has evolved. It must, however, be admitted that the inevitable brevity of these articles could not enable the contributors to present a detailed and comprehensive narrative, nor deal with all associated analytical problems. Nonetheless, the salient features of the conflicts are clearly outlined.

This introduction is meant to help the reader understand the overall flow of events and the way each chapter follows from the previous act and leads to the next one, so that a sense of the entire narrative and its continuity and fullness is provided. The manner in which I have chosen to relate the story and the choice of interpretation are my own, and do not necessarily reflect the views of any contributor.

As already mentioned, the 1936 Arab Revolt was the first large-scale and somewhat centrally organized Palestinian act of resistance to the Zionist project and to its British sponsors. The Jewish paramilitary organization, the Haganah, although still rudimentary, was sufficiently strong and organized to foil all attempts by the Palestinian Arabs to destroy Jewish colonies, deter Jewish immigration, and disrupt the further development of Jewish rural and urban settlements. Even so, as Yigal Eyal's narrative in Chapter One well reflects, the main task of suppressing the Arab Revolt fell to the British army and police. With the clouds of World War II looming on the horizon, the British Empire felt obliged to pacify the Arabs, who turned their revolt not only against the Zionists but also against the British government. By 1939 the first Arab Revolt was effectively crushed and its military and political instruments totally destroyed.

Although that conflict ended with the total failure of the Palestinians to disrupt the growth of the Zionist endeavor, it gained for the Palestinians some important political achievements. In order to court the Arabs in the Middle East, the British, in 1938, published a "White Paper" that amounted to a virtual abnegation of their pledge to facilitate the building of a Jewish "National Homeland" in Palestine. Immigration after a five-year period was to become contingent on Arab consent and the acquisition of additional land by Jews was to be drastically curtailed.

The following six years (1939–1945) witnessed an almost total arrest of all intercommunal violence in Palestine. The massive concentration of British forces within Palestine and neighboring countries during the war, the deportation or flight of many Palestinian leaders, and the erroneous decision of their leader, Haj Amin al Husseini, to side with Germany stymied the ability of the Palestinians to regroup throughout the next decade. The decision of the Jews to support the British in their struggle against Hitler rendered their incipient struggle against what they considered the "British betrayal" mute.

During this lull in the conflict, the Zionist movement concentrated all its efforts in consolidating the Jewish demographic and economic base in the country and fortifying Jewish military capabilities. During thirty years of British rule in Palestine, the Jewish population grew from 50,000 in 1918 to 650,000 by the end of 1947. By joining the British armed forces fighting against the Germans, the Jews of Palestine gained military expertise and experience. Some 30,000 of them were enlisted within different British services, which included a "Jewish Brigade" that gained combat experience in Italy. With an excessive concentration of weapons and other war materiel being located in the Middle East, the Jews were able to illicitly enhance their clandestine stock of armaments.

The end of World War II coincided with the traumatic exposure of the Zionists to the horrors of the Holocaust, a fact that enhanced their resolve to establish a Jewish State in Palestine. Their main military engagements in 1946 and 1947 were directed against Britain, which still refused to alter its "White Paper" policy. Attacks on British targets, acts of terror against British personnel, and large-scale illegal immigration compelled the British to maintain a large military and police force in Palestine, which soon became prohibitively expensive.[7] When the British decided in 1947 to relinquish their responsibilities in Palestine and cede their mandate to the United Nations (UN), the discredited Arab leadership found it difficult to regroup and reorganize their national movement. In anticipation of an armed conflict, the Haganah was well organized, if inadequately equipped, while the Arabs, by contrast, were in total disarray.

The next chapter in the unfolding conflict, which spanned eighteen months, was bloody and decisive. The 1948 war, which the Jews call their "War of Independence" and the Arabs call their "Disaster" (Al Naqba), erupted immediately after the adoption of the UN General Assembly Resolution 181, on November 29, 1947. That resolution called for the partition of Palestine into a Jewish State in 60 percent of the land and an Arab state in the remaining 40 percent, with an international enclave around Jerusalem to be controlled by the UN. Quite understandably, the Palestinian Arabs, who despite the impressive growth of the Jewish community still comprised an overwhelming majority of the country's population (1,250,000), rejected the UN resolution. With the help of neighboring Arab states, they opted to oppose the creation of a Jewish state, by force if need be.[8]

As Professor Gelber indicates in Chapter Two, the Arabs misjudged the real and potential balance of power between the contending forces. Despite some setbacks during the early months of the war and an initial Arab advantage in the possession of advanced weapons, the smaller Jewish community managed to mobilize its manpower and eventually redress the armaments imbalance. This ultimately enabled it to deploy field forces superior to those that the Arabs were able to muster. As Gelber notes, both sides were novices in warfare and committed many blunders leading to needless casualties, yet it seems that the Arabs erred more and were less animated in the struggle in comparison with the Israelis, who felt that they were fighting with their backs to the wall.

The outcome of the war was disastrous for the Palestinians. Not only did they fail to abort the establishment of the Jewish State, but Israel managed to expand its hold on territories beyond the area allotted to it by the UN resolution. Some 60 percent of the Palestinian population were uprooted and became refugees. The territories in western Palestine that remained in Arab hands fell under the control of Abdulla, the king of Transjordan who was to become the sovereign of the Hashemite Kingdom of Jordan. By incorporating into his dominion the Arab parts of the West Bank of the Jordan River and of Jerusalem,[9] he denied the Palestinians national independence and political sovereignty. For an entire decade, they totally disappeared as a political entity.[10]

The human cost of the war was horrendous. The exact number of Arabs killed has not been ascertained but is estimated as being over 20,000. The Jews lost 6,000, which amounted to 1 percent of their population at the time. However, by their victory, they secured their sovereignty, which enabled them to enhance the pace of Jewish immigration and intensively populate the land that was largely emptied of its indigenous Arab population.

The 1948 war did not end in peace. The armistice agreements signed by Israel with the four neighboring Arab states (Egypt, Lebanon, Jordan, and Syria) demarcated the lines that Israel wanted to hold as de-facto permanent borders but that the Arabs regarded as temporary cease-fire lines. Based on a group of observers that the UN had sent to Palestine during the war, the United Truce Supervision Organization (UNTSO), a fragile mechanism, was set up to monitor compliance with the armistice agreements and to mediate disputes regarding the exact interpretation of the armistice agreements.

Neither Israel nor the Arab states were ready to conclude permanent peace treaties. A conference convened by the UN Palestine Reconciliation Committee (PRC) during the winter of 1949 in Lausanne, Switzerland, ended in failure.[11] Even for the most moderate of Arabs, withdrawal from the excess territories Israel had gained during the war and the return of hundreds of thousands refugees to their homes inside Israel was a minimal requirement. From Israel's point of view such demands were totally unacceptable. On their part, the Arabs were unable to countenance the existence of the Zionist State and retained the hope that sooner or later they would be able to undo what they considered as Zionist aggression.

The third chapter of the story, which Dr. David Tal aptly describes as the Armistice Wars,[12] mostly involved a low level of violence lasting seven years

(1949–1956). Small and local clashes took place daily along all armistice lines. Occasionally they developed into larger-scale encounters, triggered mostly by Israel's retaliation policy. The basic cause of this prolonged, low-intensity warfare was the two sides' underlying difference in the interpretation of the meaning of the armistice agreements. While Israel saw the agreements as finitely terminating the state of war and forbidding all belligerent acts, the Arabs interpreted them as a temporary truce that did not deny them the right of belligerents, as traditionally specified by international law, as long as peace treaties were not in force.[13] This controversy was reflected in a number of specific disagreements. For example, Israel considered the Arab economic boycott imposed by the Arab League and the closure of waterways under Arab control to Israeli navigation as violations of the agreements.

There were also some controversies with regard to specific clauses of the armistence agreements. Both Jordan and Israel did not comply with the article that was supposed to provide for free passage though some territories held by the other side. This included Israeli access to Jerusalem via Latroun and the Arab rights of passage to Bethlehem via some Israeli-held suburbs of Jerusalem, as well as access of Jews to the Western Wall in the old city of Jerusalem. Syria considered the demilitarized zones scattered along its border with Israel as falling under the jurisdiction of the UN and sought to prevent Israel from altering the situation in these areas. For its part, Israel demanded full sovereignty, barring a military presence, over these strips.

As Tal informs us in Chapter Three, the most pervasive daily phenomenon that became widespread along all armistice lines was the numerous and occasionally violent infiltrations of uprooted Palestinians across the lines. These infiltrations were motivated by different factors, mostly economic (harvesting, retrieval of left-behind property, theft, etc.), but they also were based on a desire to murder Jews as a means of avenging the dispossession of many Palestinians. Some of these violent excursions were organized and utilized for political reasons by different unofficial parties and, later, also by Arab governments. Israel's defensive measures could not stem the rising tide of lethal infiltrations and it soon reverted to reprisal raids in an attempt to coerce Arab governments to adopt more stringent measures to stop the marauders.

In Chapter Three, Tal argues that Israel's retaliatory raids achieved, at best, only a temporary respite, and in the case of the Gaza Strip caused a further escalation of violence. In the spring of 1955, Ben-Gurion and General Moshe Dayan, the key players in the formulation of Israel's security policy, concluded that the armistice agreements ceased to serve Israel's interests. This occurred after the conclusion of a massive arms deal between Egypt and the Soviet Union, announced by President Abdul Nasser on September 27, 1955.[14] That deal, which signified a far-reaching diminution of Israel's deterrence capability, persuaded Israel to seriously consider a military showdown with Egypt that might improve its demarcation lines and lead to a more acceptable cease-fire arrangement. However, Ben-Gurion hesitated. He preferred to redress the adverse balance of power by a dramatic arms deal with France towards the end of June 1956. That deal constituted part of a multiple intelligence and operational collaborative counter to fight Nasser's ambitions in the region.

The 1956 Suez War was seen by Israel as a continuation of its struggle against Arab belligerency. It could not have occurred in the absence of the international crisis triggered by Gamal Abdul Nasser on July 26, 1956, when he nationalized the Suez Canal Company. That act provoked the French and the British to collude with Israel and make the strangest and most unexpected coalition feasible—a coalition of nations who went to war with Egypt and failed to attain their objectives, without ever admitting their coordination and priorly agreed-upon joint goals.

In Chapter Four, Dr. Motti Golani, who is the author of a detailed, two-volume account of the Sinai War,[15] dwells on an interesting but somewhat secondary aspect of this event. He describes the convoluted relations between the three partners of the coalition that had set out to destroy Nasser and reinternationalize the Suez Canal. From the point of view of the French and British, it was from the outset a foolhardy attempt that reflected a total misunderstanding of the new international norms in a post-World War II era. The two European powers were prevented from completing their military campaign and were forced to withdraw. It was patently clear that France and Great Britain lost their standing as "Great Powers." The world became distinctly bipolar.

The story just related was quite different from the point of view of Israel. Israel managed to complete its military undertaking by conquering the entire Sinai peninsula. But under heavy international pressure and after three months of futile diplomatic maneuvering, the Israelis, too, had to relinquish all the territory they occupied. They did, however, manage to change the rules of the game, which prevailed for the next ten years in Israel's relations with Egypt and gained a new sense of security and prosperity. The deployment of the UN Emergency Force along its southwestern borders provided Israel freedom of navigation in the Strait of Tiran and ended the vicious cycle of violence and counterviolence in the area.

The main winner of this war was doubtlessly the Egyptian president, Gamal Abdul Nasser. He was able to explain away the defeat of his troops in the Sinai as a preplanned retreat initiated in order to concentrate his forces against the invading French and British troops from the north. With some justification, he could claim that on the whole he emerged from the crisis with flying colors. During the next few years Nasser became the unchallenged leader of the Arab world. Within the entire Third World, his prestige soared. Displaying some caution, for the next ten years he meticulously refrained from provoking Israel into another confrontation.

The relaxation of Israel's security concerns was incomplete. More radical nationalist elements in the Arab world, especially the Palestinians, resurfaced in the middle of the 1960s under the banner of the Palestine Liberation Organization (PLO) and later under the leadership of Yasser Arafat. Young Palestinians, who grew up in refugee camps, understood full well that with every year Israel enjoyed a de-facto peace, Zionism would become more entrenched. Israel's Jewish population was able to expand and its economic and social conditions were constantly improving. The diversion of the river Jordan's water from it source in the Lake of Galilee to Israel's arid south, completed in 1964, symbolized for the Arabs Israel's successes. Syria, after the failure of its union with Egypt in 1961, took the lead. It intensified its resistance to Israel's attempts to impose its unilateral interpretation on the demilitarized zones. It sponsored raids of Palestinian guerrillas and tried to divert the headwaters of the Jordan that originated from sources located in areas under its control.

This was the background of "The War on the Jordan's Water," which Ami Gluska discusses in Chapter Five.[16] Israel succeeded in foiling all attempts at diverting the headwaters of the river, but was unable to stop Syria from assisting the Palestinian guerrillas and avoid continuous flare-ups of violence along its borders.

A reading of the narrative of this conflict is therefore necessary for understanding the mounting tension between Israel and the new radical nationalist, socialist, and pro-Soviet regime in Syria, which eventually brought about the Six-Day War in June 1967. In Chapter Six, Michael Oren, who recently provided the most updated and comprehensive account of this war, summarizes the intricate chain of events that led to the outbreak of hostilities, the stunning victory of the Israeli forces, and the dramatic change in the political and military realities of the Middle East. As Oren mentions, this was a war that initially nobody desired or expected and was wrought with an amazing chain of misconception, disinformation, and miscalculation.[17]

The Six-Day War had many intriguing outcomes. It changed entirely the landscape of Israel's internal politics; it caused the eventual demise of a significant segment of Egypt's elite; it changed irreversibly the fortunes of Jordan, while catapulting the Palestinians back into the center of the conflict. To this day, the role played by the Soviet Union remains in some degree an enigma. The Soviet Union was probably genuinely concerned for the future of the Ba'ath regime in Damascus, and was eager to deter the Israelis from any adventure along the Syrian border. But the Soviet Union's concocted information about massive concentrations of Israel Defence Force (IDF) reserve units in the north could easily have been seen through. Why, then, did Nasser swallow the bait? Was it a ploy aimed at extricating his army from the quagmire in Yemen? Or was it just an excuse to gain the long-cherished land connection with the Arabs in Asia, via the Israeli Negev? Oren addresses some of these questions in Chapter Six, yet others must remain unanswered as long as the relevant Arab archives are still closed.

The ease with which the Israeli air force decimated the Arab air forces within six hours and the destruction within six days of Arab ground forces confronting Israel in the Sinai, the West Bank of Jordan, and the Syrian Golan Hights brought many Arab leaders to the conclusion that Israel could not be defeated militarily and that it ought to be recognized as a permanent entity. It was clear, however, that this could be agreed upon only if Israel would give up all of the territories it had just recently acquired. Moreover, not all Arab leaders were able to come to such sober conclusions. The Palestinian young guerrilla leaders, who in 1969 managed to take control over the PLO, were not ready to relinquish their hope that sooner or later the Zionists would be defeated and a Palestinian state would emerge within the entire historic territory of Palestine. Palestinian groups, such as Arafat's Fatah, were created long before the Israeli conquest of the West Bank and the Gaza Strip. Defining their aim as "destroying the Zionist entity," they found it difficult to mitigate their radical postures. It took many more years to bring them to a more realistic appreciation of the general situation.

Many Israelis, conversely, were prone to a strong sense of hubris. Moreover, the areas recently conquered by Israel included locations that were considered the holiest in the eyes of Jews for two thousand years, notably the old city of Jerusalem and the Temple Mount in its center. It became very hard for most Israelis to acquiesce to the adamant demand, even of the more moderate Arabs, to relinquish sites that they regarded as the cradle of Judaism. Whether for strategic reasons or out of sentimental motivations, Israel unilaterally annexed East Jerusalem and started to settle some of the newly acquired lands.

Soon after they overcame their initial shock of defeat, the Palestinians resumed their guerrilla and terrorist activities. Meanwhile, the Egyptians, and to a much lesser extent the Syrians, initiated what was later referred to by President Nasser as "A War of Attrition" against the Israeli forces that were now deployed along the Suez Canal and on the new cease-fire lines on the Golan Heights. After a brief, futile attempt to instigate an armed uprising within the West Bank, the various Palestinian "popular struggle" organizations based themselves on the eastern banks of the Jordan River. From there they attempted to make recurrent incursions across the river in order to mine roads, ambush traffic, or attack Jewish installations in the occupied territories. However, geographic and topographic circumstances did not enable the Palestinians to mount a significant challenge to the Israelis. By a combination of defensive devices, including rapid airborne responses and retaliatory raids deep inside the eastern bank of Jordan, the IDF frustrated Palestinian attempts to undermine its hold on the territories occupied in 1967. On the other hand, a Palestinian terror campaign reaching Israeli towns and Israeli and Jewish targets outside the country was more telling.

In Chapter Nine, Benny Michelsohn gives a detailed account of Palestinian insurgency operations around the world and inside Israel's heartland. These operations included attacks on Israeli diplomats in Europe and Asia, airline highjacking, and suicidal incursions of guerrilla squads into Israel. Such actions exacted a high price in blood from the Israelis and kept the Palestinian issue alive before the world at large.[18] During the late 1960s and early 1970s, Israel found it hard to eradicate the guerrillas or even counter them effectively. This was so even after King Hussein suppressed the guerrilla movement in his kingdom and expelled their cadres from his realm in September 1970.

The War of Attrition along the Suez Canal, as Dan Schueftan makes clear in Chapter Seven, took a different course: The IDF succeeded in stabilizing its lines along the Suez Canal by means of a chain of heavily fortified bastions, which were named, after the chief of general staff at the time, the "Bar-Lev Line." This minimized the level of casualties inflicted by the artillery and mortar shelling, ambushes, and mining that the Egyptian army initiated. Israel failed, however, to deter the Egyptians by means of retaliatory raids and air strikes ever-deeper inside the Egyptian heartland. The penetration of Egyptian air space persuaded the Soviet Union to provide Egypt with a variety of ground-to-air missiles. It also increased dramatically the involvement of Soviet military personnel in Egypt, which climaxed in a "dog fight" between Israeli and Russian pilots that led to the downing of five Soviet planes. The virtual stalemate exhausted both sides. By August 1970, it gave rise to a U.S.- and UN-sponsored temporary truce. After 1,000 days of incessant fighting, the end of the "War of Attrition" between Israel and Egypt was reached. Territorially, this war concluded on the same lines in which it began, but during the last hours, taking advantage of the end of hostilities, the Egyptians managed to bring forward many of the Soviet anti-air missiles, which soon proved to be fatal for the Israeli air force. Also, the hope for a diplomatic breakthrough was not realized. No progress was made during the next three years towards conciliation.[19]

Although no respite could be enjoyed by Israel from Palestinian terror, the relative calm that prevailed along all its frontiers during 1971–1973 gave birth to a dangerous illusion and spawned a sense of complacency. A widespread conception prevailed among the Israeli public, and the military establishment in particular, that because Israel consolidated its hold on the territories occupied in 1967, no military option remained in the hands of the neighboring Arab states to coerce it into making unwanted concessions. In this light, various proposals suggested by UN and other mediators, and even by some Israeli leaders, were not taken up. The principle enunciated by General Moshe Dayan, the powerful minister of defense, that "Sharm al Sheikh without peace is better the peace without Sharm al Sheikh," well reflected the prevailing mood. Israel also continued to settle Jews in the recently occupied areas. Dozens of new settlements were established on the Golan Heights, along the Jordan Valley, and even inside the Sinai, where a new town, Yamit, arose on the Mediterranean coast west of the Gaza Strip. As for East Jerusalem, it was officially, though unilaterally, annexed by an act of the Knesset.

It seems that Anwar Sadat, who in September 1970 succeeded the late Nasser as the president of the Republic, well understood that over the passage of time, Israel would further entrench itself in the occupied territories and that world opinion would adjust to the changing situation. Despite his assessment that his army was unable to defeat the Israelis or even to reoccupy the entire Sinai peninsula, he came to the conclusion that he had to order his forces to cross the canal to the east. He must have believed that Egypt stood some chance in regaining a foothold east of the waterway or at least upsetting the political status quo and compelling the international community to press Israel into making the concession it was thus far unwilling to make. A simultaneous offensive of the Syrian armor brigade on the Golan frontier was necessary to limit the capacity of the Israelis to concentrate most of their forces on its southern front.[20]

The eighteen-days-long war in October 1973 that the Israelis call the Yom Kippur War, of which Shimon Golan presents a summary in Chapter Eight, came to the Israelis as a traumatic surprise and totally upset their hitherto prevailing complacency. Much has been said and written on the failure of the intelligence services to give Israel a proper warning.[21] Less attention was given to the much greater surprise that awaited the Israeli troops within the first few days of the Suez Canal crossing. That surprise had to do with the dramatic changes in the character of the battlefield which took place during the six years that elapsed since 1967. The Israeli war planners assumed that the Egyptians would one day try to cross the canal, but they also were confident that they would not find it too difficult to frustrate such an attempt, after having mobilized their reserve armored units and rushed them to the front. Indeed, with amazing speed, two Israeli armor divisions were deployed along the main approaches to the Canal Zone and within thirty-six hours began their pre-planned counteroffensive. However, a combination of massive artillery barrages and the use of highly effective and intensive antitank missiles (the Sagers) enabled the Egyptians to hold their newly gained positions along the canal on its eastern side. The Israeli air force could not, as expected, give ground support to the armor division since the Egyptians had managed to deploy their missiles in the vicinity of the canal in the final stages of the War of Attrition. This enabled them to build a massive umbrella composed of the most modern Soviet ground-to-air missiles, covering a full array of altitudes over the battle zone. In short, they had prepared an effective defense for their ground forces against Israeli planes.

Only after the repulsion of the Syrians from the Golan, in the wake of a failed attempt of the Egyptian armor division to advance deeper into the Sinai and after the costly destruction of most of Egypt's ground-to-air missiles sites, was the IDF ready to show its mettle. Three armor divisions managed to cross the canal westwards, threatening to encircle the two Egyptian armies deployed along the eastern bank. Strong international pressure saved an entire Egyptian army from total encirclement. When cease-fire negotiations brought the fighting to a close, the Israeli's armor division reached points sixty miles from Cairo and almost thirty miles from Damascus.[22]

Considering the enormous difficulties that the IDF faced at the outbreak of fighting, these were impressive achievements. But the initial setbacks, the heavy toll of blood (over 3,000 Israeli killed and three times more injured), and the fact that two Egyptian armies were still deployed east of the canal at the end of the war made most Israelis regard the war as a debacle. The Hebrew word *mehdal* (which means "an omission" or "an oversight") was attached to the initial complacency that ruled Israel's mistaken appreciation of the political and military situation leading to the war and its mismanagement in its early stages. A spontaneous movement led by demobilized reserve soldiers staged large and continuous street demonstrations and vigils. Under mounting pressure, the government felt obliged to establish a committee of inquiry chaired by Chief Justice Shimon Agranat, which in its final verdict called for the dismissal of General Elazar, the chief of staff; General Gorodish, the commander of the Southern Command; and General Ze'ira, the head of the Intelligence Division. The Agranat committee abstained from passing judgment on the political echelon but public anger eventually led to the downfall of Golda Meir, the prime minister, and Moshe Dayan, the minister of Defense.

Despite the IDF's eventual military successes, President Sadat's gambit proved to be successful and gained for Egypt a great psychological and political victory. Their audacious defiance of the Israelis enabled them to recover their national pride and self-esteem, which had been shattered by their defeat in 1967. These contradictory changes of moods on both sides facilitated a long-delayed march towards peace. The Israelis were now ready to conclude interim agreements that provided the Egyptians with a wide belt along the Eastern Sinai and the Syrians Kuneitra, the main town on the Golan Heights. Within another four years, in the wake of a dramatic visit of President Sadat to the Israeli parliament, and the energetic mediation of American President Jimmy Carter, peace between Israel and Egypt was finally reached. Israel withdrew from the rest of the Sinai peninsula, though not from the Gaza Strip. No similar breakthrough was recorded with the Syrians.[23]

The Egyptians assumed that the peace agreement they concluded with Israel in 1978 would solve the Palestine problem which, after all, was the main source of their thirty years' quarrel with Israel. The 1978 Camp David Accord indeed included a formal recognition by Israel of the "political rights of the Palestinian people," but negotiations on autonomy for the Palestinians, which were held between Israel and Egypt during 1979–1980, failed to yield an agreed-upon formula. The Palestinians in the Gaza Strip and the West Bank of the Jordan remained under Israeli conquest while land expropriations and Jewish settlements in the occupied territories expanded by leaps and bounds. As expected, the Palestinians continued their guerrilla and terror attacks against Israel.

After the expulsion of the Palestinian guerrilla groups from Jordan in September 1970, the PLO and its various affiliated groups entrenched themselves in the refugee camps in Lebanon. In addition to military training sites, armament depots, and headquarters, the PLO had, during the 1970s, built an impressive array of educational, medical, social, cultural, and other civic institutions in Lebanon. The Palestinian presence in the country acquired many traits of self-governance, which was facilitated by constant friction between different religious and ethnic groups within Lebanese society and by the fragile authority of the Lebanese state.[24] To many observers, the Palestinians seemed to have created in Lebanon a "state within a state." These developments came to a head when, in 1975, the internecine discord that was simmering for a long time in Lebanon spilt over into a full-scale civil war. The main contending forces were the Christian Maronites, the Druse, and the Moslem Sunnis (The Shi'ites remained, at this stage, somewhat in the background). The Palestinians, who controlled their camps, much of the southern part of Lebonon, and parts of the city of Beirut, were well organized. They participated in the struggle, pitting themselves against the Maronite militias. The Syrian army, too, entered the fray and soon controlled the entire Beq'a Valley and the eastern approaches of Beirut.

Despite the heavy losses that the Palestinians sustained, they held onto most of their bases. Moreover, these developments further established their self-rule, fortifying their resolve to continue their struggle against Israel. In Chapter Nine, Benny Michelsohn accounts for the different methods used by the Palestinian guerrillas during the 1970s to harass Israel. These involved raids from the sea (including one raid into the heart of Tel Aviv), ambushes across the border, skirmishes against Israeli military garrisons and civilian villages, and Katyushka shelling of towns such as Nahariya and Kiryat Shmona. The large-scale excursions and deep penetrations that the IDF launched during those years against the Palestinian forces in Lebanon were mostly operational successes but could not bring respite from Palestianian harassment. The formation of the mostly Christian South Lebanese Army, commanded by Major Sa'ad Hadad and after his death by General Antoin Lahad, who fully collaborated with the Israelis, brought only relative and local relaxation of the troubles in the north.

The circumstances in Lebanon and the continued war waged by the Palestinians based in Lebanon forced the Israelis into an undeclared but rather intensive alliance with the Maronites, who considered the Palestinians as the prime cause of their diminishing power in Lebanese society. Israel provided the Maronite militias with indirect but massive support consisting of training of personnel, the provision of military equipment, intelligence information, and financial assistance. Despite all this, the Maronites were unable to dislodge the Palestinians from their bases. By June 1982, the Israeli government, led by Menachem Begin and goaded to action by Ariel Sharon, the aggressive minister of defense, launched a large-scale invasion of Lebanon. They aimed to totally destroy the Palestinian "State," eject Syrians from Lebanon, and reinstall the Maronites as the strongest and most decisive force in the "Land of Cedars." Self-righteously, Begin code-named this operation as the "War for the Peace of the Galilee."

The highly complex military and political developments of this war, which lasted longer than anticipated, is analyzed by Eyal Zisser in Chapter Ten.[25] Though the IDF managed to push the Syrian forces from the approaches of Beirut and destroy their air defenses, it failed to remove them from their hold in the Beq'a Valley. On the other hand, the destruction of the Palestinian civil and power structures in Lebanon was total and complete. Yasser Arafat, chairman of the PLO, who for a while held on under siege and heavy Israeli fire in West Beirut, eventually had to evacuate Lebanon. He was escorted by many of his guerrilla fighters, who were dispersed in different Arab countries, while he established his headquarters in Tunis. The Lebanese chapter in the PLO's saga was over.[26]

On the other hand, the main failure of the Israeli strategy was its inability to cash in on its alliance with the Maronites. Bashir Joumael, who was elected "under Israeli bayonets" as president of the republic, was shortly thereafter assassinated. His brother Amin, who replaced him, was pressurized by Syria not to endorse a hastily concocted peace agreement between Lebanon and Israel. The policies pursued by Israel alienated all other elements in Lebanon, such as the Druse, the Moslem Sunnis, and the Shi'ites. The latter's burgeoning guerrilla groups, first the Amal and then, with greater audacity, the Hezbollah, superseded the Palestinians in their never-tiring attempts to harass Israeli forces deployed in the country. Under such pressure, the IDF was forced step-by-step to retreat from areas conquered during the war. By the spring of 1984, the IDF withdrew from its main positions in Lebanon except for the so-called "Security Belt," in the south, which remained under the control of the South Lebanese Army (SLA). Some Israeli troops maintained strongholds and sent patrols into South Lebanon to help the SLA displace the Shi'a guerrillas from the border.

The unhappy Israeli alliance with the Maronites also adversely affected Israel's moral image—Maronite militias were allowed by IDF's command in Beirut to penetrate the Palestinian suburbs of Sabra and Shatila, while Israeli troops kept their distance. Given a free hand, the Maronite militiamen perpetrated a most cruel and shameful massacre.

The entire venture in Lebanon became a highly controversial issue inside the Israeli political and public arena. As its full scope unfolded it became clear that the prime minister's early pronouncements were being borne out. Menachem Begin claimed that the IDF's objective was limited to a temporary incursion into Lebanon of an area no deeper than forty kilometers, and the destruction of the Palestinian military establishment in that area. The fateful involvement with the Maronites and the siege of Beirut met with mounting criticism from growing segments of the Israeli population. In response to the Sabra and Shatila massacre, the Israeli peace movement in collaboration with the Labor Party and other social and political forces, held the largest demonstration ever held in Israel. More then a quarter million people swarmed into the municipal square in Tel Aviv demanding the dismissal of Ariel Sharon, who was regarded as the main architect of the entire fiasco. Early in 1983, under the interdiction of a state inquiry committee established by the government and headed by Justice Kahan, Sharon resigned his position as minister of defense but retained his seat in the government. Shortly thereafter, Prime Minister Menachem Begin also resigned to live out his final days in total reclusion. In the 1984 elections, Begin's party lost some of its public support and was compelled to share power with the Labor Party headed by Shimon Peres. Itzhak Rabin was nominated as minister of defense.[27]

By 1987, a growing number of Palestinians inside the territories controlled by Israel, who continued to suffer great economic setbacks and who were constantly humiliated by the Israeli occupation, despaired of being delivered by outside forces. While the PLO remained in their eyes "the sole representative of the Palestinian people" and Arafat was still considered by most as their venerable leader, many realized that the PLO was incapable of redeeming them. A younger generation of inspired students decided to take their fate into their own hands. In December 1987, a spontaneous uprising of mainly young Palestinians erupted all over the towns and villages of Palestine. It soon became known as "the Intifada" (in Arabic

"Shaking up"). Young men and women, even children, took to the streets chant-
ing, hoisting their national flags, and throwing stones and occasionally hurling
incendiary bombs at the Israeli troops who tried to contain them.[28] The Israeli
army, ill-prepared for such a confrontation, was taken by surprise and overreacted.
Lacking the appropriate means to disperse unarmed demonstrations, they resorted
to shooting and the rate of Palestinian casualties, consisting mostly of the young,
began to soar. This resulted in a further escalation of resistance, causing Israel
great setbacks in the international arena. Gruesome scenes of Israeli brutality were
portrayed throughout the world by means of electronic and other media. It was as
if the young Palestinians were exclaiming to the Israelis and the world at large:
"We know we cannot kill the Israelis but we can make them kill us and thus shake
the stalemate and bring about the end of occupation."

As Reuven Aharoni explains in Chapter Eleven, the Palestinian resistance during
the first Intifada found its expression in sustained street skirmishes of youngsters
who defied the Israeli forces. The Palestinians proudly called the youngsters "the
stone children." This was accompanied by an intensive campaign of wall graffiti.
Palestinian quarters and public property were plastered from top to bottom with
lengthy texts and animated slogans painted in red, black, and green, according to
the party that painted them. Also there were numerous commercial and labor
strikes. Palestinian workers of the Israeli civil administration resigned en-masse. In
order to relieve the people from the need to apply to the hated Israeli authorities,
self-help institutions in different social, medical, educational, and administrative
areas were organized by various local and national groups. The Palestinian civil
society received an important boost. The Intifada that began as a spontaneous
uprising also enhanced the local leadership and the national leaders who lived
inside the occupied areas. Shortly after its outbreak a group of leaders began to
publish "official" communiques in encouraging rhetoric that contained instructions
concerning strikes, demonstrations, and other ways of running the campaign.
However, the unrest and public excitement also deepened inner dissent and gave a
strong boost to the more uncompromising Islamic groups, in particular the Hammas. In an attempt to regain leadership, the PLO National Council declared in
December 1988 the virtual founding of a Palestinian State and its recognition of
the State of Israel.[29]

The political stalemate between the left Labor Party and the right Likud that
resulted from the 1984 elections immobilized Israeli politics and prevented an
appropriate Israeli political response during the first year of the Intifada. In the elections held in October 1988, the intransigent incumbent Likud, Prime Minister
Shamir, gained a slight margin over his rival Shimon Peres, but the political stalemate remained intact. Only under heavy U.S. pressure did Shamir began to consider
a political response to the Palestinian uprising. He did not relinquish his definitive
opposition to the creation of a Palestinian state or his total rejection of any recognition or negotiations with the PLO. On the other hand, he had to reconsider his
refusal to participate in an international conference, jointly convened by the United
States and Russia, to discuss the political future of the Palestinian people.

During the Gulf War in the winter of 1991, Israel was attacked by some forty
Iraqi long-range missiles. Extensive material damage was caused in Tel Aviv and
other locations in Israel's centers of population. The Palestinians rejoiced and
hailed Saddam Hussein, while the PLO officially declared its support of the Iraqi

regime and its invasion of Kuwait. Nevertheless, the victorious Americans, who were assisted by a coalition of a number of Arab states (including Syria, Saudi Arabia, and Egypt) felt compelled to sponsor a serious peace process.

Under a U.S. threat of economic sanctions, Prime Minister Shamir was reluctantly dragged to the Madrid Conference, convened in 1991, where he was not prepared to countenance the participation of the PLO. The Madrid Conference, which was in itself little more than an occasion for declamatory speeches, gave rise to further negotiations, held in Washington, D.C., between Israel and its enemies, Syria, Lebanon, and a Jordanian delegation which included Palestinians from the occupied territories. What seemed at the time to be the beginning of a serious peace process brought the first Intifada to an end. Unfortunately, a positive outcome did not materialize.

By the end of 1992, after having regained the leadership of the Labor Party and as a result of a constitutional change that provided for direct popular elections of the prime minister, General Itzhak Rabin headed a new coalition in which his old rival, Shimon Peres, became the minister of foreign affairs. Likud was relegated to the opposition. Rabin tried at first to continue the pattern of negotiations established in Madrid, but it soon became clear that his Palestinian interlocutors lacked powers to make decisions independently of the PLO leadership based in Tunis.

Arafat, who was drastically weakened by his pro-Saddam orientation during the Gulf War and who lost much of his financial support from Arab oil-producing countries, retained the loyalty of his own people. Rabin and Peres came to the conclusion that only direct negotiations with the PLO could ensure a serious peace process. Secret negotiations in Oslo resulted in the August 1993 signing on the White House lawn of the now famous Oslo Accords and the no-less-famous handshake between Arafat and Rabin.[30] The bestowal of the Nobel Peace Price upon Arafat, Rabin, and Peres created the semblance of a promising beginning which might have heralded the end to the 100 years of strife between Arabs and Jews in Palestine. But as Chapter Twelve of this text makes clear, the fanfare in Stockholm was perhaps premature, for yet more bloodshed and suffering was to follow.

Implicitly, the Oslo Accords amounted to an exchange of security for Israel against independence for the Palestinians, but the agreements were flawed in that their ultimate objectives were not clearly specified. They were formally no more than agreements for some interim arrangements while a final settlement was to be hammered out to embrace all the main outstanding issues such as borders, the future of Jerusalem, and the problem of the Palestinian refugees. The essential practical change that the Oslo Accords caused was the establishment of the Palestinian Authority, first in the Gaza Strip and Jericho and then within the major Palestinian towns in the West Bank. Arafat and his lieutenants returned to Palestine from Tunis and elsewhere, expecting to pave the way for their independent state.

At first a mood of optimism prevailed, but the rise of the nonconforming groups inside the Palestinian community spearheaded by the Hammas continued to perpetrate acts of terror and provoked punitive reprisals by Israel. The assassination of Rabin in November 1996 and the eventual return to power of Likud, now headed by Benjamin Netanyahu, prevented all prospects of the Oslo Accords from succeeding. The rising wave of suicide bombers in the midst of Israeli towns hardened Israeli security measures and made life in the occupied territories unbearable. The replacement of over 120,000 Palestinian workers, employed in Israel by foreign laborers, dramatically increased unemployment and poverty among the Palestinians. Closures of Palestinian towns and villages and a network of roadblocks manned by Israeli soldiers heightened the level of humiliation experienced by the Palestinians.

A brave but mishandled attempt by Prime Minister Barak at his meeting with Arafat, hosted by President Clinton at Camp David in June 2000, failed to produce a compromise. The provocative visit of Ariel Sharon, the new head of Likud, on the Temple Mount in October that year resulted in the spontaneous rioting of young Palestinians. In an attempt to quell the unrest, several of the young rioters died. This triggered a new wave of demonstrations and violent attacks by Palestinian guerrillas, provoking severe repressive measures by Israeli forces. The renewed Palestinian uprising soon acquired the name "Intifada II," or "Indifadat al Aqsa" (named after the old mosque on the Temple Mount, where it began).

Unlike the first Intifada, which was characterized mostly by civil disobedience and low-level street violence, the second uprising soon became lethal. Suicide bombers attacked Israeli busses, restaurants, cafes, and bus stations, causing the death of hundreds of innocent people including women and children. In addition, there were numerous road ambushes and some audacious penetrations into Jewish settlements in the occupied areas, all of which undermined the sense of security felt by most Israelis.

Harsh countermeasures taken by the IDF and the Israeli police included large-scale and recurrent invasions of towns and villages, which in terms of the Oslo Accords were under the control of the Palestinian authority. These were accompanied by large-scale arrests, the demolition of houses, missile attacks by helicopters targeted to kill instigators of acts of terror (which also included innocent bystanders), the continuous closure of entire Palestinian zones, and the confinement of Yasser Arafat to his headquarters in Ramalla. Those measures, which failed to end the Palestinian resistance, resulted in thousands of Palestinian fatalities and injuries and imposed extreme poverty and suffering on most of the Palestinian population. During the three years of the new Intifada, close to 1,000 Israelis and over 3,000 Palestinians were killed and at least triple such numbers were wounded.

Shaul Shay's attempt, in Chapter Twelve, to analyze a still-ongoing conflict has perhaps been the most taxing. The unavoidable lack of a proper perspective; the intensity of emotional, political, and ideological strife, both within Israeli society as well as in the international arena; the variety of the incidences that have occurred; the complex fusion of military and political factors; and the constant oscillation between hope and despair have all contributed to making his task exceedingly difficult. In addition, more than any other conflict, this one has totally polarized Israeli public opinion. It is almost impossible to present a narrative that would be received by all readers as an unbiased assessment of the events in question. Even so, the reader is provided with sufficient facts to make his or her own judgement.

The ongoing conflict dealt with in this text is in essence a struggle between Jews, seeking to establish their right of self-determination in the land considered to be the cradle of their nation, and indigenous Arab aspirations regarding the same land, where incidentally, they have been present for centuries.[31] As a result of the initial weakness of the Palestinians and the defeats they suffered from the hands of the better-organized Israelis, the entire Arab world, especially the four Arab states adjacent to Palestine as well as Iraq, stepped into the breach. Between May 1948 and October 1973, the wars described in Chapters Two through Eight primarily involved Arab regular armies, while the Palestinians remained to a large extent on the margins. What had started out as a Palestinian resistance to the Zionist endeavor in the 1936 revolt and during the first half of 1948 came back to haunt the land. The Palestinian comeback began in 1965 as a result of guerrilla insurgency. It gathered momentum on account of the popular uprising of the first Intifada (1987–1990) and more so with the commencement in October 2000 of the second and more lethal Intifada. The peace agreements that Israel signed with Egypt and Jordan and the relative weakness of Syria and Lebanon, as well as the collapse of Iraq in 2003, had originally left the Palestinians to their own devices. At the same time, it brought home to them the fact that only a painful historic conciliation between the national aspirations of the Israeli Jews and the Palestinian Arabs, entailing a fair and mutually agreed-upon division of the land, would resolve the conflict.

Recurrent polls taken among both Palestinians and Israelis have shown that a clear majority of both nations had already arrived at that conclusion. Of course this has not applied to all of them. Strong, armed, and violent minority groups among the Palestinians still cherish the hope of being able to bring about the dismemberment of the Jewish State. Strong and still-influential segments within the Israeli ruling elite still strive to retain Israeli control over the entire land west of the river Jordan, which would of course deny the Palestinians their rights and aspirations. No conciliation can be achieved between these two extremes and therefore no end to the conflict can be achieved so long as these extremes remain influential.

The simple historic fact should be recognized that the entire conflict was initially caused by the uninvited arrival of masses of Jews in a land already inhabited by the Palestinians. But the Zionist project had arisen two generations before the Palestinians began to develop their own separate national consciousness and was conceived in a different world in which European colonialism was not considered a sin. By 1948, three years after the Holocaust in which six million Jews were exterminated, the 650,000 Jews already living in Palestine, of whom many, like myself, were born in the country, faced no alternative other than to fight for their personal survival and collective right of self-determination.

That war resulted in a de-facto compromise: The land was in fact partitioned between the Jews and the Arabs. Extremists on both sides declined to acknowledge that compromise. The Arabs who demand the return of all the Palestinian refugees to their homes do not accept the verdict of history that gave the Jews a state in which, as a majority, they may develop their own national identity. On the other hand, the Jews who still aspire to hold on to all the territories west of the Jordan do not accept the verdict of history that has left some space for the Palestinians to develop, in freedom and independence, their own national identity.

In reading through this text one may easily detect mistakes committed and opportunities lost to redress wrongs omitted. One may detect many ill-advised measures taken that cannot but be defined as evil perpetrated by one side or the other. Yet it is not a story of an encounter between villains and righteous people. It is the story of a tragic clash between patriots dedicated to the welfare of their own people, the story of a tragic confrontation of two national movements contesting the same small piece of land, that has transformed it into one of the most intractable issues in modern times. A war between villains and a righteous people can more readily be ended when the good defeat the bad with the assistance of a well-meaning international community. Tragedies will continue to haunt people as long as they are unable extricate themselves from their causes and learn to live within more realistic limits in the fulfillment of their hopes and dreams.

It seems that in recent months, the conflict between the Palestinians and the Israelis has reached a moment of truth. Every sober person, on both sides of the barricades, appreciates what is required for an historic conciliation—the creation of a Palestinian state in the Gaza Strip and the West Bank more or less within the limits of the June 5, 1967 borders. Jerusalem ought to be the shared capital city of both the state of Palestine and the state of Israel. The Palestinian refugee problem should be solved by allowing the refugees to settle in the new Palestinian State, in the states where they are already present, and in other states which may open their gates to them. Naturally, they ought to be fully compensated for losses to property that occurred during the conflict. Some already discern the light at the end of the tunnel, but it requires leaders of vision on both sides to persuade their people that despite all the anguish of forfeiting futile dreams, it is far better to come to terms with reality and accept the only possible way out.

NOTES

1. In a speech Prime Minister Yitzhak Rabin held in Cairo on the occasion of the signing of the second Oslo Agreement, he mentioned Avrham Yalovsky, my wife's great-grandfather, who was assassinated by Arabs on the outskirts of Nes Ziona in 1886, the first Jewish victim of the 100 years' conflict over Palestine.

2. For a discussion of the early phases of Palestinian nationalism, see Rashid Khalidi, *Palestine Identity: The Construcion of National Consciousness,* New York: Columbia Universtity Press, 1997. Joel Migdal and Baruch Kimmerling recognize an earlier expression of Palestinian aspirations in the revolt against Mohamed Ali, the Egyptian ruler of Palestine during the 1830s. See B. Kimmerling and J.S. Migdal, *Palestinians: The Making of a People,* New York: Free Press, 1993.

3. For a comprehensive discussion of development of the Zionist movement, see Walter Z. Laquer, *A History of Zionism,* New York: Schocken Books, 1989. For a discussion of the beginning of the British mandate over Palestine and the development of the Jewish community in Palestine in the 1920s, see Howard M. Sachar, *A History of Israel,* New York: Knopf, 1987.

4. For good analysis of the early phases of Palestinian resistance to the Zionist project, see Yehoshua Porath, *The Palestinian Arab National Movement, 1929–1939,* London: Frank Cass, 1977.

5. Benny Morris, *Righteous Victims: A History of the Zionist-Arab Conflict, 1881–1999,* New York: Vintage Books, 2001; Avi Shlaim, *The Iron Wall: Israel and the Arab World,* London: Allen Lane, 2000.

6. For brief biographical notes on the contributors and their publications, see Appendix A.

7. For some treatment of the last days of the British rule in Palestine, see R. Louis and R. Stookly (eds.), *End of the Palestinian Mandate,* Austin, Texas, 1986; and Richard L. Jasse, *Zion Abandoned: Great Britain's Withdrawal from Palestine Mandate, 1945–1948,* Ph.D. thesis at the Catholic University of America, Washington D.C., 1980 (University Microfilm).

8. For a comprehensive survey of the 1948 war, see N. Lorch, *Israel's War of Independence, 1947–1949,* Hartford, CT: Hartmore House, 1968.

9. The Egyptians remained in control of the Gaza Strip.

10. Professor Avi Shlaim of Oxford described these events as a collusion between King Abdulla and the Zionists under the tacit auspices of the British to divide Palestine amongst themselves to the exclusion of the Palestinians. See A. Shlaim, *Collusion across the Jordan: King Abdullah, the Zionist Movement, and the Partition of Palestine,* Oxford: Oxford University Press, 1988. On the involvement of the Jordanian army in the 1948 war, see J. B. Glubb, *A Soldier with the Arabs,* London: Hodder & Stoughton, 1957, and B. Morris, *The Road to Jerusalem: Glubb Pasha, Palestine and the Jews,* London, Tauris 2002, Ch. 5, pp. 145–208.

11. For a good summary of the PRC efforts, see N. Caplan, *Futile Diplomacy, Vol. 3, The United Nations, The Great Powers, and Middle East Peace Making 1948–1954,* London: Frank Cass, 1997. A shorter version *in idem, The Lausanne Conference, 1949,* Tel Aviv, 1993.

12. Benny Morris preferred to call it "Border Wars." See B. Morris, *Israel's Border Wars 1949–1956,* Oxford: Oxford University Press 1993. See also M. Oren, *The Origins of the Second Arab-Israeli War: Egypt, Israel, and the Great Powers,* London: Taylor & Francis, 1992, Ch. 8.

13. Even in the 1952 edition of the most prestigious compendium of international law, *armistice* is defined as a temporary truce, rather as a finite end of belligerency. See F. L. Oppenheim, *International Law,* London: Longman, 1952, pp. 546–547.

14. The deal was ostensibly concluded with Czechoslovakia but was in fact a Soviet deal.

15. The Hebrew version was titled: *There Will Be War Next Summer . . . The Road to the Sinai War, 1955–1956,* Tel Aviv, 1997. The English shortened version carries the title *Israel in Search of War: The Sinai Campaign, 1955–1956,* Brighton: Sussex Academic Press, 1998. Scores of books were published on this war. For one, see M. Bar-On, *The Gates of Gaza: Israel's Road to Suez and Back, 1955–1957,* New York: St. Martin's Press, 1994.

16. Ami Gluska completed his Ph.D. thesis on this subject and is currently preparing it for publication.

17. Even more than the 1956 Suez War the Six-Day War attracted the attention of many writers. For a comprehensive bibliography, see the end of Michael Oren's book, starting with page 405. Six Days of War: June 1967 and the Making of the Modern Middle East, New York: Presido Press, 2003.

18. For an animated narrative of these events from a Palestinian perspective, see Salah Khalaf (Abu Iyad), *My Home, My Land: A Narrative of the Palestinian Struggle,* New York: Times Books, 1981. For a good analysis of these developments, see H. Cobban, *The Palestinian Liberation Organization: People, Power and Politics,* Cambridge: Cambridge University Press, 1984.

19. For another source on the War or Attrition with Egypt, see Y. Bar-Siman-Tov, *The Israeli-Egyptian War of Attrition 1969–1970,* New York: Columbia University Press, 1980.

20. On the Egyptian calculations leading to the war, see Field Marshal Mohamed Abdel Ghani El Gamasi's memoirs, *The October War,* Cairo: American University in Cairo, 1993. Gamasi was the Chief of Operations during the war. A critical view from Egypt was presented by then-chief of staff General Sa'ad el Shazly in *The Crossing of Suez: The October War (1973),* London: Third World Center for Research, 1880.

21. A recent, thorough investigation of the surprise was published in Hebrew by Uri Bar-Joseph, *The Watchman Fell Asleep: The Surprise of Yom Kippur and Its Sources,* Tel Aviv, 2001.

22. For a good jounalistic survey of the war, see Z. Schiff, *October Earthquake: Yom Kippur,* Tel Aviv, 2001. For an American view, see Henry Kissinger, *Crisis: The Anatomy of Two Major Foreign Policy Crises,* New York: Simon and Schuster, 2003.

23. On the negotiations of the peace treaty between Israel and Egypt, see W. B. Quandt, *Peace Process: American Diplomacy and the Arab-Israeli Conflict Since 1967,* Washington, D.C.: Brookings Institution, 1993. For an Egyptian perspective, see Mahmoud Riad, *The Struggle for Peace in the Middle East,* London: Quarted Books, 1981.

24. For a good analysis of the civil strife in Lebanon, see Samir Khalaf, *Civil and Uncivil Violence in Lebanon,* New York: Columbia University Press, 2002.

25. A good journalistic narrative of the war may be found in Z. Schiff and E. Ya'ari, *Israel's Lebanon War,* New York: Simon and Schuster, 1984.

26. For the full story of the last chapter of the PLO in Lebanon, see R. Khalidi, *Under Siege: PLO Decisionmaking During the 1982 War,* New York: Columbia University Press, 1986.

27. On the antiwar activities, see M. Bar-On, *In Pursuit of Peace: A History of the Israeli Peace Movement,* Washington, D.C.: U.S. Institute of Peace, 1996, Chapter 7, pp. 137–156.

28. For a good analysis of the first Intifada, see F. R. Hunter, *The Palestinian Uprising: A War by Other Means,* London: Tauris, 1991. For a compilation of articles, mostly from a Palestinian perspective, see Zachary Lockman and Joel Beinin (eds.), *Intifada: The Palestinian Uprising against Israeli Occupation,* London: Tauris, 1989. For an interesting though somewhat marginal view, see Meron Benvenisti, *Intimate Enemies: Jews and Arabs in a Shared Land,* Berkeley: University of California Press, 1995.

29. The "Leadership Communiques" were published and commented on by Shaul Mishal and Reuben Aharoni in *Speaking Stones: Communiques from the Intifada Underground,* Albany, NY: SUNY University Press, 1994.

30. For a good analysis of the Oslo process from an Israeli perspective, see David Makovsky, *Making Peace with the PLO: The Rabin Government's Road to the Oslo Accord,* Boulder, CO: Westview Press, 1996. For a Palestinian narrative, see Mahmoud Abbas (Abu Mazen), *Through Secret Channels: The Road to Oslo,* Reading, UK: Garnet Books, 1995.

31. In recent years Palestinian propaganda claims continuity of ancient people who lived in Palestine even before the Israelites came there in biblical times, but the real presence of Arabs in Palestine cannot be established before the conquest of the Islamized Arabs in the year 638 A.D., that is, 1,250 years before the advent of modern Zionist immigration in the country.

1

The Arab Revolt, 1936–1939: A Turning Point in the Struggle over Palestine

Yigal Eyal

The Palestinian uprising of 1936–1939, which is popularly known as the "Arab Revolt," was a salient and significant turning point for both the Arab and Jewish communities, as well as for the British administration of Palestine. Through its struggle against the British rule, the Arab community had explicitly declared that it had chosen to use a violent uprising, in which guerrilla tactics and acts of terror were employed, to impose its favored political solution in its struggle with the Jewish community over the same land.

A combination of international, regional, and local circumstances joined to bring about the eruption of the revolt in 1936. By the end of 1935 and during the first half of 1936, the Palestinian community arrived at some measure of national maturity when the heads of five Arab parties in Palestine presented a joint "Three Points" document to the British High Commissioner. They demanded:

1. The establishment of a majority rule in the country;
2. A ban on transfer of lands to the Jews; and
3. An immediate cease of Jewish immigration and the establishment of a committee to investigate the country's capacity to absorb further immigration.

Their aim was to impel the British government to change the policy established in 1917 by Lord Balfour's promise to facilitate the creation in Palestine of a "National Home" for the Jews, an undertaking that was confirmed by the League of Nations mandate given to the British to administer Palestine. However, at this stage a consensus within the British administration existed that Palestine was not yet ready for self-rule.[1] The rejection of the Arabs' demands seemed to confirm their perception that the influence of the Jews in London gave them great political advantages.

The failure of the Palestinian leaders to initiate a political process that would have changed their constitutional position, in view of the impressive political gains of the leaders of the neighboring Arab countries and the continuous growth and development of the Jewish National Home, strengthened their fears that further inactivity would be to their greatest disadvantage.

The Palestinians drew encouragement from the political developments that took place at that time in Egypt and in Syria. The British were obliged to negotiate a new treaty with the Egyptian government. The treaty, signed in August 1936, required the British to consult with the Egyptians in times of an international crisis and concentrate all their military bases in the vicinity of the Suez Canal. This in turn moved the Syrians to stir up some unrest and demonstrations against the French, which also impressed the Palestinians.[2]

During the years 1933–1936, the Jewish community of Palestine grew significantly in population, became firmly established, and managed to prove that the Zionist project in Palestine was there to stay and could not be discarded. The stream of immigrants increased and by 1936 the Yishuv (the Jewish community in Palestine) numbered 400,000. The demographic growth and the sharp increase in economic, industrial, and agricultural activities proved that the Zionist dream of turning Palestine into a haven for masses of Jews was sustainable.

National consciousness among Palestinian Arabs, which was simmering for some time, surfaced. In response to the unrest in Syria, solidarity meetings were convened throughout the country, financial contributions to support the Syrians were raised, and the Arab newspapers called upon the Palestinians to march in the footsteps of their "great sister Syria" and fight for the same goals. The fact that Palestine remained the only Arab country still under foreign rule added fuel to the growing dissatisfaction. A small spark was enough to ignite the explosion. Sir Arthur Wauchope, the high commissioner, well understood that those events in the Middle East had great impact on developments inside Palestine and that the Arab population was ready to transcend from words to action. In a letter to the state secretary for the colonies, he quoted David Ben-Gurion, who also estimated that "the political actions recently taken in Syria and Egypt will be a powerful factor in this country." In another letter two weeks earlier, he warned that if Egypt and Syria would receive greater independence and if the proposal to establish in Palestine a legislative council would not be honored, the storm in Palestine would be aggravated.[3] Despite these warnings the storm that erupted on April 19, 1936, took the British by surprise.

The three years of continuous military struggle that ensued witnessed many ups and downs, recurrent crisis, many casualties, and much loss of property. Only at the end of that period did the British army manage to quell the revolt. The winds of war were already blowing over Europe, therefore, despite their military success, in order to avoid another front in the Middle East, the British decided to adopt a policy appeasing to the Arabs. The "White Paper" of May 1938 cast a heavy shadow on the future of the Jewish National Home and made Great Britain its great enemy.

PHASE ONE

In the early afternoon of April 15, 1936, a convoy of trucks travelling on the Tul Karem-Nablus road was halted by a makeshift stone barrier. One of the trucks was driven by two Jews, Danneberg and Hazan. They were on their way from Haifa to

Tel Aviv. A group of masked and armed Arabs collected money from passengers, claiming that they needed to buy more arms to avenge the assassination of Izz-a-Din al Kassam, the fundamentalist Moslem leader, who was killed by the British police in November 1935. The two Jews were shot dead at point blank. The next day, two Arabs were shot by unknown persons in a hut near Petah-Tikva. The police opined that this was an act of revenge for the killing of Danneberg and Hazan. These were the opening shots in a chain of provocative acts of revenge and counterrevenge between Jews and Arabs in Tel Aviv and Jaffa. The clashes occurred as a backdrop to a recent Jewish campaign against the employment of Arab workers in Jewish enterprises, which was launched in response to the growing unemployment among Jews at the time.[4]

The funeral of Hazan on April 17, 1936, turned into a stormy nationalist Jewish event and the police were obliged to restrain some hot-headed mourners. Acts of cruelty perpetrated by Jewish fanatics shook the leadership. Ben-Gurion, the chairman of the Jewish Agency's Executive Committee, expressed his disgust: "What happened in Tel Aviv last Friday and Saturday, the beating of shoe shine children, breaking into a closed Arab shop, amount to blasphemy."[5]

Dark storm clouds also gathered in Jaffa. Wild rumors spread regarding the clashes in Tel Aviv in the wake of Hazan's funeral. The attempt of the police to dispel these rumors and calm spirits was met with utmost disbelief by the Arab masses. A large crowd besieged the police station in town, demanding to be shown the bodies of four Arabs who according to the rumors were killed by Jews. The police lost control of the situation, with riots breaking out throughout Jaffa. The train of violence now raced full steam and could not be stopped. Within the two first days, sixty-one Jews and six Arabs were killed (seventy-six Jews and seventy-one Arabs were wounded).[6] As these spontaneous events were unfolding, first measures to organize and control the developments were taken by the Palestinian leadership. When the news from Jaffa spread, sprits were aroused and more demonstrations were staged in other Arab towns. In Nablus and Tul Karem, police dispersed the crowds consisting mostly of youngsters and school children. On April 20, 1936, a pamphlet was distributed in which the leadership called the Arab public to a general strike.

The high commissioner summoned five Palestinian leaders and presented them with five demands:

1. To use their influence to stop the illegal acts.

2. To dispel all unfounded rumors.

3. To avoid damages to property and attacks on people.

4. To clarify that the police will suppress every case of violence.

5. To reopen the schools and permit the children to return to their studies.

Ghareb Nashashibi, the head of the National Defense Party, delivered the group's response. He claimed that the riots broke out spontaneously, without any guiding hand, and that they expressed the anger of the masses against continued Jewish immigration.[7]

On April 23, 1936, "National Committees" were established in several Arab towns in order to coordinate the strike. The larger national parties, afraid of losing control and as a token of national unity, founded the "Arab Supreme Committee"

(ASC). Haj Amin al Husseini, the Mufti of Jerusalem, was elected as its chairperson. The ASC adopted as its main platform the three demands that had been presented to the high commissioner earlier in the year. The demands represented a threat to the Jews in Palestine. For had there been democratic elections, the Arabs would have emerged victoriously and would have instituted anti-Jewish policies.

The ASC decided that a memorandum containing the Arab demands be sent to the high commissioner, that contacts with all local National Committees be established, and that the possibility of Arabs employed by the British administration joining the strike be canvassed. These directives completed an important stage in the consolidation of the unfolding revolt: Organs of leadership were created and the political demands, acceptable to the entire Palestinian society, were formulated. Wauchope notified London that he had no intention of recognizing in any formal way the ASC, "since it is a body which was not elected according to the law."[8] The British did try to contain the spread of violence by maximum separation of the two communities and by threatening to punish the perpetrators of illegal acts without alienating innocent segments of the population. But that did not contain the unrest that spread across the country like brushfire.[9]

Two important new characteristics were added to the uprising in May. Farmers from the villages joined and guerrilla groups were activated throughout the country, especially in the hills. The passage of the revolt from the towns to the hills was accompanied by an increase of illegal acts. These included bomb throwing,[10] public incitement, the ambushing of Jewish convoys and British patrols, firing at military camps, the burning of Jewish crops, attacks on isolated Jewish settlements, and the cutting of telephone and telegraph lines.[11] In response, the government detained six Palestinian leaders and banished them to different parts of the country. The deportees gained immediate glory. Before their departure, they published a farewell address worded in a shrill, nationalistic style. Thus the administration inadvertently created "new heroes."[12] 1936 also witnessed an awakening of and sharp increase in the activities of the Haganah, the Jewish paramilitary organization. Riots and unrest always encouraged activities in this organization, yet this time it also made a qualitative difference.[13]

The central Jewish defense organization was at first taken by surprise by the timing of the Arab uprising, its scope, its rapid spread, and its persistence. During the first days the Haganah remained mainly passive. Its functions were limited to defense from "inside the fences." The members usually waited passively for the appearance of the incited Arab crowds and then repelled them by shooting from their fortified trenches. The Haganah command reacted according to traditional outdated strategies that called for the defense of Jewish towns and villages until British security forces arrived and took over.

Sir Arthur Wauchope reported to London that the situation had dangerously deteriorated. He believed that only the dispatch of a royal commission to investigate the situation in depth could prevent further escalation and save the day. In the meantime, the British military garrison undertook three functions: the defense of essential installations, the patrolling of roads and railways, and the escorting of convoys. The situation demanded the use of military guards in many locations such as the railway workshops in Haifa, fuel depots in Jerusalem, the central post office, electric power stations, the broadcasting station in Ramalla, and the telephone center in Ramleh.

Even after the main activities were moved to the hills, Jaffa remained the hotbed of the rebels. Its old, narrow, and winding streets provided an excellent cover from which terrorists could emerge and to which they could escape. The police estimated that large quantities of arms were secreted there. From the ramparts of the old town the rebels could also overlook the harbor and foil all attempts to employ Jewish or Egyptian strike breakers. Wauchope saw an urgent need to control the town, limit its space, and minimize its influence as a furnace of terror and a model for emulation. A plan was prepared to reoccupy the old town and widen four streets, which would then facilitate an easy access to the harbor. The plan necessitated the destruction of many houses. The government maintained that the opening of the broad streets was necessary for "reasons of sanitation and security." On May 28, 1936, a warning was published calling on the residents of the old quarter of Jaffa to stop shooting at the security forces, but sniping and bomb throwing persisted. On May 30, the army went into action with massive fire power but the destruction of the quarter could not be accomplished until military reinforcement arrived in the country eighteen days later.

August was a "hot month." At the end of July the Palestinians attempted to place the disparate guerrilla groups under a unified command. On August 7, the heads of the groups agreed to establish three command zones: the hills of Nablus, the Tul Karem zone, and the area around Haifa and Acre. A "Supreme Court" empowered to try traitors was established. During that month the rebels fortified their hold in the hills, especially in what was named "The Dangerous Triangle" of Tul Karem, Nablus, and Jenin. Their audacity increased day by day. They started to operate in full daylight and attempted to destroy the entire communications network. Assaults on railways, telephone and telegraph lines, and road and railway bridges became a daily occurrence. Terror squads that arose in the cities of Nablus, Haifa, and Jerusalem caused the authorities great concern.[14] These concerns multiplied when information was received of the arrival of mercenaries from neighboring Arab countries under the command of Fawzi el Kawakji, a veteran Syrian rebel who had formerly served in the Iraqi army. These forces were dispatched by the "League for the Defense of Filasteen," recently founded in Bagdad, in order to give the revolt a new momentum and convert the guerrilla warfare into a frontal encounter with the British army.[15]

Kawakji crossed the river Jordan with 100 of his Iraqi supporters and chose the hills near Nablus, which were difficult to access, as the seat of his command, which he termed the "General Command of the Arab Revolt in Southern Syria." He also empowered a so-called "Supreme Court" to adjudicate in civil cases of financial, familial, and agricultural disputes. This tied in with his intention of establishing a governing system that would replace that of the British. His forces were divided into four subunits according to the origin of their fighters: Syrian, Iraqi, Druse, and Palestinian.

The situation obliged the British government to alter its strategy. When the cabinet met on September 2, the concern that the Empire would be humiliated inspired the ministers to resolve to quell the Palestinian violence and reimpose Britain's prestige. The minister for the colonies explained to his colleagues that the limitation of Jewish immigration at that stage would have amounted to a surrender to crime and violence. The minister of war recommended the dispatch of an infantry division under the command of a senior general, who was to be independent of the high commissioner's authority.[16]

The cabinet's conclusion changed the entire picture. It was decided to postpone any decision regarding the limitation of Jewish immigration, to take energetic measures to quell the Palestinian uprising (without bombing civilians), and to restore governing services relating to the police, commerce, and tax collection as soon as law and order was reimposed. The cabinet accepted the principle that a military regime could be instituted in the country or in certain parts of it, if necessary.[17]

For such purposes, a military division (without its artillery) was sent from the United Kingdom to Palestine. It included three brigades (thirteen battalions) and auxiliary units. Control over military affairs in Palestine, which was until then maintained by the Royal Air Force, was entrusted to the army under the command of General John Dill.[18] It soon turned out that the military command and the high commissioner interpreted the cabinet's resolution differently. While the army saw it as an opportunity to employ its forces under a military regime, Wauchope took it only as a warning to the Arab leadership to take action to reduce violence. He wanted to leave them an opening to withdraw and allow them some time, albeit a limited time, for political action. In any case, he certainly intended to continue to handle the affairs of the country. This disagreement soon developed into a bitter controversy.

The first battle between the army and Kawakji's troops took place on September 3, 1936, near the village of Bal'a on the highway between Tul Karem and Nablus. The British managed to encircle Kawakji's forces in his mountain stronghold. At that point the Palestinian leadership, impressed by a call from several Arab monarchs and rulers, decided to call off, for the time being, the general strike. After 176 days, six thousand Moslems gathered for a special prayer in the Haram a Sharif in Jerusalem, at the end of which shops were reopened and public transport was resumed. The first phase of the revolt was over.

The ending of this phase in the revolt came as a result of a number of factors. The strike began to boomerang and exacted heavy losses from the Palestinian population. Commercial and economic interests began to exert pressure on the High Arab Command (HAC) to call the strike off. Leaders in neighboring Arab countries counseled for an end to violence, while the British threatened to mobilize even more forces from England.[19]

With the uprising winding down, General Dill wished to pursue and destroy remaining guerrilla gangs. He was opposed by the high commissioner, who feared that such tactics would have provoked a renewed cycle of violence. The controversy between the civil administration and the military came to a head over the issue of handling Kawakji's troops. The HAC and the mayor of Nablus, surprised by the scope of the military operations and concerned for the fate of Kawakji and his men, who were trapped in the hills, appealed to the high commissioner. An agreement was obtained, by which Kawakji and his men would be allowed to leave the country unharmed. Reluctantly, the army complied. Kawakji and his men forded the river Jordan bearing all of their arms. In a letter to the secretary for the colonies, Wauchope wrote that Dill was disappointed in not being given a free hand in imposing a clear-cut military solution.

The lull in the revolt lasted until September 26, 1937, ending in a general stalemate. The Palestinians gained the backing of all Arab states for their cause. Britain managed to preserve its interests in Palestine and the Middle East at large. The Jews, under British protection, managed to defend their "National Home" and even strengthened it. The main loser was the British army, which felt betrayed and used by politicians for their own purposes. Many officers believed that the high commissioner had subverted the cabinet's decision and that ending the revolt without crushing all guerrilla resistance simply paved the way for a resumption of insurgency.

SECOND PHASE

The second phase of the revolt started on November 11 with the arrival of the Royal Investigation Commission, led by Lord Peel, in Jerusalem. The next day a festive opening session was held in the Government House, in the presence of many civil and military dignitaries. The appointment writ was read in the three official languages and the high commissioner blessed the Commission and wished it success. The British cabinet had in fact decided to dispatch a commission in the early stages of the revolt, but in May 18, 1936, it made it contingent on the "resumption of law and order and the cessation of hostilities."[20]

While the Commission was working on its final report, the army sought to utilize the truce in order to prepare a wide operational infrastructure for a comprehensive struggle against guerrilla and terror tactics. New roads, leading right into the heart of the Palestinian rural hinterland, were paved. The construction of a security fence along the northern borders was inaugurated to isolate Palestine from Syria and Lebanon. General Spicer, the chief of police, also began to disarm the entire population in a belt, ten miles wide, on the eastern side of the river Jordan. He instructed the border police to keep a constant vigil over the western side of the river and to draw fences across all access roads leading to the river. Intensive patrolling was introduced along the northern border and "blockhouses" were built to serve as mini-police stations along the fence.[21]

However, the controversy between the civil administration and the military became so intense that London had to intervene. The cabinet was aware that the bitter relations between Dill and Wauchope would not have enabled them to deal with the likely challenges inherent in the Peel Commission's pending recommendations. It was decided that the command powers of the high commissioner would apply only during normal times. Should a military regime be promulgated, the senior commander of the military force would assume the supreme power in the country. Nevertheless, for the time being the army's mission was not changed and the high commissioner remained the decisive figure dictating the rules to be implemented in handling the revolt.

The Jews, too, began to learn lessons from the first phase of the revolt. They reorganized their defenses and improved their military capability. A conference of all commanders of the Haganah convened in Tel Aviv, assessed likely future developments, and identified the measures required for such challenges.[22] The events of the revolt placed security matters at the center of attention of the Jewish public. The flow of new volunteers to the ranks of the Haganah increased dramatically. By the end of 1937, the Haganah numbered 25,000 fighters. Special attention was given to modern military training. "In many cases failures resulted from the fact that men were not accustomed to deploy their weapons quickly enough and with confidence."[23]

The Haganah also began to develop new fighting frameworks and changed the tactics of defense. A wide network of the new "Jewish Settlement Police" (JSP) was established. These were squads of young Jews whom the British authorities fitted with guns and special uniforms. Provided with light trucks and some machine guns, these legalized police auxiliary forces, who were formally supervised by British police officers, were in fact guided by the Haganah. They gave the Jewish paramilitary organization the opportunity to control entire sections of the land that were intensively populated by Jewish Kibutzim and villages. In many villages and colonies weapons were stored in special JSP "Stations" and members of the Haganah were able to use them for training and guard duties. It also gave the Haganah the opportunity to give its low- and middle-ranking commanders some command experience. Many of the later cadres of Israel's Defense Forces began their military career in the JSP.

A new procedure evolved for rapidly establishing new tower and stockade (Homa u Migdal) settlements. It entailed a convoy of trucks, loaded with hundreds of volunteers and all necessary equipment, setting out at dusk to a chosen location. A number of wooden houses and tents would be erected overnight, surrounded by a double wall comprising two panels of wood filled with pebbles. In addition, a tall watchtower would be positioned in the settlement's center to serve as a lookout and to transmit light signals. By dawn a new village would have been completed, ready to meet any attacker from behind fortified walls.[24]

A few daring young commanders, notably Itzhak Sadeh and Eliahu Ben Hur, who in later years became generals in the Israel Defense Forces, experimented with more aggressive and offensive tactics. Under British rule, the Jewish community in Palestine could not undertake the responsibility and was not able to suppress the Arab revolt. During 1936–1939 the war raged primarily between the Palestinian guerrillas and the British army. Nevertheless, since the Arabs directed many of their attacks against Jewish targets and the British forces were not always available to repel those attacks on time, the Haganah had to, as was expected by the authorities, take on many defensive functions, at least until the British army or police arrived on the scene. Sadeh and Ben Hur offered a wider interpretation of this primarily defensive function. Instead of waiting inside the perimeter of the Jewish settlements until the Arabs arrived and only then repelling by firing from fortified positions, they decided to preempt such attacks by ambushing Arab gangs and even attacking the Palestinians in their own bases. These new tactics were termed "emerging from the fences" by their initiators and afforded an opportunity for growing numbers of young Jews to gain field combat experience. The Haganah supreme command, recognizing the advantages inherent in that approach, soon organized a few special mobile units throughout the country manned by permanently recruited fighters. These units were called "Field Companies" (known better by their Hebrew acronym "FOSH") and were unofficially recognized by the British authorities.[25]

The Arab Revolt also spurred the Haganah to upgrade its overall organization and planning. During the 1920s and early 1930s, the Haganah was a loose national conglomerate of local defense groups. The central command was weak and did little more than provide the local units with some centrally procured armaments and sporadic specialized training. During the revolt, the first military planning on a national scale was drafted. Regular national courses for commanders on different levels became routine. The central command began to assert its authority. For the first time the national defense plan allowed for the possibility that the Jews themselves would have to face, head on, the Palestinian forces committed in their fight against the Zionist project. For the first time the notion that the defense of the Jewish community might require the military conquest of the entire country or large parts of it was taken seriously by the Jewish military planners.[26]

The growing international tension around the expansionist policies of Hitler and Mussolini in Europe and Africa during 1937 and the relative calm that resulted at the end of the general strike in Palestine drove the British to decrease its garrisons in the country. The plans for the erection of fences along the borders and other precautionary measures that emerged from the lessons the British drew from the uprising were now shelved. The withdrawal of a large segment of the British army created a vacuum and the government decided to fill it by augmenting the local police force. Financial difficulties in London and the lack of available trained personnel in England opened for the Jewish community the opportunity to participate actively and officially in the defense of the country as a whole. Roy Spicer, the police chief superintendent, suggested that local policemen "especially Jews" be recruited to fill the gaps. Wauchope agreed and at the beginning of 1937 the Colonial Office authorized the creation of a new force of "Special Auxiliary Police," which was used for the defense of several points along the railways and other vital installations.[27] This was a splendid opportunity for the Jewish community to legally train and arm additional young men, whose numbers ran into the hundreds.

The Peel Commission did a thorough job in analyzing the different aspects of the Arab-Jewish strife and presented a number of recommendations, the most important of which was their suggestion to partition the country between the Arabs and the Jews. It was a revolutionary turn in British policy over Palestine, which so far had adhered to the development of a unified bi-national state.

The atmosphere in the country, in expectation of Peel's report, was highly charged. The HAC was alarmed by rumors suggesting that the Peel Commission would recommend partition. Envoys were sent to all Arab countries to drum-up opposition to such a proposal. The Mufti, Haj Amin himself, travelled to Damascus for the same purpose. At this stage all concerned wanted to avoid a renewal of violence, but were fully aware that a small spark would suffice to reignite the entire country. The members of the Peel Commission themselves were also cognizant that "The more we saw and the more we heard in the days that followed, the clearer it became that this armistice was only a suspension of hostilities, not a preliminary to peace. . . . It was believed in many quarters that another outbreak might occur at any moment. Several isolated murders or assaults occurred during our stay."[28]

Haj Amin's efforts were crowned by a conference convened on September 8, 1937, in the Syrian resort town of Blodan. Although the conference was not officially endorsed by the Arab states, it became an impressive occasion and a turning point in the affairs of Palestine, since it indicated a clear intensification of the involvement of all Arab sovereigns in the Palestinian conflict and signalled the resumption of the revolt. There were 400 representatives from Egypt, Iraq, Transjordan, Lebanon, Palestine, and of course, from Syria, which hosted the event. The conference served as a platform for virulent attacks against Great Britain and Zionism. Four committees were established to handle the political, financial, economic, and propaganda issues destined to encourage the Arab states to support the Palestinian cause. Five decisions were arrived at:

1. Palestine was regarded as an inseparable part of the Arab world.
2. The partition of Palestine and the creation of a Jewish state was to be utterly rejected.
3. Financial resources were to be raised to support the Palestinians.

4. Jewish and British merchandise was to be boycotted.

5. Pro-Palestinian propaganda was to be disseminated.

Some of the proceedings dealing with military affairs were held behind closed doors. No official decision to resume the revolt was taken, but on September 10, the Mufti and his personal guards enclosed themselves in the Haram e Sharif, the holy Moslem shrines on the Temple Mount in Jerusalem. This move signalled the end of the truce.

The Jews also made some moves in response to the Peel Commission's recommendation. It was decided to rapidly expand the boundaries of the area settled by Jews to preempt a final decision on the exact lines of partition. More land was purchased in different parts of the country, including some traditionally Arab sections. Between 1936 and 1939, fifty-two new settlements were established, mostly in the Homa u Migdal method, in remote and outlaying regions.

THIRD PHASE

On September 26, 1937, around 6 P.M., the spark was ignited that enflamed the entire country. Louis Andrews, the governor of the Galilee, and his bodyguard McEwan were shot dead by four Arabs, walking, as always on Sundays, towards the Anglican church in Nazareth. The British cabinet was shocked and decided to take firm action in response. The HAC denounced the murder, but its denouncement was rejected by the government. It was the first time a British official was murdered in Palestine and the British considered the deed as a declaration of the renewal of the revolt.[29]

The authorities in Jerusalem took some immediate actions, and for a while it seemed as if they had moved away from an appeasement policy and decided to nip the revolt in its buds.[30] A heavy police force placed Nazareth under curfew. The government "Executive Council" decided to ask London for permission to annul the legal status of the HAC and some local national committees and arrest the Mufti and other prominent members of the HAC. Buttershill, the general secretary of the Palestine administration, while acting as high commissioner, not waiting for the reply from London, ordered the prompt arrest of more than 100 Arabs in the Galilee, Haifa, and Samaria. These were largely terrorists and inciters blacklisted by the police on account of their previous activities.

The secretary for the colonies approved the arrest of members of the HAC and their exile to the Seychelles Islands in the Indian Ocean. He informed Buttershill that rapid and unimpeded action was needed. The government was to explain that such measures were adopted in the interest of public security.[31] Early in the morning on Friday, October 1, all telephone lines were cut off while the police raided the homes of all HAC members. However, due to faulty intelligence only some of the members were arrested and deported. The rest managed to hide or escape to Syria.

The most decisive action was the dismissal of Haj Amin el Husseini from his position as the head of the High Moslem Council, a position to which he was nominated by the British authorities in 1921. The disbanding of the HAC did not eliminate Palestinian leadership. The leadership void was soon filled. Those left behind, especially members of the Husseini clan, called for the renewal of the general strike, but the public response was cool and the Mufti, from his refuge on the Haram e Sharif, called it off. The authorities, too, procrastinated and did not take advantage of the shock and confusion that initially engulfed the Palestinian community. Buttershill well realized that any security improvements were only temporary. Even so, he decided to bide for time.[32]

Appreciating that further harsh measures might be necessary, the cabinet decided to replace the cautious Wauchope with a new high commissioner with more colonial experience.[33] In the meantime, in reaction to rumors that the Mufti was planning an escape, General Archibald Wavell, who replaced General Dill as the senior military commander, and who, like his predecessor, considered the Mufti the prime source of the troubles, sought the Mufti's arrest. However, the "Red Fox," as the Mufti was nicknamed by the British, frustrated operation "Tallyho" by descending the walls of the Holy Mount, camouflaged in bedouin attire. He was whisked away by his loyal supporters to Jaffa harbor, whence he travelled by boat to Lebanon. There he received political asylum by the French authorities, and though his actions were formally constrained, he succeeded in reconstituting the HAC and reactivating it from Damascus.

Wauchope, who temporarily resumed his post, was beguiled by his misconceptions. The cool response of the Palestinian population to the call to renew the rebellion led him to believe that the main wave of terror had subsided and that political measures were preferable to military ones. Accordingly, he continued to oppose the imposition of a military regime. Many Palestinians realized that the general uprising in 1936 did not advance their interests and simply resulted in economic losses, but by the summer of 1937 the guerrilla gangs, by virtue of their renewed activity, orchestrated the music to which the British army was forced to march.

When 1937 neared its end, it was clear that the military measures taken by the authorities could not impose law and order. Buttershill admitted in his reports to the Colonial Office that life and property were not secure, the country was in general retreat, and the general picture was bleak. Violent assaults, murder, and attempts of murder were daily matters, armed gangs roamed around unimpeded and the Jews began to counterattack on a growing scale. All British civilian personnel had to be armed or put under police protection.[34] In addition, the cabinet yielded to the pressures of the Foreign Office. The head of the Eastern Department submitted to the cabinet a memorandum in which he recommended the shelving of the Peel Commission report. He argued that groups of armed Arabs from all neighboring countries were awaiting the first opportunity to join hands with the Palestinian guerrillas against Great Britain. He quoted King Ibn Saud who said that he considered the establishment of a Jewish state on the shores of Palestine a great danger to the Arabs, especially in view of the high likelihood that European Jews would swarm into the country.

The appointment of a new inquiry committee seemed to be the way out. Sir John Woodhead was asked to head it and was charged by the cabinet with investigating the practicalities of implementing the Peel recommendations.[35] The committee arrived in Palestine on April 24, 1938, and the HAC, banned from its new seat in Damascus, cooperated with it. Woodhead was met upon his arrival by some blatant acts of terror. Six Jews who travelled in a taxi between Safed and Acre were assassinated, a number of Jewish settlements came under heavy fire, and lines of communications were attacked.

FOURTH PHASE

On March 1, Wauchope was replaced by Sir Harold MacMichael, a veteran colonial civil servant. The embittered Wauchope, who had so great an influence on the events of the previous two years, summed up the situation thus: "The last two years will be remembered in history as years of difficulties and disappointments. The difference between what we have hoped for and what was achieved is discouraging . . . but where no vision exists there is no life."[36] The changing of guard was intended to improve the relations between the civil authority and the military and to enable full cooperation of the two bodies in an attempt to suppress the rebellion as quickly as possible. The cabinet in London attached great importance to those objectives since heavy clouds were casting their shadows over Europe. Malcolm MacDonald, who was about to take over as secretary for the colonies, congratulated MacMichael on his appointment and added that his new task was the most difficult in the entire colonial service and involved the most difficult problem facing the Empire. The cabinet felt a moral obligation to the Arab and Jewish residents of the country, he added. Great Britain had resolved to remain in Palestine for strategic reasons and for reasons of political prestige.[37] On April 9, Major-General Wavell was also replaced by Lieutenant-General Robert Haining as commander in chief of the military force in Palestine.

In the summer of 1938 the revolt reached its peak. The growing international tensions obliged the British to evacuate more troops from Palestine. The Palestinian guerrillas who remained as the only effective force controlled large parts of the country and some major towns as well. The government had to rely more heavily on the Jewish community and recruited more Jewish auxiliary policemen. MacMichael reported at the beginning of July that up to that point, 5,500 Jews were trained for different police duties and 1,345 were stationed in different Jewish settlements in permanent positions.[38] Jewish men were now utilized in many and diverse functions. For example, 250 Jews were employed to defend the workers who were engaged in constructing the northern fence when the work on it has been resumed. Twenty Jews reinforced the police in Safed and, as of June, security along the railway line from Haifa to Egypt was provided by Jewish auxiliary policemen. In addition, more Jews were trained to man the little forts scattered along all railways. The high commissioner told the secretary for the colonies that in time of a general rebellion the government would be obliged to recruit and arm many more Jews and use them for offensive operations. He was aware of the heavy political implications of such a move, and knew that it could have been considered only as a last resort.[39]

A symbolic step in this direction was taken already by General Wavell, who was looking for new methods to combat the Arab guerrillas. In February, a certain Captain Charles Ord Wingate, an intelligence officer with the Royal Artillery, was posted to general headquarters in Jerusalem. On his request he was granted permission to travel to the north in order to investigate the situation on the spot. Wavell considered Wingate a "strange creature" but could see, through his queer external appearance, a thoroughly nonconventional officer with unique qualities. Wingate met the brigade commander stationed in Haifa, whom he found "supportive, understanding and energetic." Wingate proposed the establishment of a special mixed British-Jewish unit to defend the pipeline that delivered Iraqi oil to the refineries in Haifa and that was often sabotaged by the Arabs. His proposal seemed to provide an appropriate response to the concerns of the British chiefs of staff over the security of the pipeline, which they considered a vital British interest. Accordingly, they approved General Haining's formal proposal to establish the "Special Night Squads" (better known by the acronym SNS) despite a previous decision that Jews were not to engage in offensive operations.

In the history of the Haganah, the foundation of the SNS is considered a landmark, despite the fact that it operated only less than a year and included only a few dozen Jews. The experience was exhilarating for the young men who participated, many of whom later formed the high command of the Haganah and the Israel Defense Forces. The "Sergeants course" that Wingate conducted at Ain Harod was the anvil on which most of the Haganah command for the next ten years was forged. His teaching became a cornerstone of the Jewish defense forces' doctrine for many years to come. The squads led personally by Wingate, which operated offensively deep in Arab territory, sought to engage the Arab guerrillas in or near their bases. Many were dispersed and suffered casualties. Wingate became a legendary figure in the Zionist collective memory. His daring leadership and friendly demeanor towards the young Jews who served under him impressed them deeply. The battle experience they gained in the SNS and the guidance (spiritual as well as tactical) they received from the bible-lover captain, known among Jews as "The Friend," left a lasting legacy within the Yishuv.[40]

Wingate's successes marked also a change of mood among the authorities. They became prepared to transfer the fight into the Arab heartland. On the other hand, many British officials were opposed to Wingate's initiatives. Most intelligence officers objected to the use of Jews in offensive operations out of fear of further alienating the Arabs. Despite his success, on December 12, 1938, after having been wounded in one of the skirmishes, Wingate was replaced by his deputy, who began to gradually liquidate the squads. The last squad was disbanded by the end of July 1939. The explanation given for this move was that the Iraqi Petrol Company stopped the financing of the unit. For captain Wingate, his activity with the Jews was not just a brief episode. He had far-reaching visions. He believed that the Jews ought to and would decide the future of the country. They did not need British bayonets to defend themselves, he argued. They had the will and the capability to become a fighting nation and were becoming the best allies of the United Kingdom in the Middle East.[41]

Perforce, the British had to continue to rely on the Jewish community in their fight against the Arabs. The role played by the Jews in the government defense plans necessitated a deep organizational reform within the Haganah. In July 1938, Yohanan Ratner, a veteran officer of the Russian army, was nominated as the first chief of staff of that clandestine organization. Up to then, the Haganah was managed by a political body of representatives of different parties in the Jewish community. This body, renamed the "Country Command Committee," became the new political civilian supervisory body acting on behalf of the entire community. It was Ratner who created the professional military General Staff of the Haganah. The organization was divided into six regional commands of the larger towns of Jerusalem, Haifa, and Tel Aviv and four rural regions. The companies of the "FOSH," the mobile standing forces, were placed under the control of the regional commanders. The official Jewish Settlement Police (JSP) afforded the Haganah a semilegal organ to advance the construction of their paramilitary units. Many of the Haganah's commanders formally served as Non-Commissioned Officers (NCOs) of the JSP but were actually nominees of the Haganah. Weapons stored in the several JSP stations were used to train Haganah members. The British, who were at this stage fighting the Arab rebels, having an interest in that arrangement, closed at least one eye to those semilegal activities of the Jews.

In the summer of 1938, in the wake of a further decrease in the size of the British garrison in Palestine, a sharp increase in acts of terror against British and Jewish personnel provoked a few retaliatory attacks perpetrated by a Jewish group which had recently splintered from the Haganah. In 1937, a right-wing political group led by Zeev Zabotinski formed an independent military organization they named "The National Military Organization" (better know by its Hebrew acronym IZL for "Irgun Zvai Leumi," or in short "The Irgun"). They denounced the policy of restraint adopted by the Haganah and did not recognize the authority of the Haganah's National Command and General Staff. Instead, they adopted an offensive approach and launched a series of retaliatory attacks against Arabs, including civilians. On July 6, 1938, a small group of IZL members penetrated the Arab market in Haifa and threw a bomb in the middle of the heavy crowd. Twenty-five Palestinians were killed and 100 wounded. More bombs were thrown in populated places in Jerusalem and Jaffa and wanton fire was opened in a number of other places against Arab crowds. IZL claimed that these attacks came as reprisals for Arab attacks, but the net effect was the heightening of tension between Jews and Arabs in Palestine. These undisciplined and cruel acts jeopardized the sympathy of the British for the Jews. They also bothered London, especially since they were popular among many young Jews who were attracted to the more radical circles.[42]

The sharp intensification of the international tension at the beginning of the summer induced London to find a way out of the crisis in Palestine. On August 6, 1938, Malcolm MacDonald, the secretary for the colonies, arrived for a one-day visit to Jerusalem. He wanted to obtain a firsthand impression of the situation in order to formulate a new policy. He urged the high commissioner to put the police under the authority of the army in order to signal to the public that the government "is resolved to suppress any opposition to the rule of law."[43] Nevertheless, the secretary still rejected putting the country under a military regime, especially in view of the lack of forces to impose it. On the other hand, the secretary was concerned lest Britain encountered troubles in the Middle East while its affairs in Europe were entangled. He began to consider a policy that would eventually lead to the relinquishment of the Peel partition plan. He believed that some gesture to placate the Arab leaders was timely. MacMichael was not enthusiastic, since he thought that the moderate leaders were at that stage more afraid of the radicals than of the British. The Arab public, he explained, was given to terrorist threats and chose the least dangerous alternative. The villagers supported the terrorists by providing them with more fighters, food, and money, and by denouncing collaborators. MacDonald recommended that the French government be called upon to expel the Mufti and his headquarters from Syria and Lebanon and to strike "at the heart of the terrorist organization."[44]

MacMichael was right. The situation had indeed totally deteriorated: The Palestinian political organs were outlawed; most of the urban leaders were either under arrest or in exile; foreign leaders, such as Kawakji, could not be reactivated. Under such conditions no effective political activity was possible. The only groups that were able to wield real and effective power were the guerrilla gangs. They managed to impose themselves on the large towns as well. The great measure of control that the gangs had on the Palestinian public was symbolized by the order they issued to men to wear the traditional rural "Kefiya and Aqal" headguard and for women to cover their faces. In fact, they managed to impose an alternative governance.[45] This symbolic act provoked the British government to take radical measures to prevent the country from falling into utter chaos.

FIFTH PHASE

The conclusion of the "Munich Agreement" on September 30, 1930, seemed for a while to have dispersed the clouds of war over Europe and made the resumption of a military build-up in Palestine possible. Field Marshal Ironside, the head of the Emperial General Staff, visited Palestine to plan a decisive strategy for the suppression of the rebellion. He did not believe that anything would be achieved by political declarations alone. In his view, the full use of military power was needed to prevent the total collapse of civil authority.

One of the British police officers most experienced in counterinsurgency warfare, Sir Charles Tegart, was sent to General Haining's headquarters and two infantry divisions were added to the local garrison. In October 1938, 18,500 British soldiers were stationed in Palestine, the 7th Division under Major-General Richard O'Conor around Jerusalem and the 8th Division under Major-General Bernard Montgomery around Haifa. The Royal Air Force was also reinforced with three more combat wings. Once those forces were deployed, London still dragged its feet in prolonged debates and planning. Only after General Haining threatened to resign were the operational orders issued. The military brief was defined as "replacing" the civil authority in the implementation of the new strategy instead of merely "supporting" it. It was not an explicit declaration of a military regime, but the army obtained wide emergency powers, with the police coming under the military command.[46] On October 19, a governmental proclamation was published in the *Official Gazette* and in the daily press to the effect that all security affairs were transferred to the military commanders. The regional civil governors were to serve as political advisors and were to continue to be in charge of civil affairs.[47]

A slow process of suppressing the revolt got underway, which was devoid of snags. In addition to military moves, limitations on civilian life, especially on Arab personal mobility, and traffic were imposed. To avoid being portrayed as vengeful by the propaganda media of the rebels, the military command took care to keep these limitations within reasonable bounds. Being fully aware that by the end of military operations civil authority was to be restored, Haining wanted to avoid a "scorched earth policy." Essentially, he wished to restore British prestige by removing the rebel threat from the population by confiscating all illegal arms.

In preparation for the reconquest of the "Old City" in Jerusalem, General Haining nominated General O'Conor as governor of that region. Over time, hundreds of Palestinian guerrillas had infiltrated into the old walled city, of which they gained effective control, even to the extent of closing its gates on October 8. British police were ejected and an Arab flag was hoisted over the Damascus gate. O'Conor determined to repossess the old quarter with minimum casualties. He intended to:

a. Surround and isolate the city.

b. Capture the Dome of the Rock that dominated the entire area both physically and spiritually.

c. Enter the entire area rapidly via alleys and rooftops, giving preference to the seizure of minarets which overlooked various sections.

The regimental commanders gave his plans quite a cool reception. They were not experienced in street fighting and were fearful of incurring heavy losses. O'Conor, suspecting that their reservations stemmed from their unfamiliarity with his tactics, felt that there was no other suitable alternative.[48] The attack commenced at 4:00 A.M. on the October 19. The soldiers were ordered to bear minimal equipment to facilitate rapid movement and wore rubber-soled shoes to avoid slipping on the slippery pavement. Two battalions encircled the old quarter while two others smashed the gates to move rapidly from house to house, pushing groups of civilians ahead as "live shields." Airplanes guided the troops from above. The opposition was weak, since most of the rebels were hiding in the Haram e Sharif. The combing of the old town lasted four days and only four Arabs and one soldier were killed.

The same day the town of Acre was also "conquered," and by October 31, the cleansing of Jaffa began. The British were assisted by Jews who were well acquainted with the area. They experienced no losses but on the Arab side four deaths and two injuries were sustained. With a large number of Palestinians detained for further investigations, the police could assume routine control of the towns. The moral effect of the successful operation was highly significant. Jaffa ceased to be the major hotbed for trouble makers.[49]

It became obvious that the rebels were losing ground. The appearance of the "Peace Gangs" in the Palestinian community gave the best indication of this transformation. Groups of Palestinians who opposed the radicals began to provide active defense to Arab citizens threatened by the guerrillas. The Arab community was now divided over three main questions relating to the leadership of the revolt, the appropriate tactics to be employed against the British army, and the measures to be taken against Arabs who collaborated with the government and the Jews.

The third issue constituted the main bone of contention between the supporters of the Mufti and his opponents. The extremists took note of the moderate Arabs and those suspected of supporting the Peel partition plan.[50] Threats and terror against moderates multiplied dramatically during 1938. This impelled the Nashashibi clan, who led the moderates, to take preemptive measures. They began to mobilize the Arab notables in and around Jerusalem in opposition to the Husseinis and organized counterterror "Peace Gangs." On November 1, the army proclaimed that every citizen had to carry an identification card. This placed the Palestinian population in a dilemma. They could either request identification cards, risking the revenge of the guerrillas, or abstain and give up every possibility of personal movement and commercial activities. At first, they mostly chose the first option, pressurizing the guerrillas to permit the drawing cards by those who needed to engage in the citrus harvest. The radicals yielded with regard to truck drivers who were transporting citrus fruits to the harbors in exchange for a special tax levied on every fruit box, ostensibly for the benefit of the revolt's treasury.

In order to encourage the moderates, MacDonald decided to take some conciliatory moves. He published the recommendations of the Woodhead committee, which spelled a backing away from the Peel partition plan. He also declared the intention of the British government to convene in London an Arab-Jewish conference, with the participation of delegates from several Arab states, to discuss the future of Palestine. The Arabs rejoiced and saw in the Woodhead Report proof of their revolt's victory. However they resented the fact that Jewish immigration had not yet been stopped and that the Mufti was excluded from the negotiations. The Jews, on the other hand, were shocked to find out that the Woodhead Report proposed to limit the future Jewish State to a narrow coastal region and recommended that the British mandate would remain intact over the entire Galilee.

By mid-November attention was drawn to two new developments. During the night of November 9, called Kristal Nacht, the Nazis unleashed a series of anti-Jewish pogroms. The concern of the Yishuv for the fate of Jews in Germany and other Jewish communities in Europe intensified. Sir Harold MacMichael commented cynically that the "primitive and cruel outburst" focused the attention of the world to the plight of the Jews at a time most appropriate for the Zionists, just when they most needed the sympathy of the world.[51]

Around the same time the internecine struggle in the Palestinian community came to head. On November 15, Fahri Nashashibi, the head of the clan, published an open letter to the high commissioner, complementing the government for its withdrawal from the partition plan. He claimed that his "Defense Party" represented the opinion of 50 percent of the Arab population in the country. He also published a brochure laying out all the Mufti's crimes. By December, the high commissioner estimated that the internecine terror had reached its peak, working to the rebels' disadvantage. He believed that the Palestinians would eventually have to choose between economic ruin and hunger or being beholden to the rebels. He also compared the Arab plight to the great prosperity that the Jews enjoyed. This economic prosperity resulted from a number of causes: the disappearance of Arab vehicles from the roads, the recurrent closure of Arab businesses, the increase in employment of Jews in the service of the police, and the contracts concluded between Jews and the British army. The economic boom brought about a significant reduction of Jewish unemployment.

In November, the towns of Be'er Sheva and Hevron, which had been under the rebels' heels since September, were freed. Despite the slowness of the operation, General Haining was satisfied with the progress achieved.[52] By the beginning of December, a third of the 1,000 Arab villages were also penetrated and the secretary for the colonies was able to report to the cabinet that the military operations were on target. Only small-scale, sporadic acts of sabotage were being perpetrated.[53] He added that these successes made it possible to consider favorably the appeal of some Arab states to release the Palestinian leaders who were exiled to the Seychelles to enable them to participate in the forthcoming conference in London.

END GAME

1939 was a year of decisions. It began with a flurry of political activities. The London conference was imminent. Before proceeding to London the Seychelles exiles arrived in Beirut on January 11, 1939, for consultation with the Mufti, despite promises given by the French government to prevent that encounter.[54] Haj Amin el Husseini regained control of the situation, for the thirteen-member delegation to London was totally under his influence. His cousin Janal el Husseini was nominated head of the delegation. It forebode an inflexible Palestinian stance likely to forestall a settlement or compromise. It was also a harsh blow to the moderates who were eager to bring the revolt to an end and resume cooperation with the British.

In the meantime, the military operation continued. At the beginning of January 1939, General Montgomery initiated a cleansing operation in the north. Thereafter, Montgomery planned to move south to link up with other forces in ultimately suppressing the revolt in the "Dangerous Triangle." MacMichael noted that on the one hand the Palestinian population began to collaborate with the authorities by providing information on the rebels' movements and by being prepared to carry ID cards; yet on the other hand, there was a marked increase in the number of assassinations of Arabs by Arabs.[55] The guerrillas maintained their hit-and-run tactics against British and Jewish targets. On January 5, they attempted to kill a number of senior British officers including Sir Charles Tegart. A convoy travelling on the Jerusalem-Nablus road was attacked by an 80–100-men-strong ambush. Tegart's assistant was killed but the convoy managed to proceed to Jerusalem. Elsewhere, on January 16, near Ben Shemen, a group of twenty guerrillas attacked three mounted Jewish guards. Two Jews and one Arab were killed in the skirmish.[56]

Despite such exploits, the rebels began to lose the sympathy and support of the Palestinian people. Contrary to the logic of guerrilla warfare, they frequently engaged in large-scale battles in which their losses were excessive. When on March 27 Abd el Rahim el Haj Mohamend, one of the outstanding guerrillas, was killed in a battle north of Nablus, it became clear that the revolt had just about run its course. The fact that the rebels began to recruit minors under the age of seventeen was a clear indication of their desperation. Several of the senior commanders of the rebellion fled to Syria and Transjordan. The exiled Mufti tried to continue the struggle by raising more money, buying weapons, and recruiting Syrian volunteers, but he was out of touch with the beaten, tired, and harassed population that no longer wished to serve a lost cause. Attempts by the Germans and Italians to stiffen the resolve of the guerrillas in order to foster their interest in the looming war in Europe were also in vain.[57]

The London conference was convened in St. James palace in March 1939. It failed to achieve any results since the parties did not budge from their original positions. A new policy statement by the British government was now inevitable. In April, General Montgomery, who appreciated that the organized revolt was destroyed, returned to England to assume command of the 3rd Division.[58] The revolt was clearly at an end. One of the opposition's active members dared to denounce the rebels' threats and murders in a public meeting in Nablus. Some isolated incidents continued, such as an attack of a 100-strong guerrilla group on the police station and governor's house in Nazareth. But all were now expecting the new British policy declaration. Jewish intelligence agencies reported that governmental circles in Jerusalem were of the opinion that that step would augur the end of the Arab Revolt.[59] For the Zionists, the future of their "National Home" was at stake.

On May 17, London published a "White Paper" that contained the expected new policy declaration over Palestine. It pronounced Britain's undertaking to set up within ten years an independent State of Palestine. No federal arrangements were mentioned. The proclamation, which was concluded after consultation with several Arab states held in Cairo, was designed to satisfy Britain's interests in the imminently expected war in Europe.

The strategic interest to avoid opening a second front in the Middle East was compelling. The "White Paper" also imposed severe constraints on the Jews in the areas of immigration and land purchase. It was a dramatic change in Great Britain's attitude towards the Zionist endeavor and brought about a crisis in the relations of the Yishuv with the British government. A short while before the proclamation was about to be transmitted over the Palestine Broadcasting Service, the electricity line of the radio station in Ramalla was severed. The government suspected that the sabotage was performed by Jews. The Yishuv was deeply frustrated and prepared itself for a tenacious struggle, but war in Europe broke out three months later and the head-on conflict between the Zionists and the British had to be postponed until Hitler was defeated five years later.

CONCLUSION

Despite the military failure, the Arab revolt was a landmark in the history of the Palestinian national movement. The Palestinians dared to challenge the British rule in Palestine and managed to insert their cause on the Empire's agenda, to commit the Arab states to their side, and to make the United Kingdom withdraw its support of the Zionist program. The revolt was the fountainhead from which the Palestinians in the following decade drew their hopes and aspirations. The revolt also had negative results for the Arab community of Palestine—the casualties and the heavy economic price they had to pay, the internal bitter rifts and the removal of an entire layer of leaders that caused severe setbacks for the future development of their national movement. The Arab states that filled the vacuum brought about by the revolt had their own interests at heart. The Palestinian cause served as a smokescreen to disguise that elementary fact.

Paradoxically, the Arab revolt gave an important incentive to the development of the Jewish homeland. The revolt spurred a leap forward in the Haganah's organization and strategic doctrine and provided a strong thrust to the development of the Jewish economic infrastructures in the country. It encouraged the creation of additional rural settlements across large parts of Palestine. The leadership of the Yishuv consolidated its representative authority despite the dispute over the mode of response to Arab terrorism and to the new British anti-Zionist policy. It became clear that a combination of political and economic activism, military force, and a broad national unity of purpose were necessary for the development of the "National Home."

The road to the suppression of the rebellion was arduous and strewn with difficulties, but the brazen insistence of the British military commanders to deploy force without constraint led to its conclusion. Without the heavy blows the military inflicted between October 1938 and March 1939, the commanders of the revolt would have escaped and the destruction of the guerrilla gangs may not have been fully accomplished. The military offensive created the conditions in which a measure of collaboration of many Arabs with the government could be reestablished, and the trust between the Palestinians and the British could be partially reconstructed.

On May 7, 1940, General Giffard, the new military chief in Palestine, announced that the revolt was finally broken. He predicted that should the revolt ever be resumed, the Jews would react differently. The outcome of that prediction had to wait for another era. As it happens, the Jews eventually directed their wrath against a different enemy—the British themselves.

NOTES

1. See *Peel Royal Commission on Palestine, 1936–1937,* pp. 64–65, London, MMSO. See also Charles R. Gellner, *The Palestine Problem,* Washington, DC, 1947.

2. For more details see Igal Eyal, *The First Intifada,* Tel Aviv, 1998 (in Hebrew), p. 57.

3. Wauchope to Thomas, 30 April, 1936, Central Zionist Archive (CZA), S25/22725 and Wauchope to the secretary of state for the colonies, 18 April, 1936, Public Record Office (PRO), CO733/297/75156, p. 11.

4. Anita Shapira, *Land and Power: The Zionist Resort to Force, 1881–1948,* Oxford: Oxford University Press, 1992.

5. David Ben-Gurion, *Memoirs,* Vol. 3, Tel-Aviv, 1973, pp. 122–124.

6. Monthly Summary of Intelligence, Palestine and Transjordan, Air Headquarters, April 19, 1936, CZA, S25/22741.

7. High commissioner to the secretary of state for the colonies, 21 April, 1936, PRO, CO733/310/1.

8. Wauchope to Parkinson, dispatch no. 261, 23 May, 1936, PRO, CO733/310/2.

9. Quoted by J. Arnon-Ohana, *The Internal Political Struggle within the Arab Palestinian Community,* Tel Aviv, 1982 (in Hebrew), p. 63.

10. According to the official history of the Jewish paramilitary organization, forty-one bombs exploded in Jaffa and thirty-five in Haifa until May 20. See Yehuda Slutsky (ed.), *History of the Haganah,* Vol. II, Tel Aviv, 1972, p. 645.

11. Situation Report, 15 October, 1936, PRO, WO32/4177.

12. For more on these developments, see Yehoshua Porat, *From Riots to Rebellion: The Palestinian Arabs National Movement, 1929–1939,* London, 1977, p. 241.

13. Slutsky, *History of the Haganah,* Vol. II, p. 735.

14. For more details see Porat, *From Riots to Rebellion,* pp. 221–222, Slutsky, *History of the Haganah,* pp. 648–652, and Eyal, *The First Intifada,* pp. 90–91, 109–113, and 148.

15. Weekly Summary of Intelligence, HQ British Forces in Palestine and Transjordan, September 11, 1936, CZA, S25/22741.

16. Charles Smith, *Revolt in Palestine: Examination of the British Responses to the Arab and Jewish Rebellion, 1936–1940,* Cambridge: Cambridge University Press, 1989, p. 81.

17. Cabinet Meeting of 2 September, 1936, PRO, CAB23/85.

18. On General Dill's military career, see "Dill 1881–1844," PRO, WO282. The Reinforcement Orders of the Emperial General Staff is in PRO, WO32/4176.

19. The military threat brought a significant reduction in the number of violent events. Vice Air Marshal Peirse estimated the reduction at 50 percent. See Peirse's Situation Report, 15 October, 1936, PRO, WO32/4177, p. 105.

20. PRO, CAB23/84.

21. Spicer report of 11 December, 1936, CZA, 25/22764.

22. For more details see Slutsky, *History of the Haganah,* Vol. II, p. 736.

23. *Ibid.,* p. 743.

24. *Ibid.,* pp. 851–880.

25. The "FOSH" was disbanded at the end of the Arab Revolt in 1939. In 1941, the Palmach, another permanently mobilized central unit, was created as part of the renewed cooperation between the British army and the Haganah on the backdrop of the dangers the Axis presented in the Middle East during the war.

26. More on the "Avner Plan" in Slutsky, *History of the Haganah,* Vol. II, pp. 748–754.

27. Wauchope to Ormsby-Gore, 26 November, 1936, PRO, CO733/325/13.

28. *Palestine Royal Commission Report, CMD 5479,* London, July 1937, p. 113.

29. R. J. Collins, *Lord Waivell 1883–1941, A Biography,* London, 1949, p. 80.

30. Buttershill to the secretary for the colonies, 29 September, 1937, PRO, CO733/332/11.

31. Secretary for the colonies to Buttershill, 29 September, 1937, PRO, CO733/332/11.

32. Buttershill to Shackborough, 12 October, 1937, PRO, CO733/351/1.

33. Cabinet Conclusion 36, 6 October, 1937, PRO, CAB 23/89.

34. Buttershill to Shackborough, 21 November, 1937, PRO, CO733/333/12.

35. MacMichael to the secretary for the colonies, 14 April 1938, PRO, CO935/21.

36. Sir Arthur Wauchope's speech on the Palestine Broadcasting Service, February 28, 1938. The Wauchope Legacy, Black Watch Archives, London.

37. MacDonald to MacMichael, 15 December, 1937, The MacMichael Papers, St. Anthony College Archives, Oxford, DC/126.2.

38. MacMichael to MacDonald, 2 July 1938, PRO, WO32/4176.

39. MacMichael to MacDonald, 2 July 1938, PRO, CO733/358/10.

40. Wingate died in action as a major general with the commando units he led in Burma during the war. Many streets, squares, and institutions in Israel today carry his name. Among the outstanding men who fought with the SNS were General Moshe Dayan and General Igal Alon. More on Wingate can be found in Christopher Sykes, *Ord Wingate,* London, 1959.

41. Slutsky, *History of the Haganah,* Vol. II, pp. 911–938.

42. MacMichael to the secretary for the colonies, 14 July, 1938, CZA, S'25/22762. For more details of these developments, see David Niv, *Battle for Freedom: The Irgun Zvai Leumi,* Vol. I, Tel Aviv, 1965.

43. MacDonald to MacMichael, 6 September, 1938, PRO, FO371/21863.

44. MacMichael to the Colonial Office, 9 August, 1938, PRO, CO733/366/4; MacMichael to MacDonald, 2 September, 1938, FO371/21863.

45. MacMichael to the Colonial Office, 7 September, 1938, PRO, FO371/21881.

46. *Palestine Gazette* No. 826, October 17, 1938. For more on the importance of Tegart in the suppression of the Arab revolt, see Y. Eyal and A. Oren, "Tegart Fortresses, Administration and Security under One Roof: Concept, Policy and Implementation, *Cathedra,* 104, pp. 95–126.

47. See, for example, *Davar,* October 19, 1938.

48. See O'Conor's 1970 testimony "1938–1939 Operations in Palestine," in O'Conor's Collection, Liddleheart Center.

49. MacMichael Report No. 716, 21 October, 1938, PRO, CO733/366/4/P3. For more on these operations, see also Slutsky, *History of the Haganah,* Vol. II, pp. 774–775.

50. See Y. Gelber, *Growing a Fleu-de-Lis: The Intelligence Services of the Jewish Yishuv in Palestine 1918–1947,* Tel Aviv, 1992 (in Hebrew), p. 236.

51. MacMichael's Report of 29 December, 1938, PRO, FO371/23443.

52. Haining to the War Office, 25 November, 1938, PRO, CO733/379/3.

53. Cabinet Conclusions, 7 December, 1938, PRO, FO371/21868.

54. MacMichael to the secretary for the colonies, 27 February, 1939, PRO, FO371/232443.

55. MacMichael to MacDonald, 2 January, 1939, PRO, CO733/398/1.

56. MacMichael Report, 27 February, 1939, PRO, FO371/232443.

57. Gils of the CID to Buttershill, 26 April, 1939, PRO, WO106/1594C.

58. N. Hamilton, *Monty, the Making of a General 1887–1942*, London: FLEET, 1981, p. 290.

59. Jewish Agency Monthly Survey, April 27–May 5, 1939, CZA, S25/22558.

2

The Israeli-Arab War of 1948: History versus Narratives

Yoav Gelber

PANDORA'S BOX

A single master's thesis submitted to the Department of Middle Eastern History at the University of Haifa opened a Pandora's box and has agitated the Israeli academe for more than three years. The author, Teddy Katz, told the story of two Arab villages in the War of 1948. Relying mostly on oral testimonies of Arab former residents and Israeli soldiers, the author argued that in one of these sites—Tantura on the Mediterranean coast—Israeli troops had committed war crimes that had caused the death of 250 villagers.

Soon, the thesis leaked to the press. Sensing an opportunity for anti-Israeli propaganda, Arab Members of Knesset (MKs) promptly demanded a judicial investigation of the alleged war crimes. The charges were widely discussed by the media. A group of veterans sued Katz for libel. An association of Arab lawyers and Jewish groups of the radical left launched a fundraising campaign to finance the defense. They aimed to turn the court proceedings into the *Naqba* trial—disgracing Israel as covering up war crimes and blaming it for the Palestinians' sufferings in 1948 and after. However, from the beginning of the court's sessions, serious doubts emerged about the author's motives, methodology, and competence, casting a heavy shadow on the scholarly weight of this thesis and about the integrity and competence of the supervisors and reviewers who gave it the outstanding grade of 97. Far from encouraging a historical debate on Israel's responsibility for the *Naqba,* the trial dealt with falsifications and distortions. The legal proceedings ended in Katz's withdrawal of his previous accusations, accompanied by an undertaking to apologize in public, on which he later tried to back down but the Supreme Court rejected his request.

Under these circumstances, the University of Haifa appointed a commission of experts in Arabic language and Middle Eastern History that listened to the original tapes of the testimonies and found in the thesis several cases of negligence, fabrication, falsification, ignorance, and disregard. The fact that all these cases reflected the same tendency eliminates the chance that they were only a matter of incompetence. Katz was given an opportunity to submit a revised version, but three out of five external reviewers rejected it, severely criticizing his lack of competence.

What would have happened if a scandal like this had taken place in a department of chemistry or psychology? Had major discrepancies been found between the experiment and the chemist's published conclusions or between the questionnaires and the psychologist's reasoning—all the more so if the researcher had intentionally tampered with the results—their academic colleagues would have unanimously condemned them as charlatans and expelled them from their ranks. In this case, however, Israeli historians have split: some have maintained that this has been an unprecedented disgrace, and others have retorted that this is a new zenith of scholarship.[1]

Pending determination of what *historical scholarship* is, and the shaping of the criteria by which it will be possible to decide whether a historical work qualifies as a *bona fide* piece of knowledge or as a piece of propaganda and historical fiction, we shall continue to roam among conflicting narratives, collective and individual memories, myths, and prejudices. In this chapter, I intend to review the growth of basic narratives of the Arab-Israeli War of 1948. Subsequently, I shall contrast them with the principal findings and conclusions of my own studies of that war, and also try to offer some observations and explanations.

SIGNIFICANCE AND UNIQUENESS

The long-lasting interest in the War of 1948 ("War of Independence" in the Israeli terminology and *Naabah* [catastrophe] in Arab terminology) has not emanated from its significance to military history or its unique features as a military campaign. Scholarly and public curiosity have derived mainly from the wider historical consequences of this war: the emergence and shaping of Israel, the persistent existence of the Jewish State as a spearhead of Western civilization in the Middle East, the protracted Arab-Israeli conflict, and the unsolved Palestinian problem. Other historical transformations also have significant causal links to this war, and these processes include the disappearance of the ancient Jewish communities in Muslim countries through emigration to Israel and elsewhere, political and social upheavals in the Arab states, and frequent changes of their global orientations after the war.

Contrary to most wars of the twentieth century, the War of 1948 has not ended yet. Historians writing on this encounter deal with an ongoing confrontation. Fighting did not resolve any of the problems that led to the outbreak of the war. Moreover, the outcomes of the military contest produced new crucial issues, such as the plight of Palestinian refugees and the status of Jerusalem. Every word written or said on that war has actual ramifications and is often interpreted and discussed outside its historical context and in terms of the continuing struggle at present. In this sense, the historiography of the Arab-Jewish conflict is as unparalleled and unprecedented as the conflict itself.

A recent anthology on the war's historiography published by the Cambridge University Press is a typical example of the pitfalls that the innocent reader seeking to learn about the history of the war must anticipate. Under a disguise of a seemingly impartial and academic volume, the editors' selection of contributors ensured the presentation of the war from viewpoints sympathetic to the Palestinians and critical of the Israelis. At the same time, they ignored a variety of scholarly studies that reject the revisionist views of the war or criticize them. Of course, this anthology cannot be considered a balanced and comprehensive presentation of the War of 1948 or its historiography, as the innocent reader may gather from its title. The editors dismissed any approach, excluding that of the "New Historians" as mythical and obsolete.[2]

The conflict's endurance focuses attention on its actual aspects and pushes aside its historical roots, increasingly dismissing them as irrelevant—a highly mistaken approach. In Western Europe, the United States, and even in Israel, memory becomes shorter, patience diminishes, and propaganda competes successfully with historical knowledge. In the postmodernist era it is hardly possible to discern between them.

THE NARRATIVES

A fundamental issue of the war's historiography has been the imminent tension between contemporary Israeli and Arab myths that later developed into the respective war narratives, and between the narratives of the protagonists and the findings of historical research. Comparative examination of the contemporary and authentic Israeli and Arab archival sources—where such comparison is feasible—reveals relatively narrow discrepancies between the relevant versions. With the lapse of time, however, apologetics and polemics have increasingly widened the breach. Originally, there was one history, albeit embracing slightly different versions. Gradually, this history has split into separate, opposing and conflicting narratives. In the process of their shaping, the so-called "collective memories" of Jews and Arabs have encrusted the war in a thick layer of narratives based on fables, stereotypes, myths, polemics, and apologies. Now, the historian's task is to unearth the real war that hides behind and below these masks.

The Israeli notions of the war have been shaped during the campaigns and in their immediate aftermath, or under the shadow of the later threat of a "second round" that hung over the Middle East for many years. Incessant skirmishing along the armistice lines and enduring political and economic warfare created a lasting atmosphere of siege that naturally affected the Israelis' writing on the war. With very few exceptions, in the 1950s and 1960s Israeli historiography, commemoration, and fiction literature exalted the war as a miracle. The writers painted the scene in black and white, and contrasting pairs of concepts characterized their writing. They perceived the war and presented it as the triumph of few over many, the weak successfully challenging the strong, a right cause winning against the wrong one, the wise guys defeating the stupid ones, the heroes crushing the cowards, and the ambitious side triumphing over the indifferent one. The common historical analogies were David's defeat of Goliath or the Maccabeans' victories over the Seleucian armies. To amplify the heroic achievement, Israeli writers blamed Britain for covertly directing the Arab onslaught on the Yishuv (the Jewish community in Palestine) and the invasion of Israel. They condemned the British for attempting to obstruct Jewish statehood and, having failed, to deny Israel the fruits of victory. As the academic study of the war and its consequences advanced, this approach changed, liberated itself from superlatives and phraseology, and turned more critical.

Poetry, theater, films, fiction literature, school textbooks, popular songs, commemorative statutes, memorial books, and political polemics molded the war narratives before the beginning of professional historical research and writing. Several narratives developed on each side: Ben-Gurion's version of the war differed from that of the Israeli left-wing parties that stressed and even exaggerated the contribution of Soviet assistance through diplomatic support and the provision of war material. The two military schools—that of the *PALMAH* and that of the British army's veterans—had their own incongruous views about the causes for the military achievements. Even the *Irgun* (IZL) had a narrative of its own. Nonetheless, certain assumptions have been common to all Israeli narratives: A profound faith in the purity of Jewish arms; a deep-rooted belief that the Arabs had enormous superiority in manpower and war material; a conviction of the Arabs' determination "to throw the Jews into the Mediterranean"; recollections of the Arab leadership's call to the Palestinians to abandon their homes and its promises of a quick return to their places in the wake of the triumphant Arab armies, and a few others.[3]

On the Arab side, each Arab country has developed its own narratives, in addition to those of the Palestinians. Until the end of the war, Arab public opinion had only a vague idea of what was really happening in Palestine. The governments did their best to conceal the essence of the armistice agreements and the military defeats that had led to their conclusion. While Egypt negotiated an armistice in Rhodes at the beginning of 1949, a poll held by the popular Egyptian weekly *Akhir Sa'a* revealed that 79 percent of the 20,000 sample believed that "Egypt won the war against the Zionist gangs." Early Arab narratives of the war—usually stories reflecting "collective memory," polemic or apologetic memoirs, and rarely scholarly research—concentrated on assigning guilt rather than on analyzing events. The authors have exonerated their own conduct, seeking to place elsewhere the blame and responsibility for the calamity that has befallen the Palestinians and for the Arab armies' defeat. Since it was inconceivable that the tiny Yishuv inflicted this catastrophe on the Arabs on its own, it was essential to mitigate the disaster by suggesting accomplices. The Arabs accused Britain of betraying them, blamed the United States for supporting the Zionists, and denigrated King Abdullah of Transjordan, who was the only Arab ruler that benefited from the general debacle.

After the war the Palestinians, in particular, had grievances against everyone but themselves. In his recently published notes from 1949, Anuar Nusseiba—chief of the Palestinian national committee of Jerusalem—complained that the Arab Legion was Arab only by name and because of its British command could not implement an Arab policy; Iraq was run by the British embassy and had an account to settle with the Palestinian leader, Haj Amin el Husseini, for his role in the Rashid Ali al-Kailany revolt in 1941; Syria and Lebanon were grateful to Britain for ejecting the French and facilitating their independence. Nusseiba accused all the Arab states for their consent to the first truce shortly after the invasion and asserted that from the beginning they acquiesced to partition and simulated the invasion to cover their impotence. Constantine Zurayq made this charge already during the war, and Mussa Alami repeated it after the war, blaming also Britain and the United States for the calamity that befell the Palestinians.[4]

Another obsession of Arab historiography of the war that has persisted to our own days has been the question of justice and unfairness. Arab scholars have scarcely endeavored to find out what really happened in that war, when did it happen, how, and why. In place of this, they have elaborated extensively on whose case was right and whose arguments were illegitimate. In these discussions, issues such as reliability of sources or accuracy of arguments, naturally, have been marginal.[5]

Except for the Palestinian version, early Arab narratives tried to conceal the scope of the military defeat, to minimize its significance, or to exonerate the fiasco by ascribing it to the intervention of the UN and the "Great Powers." Of course, the Syrian, Iraqi, Jordanian, Egyptian, and Palestinian narratives are incompatible and, sometimes, mutually reproaching but they, too, share common notions, such as the existence of a premeditated Jewish scheme to expel the Palestinians ("Plan *Dalet*"), the significance of the Deir Yassin massacre, the Jews' military superiority, and world support for the Jewish cause. A typical Arab myth was the assertion that the Arab expeditions were about to win the war when international pressure accompanied by threats imposed the first truce and saved "the Zionist entity" from total destruction.

REVISIONIST RESEARCH

Images, stereotypes, and representations are at most a part of history. Certainly, they are not all history and not a substitute for the real history. Since the opening of archives during the 1980s, most traditional Israeli narratives came under attack, both in Israel and abroad. Initially, critical examination of the war's accepted axioms ignored the Arabs and focused on domestic issues that had accompanied the transition from a community (the Yishuv) to statehood: the creation and shaping of the IDF (Israeli Defense Force), the accompanying ideological and political disputes, and the history of several campaigns. These works cast serious doubts on various war narratives that hitherto had been taken for granted.[6]

Regardless of and prior to the opening of archives, academic circles in the West changed their attitude toward Israel. Against the new backdrop of Europe's postcolonial guilt feelings, the Palestinian slogans and narratives—claiming that they were a national liberation movement struggling against oppressing Zionist colonialism, denying Jewish nationality, and demanding an exclusive right of sovereignty in Palestine—slogans that had made little impression between the world wars and in the aftermath of 1948, now gained popularity. After Israel's relations with the Arab states stabilized after the Yom Kippur War of 1973, the Palestinians returned to the center of the Arab-Israeli conflict. Concurrently, historical interest in the War of 1948 shifted from Israel's triumph over the Arab armies to the effects of the war on the fate of the Palestinians. The impact of this transforming attitude on Israeli historiography became obvious in the late 1980s, with the emergence of the so-called "New Historians." What made these historians "new," and how much they have innovated?

A distinction should be drawn between historical revision and an ideological negation of the Israeli narrative and the claims it represents. Benny Morris[7] and Avi Shlaim's[8] works are examples of the first, while Simcha Flapan,[9] Baruch Kimmerling,[10] Tom Segev,[11] and Ilan Pappe[12] stand for primarily ideological negation.

An analytical approach toward various aspects of the war narratives had developed before the emergence of "New Historians." Nonetheless, they have changed the agenda by diverting attention from Israel's accomplishments to the Palestinians' ordeal. The "New Historians" criticized the traditionally accepted Israeli narrative and helped to resuscitate the Palestinian narrative that had almost disappeared into oblivion in Israel and in the West. They shifted the focus from Israel's triumph over the Arab states' military expeditions to the earlier civil war between Jews and Arabs under the shadow of the vanishing British mandate. Studying the diplomatic and social aspects of the war such as behind-the-curtains diplomatic overtures, population movements, morpho-cultural changes, and settlements policies replaced the analysis of military moves and events.

However, the "new historiography" suffers from serious deficiencies, primarily from a conspicuous lack of balance. Most "New Historians" (as well as "critical" sociologists and geographers) have adopted the basic Palestinian narrative wholeheartedly. At the same time, their negation of the Israeli narrative is sweeping. They have portrayed the Palestinians as the hapless objects of violence and oppression (Israeli), collusion (Israeli-Transjordanian), and treacherous diplomacy (British and Arab). Some of them have described the Israelis as merciless, powerful, determined, and unnecessarily wicked usurpers who cynically used the Holocaust to gain the world's support for Jewish statehood at the expense of the Palestinians' rights to their country. Consciously or unconsciously, they have all reinforced the Palestinian narrative that Israel had been conceived in sin.

To underscore the Palestinians' plight, the revisionists' interpretation of the 1948 war has bypassed elementary facts. A simple fact, supported by plenty of contemporary archival evidence, is that the Palestinians and the Arab League— not the Jewish Yishuv, promptly rejected the UN resolution on partition. Rashid Khalidi ignores Palestinian "rejectionism" altogether and portrays the war as if it emerged out of the blue.[13] Identifying himself completely with the Palestinians, Pappe justifies their opposition to partition. This justification, of course, is open to argument but the fact of rejection is incontestable.

Following the Palestinian historians, the Israeli "New Historians" turn another blind eye to the fact that immediately after the UN resolution the Palestinians embarked on frustrating the implementation of partition by violence. The Arab League backed the campaign from the beginning and the Arab states joined in the fighting upon the end of the British mandate, invading the newly established Jewish State. During the last weeks of the mandate and throughout the two truces, the Arabs stubbornly repudiated any compromise that provided for Jewish statehood. They objected to and voted against all relevant UN resolutions, beginning with Resolution 181 (partition and the establishment of Jewish and Palestinian states) and ending with Resolution 194 (among other issues: the "right of return"). Only in the wake of military defeats did the Arabs make UN resolutions a cornerstone of their case and demand their strict fulfillment.

Any study describing exclusively Palestinian suffering is one-sided and incomplete without properly weighing this plain truth: As victims of war, the Palestinians' own conduct gives adequate cause to deny them the adjective "innocent." Truly, they have paid a heavy price in this war—and ever since. The Palestinians have been victims—but victims of their own follies and pugnacity as well as the incompetence of their Arab allies.

As the editors of a recent volume on the war historiography commented, the old aphorism that history is written by the victors does not apply in this case. All the defeated Arab states as well as the Palestinians have written their narratives of that war. It would be more accurate to say that *revisionist historiography* is the victor's privilege, and not always is it one to be proud of. So far, there is no "new historiography" of the 1948 war on the Arab side.[14] Rashid Khalidi, one of the more open-minded Palestinian historians, promises that there will not be any, since "there can be no facile equivalence between the two sides."[15] Indeed, even Arab "old historiography" can hardly exist as long as Arab historians (to say nothing of Israelis) have no access to the relevant Arab archives. In fact, what we have on the Arab side is not a historiography of the war but versions based on selective and biased readings of usually anachronistic, secondary (and, rarely, primary) Israeli sources, fragments of British and U.N. documentation, journalistic reports, and Arab memoirs, recently reinforced by plenty of dubious oral testimonies.

THE PALESTINIAN-JEWISH WAR

So far, my works on the war have tackled the shaping of the IDF and the accompanying controversies in Israel, the pre-1948 development of the Arab-Jewish conflict, and the Jews' relations with Transjordan until the invasion. Another book examines the development of the Israeli intelligence services during the war. In my last book, *Palestine 1948,* I have tried to present both sides of the hill (in 1948, not at present), while putting an emphasis on the parties' conflicting perceptions of the refugee problem.[16]

Israel's War of Independence consisted of two distinct, consecutive, but separate campaigns fought by different enemies, under dissimilar circumstances, each phase under different rules. The first encounter commenced early in December 1947 and lasted until the British mandate in Palestine expired. It was a civil war between Jews and Palestinians that took place under British sovereignty and in the presence of British troops. The second contest began with the invasion of Palestine by regular Arab armies on May 15, 1948 and continued intermittently until the conclusion of separate armistice agreements between Israel and each Arab state (except Iraq) during the first half of 1949. This was a war between Israel and a coalition of Arab states fought by regular armies. Consequently, the Palestinians—who placed their destiny in the hands of the Arab states and armies—disappeared for several decades from the military and political arena of the Arab-Israeli conflict.

Until the evacuation of British troops entered its essential phase with the withdrawal to Germany of the 6th Airborne Division early in April 1948, no territory could be gained by either side—even temporarily. Lacking proper military objectives, the antagonists carried out their attacks on noncombatant targets, subjecting civilians to deprivation, intimidation, and harassment. Consequently, the weaker, less cohesive, disorganized, and backward Palestinian society collapsed under a not-overly heavy strain. An increasing flow of refugees to the heart of Arab-populated areas and into adjacent countries underscored the defeat.

During this period, the principal Jewish paramilitary organization—the Haganah,—transformed from a militia into a regular army based on conscription. Simultaneously, the autonomous Jewish national institutions that had emerged during the mandatory era developed into a system of independent and sovereign government that centralized, controlled, and directed the Yishuv's war effort.

Palestinian society lagged behind. Unaware of the difference between anticolonial insurrection and a national war, the Palestinian leaders preferred to conduct the struggle from safe asylum abroad as they had done during their rebellion against the British in 1936–1939. The Palestinians failed to establish central political, financial, administrative, and military facilities for conducting a war. This failure resulted in a rapid deterioration of local institutions and eventually led to complete anarchy. The Arab League contributed to the chaos by being able neither to determine Arab Palestine's political future nor to let the Palestinians shape their own destiny.

From the outset, the Arab League assigned the Palestinians a secondary role only in the framework of the Arab war effort. Early in October 1947, the League Council had appointed a committee to examine the military situation in Palestine. Six weeks later, the Iraqi general Isma'il Safwat, the chairman of the committee, reported that in order to hold their own the Palestinians would need massive assistance from the Arab states in manpower, war material, and experienced command. Frustrating partition, Safwat stressed, required the intervention of the Arab regular armies. These armies were unprepared for a task of this magnitude and Safwat urged the League member-states to start preparing them at once.

In December 1947, the League undertook to raise the Arab Liberation Army (ALA) that should have carried the main burden of the Palestine campaign. This half-regular force composed of volunteers from Syria, Iraq, Lebanon, Egypt, and North Africa, in addition to Palestinian recruits, hastily assembled in Syria, and during January–March 1948 moved into Palestine. Originally, the mission of the ALA should have been defending the Arab areas until the end of the mandate, meanwhile avoiding incidents with the British and major clashes with the Jews. Yet, the rapid escalation of the civil war on the Palestinians' initiative dragged the ALA into an untimely involvement in combat and led to its disintegration. The progress of British withdrawal enabled the adversaries to change their tactics. Early in April, the Haganah took the initiative and during the next six weeks launched several large-scale operations across the country. By contrast, the Arab forces remained dispersed and disarrayed, clinging to their traditional patterns of small warfare and loose organization that had become anachronistic under the new circumstances. Between early April and mid-May 1948, the nascent Jewish army crushed the Palestinian militias and the League's expedition.

Culminating in the last days of the mandate, this civil war set a precedent. It was the first modern civil war fought between rival ethnic groups. Similarly, it was also the first national contest in the post-Ottoman Middle East. In the 1970s and 1980s, the civil war in Lebanon might have given some perspective and a better insight into the brutal nature of this kind of feud. Recent wars in the Balkans or in the Caucasus might have further revealed the cruel essence of intercommunal flare-ups and their immense impact on civilian populations.

Encounters between akin societies such as Serbs, Croats, and Bosnians; Armenians and Azeris; or Georgians and Ossetians are often indecisive. The rapid and definitive tipping of the scales in favor of one side in the civil war in 1948 was exceptional. The Palestinians' swift downfall surprised all concerned: Arabs, British, and Jews.

THE INVASION

Contrary to the Israeli narrative, the British did not help the Palestinians and did not encourage the Arab invasion. Quite the opposite, the Palestinians' collapse occurred when the British were still masters of Palestine. Britain had sufficient air and land forces in the country to stop the Haganah, had the British authorities wanted to use them. Determined to complete their withdrawal according to schedule, the British were reluctant to intervene. In April–May 1948, they looked on while the Haganah crushed the Palestinians and the ALA. At most, they provided the Arabs with transport and escorts to facilitate their exodus.

Britain's position did not stem from any sympathy with the Jewish cause. Its main purpose was preparing the ground for Abdullah's seizure of the country's Arab areas after termination of the mandate. The British decided to endorse the king's ambition although it violated the UN resolution to establish a Palestinian State. Yet, Abdullah's aspirations were unpopular among the Palestinians and the other Arab states were likely to oppose their implementation. The Palestinians' defeat should have made them, and the Arab states as well, more amenable to annexation to Transjordan—in the absence of any practical alternative.

This British-Transjordanian conspiracy against the Palestinians produced another intrigue to modify the partition plan at Israel's expense. Wishing to allay the Arab states' probable opposition to Transjordan's expansion, Britain sought to excise the Negev—Palestine's southern desert area—from the Jewish State. The prospect of preserving the Arab world's territorial continuity appeared to the British sufficiently attractive to ease Egypt's opposition to merging Arab Palestine with Transjordan. A possible Saudi-Transjordanian condominium in the Negev might have compensated Ibn Saud for his Hashemite foe's aggrandizement by granting Saudi Arabia an outlet to the Mediterranean. For his part, Transjordan's king could show a spectacular achievement on behalf of the general Arab cause, justifying his occupation of Arab Palestine and abstaining from war with the Jews. Israel, of course, was expected to pay the price for this scheme.

The British machinations, however, did not materialize. Late in April 1948, it seemed that without outside intervention to stop the Haganah's offensive, the Jews might take over the entire country. This implied the imminent demise of Arab Palestine and more refugees pouring into the adjacent states. Thus, the Palestinians' debacle in the civil war activated the regular armies' invasion and the Arab-Israeli war.

The Arab states' military intervention in Palestine had been a feasible contingency since the Arab League's conference at Bludan in June 1946. Nonetheless, the Arab governments had hesitated for a long time before deciding to employ their armies for that purpose. These armies were young, untrained, inexperienced, and poorly equipped. Their principal task was defending the regimes against domestic subversion. Dispatching the troops to Palestine was likely to expose the rulers to internal dangers. The expeditions' possible failure might have triggered further risks when embittered soldiers would return from the battlefields to endanger political stability—precisely what happened after the war.

Competition and animosity within the Arab League made the creation of a military coalition a difficult task. Aware of their domestic necessities and military defects, the Arab leaders discarded invasion by their regular armies. As a substitute, they embarked on the hasty formation of the ALA, which was a common

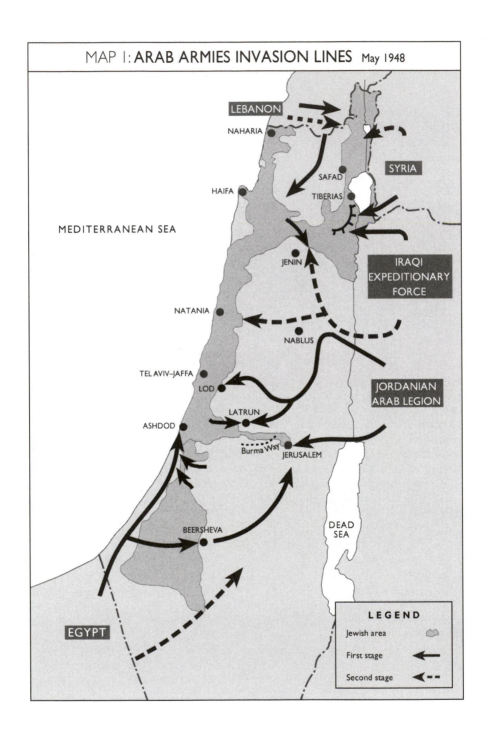

MAP 1: ARAB ARMIES INVASION LINES May 1948

LEBANON

NAHARIA

SAFAD

SYRIA

HAIFA

TIBERIAS

MEDITERRANEAN SEA

JENIN

IRAQI EXPEDITIONARY FORCE

NATANIA

NABLUS

TEL AVIV–JAFFA

LOD

JORDANIAN ARAB LEGION

LATRUN

ASHDOD

Burma Way

JERUSALEM

BEERSHEVA

DEAD SEA

EGYPT

LEGEND

Jewish area

First stage

Second stage

enterprise of the League as a whole. In April 1948, the ALA's setbacks and the Palestinians' defeat thrust the issue again into the Arab leaders' laps. Under pressure of public opinion aroused by news from Palestine and incited by wild rumors spread by Palestinian refugees, they reluctantly decided to invade the country.

Israeli narrative claims that the invasion had been planned from the beginning of hostilities in Palestine (namely the resolution on partition) and that its purpose was "to throw the Jews into the sea." However, the invading Arab expeditions were incapable of and insufficient for taking over the whole country. Despite the wild rhetoric that had preceded and accompanied the invasion (and fostered the Israeli narrative), the invaders' goal was not and could not be "pushing the Jews to the Mediterranean." The aim of this propagandist slogan was mobilizing domestic support for lame politicians who had undertaken a crucial decision and feared its consequences.

Drawn into the war by the collapse of the Palestinians and the ALA, the Arab governments' primary intentions were preventing the Haganah from occupying the whole of Palestine, saving the Palestinians from total ruin, and avoiding the flooding of their own countries by more refugees. According to the Arabs' perception, had the invasion not taken place, there was no Arab force in Palestine capable of checking the Haganah's offensive and, eventually, the majority of the panicked Palestinian population would have wandered into adjacent Arab countries.

The Yishuv's comprehension of the Arab onslaught was, of course, totally different. Against the backdrop of the Palestinians' violent opposition to the Zionist enterprise since the early 1920s, and the Arab states' support for their struggle since 1936, the Yishuv genuinely perceived the menace of an Arab invasion as threatening its very existence. Having no real knowledge of the Arab armies' true military efficiency, the Jews took Arab propaganda literally, preparing for the worst and reacting accordingly.

THE BALANCE OF POWER

Miracles rarely, if ever, occur in wars. Usually, the stronger belligerent wins, and the Israeli War of Independence was no exception. A detailed examination of the balance of power reveals that throughout most of the 1948 war, the Jews were superior in personnel, equipment, logistics, and organization. The sole exception to this rule was the period from the outset of the invasion on May 15 to the first truce in June 1948. During that period the Arab armies enjoyed a considerable superiority over the IDF in the air, artillery, and light armor forces. Moreover, Jewish troops were exhausted after six months of combat and had already sustained heavy losses. By contrast, the invading formations were all fresh and complete. Nonetheless, even at this stage, the expeditionary forces and their local auxiliaries were quantitatively inferior to the Yishuv's mobilized manpower. Throughout the rest of the war, the Haganah and the IDF were stronger.

Jewish material superiority was also significant, though never admitted. During the civil war, the Palestinians' performance and the information on available arms in various places did not support the orthodox evaluation of the arsenal at the Arabs' disposal. The shortage of arms and munitions was the Palestinians' principal source of anxiety, fueled both by scarcity inside the country and difficulties of obtaining weapons abroad.

Most Arab armies depended on Britain for supply of arms, munitions, spare parts, and other war material. Hence, they suffered heavily from the embargo that the UN Security Council imposed in May 1948. Only towards the end of the war did Arab governments find alternative sources of supply on the free European arms market and means of shipping purchased armaments to Arab ports. This was too little and too late to have a significant effect on the situation at the front lines. By contrast, the Israelis—having a long-time experience in clandestine purchase and shipment of weapons—efficiently circumvented the embargo. Since April 1948, small deliveries arrived by air from Czechoslovakia and elsewhere but the large influx began only after the close of the British mandate. By July, the IDF had balanced the initial superiority of the Arab armies in heavy equipment, later regaining the lead in several types of weaponry.

Like other claims, by asserting that the Haganah was stronger than the Palestinian militias and the IDF was superior to the Arab expeditions, the "New Historians" broke into an open door. The Israeli myth of "few against many" has been a popular, not an official one. Officially, Ben-Gurion had denied it during the war and repeated the denial long after it ended. In the minutes of the *Knesset* Committee on Defense and Foreign Affairs, I have found the following historical explanation of Ben-Gurion, still prime minister at the time.

In the War of Independence the Arabs were divided. . . . They were also poorly equipped. Indeed, in the first thirty days after the invasion they were superior in equipment because ours was still abroad. However, when our war material arrived it was better than theirs. Besides, although it may look strange, we then had a larger army than theirs.[17]

Ben-Gurion said similar things already at the end of the war, at the provisional government's meeting prior to the IDF launching Operation *Horev*.[18] Nonetheless, the popular myth reflected an authentic anxiety in the Yishuv. This concern was natural in a small community surrounded by a hostile Arab world that appeared to most Jews strange, savage, and threatening. The "few against many" narrative did not emanate necessarily from the battlefield's reality but from the existential situation of the Jews in the region.

Beyond the quantitative calculations of bodies and weapons, throughout the war the IDF and the Arab armies underwent opposing processes: The Haganah/IDF developed from a territorial militia whose operational formation's freedom of action was restricted and they were tied to specific areas for which they were responsible, into a regular army of mobile formations, relieved of territorial responsibility for the civilian population and installations. The culmination of this process was the establishment of front commands at the beginning of the second truce. The new front and district headquarters relieved the brigades from their regional responsibilities, and the new troops that the districts raised locally replaced the infantry brigades in performing static duties such as holding the frontline positions. This reform enabled the IDF to concentrate its forces against the Egyptian army and crush it in the campaigns of October and December 1948.

When the Arab invading armies entered Palestine, they were free of static duties, civil commitments, and territorial responsibilities and could focus on their military mission of taking over the Arab parts of Palestine and defeating the Jewish forces. However, as the thrust of the Arab offensive waned, and in the absence of any civil administration worthy of this name in the Arab areas, the military commanders of the expeditions found themselves encumbered with ever-growing nonmilitary responsibilities and commitments. The troops dispersed thinly along lengthy lines and were tied up with static duties in defense of what was left of Arab Palestine. The Israeli military planners skillfully took advantage of this dispersion, particularly of the Egyptian and Iraqi expeditions, while planning the operations of autumn and winter 1948.

Having said all that, Israel's military superiority was still insufficient by itself to explain the final outcomes of the war. Ultimately, the enormous Jewish advantage laid in the social, cultural, moral, organizational, and technical infrastructure behind the warriors and successful transformation and application of these factors in the military sphere. The disparity between a modern, but still not pampered society, and a traditional, patriarchal community was a principal factor in deciding the outcome of the war.

THE TOLL

The military triumph notwithstanding, the war was also the most costly that Israel has ever fought. The number of fatal casualties exceeded 6,000 and was about 1 percent of the Jewish population in Palestine at the beginning of the war. Lack of preparedness, dilettantism, and mistaken conceptions—not Arab might— were the main reasons for the high death toll.

Before the war, the Yishuv's political and military leadership believed that the "Great Powers" should safeguard implementation of the partition solution adopted by the General Assembly against any outside onslaught. Ben-Gurion was the only exception to this rule. His colleagues, however, did not share Ben-Gurion's vision of the approaching war and consistently objected to his demands to prepare the Yishuv for a total war and modify or reform the Haganah accordingly.

Until 1948, the Haganah anticipated an enhanced repetition of the Palestinian revolt of 1936–1939, ignoring potential dangers from across the border. Various setbacks that the Haganah sustained in the course of the civil war demonstrated that it had not been adequately prepared even for that contingency. Learning and recovery were quite rapid, but drawing the lessons, devising appropriate operational responses, mass training, and reorganization in the midst of fighting required time and departure from long-established traditions. The high proportion of casualties was the price paid for lack of preparedness. Several myths surrounding the war have masked guilt-feelings about this undoing and represented polemics about who were to be blamed for the negligence.

THE EMERGENCE OF THE REFUGEE PROBLEM

Since the abortive talks at Camp David in July 2000, the Palestinian refugee problem has reemerged as the hard core of the Arab-Israeli conflict. For five decades, the Israelis have swept the problem under the carpet, while the Palestinians have consistently developed their national ethos around the "Right of Return" (al-Auda). Assisted by a few Israeli historians and sociologists, they have composed a false narrative of deliberate expulsion, inventing the centrality of the transfer idea in Zionist thought before the war and stressing the role of Deir Yassin and Plan Dalet in their exodus.

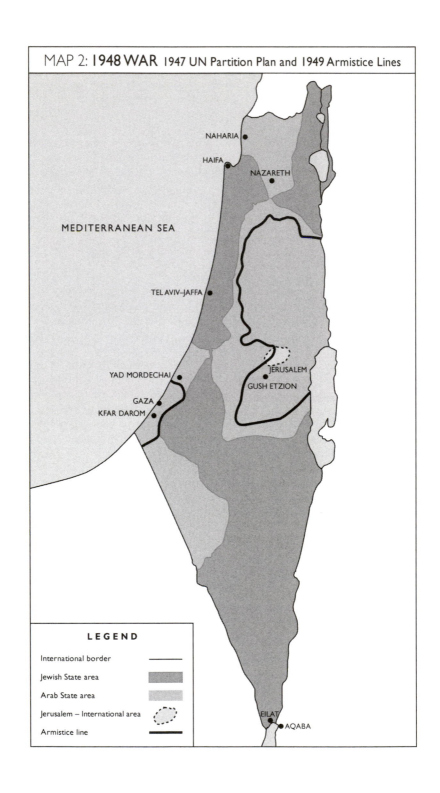

MAP 2: **1948 WAR** 1947 UN Partition Plan and 1949 Armistice Lines

NAHARIA

HAIFA

NAZARETH

MEDITERRANEAN SEA

TEL AVIV–JAFFA

YAD MORDECHAI

JERUSALEM

GUSH ETZION

GAZA

KFAR DAROM

LEGEND

International border

Jewish State area

Arab State area

Jerusalem – International area

Armistice line

EILAT

AQABA

Unfortunately, writing or saying it—even endlessly—does not make it so. During the civil war the Palestinians ran away and were not deported. Throughout most of the next stages, until the liberation of the northern Negev and central Galilee in October 1948, local deportations were the result of military needs, mainly denying the invading Arab armies bases in the vicinity of Jewish settlements and securing control of important roads. Even in October 1948, massacres and lesser atrocities were sporadic and exceptional and expulsions were partial.

Unlike the Jews, who had nowhere to go and fought with their back to the wall, the Palestinians had nearby shelters. Escape accompanied the fighting from the beginning of the civil war and an increasing flow of refugees drifted from mixed Jewish-Arab towns into the heart of Arab-populated areas and the adjacent countries. The Palestinians did not recover yet from their revolt in 1936–1939. In this early phase of the war, their fragile social structure tumbled not because of military setbacks but owing to economic hardships and administrative disorganization that deteriorated further as the fighting intensified. Contrary to the Jews who built their "State in the Making" during the mandate period, the Palestinians had not created in time substitutes for the government services that vanished with the British withdrawal. The absence of the leaders, the collapse of services, the lack of authority, and a general feeling of fear and insecurity generated anarchy in the Arab sector.

When riots broke out early in December 1947, middle-class Palestinians sent their families to neighboring countries and joined them after the situation deteriorated. Others moved from the vicinity of the frontlines to less exposed areas in the interior of the Arab sector. Non-Palestinian foreign laborers and businessmen returned to Syria, Lebanon, and Egypt to avoid the hardships of war. First-generation emigrants from the countryside to urban centers, who had no roots in the cities yet, returned to their villages. Thousands of Palestinian government employees—doctors, nurses, civil servants, lawyers, clerks, and so on—became redundant and departed as the mandatory administration disintegrated. They all set a model and created an atmosphere of chaos and desertion that rapidly expanded to wider circles. Between half to two-thirds of the inhabitants in cities such as Haifa or Jaffa had abandoned their homes before the Jews stormed these towns in late April 1948.

In the last six weeks of the British mandate, the Jews occupied most of the area that the UN partition plan allotted to the Jewish State. They took over five towns and 200 villages; between 250,000 to 300,000 Palestinians and other Arabs ran away to Palestine's Arab sectors and to neighboring countries. The Palestinian irregulars and the League's army disintegrated, becoming militarily immaterial.

This rapid and almost total collapse astonished all concerned. It was unbelievable that plain defeatism lacking any ulterior motives had prompted this mass flight. The Jews suspected the exodus was nothing but a conspiracy—concocted by the Palestinian leadership—to embroil the Arab states in the war. Later, this guess would become the official line of Israeli diplomacy and the gist of the Israeli explanation. However, the documentary evidence clearly shows that the Palestinian and other Arab leaders did not encourage the flight. On the contrary, they tried in vain to stop it. The old Israeli narrative about conspiracy is as wrong as the new Palestinian one about expulsion, and the historical picture is far more complex.

At this point in time, running away was for the most part "voluntary" and preceded the conquest of most Arab towns. Dependence on towns that had fallen, the quandaries of maintaining agricultural routines, and rumors of atrocities exacerbated mass flight from the countryside. Many hamlets that the Haganah occupied in April and May were empty. No premeditated deportations had taken place at this stage, and the use of intimidation and other methods of psychological warfare were sporadic. Quantitatively, the majority of Palestinian refugees fled under these circumstances of an intercommunal civil war. The Arab armies' invasion on May 15, 1948, terminated this phase of the flight. In certain places, fugitives who had not gone far from their hamlets returned to their deserted homes in the wake of the invading troops.

During the civil war, the Palestinians' demeanor stood in sharp contrast to the Yishuv's performance. Not a single Jewish settlement was deserted before the invasion. Only a dozen remote or besieged settlements sent mothers and children to safer places in the interior. The central leadership took measures to reinforce vulnerable posts and secure their capacity to survive. Unlike the Palestinians, the Yishuv's main centers displayed a proven solidarity with its periphery.

Unlike the civil war period, certain IDF actions on the eve of and after the invasion aimed at driving out the Arab population from villages close to Jewish settlements or adjacent to main roads. These measures appeared necessary in face of the looming threats by the invading Arab armies. The Israelis held the Palestinians responsible for the plight that the invasion caused and believed they deserved severe punishment. Local deportations in May–June 1948 of villages along the anticipated route of the Egyptian army and in the vicinity of Haifa appeared militarily vital and morally justified. Confident that their conduct was indispensable, the troops did not attempt to conceal harsh treatment of civilians in their after-action reports.

By July 1948, the Israelis' previous restraints about crossing the UN partition line had disappeared, and during the Ten-Day Campaign (July 9–18) the IDF occupied three Arab towns and tens of villages. It became clear that instead of saving the Palestinians, the Arab armies' invasion doubled their territorial losses and the number of refugees. Later waves of mass flight were the result of the IDF's counteroffensives against the invading forces. The position of these new escaping or expelled Palestinians—such as the inhabitants of Lydda and Ramle—was essentially different from that of their predecessors who had run away in the preinvasion period. The resuming mass flight was not the outcome of the Palestinians' inability to hold on against the Jews. The Arab expeditions failed to protect them, and the new refugees remained a constant reminder of the armies' military fiasco. These refugees were sometimes literally deported across the lines. In certain cases, IDF units terrorized them to hasten their flight, and isolated massacres took place that might have expedited the flight.

After the conquest of Galilee, the feasibility of the West Bank's occupation depended to a large extent on the likely reaction of the civilian population to the advent of the IDF in this region. Ben-Gurion pondered the inhabitants' reaction: whether they would run away as their predecessors had done before the invasion, or stay put and encumber Israel with countless political, economic, and administrative problems. The lessons of the campaigns in Galilee and the Negev implied that the Palestinians might not flee of their own will. An occupation of the West Bank meant, therefore, either plenty of atrocities—provoking domestic and international repercussions—or the absorption of a large Palestinian population, which was equally dreadful. Mainly to avoid these unattractive options, Ben-Gurion decided to give up the conquest of the West Bank and to embark on negotiations with Transjordan.

When they ran away, the refugees were confident of their eventual repatriation at the end of hostilities. This "end" could mean a cease-fire, a truce, an armistice and, certainly, a peace agreement. The return of refugees had been customary in the Middle East's wars throughout the ages. When the first truce began in June 1948, many tried to resettle in their hamlets or at least to gather the crops. However, they were fated for a surprise.

Their Jewish adversaries belonged to an alien European civilization whose historical experience and concepts of warfare were different. Three years after the end of the World War II, it was inconceivable that Germans who had been expelled by the Czechs, Poles, and Russians would ever return to the Sudeten, to Pomerania, to Silesia, or to East Prussia. The mass repatriation by the allies of millions after the war concerned their own nationals, while refugees or deportees of defeated belligerents resettled to begin new life elsewhere. People still remembered the exchange of populations between Turkey and Greece in the early 1920s. Europe was full of White Russians who had left their homeland after the revolution and the subsequent civil war. The vast majority of Israelis did not think that the Palestinians should fare better and wanted to apply this principle to the Middle East, naively ignoring its different cultural concepts and historical experience.

In Europe, war refugees seldom returned to their former places of residence if the victorious enemy had occupied their homes. Usually, they resettled and began new life elsewhere. This was particularly true after World War II. Hailing mostly from Europe, the Israelis applied this principle to the Middle East. In the summer of 1948, the Israeli provisional government decided to object to any repatriation of refugees before peace. Truces and armistices were considered a part of the war, not of a peace settlement. The IDF forcibly blocked infiltration during the truces and after the war, and demolished abandoned hamlets to deny infiltrators using them as shelters. Concurrently, the Israeli authorities seized abandoned lands and accommodated evacuees from Jewish settlements that had been occupied by the invading Arab armies in the deserted Arab quarters. Later, new immigrants and demobilized soldiers settled in deserted Arab towns and on lands formerly cultivated by Arab villagers. Thus, the presumably temporary flight turned into a permanent, almost eternal, problem of refugees.

THE COLLUSION THAT NEVER WAS

With the exception of the Gaza Strip, at the end of the Israeli-Arab war of 1948, Israel and Transjordan shared the whole of Palestine. Against the backdrop of the Arab coalition's defeat, Abdullah's success in retaining what had been left of Arab Palestine extremely annoyed his allies. The king's success stood in sharp contrast with his Arab partners' profound sense of failure and frustration after the war. This gap spawned a wave of charges, accusing Abdullah of collaborating with the Jews and betraying the Arab cause. Palestinians, Egyptians, Syrians, and Transjordanian exiles joined hands in vilifying the king and in conspiracies to eliminate him.

Except for Jordanian official historiography, Palestinian and Arab writing on the war totally avoids the fact the Abdullah saved the Palestinians twice from a total collapse. First, when he invaded Palestine—his participation was a precondition for the creation of the coalition and the invasion of the other Arab armies. Second, by his timely decision to quit the coalition, withdraw from the war, and sign an accord with Israel preventing thereby the occupation of the West Bank. Not only Arab writers but also Avi Shlaim ignores the Palestinians' ingratitude and regards Abdullah's actions as a plot intended against the Palestinians rather than for their rescue.

Similar allegations about a previous agreement that the Jewish Agency had made with Abdullah to partition Palestine spread in Israel. The sponsors were mainly rivals of David Ben-Gurion and adherents of "One Palestine Complete" on both the left and right wings of the Zionist movement and the Yishuv who opposed partition. They spoke about *Bechiya LeDorot* ("a source of lament for generations"). Originally, this was an idiom that Ben-Gurion used after the government rejected his demand to attack the Legion and occupy Samaria in the wake of a *Mujahidin*'s attack near Latrun in September 1948. The anti-Ben-Gurion version of this idiom referred either to his decision to accept the UN Security Council's demand for a cease-fire after Operation *YOAV*, and abstain from occupying Mount Hebron in the wake of the Egyptian army's retreat, or to his later resolution to refrain from occupying Samaria in the end of the war.

Until the mid 1960s, strict censorship prevented public debate in Israel on these issues, but the story spread via the grapevine. The "collusion" story became one of the war's countermyths. The first to publish the allegation openly was Israel Ber. In 1948, Ber held a senior post in the IDF General Staff, and as director of planning and operations was promoted to lieutenant-colonel after the war. At that time, he belonged to the left-wing United Workers Party *(Mapam)* and sharply criticized Ben-Gurion's conduct of the war. In the midst of the campaign, Ber claimed at a party's closed consultation that Ben-Gurion should be removed from his post as minister of defense because he was a danger and damaged the proper conduct of the war. Ber also alleged that Ben-Gurion had a secret understanding with Abdullah on partitioning the country and for this reason the he forbade the IDF to crack down on the Legion. Eventually, Ber transferred his loyalty to Ben-Gurion who appointed him official historian of the war. He was also the first holder of the chair of military history at Tel Aviv University. In 1961, however, Ber was arrested and sentenced to ten years imprisonment for spying on behalf of the Soviet Union. He died in prison before completing his term.

In jail, Ber wrote a book—*Bitchon Israel: Etmol, Hayom Umachar (Israel Security: Yesterday, Today and Tomorrow)*—that was published posthumously in 1966. In this book, he developed the allegation of an Israeli-Transjordanian collusion to let Abdullah take over the West Bank and annex it to his kingdom. Ber's dubious record and personal involvement did not lend much credence to these theories. However, they were compatible with similar contemporary accusations on the Arab side, raised in the memoirs of a former Legion officer, Colonel Abdullah al-Tal, and the former Iraqi chief-of-staff, General Salih Juburi.

For twenty years, the collusion theory lay dormant. In the late 1980s, however, Avi Shlaim adopted it in his comprehensive study *Collusion across the Jordan*. In certain details he departed from Ber's original allegations and in others he elaborated on his predecessor. Since the summer of 1946, Shlaim argued, the Jewish Agency and King Abdullah had a secret agreement to share Palestine at the expense of the Palestinians. When the time came to implement this agreement after the UN resolution on partition, both sides feigned a short war and then embarked on executing their previously agreed-upon scheme.

Certainly, the Jews and Abdullah had a common interest in opposing the ambitions of the Mufti of Jerusalem, Haj Amin el Husseini. Many Jews openly preferred Abdullah as their neighbor to a Palestinian irredentist state. Yet, Shlaim's conjecture of a deliberate and premeditated anti-Palestinian "collusion" does not stand up to a critical examination. The documentary evidence on the development of contacts between Israel and Jordan in 1948 and after simply and unequivocally refute his surmises and conclusions. If there was any collusion against the Palestinians in 1948, it was not concocted by Israel and Abdullah but by Britain and Transjordan. Even if this was the case, the outcomes reveal that the Anglo-Jordanian understanding about Transjordan taking over Arab Palestine was rather a choice by default, not a plot.

Abdullah's long history of contacts with the Jews that had begun in 1921 led to the agreement between the king and the Jewish Agency in the summer of 1946. The king undertook to support partition as the preferable solution to the Palestine problem. The Jewish Agency stated its preference for sharing the country with Abdullah and granted him financial aid to promote his status among the Palestinians and encourage his subversive activities in Syria.

This agreement was the culmination of a protracted bond, not the beginning of a new conspiracy as Shlaim portrays it. Since the mid-1930s, Abdullah appeared to the Jewish leaders to be the only alternative to the intransigent Palestinian opposition to the Zionist enterprise, backed by the rest of the Arab world. For his part, the king (then still Amir) needed Jewish backing to accomplish his territorial ambitions in Arab Palestine and fulfill his dream to become king of Greater Syria.

Until 1948, Jewish backing was the only outside support Abdullah might have gained for attaining his goals in Palestine. Most Palestinians opposed his ambition to rule them, and even his followers objected to his contacts with the Jews. All Arab states were likely to disapprove of Transjordan's aggrandizement: Saudi Arabia viewed Abdullah as a dynastic rival. Egypt—in the height of its anticolonial struggle to oust the British from the Suez Canal and Sudan—regarded the king as a puppet of Britain. Syria and Lebanon were hostile to the king's dream of Greater Syria. Even Iraq competed with Transjordan for leadership of the Hashemite House; Abdullah was senior, but Iraq was the stronger and larger state and would not admit his seniority or accept his hegemony.

Familiar with the king's capabilities or lack of them, and aware of the attitude of most other Arabs towards Abdullah, Britain refused to back his expansionist ambitions. Such support might jeopardize Britain's relations with other Arab countries. Abdullah's British advisors, the ambassador Sir Alek Kirkbride and the Arab Legion's commanding officer General John Glubb, were the only exception to this joint opinion of all other British diplomats in the Middle east and officials in Whitehall. Since the summer of 1946, both had recommended a policy based on extending the king's rule to Arab Palestine.

On November 17, 1947, twelve days before the vote on the United Nations Special Commission on Palestine (UNSCOP) report, Abdullah met with Golda Meyerson (Golda Meir), deputy head of the Jewish Agency's political department, and two of her aides, Eliass Sasson and Ezra Danin, with whom the king had met previously several times. The anticipated report reshuffled the cards by recommending the creation of a Palestinian state in the Arab part of Palestine and avoiding the issue of annexing it to Transjordan. The conferees discussed the new situation, reaffirmed their commitment to previous understandings, and contemplated means of bypassing the part of the pending UN resolution that was incompatible with the king's ambitions. Golda Meir carefully refrained from any explicit commitment to assist Abdullah in annexing Arab Palestine and suggested that the king should mobilize popular support among the Palestinians for such a merger in preparation for a plebiscite that would represent it as a voluntary Palestinian step. Both sides pledged to maintain regular contacts and meet again when circumstances clarified.[19]

The pace of events after the vote in the UN was faster than the parties had foreseen. In the face of the rapid spread of hostilities in Palestine, Abdullah faltered in fulfilling his part of the understanding. Intermediaries maintained contacts between Amman and Jerusalem, but no high-level parley took place. The king's inability or unwillingness to prevent the invasion of Palestine by the ALA via Transjordan in January 1948 shook the Jews' confidence in Abdullah and strengthened the hands of the skeptics who had distrusted him from the beginning.

The break up of contacts between the Jewish Agency and Abdullah at the beginning of the war was mutual. Since February 1948, Abdullah appeared less dependent on Jewish support for accomplishing his goals. During the visit of Premier Tawfiq Abu al-Huda to London, the king obtained the tacit support of Britain for his plan to occupy the Arab part of Palestine upon termination of the mandate. His army was already in the country as part of the British garrison, although its involvement in combat was still marginal. To help Abdullah prepare the ground for his takeover of what later came to be known as the West Bank, the British stationed Legion companies in the main Arab towns. Being a permanent member of the UN Security Council notwithstanding, Britain consciously assisted Abdullah's efforts to frustrate the UN resolution on partition as far as it concerned the establishment of a Palestinian state. In view of the Palestinians' recalcitrance to accept partition and inability to take over administration of their own sector from the mandatory regime, the British could not devise a better alternative for the Arab parts of the country than Transjordanian occupation.

The defeats of the Palestinians and the ALA in April 1948 enhanced the king's status as the only feasible savior of Arab Palestine. Trepidation among the Palestinians grew as termination of the mandate approached and with it an end to British protection, prompting ever-more Palestinians to see Abdullah and his Legion as their last hope. Delegations of notables—some of them old rivals of the king—went to Amman to ask Transjordan to intervene. This time their appeals appeared genuine.

The collapse of Palestinian society in the last six weeks of the mandate weakened considerably any potential resistance to the king's ambitions on the part of the Palestinians and increased their dependence on the Arab Legion's protection. After the defeats of the Arab Liberation Army, even the Arab League had no alternative but to reconcile itself to the idea of the Legion's occupation of the major part of Arab Palestine. All the other Arab states could hopefully do was to restrict Abdullah's political freedom of action in the occupied regions by adopting resolutions on the Palestinians' right to determine their own future when the war would be over.

At the end of April 1948, the Arab League prevailed on the king to interfere immediately in the fighting. Azzam Pasha, the League's secretary general, urged Abdullah to save the Palestinians from the fiasco of the ALA and check their panicked mass-flight. Abdullah put forward several military and political conditions. When the Arab states decided reluctantly to invade Palestine upon the end of the mandate, they practically removed their objections to the conquest of the West Bank by the Legion. They did not, however, consent to any political design of the king in the occupied area.

The Jews contributed their share to this mutual disengagement by erroneously belittling Abdullah's significance throughout the early months of the war. During that period the Yishuv was fighting the Palestinians and the Arab League's volunteer army, and under the pressure of current exigencies neglected Transjordan and the Legion, which for the time being watched the campaign from the sidelines. Indirect contacts through go-betweens ceased in the end of January 1948. The Jewish Agency was unaware of Britain's tacit support for Abdullah's designs in regard to Arab Palestine and even later did not grasp their true essence. When efforts to resume the broken contacts with the king commenced at the beginning of May, it was too late to turn the tide—Abdullah had meanwhile become the spearhead of the invading coalition and it was unthinkable that he would quit at the last moment.

Having secured British, Arab, and Palestinian support or acquiescence, Abdullah apparently no longer needed the Jews to advance his objectives in Palestine. A last ditch effort by the Jewish Agency to resume direct communication with the king and dissuade him from joining the invading Arab coalition failed. Fueled by new circumstances, the king explained to Golda Meir, who rushed to meet him in Amman on the eve of the invasion, that now Transjordan was part of a wider alliance and he could not make separate bargains or adhere to previous understandings.[20]

Upon the end of the British mandate, Israel and Transjordan went to war against each other. They did not have any secret deals that limited their military activities. The agreement of 1946 was void. It had not related to the situation created by the U.N. partition plan, and when the war was over Israel refused to accept it as a starting point for negotiations.

The campaign of May–July 1948 was inconclusive, but far from being a feigned confrontation. Military exigencies compelled Abdullah to hand over large parts of Arab Palestine to Egyptian and Iraqi military administration. At the beginning of the second truce, the king realized his inability to retain his conquests by force and started looking for a political solution to secure his grip of the West Bank. Britain's failure to promote the plan devised by Count Bernadotte—the Swedish mediator on behalf of the Security Council, the creation of "All Palestine" government under the auspices of the Arab League, and growing friction with Egypt over Transjordan's intentions in Palestine drove Abdullah to seek understanding with Israel and resume direct contacts with the Jews.[21]

Nonetheless, the war was not a temporary interruption between two phases of the same dialogue. It was the end of the old bond between the Jews and Abdullah and the beginning of a new attempt to resolve the Palestine problem between Israel and Jordan, free from any past commitments. The starting point was the military situation after the defeat of the Egyptian army in the fall of 1948. Abdullah's main concern was preventing his Legion from becoming the IDF's next prey.

Ben-Gurion arrived at the negotiations table after having realized that the Arab population would not run away from the West Bank in the manner of the mass-flight witnessed in previous stages of the war. Yet, Ben-Gurion still wavered between Transjordan and the Palestinians. An armistice was feasible only with Transjordan. The prospect of peace, however, presented different problems and drove Israel to reconsider the Jordanian vis-à-vis the Palestinian option. In the years that followed, Israel fluctuated between the opposing poles of negotiating comprehensive peace or partial arrangements with Jordan and an escalating border war against the Palestinians under Jordanian rule in the West Bank and under Egyptian rule in the Gaza Strip.

THE LEGACY

All reservations notwithstanding, the War of Independence was, at least in certain respects, Israel's most successful campaign against the Arabs. It was the only contest in which Israel succeeded in translating a military victory into a political settlement, one that survived for eighteen years. At first, Israel regarded the armistice agreements of 1949 as an interim phase leading to a permanent peace settlement. These hopes did not materialize. The armistice regime persisted until 1967, and a permanent settlement is still remote.

Following the war, for a period that lasted from 1949 to 1967, the Palestinians receded from the scene. Those who stayed put became Israeli citizens. The indigenous Palestinians in the West Bank and the refugees on both banks were incorporated into Jordan and became Jordanian citizens. There were also "Egyptian" Palestinians in the Gaza Strip as well as "Syrian" and "Lebanese" Palestinians in refugee camps in Syria and Lebanon, though without citizenship. The concept "Palestinian" as such vanished, unless it was linked to the word "refugee."

In the wake of the Six-Day War, the Palestinians returned to the political arena under their own banner and began to reshape and revise their narrative of the war that previously had been obliterated by the narratives of the Arab states. Since Israel occupied the West Bank and Gaza Strip but did not annex these territories, their inhabitants ceased to be "Jordanian" and "Egyptian" but did not become "Israeli." They reappeared as simply "Palestinians"—a term that had been forgotten for eighteen years.

In the Yom Kippur War of 1973 the Palestinians were still immaterial. However, when Israel's relations with the Arab States stabilized in the wake of that war the Palestinians returned to the focus of the Israeli-Arab conflict. The war in Lebanon was fought primarily because of the Palestinians and against them, and only in the late 1980s the Hizbullah replaced them as Israel's principal foe on the northern frontier. The first Intifada that broke out late in 1987 eventually led to the Madrid Conference and later to the Oslo Accord. This accord was an attempt to address the problems created in 1967 by the Six-Day War and Israel occupation of the West Bank and Gaza Strip, and to bypass the legacy of the War of 1948. This deliberate avoidance was the principal cause for the accord's spectacular collapse at Camp David 2000, when the parties began to discuss in earnest the basic issues of that legacy.

The War of 1948 left four open issues that so far have curtailed all ventures to reconcile the Arab states and the Palestinians with Israel. These issues still constitute a hindrance to any permanent settlement. The first issue has been territorial. Israel inherited Mandatory Palestine's international borders with the adjacent Arab states. The Arab armies violated these lines, but Israel accepted them. In 1949, Israel withdrew from Egyptian and Lebanese territories that had been occupied in the last phase of the war in preparation for or in the wake of the armistice negotiations. Israel's border with Syria has posed a different problem. Syria has never recognized its international border with Palestine and has claimed "the water line" equally dividing the Jordan River and lake Kinneret between the parties. The most crucial territorial problem, however, has been the border between Israelis and Palestinians. The armistice lines demarcated Israel on the one hand, and Egypt and Jordan on the other hand. From a Palestinian standpoint, these lines—now called "the 1967 borderlines"—have been meaningless and noncommitting. Continuous infiltration into Israel throughout the 1950s and 1960s manifested this attitude. The only internationally recognized line that separates Israelis from Palestinians has been the 1947 partition line. The Arabs also linked the claim for Israel's withdrawal to the partition lines with the refugee issue. They maintained that the more territory Israel would cede, the less would be the scope of the remaining refugee problem after the return of some to the vacated area.

Apparently, the second issue, which has been posed by the Palestinian refugees, is the most crucial. Several other major refugee problems emerged in the world during the twentieth century—in Germany, Poland, Czechoslovakia, the Balkans, India and Pakistan, Vietnam, and various countries in Africa. Most found their solution long ago. Only the eternal Palestinian refugee problem has endured. More than any other single factor of the Israeli-Arab conflict, the Palestinian refugee problem manifests its unique features as a confrontation between opposing civilizations, extending beyond the ordinary national or religious level of other historical encounters.

Blaming the Arab League for the refugees' fate, Israel expected the Arab governments to resettle the Palestinians in their countries as Germany had absorbed *Volksdeutsche* after World War II and Israel itself absorbed refugee-immigrants from the Arab countries. Israel's efforts to convince the Palestinians, the Arab states, and the entire world that this problem should be solved by resettlement have been sincere, but out of context. The Arab world has insisted on the refugees' "right of return" as a precondition for any reconciliation with Israel. During fifty years since the end of the war, the Arab states—with the exception of Jordan— have not absorbed the refugees. While individual refugees settled to begin life anew in and outside the region, the majority barely mixed with their hosts—neither in the West Bank and Gaza Strip nor in the Arab countries. They have remained aloof from the indigenous population, socially and geographically, living in separate camps and expecting their return.

In the wake of the war, Israeli diplomacy successfully neutralized the refugee problem's explosive political potential and turned it into a human problem of aid that the UN undertook to provide. "The Great Powers" acquiesced to this change, but the Arab world—the refugees themselves, other Palestinians, and the Arab states—refused to follow. The Arabs rejected forthwith the Israeli approach to the problem and Israel's proposals to resolve it.[22] The implied message has been unequivocal: First, the Palestinian refugees are Israel's creation and responsibility, and it should not expect the Arab world to help solving the problem or share the responsibility for their ultimate fate. Second, the Arabs have not been able to crush

Jewish statehood, but Israel should not expect them to comply with its alien code of conduct. Unlike Europe, the pattern in the Middle East has been that war refugees do not resettle elsewhere but return to their homes when hostilities end, and hostilities do not end until they return. Israel has to reckon with this twofold message, and it is difficult to foresee how the problem can be solved.

A third focal issue has been Jerusalem. In Palestinian eyes, Jerusalem embodies the whole conflict because apart from its religious and historical significance, the fate of the holy city also concerns the territorial and refugee issues. Although Jerusalem has had a Jewish majority since the middle of the nineteenth century, the town was also the seat of the Arab elite in Palestine and the traditional center of Arab political life.

In Jewish eyes, Jerusalem is primarily the historical capital of the Jewish people, the holy city, for generations the focal point for historical yearnings for a return to Zion. The town's fate in 1948 symbolized the UN's failure to implement the partition plan. Israel therefore preferred sharing the city with Jordan rather than internationalization as the lesser evil, and both states cooperated in frustrating UN attempts to revive internationalization after the war. With Jordan's disappearance from the West Bank in 1967, Israel annexed Jerusalem. Ever since it has tried hard to deny the Palestinians any political foothold in the town, claiming that they have neither historical nor political status in Jerusalem.

Once more, despite the goodwill of individuals on both sides, this seems to be an unbridgeable gap. The fourth key issue concerns Arab recognition of and reconciliation with Israel. After their defeat in 1948, the Arab states adopted the same UN resolutions—mainly Resolutions 181 and 194—to which they had vehemently objected prior to their military debacle, as the cornerstone of their political case against Israel. While insisting on strict fulfillment of these resolutions, the Arab states refused to commit themselves in return to recognition of and peaceful and friendly relations with their new neighbor. Political and economic relations with Israel, Arab leaders maintained, were the Arabs' own business and should not be linked to implementing UN resolutions that should be an international commitment.

This attitude persisted until Anwar Sadat's visit to Jerusalem in 1977. In recent years, parts of the Arab world have changed their attitude to Israel, although genuine acceptance of its "legitimacy" remains fundamentally unresolved. The cardinal issues concerning Israeli-Palestinian relations have not been tackled yet and continue to cast a shadow on Israel's relations with the Arab states as well.

During the last decade, the Israeli-Palestinian dialogue has been conducted on two separate levels that, unfortunately, did not converge: Ultimately, the vast majority of Israelis sought coexistence with the Arabs and understood that such coexistence required compromise and concessions on Israel's part. The domestic controversies among Israelis did not concern the principle of compromise and concession, but its implementation: how far to compromise and what should be the limit of *accommodation*. The Palestinians strove for neither coexistence nor compromise but for *justice*: The final and permanent settlement with Israel should remedy the wrongs that have allegedly been done to them, at least since the UN partition plan of 1947 if not since the Balfour Declaration of 1917. As long as Israeli concessions met the Palestinians' perception of justice, the dialogue persisted. When Israel stopped conceding and insisted on certain positions, the Palestinian struggle for what they perceive as their "just rights" erupted again, and this is precisely where we are at this point in time.

NOTES

1. All the written material on the Tantura affair, including the thesis' two versions, the reviewers' reports, the court proceedings, media coverage, polemics, and so on has been assembled by Prof. Dani Censor in his website http://www.ee.bgu.ac.il/~censor/katz-directory

2. Eugene L. Rogan and Avi Shlaim (eds.), *The War for Palestine: Rewriting the History of 1948* (with an Afterword by Edward W. Said), Cambridge: Cambridge University Press, 2001.

3. Israel Ben-Dor, "The Image of the Arab Enemy in the Jewish *Yishuv* and the State of Israel in the Years 1947–1956," Ph.D. dissertation submitted to the University of Haifa, 2003.

4. "Memoirs of Anwar Nusseibeh," *Jerusalem Quarterly File*, 11–12, 2001; Constantine K. Zurayk, *The Meaning of the Disaster*, Beirut, 1956 (originally published in Arabic in August 1948); Musa Alami, "The Lesson of Palestine," *The Middle East Journal*, October 1949, pp. 373–405.

5. Abraham Sela, "Arab Historiography of the 1948 War: The Quest for Legitimacy," in Laurence J. Silberstein (ed.), *New Perspectives on Israeli History: The Early Years of the State*, New York, 1991, pp. 124–154.

6. Elchanan Oren, *Baderech El Ha'Ir* (Hebrew, "On the Road to the City"), Ma'arachot, Tel Aviv, 1976; Meir Pa'il, *Min HaHaganah Letzva HaHaganah* (Hebrew, "From the Haganah to the IDF"), ZBM, Tel Aviv, 1979; Anita Shapira, *Mipiturey Ha Rama Le Piruk Ha Palmach* (Hebrew, "From the Discharge of the Haganah's Chief of Command Council to the Disbandment of the Palmach"), Hakibbutz Hemeuchad, Tel Aviv, 1984; Yoav Gelber, *Gar'in Le Tzava 'Ivri Sadir* (Hebrew, "The Emergence of a Jewish Army: The Veterans of the British Army in the IDF"), Yad Ben-Zvi, Jerusalem, 1986; *Idem, Lama Pirku Et Ha Palmach* (Hebrew, "Why the Palmach Was Disbanded"), Schocken, Tel Aviv, 1986.

7. Benny Morris, *The Birth of the Palestinian Refugee Problem*, Cambridge: Cambridge University Press, 1989.

8. Avi Shlaim, *Collusion across the Jordan—King Abdullah, the Zionist Movement, and the Partition of Palestine*, Oxford: Oxford University Press, 1988.

9. Simcha Flapan, *Zionism and the Palestinians*, London: Croom Helm, 1979; *idem, The Birth of Israel: Myths and Realities*, London: Croom Helm, 1987.

10. Baruch Kimmerling, *Zionism and Territory: The Socio-Territorial Dimensions of Zionist Politics*, Institute of International Studies, University of California, Berkeley, 1983; *idem* and Joel Migdal, *Palestinians: The Makings of a People*, New York: Free Press, 1993.

11. Tom Segev, *The First Israelis*, New York: Free Press, 1986.

12. Ilan Pappé, *The Making of the Arab-Israeli Conflict, 1947–1951*, London: I. B. Tauris, 1994.

13. Rashid Khalidi, "The Palestinians and 1948: The Underlying Causes of Failure," in Rogan and Shlaim (eds.), *The War for Palestine*, p. 13.

14. Introduction, *ibid.*, p. 7.

15. Khalidi, *ibid.*, p. 17.

16. Yoav Gelber, *Shorshei Hachavazelet* (Hebrew, "Growing a Fleur-de-Lis: The Intelligence Services of the *Yishuv* in Palestine, 1918–1947"), 2 Vols., Ministry of

Defense Publications, Tel Aviv, 1992; *idem, Jewish-Transjordanian Relations, 1921–1948,* London and Portland: Frank Cass, 1996; *idem, Nitzanei Hachavatzelet* (Hebrew, "A Budding Fleur-de-Lis: Israeli Intelligence Services During the War of Independence, 1948–1949"), 2 Vols., Tel Aviv: Ministry of Defense Publications, 2000; *idem, Palestine 1948: War, Escape and the Emergence of the Palestinian Refugee Problem,* Brighton and Portland: Sussex Academic Press, 2001; *idem. Tkuma Veshever* (Hebrew, "Independence versus Nakbah") forthcoming, Zmora-Kinnereth, 2004.

17. Protocol of the Knesset's Foreign Affairs and Defence Committee meeting, 23 February 1960, Israel State Archives.

18. Protocol of the Provincial Government meeting, 19 December 1948, p. 3, Israel State Archives.

19. Gelber, *Jewish-Transjordanian Relations,* pp. 234–236.

20. *Ibid.,* chapters 8 and 9, and *idem, Nitzanei Hachavazelet,* chapter 7.

21. Gelber, *Palestine 1948,* p. 172 ff.

22. Jacob Tovi, "Israel's Policy towards the Palestinian Refugee's Problem, 1949–1956," Ph.D. dissertation submitted to the University of Haifa, 2002.

3

Israel's Armistice Wars, 1949–1956

David Tal

Israel was born in war and was involved in wars throughout its years of existence. This reality affected the periodization of Israel's security history, which usually is divided according to the years of war: from 1949 to 1956, from 1957 to 1967, and so on. However, this division is a bit arbitrary, as the in between years were not that homogenous, from the security point of view. A subtler division seemed to be in place, and a more accurate division would be from 1949–1955 and the year 1956. The first period should be called Israel's Armistice War and it was a time when Israel fought to maintain the armistice agreements. In the second period Israeli commitment to the armistice regime loosened, and it was ready to consider its abolishment. Several features characterized the period of the Armistice War: the problems in hand were not purely military; the IDF operational capabilities were tested in a postwar era, and the test exposed the army's weaknesses; and the diplomatic aspect of the Armistice War was as important as the military. All of these features will be described in the following pages.

ISRAEL SECURITY CONCEPTION AFTER THE 1948 WAR

Israeli security conception after the 1948 war was comprised of three layers: the first related to national security in the most broad manner, the second to the concrete threat and preparedness to war, and the third to current security problems that Israel had to deal with.

The first layer, amorphous and general up to the point of abstraction, was affected by the history of the Jewish-Arab conflict in general and the experience of the war that just ended in particular. It was based on the assumption that the Arabs did not recognize Israel's right to exist, that they would act on the first occasion to undo the results of the 1948 war, and that Israel was thus still under an existential threat.[1] The fear from the existential threat had no effect on the daily preoccupation with security matters, and its influence was found in the shaping of the Israeli attitude toward peace. It decided Israel's policy regarding the price it would be ready to pay for peace, and it led the Israeli government to interpret the demand for territorial concessions and the return of the Palestinian refugees to Israel not as a price for peace but as a scheme devised by its enemies to bring about its destruction. Israeli assumption—or better put, belief—that the Arab governments were determined to launch another war against Israel, "the second round," was unfounded, as the Arab states took no action toward that goal, and made no move in that direction. The words of the assistant to the Saudi foreign minister, Sheikh Yusuf Yassin, to the American ambassador in Riad in 1950 are typical: "the Arabs had no aggressive intentions against Israel, but they will treat it as if it was surrounded by a high wall."[2]

The second layer related to the evaluation of Israel's strategic position in concrete terms, and it related to the actual threat of war. The Israeli security and military leadership assumed until 1955 that the actual danger of war was not imminent. The security minister, David Ben-Gurion, assumed in 1952 that there was no danger of war at least until 1954, and the IDF chief of staff, Moshe Dayan, claimed in 1954 that war was not expected at least for the next ten to fifteen years. The most emphatic evidence to this sense of security was Dayan's decision in 1954 to dismember the Southern Command, which was considered at that time as redundant.[3] It is interesting to note that the same feeling existed in the Arab world.[4]

The third level was the one centered over current security, and it related to the problems the Israeli security forces had to deal with on a daily basis during this period. There were three kind of problems in this category: the dispute over demilitarized zones, the military administration imposed on the Israeli Arabs, and the struggle against the infiltration to Israel from the neighboring Arabs countries, mainly from the Egyptian-controlled Gaza Strip and the Jordanian-controlled West Bank.

Out of these three problems, the most disturbing was the last one. The phenomenon was diverse and heterogeneous, as the motive of the infiltrators varied. Many of them were Palestinian refugees who had fled during the 1948 war and sought to return to their homes (illegally, of course) or to retrieve property they had left behind. Some wanted to visit relatives who had remained in what was now the state of Israel, or visit the graves of their forefathers. Others, facing severe economic problems, entered Israel to steal. The infiltrators included inhabitants of the West Bank who "specialized" in such activity and were organized in gangs. They carried out plundering raids, in some cases as "contractors" for Arab merchants.[5]

The armistice lines with Jordan and Egypt produced infiltrators of another type: individuals who, by the end of the war, found out that their land remained on the other side of what was now a border that they were not allowed to cross. Wishing to nevertheless cultivate their fields and harvest the fruits of their orchards or crops from their fields, they became infiltrators by trying to do so. Another aspect of the same phenomenon was attempts by Arabs in the border areas to seize and till land on the Israeli side, or even to harvest crops sown by Israeli settlers.[6]

Few of the infiltrators from Jordan and the Gaza Strip were what we call today "terrorists" who infiltrated Israel for political reasons. They included Palestinian activists who carried out sabotage and murder raids inside Israel, wishing to maintain constant military tension along the borders, preventing the consolidation of the status quo generated by the armistice lines, and generally keeping the conflict alive.[7] It should be emphasized that this "political" infiltration represented the lesser part of the phenomenon. It was the Israeli reaction that overlaid the infiltration phenomenon with a political dimension, since Israel did not treat the infiltrators for what they were but linked them to the broad Arab-Israeli context and to the country's political and security problems.

Why did Israel treat the subject as a security one? In fact, when the first signs of the phenomenon were noticed, Israeli leaders referred to it as a civil problem. Ben-Gurion said in September 1949 that "the theft case [committed by the infiltrators] are crimes against the civil law, and it will be treated as any other theft case."[8] However, neither at this early stage nor later was the issue treated as a civil matter. The IDF was assigned to prevent the entry of the infiltrators as soon as the phenomenon was noticed during the 1948 war, and it remained its important assignment throughout the first half of the 1950s. The assignment of the IDF to this task was no coincidence, and it was the result of the way the Israelis interpreted the infiltration phenomenon and its connection to the armistice regime. Israel ended its war of independence with three major achievements. The first was its ability to survive the attacks of its Arab neighbors, who tried to prevent the establishment of a Jewish state in Palestine. The second achievement was territorial. The Arab refusal to accept the UN partition resolution and the ensuing war led to the expansion of the state of Israel, compared to its size, as was set by the partition resolution.

Furthermore, in this enlarged area, the demographic ratio between Jews and Arabs improved—from the Jewish point of view—and that was the third accomplishment. Within the territory allocated to the state of Israel by the UN, there were supposed to be about 450,000 Jews and 300,000 Arabs. During the war, hundreds of thousands of Palestinians either fled away from their homes or were deported by the IDF soldiers, and consequently, within the expanded Israeli territory the ratio had changed to 600,000 Jews against less then 100,000 Arabs. When this trend was identified, the Israeli leadership viewed it as a major achievement. It soon became a policy cornerstone that under no circumstances should the refugees be permitted to return to the Jewish state.[9]

Israel adhered also to the geographical achievements gained in the war. The armistice lines (armistice demarcation lines—ADL) were considered both by the world and the Arab states as temporary, a situation that led Ben-Gurion to declare in June 1950 that "Israel ended the war with borders that were different than those set for us. . . . There was objection to the expanded borders, and this objection has not disappeared."[10] The voices of objection were heard during the war, with the proposal of the UN mediator, the Count Folke Bernadotte, who called in summer 1948 to perpetuate the current territorial status quo that would replace the partition resolution lines. Bernadotte meant that the territories under Jewish control, which included territories that were not assigned to the Jews, such as the Jerusalem corridor and the western Galilee, would be part of the new Jewish state, while the southern Negev that was supposed to be part of Israel according to the partition resolution and was under the control of the invading Egyptian army, should be handed to an Arab country.[11] Israel rejected the idea to trade the Negev for the western Galilee and demanded to include both areas within Israel, one in the power of its military achievements, and the second through the right given to it in accordance with the partition resolution.[12]

As the armistice agreements implied an Arab recognition—even if de facto—of its territorial and demographic achievements, Israel felt that the agreements served its interest in the best way. Peace negotiations would lead to the opening of the issues that, after all, were controversial, and hence, the state of no war-no peace embodied in the armistice agreements served Israel's strategic interest in the best way. This was the reason that Israel insisted on the preservation of the armistice regime . . . and its security policy during the years 1949–1955 served that purpose.

In addition, the damage that the infiltrators inflicted upon Israel was quite heavy. The infiltrators-thieves also murdered civilians, mainly in cases in which the settlers interrupted the infiltrators. And there was another aspect to the damage sustained by the Israeli settlers along the borders: many of them were new immigrants who were unfit to deal with the infiltration problem. From 1948 to 1950, 250 new settlements were established, most of them along the borders, and many of them were settled by new immigrants. The government was afraid that the settlers, unable to cope with the infiltrators' threat, would leave their places and would leave the border area unpopulated.[13]

BUILDING THE ORGANS OF STRUGGLE

The struggle against the infiltration was conducted along various fronts and various means were deployed. However, all of these were developed not in an orderly manner, but in a process of trial and error, in which organs, methods, and modes of operation were tested. As the phenomenon was first identified during the 1948 war, the IDF forces that were deployed along the lines were instructed to prevent the infiltrators from crossing the battlefield lines.[14] It was natural to assign IDF forces to fight the infiltrators at a time of war. However, with the end of the war and signing of the armistice agreements, confusion prevailed. No official organ was charged with the responsibility of conducting the fight against the infiltrators. Without a central body dealing with the subject, local solutions were offered, mainly by local authorities and local police forces. However, the efforts to build regional forces comprised of police and civil guard units failed, mainly because many of the residents in the border area were unfit and unready to cooperate.[15]

The issue was discussed in governmental level, but without results. During this time the IDF conducted the fight against the infiltrators, against the will of its high command. There were two main reasons for the reluctance: the struggle against the infiltration was frustrating and inconclusive, as it was impossible to completely seal a 900-kilometer-long border and to prevent desperate and determined Arabs from crossing it. In addition, in the end of the war, the IDF demobilized most of its troops, and the more than 100,000-soldier army was reduced to a 25,000-soldier army. With that, the deployment of the IDF forces along the borders was significantly thinned, making it easier to the infiltrators to cross the border. The second reason was that this activity diverted the IDF energy from what its command considered as its main task: preparing the army for the prime challenge, a war against one or all of the neighboring countries.[16]

Trying to lift off the burden of the fighting against the infiltrators, the IDF command tried to make a conceptual and practical distinction between "basic security"—

the preparation to general war—and "current security," the daily engagement with various security problems, the struggle against the infiltrators among them. The IDF high command sought to be relieved from the second task in order to be able to take all the measures toward the first task.[17] However, the distinction was artificial, as the IDF was not ready to be discharged from responsibility to the fighting against the infiltrators, as it saw as its task "to guarantee the border security." Claiming that ensuring the border security demanded military actions, it was unready to give the other organ responsibility over the armistice lines. And so, even when it was agreed that it should be the police task to fight the infiltrators, the IDF still remained involved in this struggle. Considering its status and position within the Israeli security establishment, it was obvious that the supreme responsibility would remain in the hands of the IDF.[18]

Another attempt to relieve the IDF forces from the struggle against the infiltrators was the assigning of specializing formations within the IDF with the task of the fighting against the infiltration. The first of these was the Military Government. Its formal role was to run the lives of the Israeli Arabs, but the IDF command hoped that it would be possible to assign it also to guard the border. That was impossible, as the Military Government had no forces of its own, and whenever it launched military operations within the Arab areas, such as in pursuit of infiltrators that found shelter in the Arab villages in Israel, it had to call for reinforcements from the IDF or from the police.[19]

Another structural solution that was tested was the Spatial Defense. The Spatial Defense was an organ built by the IDF as a means to solve one of the most disturbing security problems of Israel, the lack of strategic depth. The small size of Israel and the proximity of populated areas to the border lines did not allow any surrender of territory to Arab forces, in case they launched a surprise attack on Israel. The solution was the construction of the border settlements, civil settlements by all respects, as garrisons that would be able to absorb the shock of a surprise attack and contain it until the arrival of IDF reinforcement that would push the enemy forces across the border. The settlements were organized as semimilitary formations, with the settlers armed and equipped to face such an attack. Being structured to fill military missions, it was assumed that the settlements would also take part in the struggle against the infiltrators. However, for many reasons they proved to be unfit for that mission.[20]

With the failure of the attempt to use existing organs, an effort was made to build designated organs for that mission. The first such organ was the Gendarmarie, created in summer 1949. Its engineer and first commander was General David Shaltiel, the controversial commander of Jerusalem in the 1948 war. Shaltiel proposed to establish a force that would be engaged in police activity, but would be under the direct responsibility of the defense minister and not under the IDF or police command. The force's missions would be guarding and sealing the state's borders and maintaining order along the border area. The force was established, but various problems led to its dissolution within short time. The IDF and the police argued over the question of who should budget the force, and Ben-Gurion could not bring the sides to reach to an agreement. A decision was made easier as the other problems plaguing the force decided its fate. Shaltiel's personality together with the low quality of the recruits did not allow the force to function as expected, and Ben-Gurion decided to disband it, effective in summer 1950.[21]

With the failure of the border force, the IDF assumed once more the responsibility of fighting against the infiltration, an eventuality that Ben-Gurion was unhappy to see. He appointed a committee that was assigned to present its recommendations on this matter, and in the mean time the IDF continued acting along the borders in the struggle against the infiltration.[22] It is unknown what happened with this committee, but in March 1953 Ben-Gurion appointed another committee, which was comprised of police and IDF representatives, to formulate a plan for the guarding of the border.[23] The appointment of the committee was the result of the growing tension along the Israeli-Jordanian border. During that year there was a rise in the number of the Israelis killed by infiltrators, and in result the number of reprisal attacks conducted by the IDF increased, and consequently to the international criticism against Israel sharpened. The joint committee submitted its report in a short time, and its main recommendation was to establish a police force-border guard that would act under the IDF command—its role would be as its name implied: fighting against the infiltration. The new force was established in May 1953, being deployed along the Lebanese-Syrian-Jordanian border. Its deployment was completed in April 1954, and experience showed that the new force was one reason for the notable decrease in the number of infiltrations to Israel.[24]

SHAPING THE MEANS OF STRUGGLE

Israel had employed three main means of actions in its Armistice War: sending messages to the Arab governments though various existing communication channels, taking military preventive measures along the armistice lines, and reprisal attacks. The first and the third measures were directed to the local governments, and the second measure was directed against the infiltrators themselves.

Channels of Communication

There were three channels through which Israeli and Jordanian and Egyptian officials exchanged messages: one was informal, in which police officers from both sides of the border approached each other in order to solve outstanding problems. The phenomenon existed mainly along the Israeli-Jordanian border, which was the prime source of friction until 1954. Police officers from both sides of the border met frequently in an attempt to resolve problems and to reduce the tension caused by the infiltrators. The other channel was the Mixed Armistice Committee (MAC), whose creation was stipulated by the General Armistice Agreements (GAA), and its role was to monitor the implementation of the armistice agreements. There were four such committees: Israel-Lebanon, Israel-Syria, Israel-Jordan and Israel-Egypt, three members in each: two military officers, an Israeli and an Arab, and a UN officer, member of UNTSO (UN Truce Supervision Organization), who served as the MAC chairman. The MAC was meeting frequently, but its effectiveness decreased as it did not take long before it became a propaganda battlefield in which each side made charges against the other. At the same time it was the only forum in which Israeli and Arab officials met, and the forum was used also to exchange views by both sides.[25]

The last channel was a diplomatic one. Diplomats stationed in Israel and in the neighboring Arab countries rendered their good services to the local governments and delivered messages from one to another. The messages related to vast outstanding issues, and Israel's firm demand from Arab governments to prevent infiltrators from their territories from crossing the border was one recurring issue. This channel was also used to exchange messages aiming to tranquilize a tense situation and even to deliver what some scholars refer to as messages of peace.[26] As will be seen later, the question of the main tool to be used to convince the Arab governments to increase their anti-infiltration actions, either diplomacy or through the practice of military means, was a matter of controversy in 1955 between Ben-Gurion—minister of defense at that time—and Moshe Sharett, the prime minister and foreign minister.

The main message that Israel delivered to the Jordanian and Egyptian governments was that the armistice agreements forbade the crossing of the ADL, and that they should enforce that ban. The Arab governments did act to prevent infiltrators from crossing the border into Israel, but they also claimed that Israel should deal with the matter as a civil/criminal one, and should not employ the IDF in the struggle against the infiltrators.[27] Israel rejected that claim. The Israeli leaders knew that the Jordanian and Egyptian authorities did not encourage the infiltrators, and even acted to prevent them from crossing the borders, but the Israeli government charged that the two Arab governments' attitude toward the phenomenon was lax, and it demanded that the Arabs take firmer actions in their struggle against the infiltrators.[28] The strange thing was that the Israeli law did not define infiltration as an illegal act. It was only in 1954 that the Knesset passed a law that defined the infiltration as a criminal act. Until then, the infiltrators that were caught were either deported or were sentenced on crimes that were related to the infiltration act, such as theft or crossing through areas defined as closed military zones.[29]

Preventive Measures

One of the earliest measures that was taken in the struggle against the infiltration was the declaration of a strip along the border as "security zone" that nonmilitary civilians were not allowed to enter. Various strips along the Israeli border with Lebanon and Jordan were put under this category. The practical meaning of the measure was that every intruder was shot on sight.[30] Other measures included patrols and ambushes across the borders, and from time to time search operations were conducted within the Israeli territory, in places where infiltrators could find refuge. The instructions of the Israeli soldiers in the patrols and the ambushes were to shoot at sight any infiltrators, regardless who he or she was, and even if the infiltrator was unarmed. The IDF sought, through these resolute actions, to deter would-be infiltrators.[31]

Israeli Commanding Officer of the IDF Southern Command, Lt. General Moshe Dayan, explained in 1950 the means employed by the IDF and the reasons for those means: The Arabs . . . harvesting crops on our side of the border, they and their women and children, and we shot at them. . . . Vast territory, ten kilometers in depth, upon which a Jewish laid no foot, full with graze, while on the other side of the border there are 200,000 hungry Arabs, [and if] they crossed through the fields . . . we will shoot them. Arabs crossing to retrieve crops they left in their deserted villages, . . . we make them step over mines, and they return mutilated. . . . And I know no other mean to protect the borders. If the shepherds and the harvesters crossed freely, tomorrow there will be no borders to the state of Israel.[32]

Dayan laid here the foundation of the logic of Israel's reaction to the infiltration problem. A civil problem turned out to be a political one because Israel was afraid of the political repercussions of the phenomenon. The questions of whether the threat was real and whether the state of the border was so vague that it might be eradicated notwithstanding, Israeli paranoia at this stage was enough to assume that, indeed, this was the case.

Reprisal Attacks

The most known method used in the struggle against the infiltration was the reprisal attacks conducted by Israel against Jordanian and Egyptian targets throughout the years 1949–1956.[33] The impact of the attacks was so great that some scholars describe the second Israeli-Egyptian war in 1956 as the climax of the cycle of violence between the two countries in which murderous infiltration and Israeli reprisal attacks has culminated in a war.[34] However, as will be argued later, this linkage between the infiltration, Israel's reprisal attacks and the 1956 Sinai war, is inaccurate.

Initially, the reprisal attacks were small in scale, carried out by IDF regular forces, as part as their day-to-day missions. The decision to launch a reprisal attack was made, in most cases, following the murder of an Israeli citizen by infiltrators. The number of the Israeli casualties was the decisive factor in the decision to launch a reprisal attack. In 1949 infiltrators from Jordan murdered eleven Israeli citizens and in 1950 they murdered eighteen. In result, in each of these years one reprisal attack was carried out, while in 1951, with the rise in the number of Israelis killed by infiltrators, ten reprisal attacks were launched. In 1952 the numbers decreased, but in 1953 forty-six Israeli citizens were murdered.[35] In response, Israeli troops launched more than twenty reprisal attacks against Jordanian targets. The most spectacular attack, which proved to be a crossroad in the history of the reprisal attacks, took place in October. That was the Qibiya attack. On October 12, 1953, infiltrators murdered a mother and two of her sons at their home. The attack was the peak of a trend that was noticed since April. During these months infiltrators murdered twenty-nine civilians and two soldiers.[36] Two days later a large Israeli force attacked the Jordanian village of Qibyia. Seventy of the village residences were killed by the troops who demolished the village houses and shot at their occupants.[37]

The Qibyia attack had several repercussions. First, it marked a watershed in the Jordanian attitude toward the infiltration. Although the Jordanian government had tried to prevent the infiltration to Israel before the raid, it did not put everything in its disposal in the fight against it. Until that event, the Jordanian government rejected Israel's demand that the Legion forces would be deployed along the Israeli-Jordanian border and hence would seal it. The Legion's commander, Glubb, was afraid of both the possible friction between Israelis and his forces and also that putting the small Legion in the West Bank would allow Israel to strangle it, if hostilities erupted. However, following the Qibyia attack, more and more Legion forces were deployed in the West Bank, taking an active part in the struggle against the infiltrators.[38] This measure, together with the deployment of the Israeli newly formed border-guard force along the Israeli-Jordanian border, led to a noticed decrease in the extent of the infiltration from Jordan to Israel from 1954, and more significantly, to the decrease in the number of Israelis being murdered by infiltrators from Jordan. Compared to forty-six and fifty-seven murdered Israelis in 1952 and 1953, respectively, infiltrators from Jordan murdered only twenty-three and eleven Israelis in 1954 and 1955, respectively.[39] The change was mostly felt in Israeli reprisal attacks: from September 1954 to September 1956, Israel attacked no targets in Jordan.

Another repercussion was a change of policy within the IDF. The Qibiya attack in which nearly seventy civilians were killed was the last of its kind. The attack against a civilian target was not a coincidence or a mistake. Israel deliberately directed its reprisal attacks against civilian targets from the time this method was first employed. Moshe Dayan explained the logic of this choice:

The only method that proved to be effective—not justified or moral—but effective, in response to the placing of mines along the borders by Arabs . . . is to attack the nearby village on its women, children, and elders. Then the people there react against the breach of the border and force the local government to act and prevent such occurrences, as it is a test to the government prestige. Here come the Jews, opening fire, and since they unwilling and unready to go to war in response, they must take measures to prevent the deeds that provoked the Jewish actions. The collective punishment method proves to be most effective.[40]

And so, almost all the reprisal attacks that were launched since 1949 were directed against civilian targets. The conception was that there was no use attacking military targets, as it is their mission to sustain such attacks, and it would not raise sharp public reaction that would trigger governmental response. The operation order to the Qibiya attack was no exception. The forces were instructed "to attack the village and temporarily occupy it; to demolish houses and to cause maximum casualties among the village residents and by that to encourage them to leave their village."[41] However, the international reaction to the operation consequences was overwhelming. The Israeli government denied any responsibility, claiming that vigilantes did it.[42] However, in the aftermath of the Qibyia attack, Dayan, the main proponent of the attacks against civilians, admitted that the damage exceeded the benefit. Dayan, at that time the head of the IDF operation branch, was sent to New York to assist the Israeli delegation to the United Nations in its diplomatic struggle against the sharp reaction to the Qibiya attack. There he witnessed the great damage that the operation caused to Israel in the international arena, and he admitted regretfully that it would be impossible to continue attacking civil targets although he remained convinced that from the strict military point of view, this was the most effective method in the struggle against the infiltrators.[43]

The third repercussion of the operation was the realization that after years of frustration, the IDF military unit that launched the attack performed as was expected. Until the summer of 1953, the regular IDF forces that were deployed routinely along the borders carried out reprisal attacks. The unit that was assigned to a certain sector was the one to conduct the attack when one was called for. However, the performance of these units was quite poor. IDF forces failed to reach their targets, and when they did, they retreated in the face of the slightest resistance from Jordanian armed civil guard forces and or if they sustained very few casualties. The growing number of failures led the IDF to investigate the situation of the IDF infantry forces, and the IDF investigating officer presented in April 1953 a most disturbing report. The officer found that the infantry battalions were undermanned and the quality of the infantry soldiers was very poor. Junior commanders, NCOs, and officers were poorly trained, as the training program was poor and flawed.[44] The IDF high command took two immediate measures to mend things: first, it channeled better-quality soldiers to the infantry units. Among those were high school graduates that hitherto were sent to service units. The second measure was the creation of a special unit whose mission would be carrying out reprisal attacks. This was Unit 101, who together with the IDF parachute battalion carried out successfully the Qibiya attack.[45] In January 1954, Unit 101 was merged with the parachutes, who carried out all the reprisal attacks until 1956.

It is in this connection that the question should be asked: What was the real purpose of the Israeli retaliation attacks? Was it really only a tool in the struggle against the infiltrators, or did it serve another purpose? The question seems in place mainly when one wonders whether the mean was proportional to the cause. Was it really a response to the crossing of the border—even if illegal—by poor and food-seeking refugees, or were there some other hidden functions too? Many assume that there were more reasons for the practice of the retaliation attacks. Some assume that it was a means to force the Arab states to sign a peace agreement with Israel. Others argue that the attacks aimed also to force confrontation with the Arab states, to ameliorate internal morale, and to improve the operational and offensive abilities of the IDF forces.[46] There might have been, indeed, various justifications and hidden functions. However, it is quite clear that regardless of any other possible motive, the direct incentive, goal, and purpose was the struggle against the infiltration, and more accurately, against its lethal aspects. Almost every reprisal attack was carried out in the aftermath of the assassination of an Israeli by infiltrators. Not every assassination was followed by a reprisal attack, but every reprisal attack came after a murderous infiltration incursion. The list is too long to cite, but the following table will indicate in a clear manner the linkage between the killing of Israeli civilians by infiltrators and reprisal attacks in the Jordanian front.[47]

Year	Israelis Killed	Reprisal Attacks
1949	11	—
1950	18	1
1951	44	7
1952	46	12
1953	57	21
1954	23	12
1955	11	—

The same is true as to the linkage between the murders of Israeli citizens by infiltrators from Egypt and the number of retaliation attacks directed against targets at the Gaza Strip (from which most of the infiltrators came).

THE HEATING OF THE ISRAELI-EGYPTIAN BORDER

In the immediate aftermath of the Qibiya operation, tension raised sharply along the Israeli-Jordanian border, and war seemed imminent. Actually, neither side wanted war. The context of the Qibiya operation was obvious—Jordan was informed about the murder that triggered the operation, and the Jordanians knew very well why Israelis launched the attack. Consequently, the tension decreased as fast as it emerged, and with the security measures taken by both states along the border, calm was gradually restored. However, while the situation along the Israeli-Jordanian border stabilized, the Israeli-Egyptian border, mainly along the Gaza Strip, which was the populated area along the joint border, started to heat up. Up to 1954, the border was relatively calm, if the indication is the infiltration's lethality and the resulting Israeli reprisal attacks. During the years 1949–1953, infiltrators from the Egyptian border murdered some half dozen Israelis every year, and consequently, very few reprisal attacks were carried out.[48]

The growing conflict in 1954 was the result of clashes between Israeli and Palestinian soldiers that were deployed along the Gaza Strip border. The Palestinians used to shoot at passing Israeli patrols just across the border, and representatives from both sides acted to quell the tension. In early 1955, Egyptian and Israeli military officers were close to signing an agreement that would quell the tension, but several events terminated the talks before their conclusion. One event was the death sentences announced in Cairo for Israeli agents who tried to place bombs in American and British installations in July 1954. The agents acted in an attempt to sabotage the just-announced Egyptian-British agreement for the evacuation of the British bases along the Suez Canal. Israel wanted to see the British remain, as their presence was considered an effective buffer between Israel and Egypt, and through the sabotage campaign Israel hoped that the British government would announce that it would postpone the evacuation in light of the unrest in Egypt. That entire affair was a blunder, and the Israeli agents were caught. Two of them were sentenced and put to death in January 1955, as a result the Israeli-Egyptian military talks were suspended.[49]

The tension was aggravated by an Israeli reprisal attack on an Egyptian military barracks on February 28, 1955. The attack is considered by many as a watershed in the history of the Israeli-Arab relations, and as the first shot in the 1956 Sinai War. The common argument is as follows: In 1953 Ben-Gurion resigned from the government, Moshe Sharett taking his position as prime minister and Pinhas Lavon the defense portfolio. In February 1955, Lavon was forced to resign, and the retired David Ben-Gurion returned to the ministry of defense. Asking to put his mark on Israel's security policy that was dominated during his absence by the moderate Sharett, he was ordered to execute the attack in which forty Egyptian soldiers were killed. Egyptian President Abdul Nasser felt offended by the attack and defenseless. As Britain and the United States would not provide him the arms that would allow him to stand against the Israeli challenge, he resorted to the Soviet Union, and Moscow approved his request for the largest arms deal that was ever signed in the Middle East.[50]

As will be seen later, the linkage between the Gaza operation and the arms deal, which Nasser worked so hard to establish, did not actually exist. The Gaza operation, on the other hand, was just another reprisal attack. A few days before the attack, Egyptian intelligence agents that infiltrated Israel killed an Israeli citizen on their way back to Egypt. Ben-Gurion, who had just reassumed his position as minister of defense, proposed to carry out a reprisal attack, and Sharett, the prime minister, concurred. The chosen target was a military base, as was the practice since the Qibiya attack.[51] However, all this said, other motives than the prime one—the response to a murderous infiltrators' incursion—were also present when the decision was made. One was Ben-Gurion's desire to bring a shift in Israel's security policy from the path his successor, Moshe Sharett, directed.[52] The signing of the Western-oriented Baghdad Pact and Israel's failure to achieve security guarantees from the United States made Israel determined to make a show of power. Egypt's refusal to allow Israeli ships to cross the Suez Canal, a policy that Israel tested in 1954, and which resulted in the confiscation of a boat that tried to cross the canal and the arrest of its crew, and the death sentences for the Israeli agents that were involved in the mishap in July 1954, all provided an incentive to attack an Egyptian target.[53]

However, one should not confuse the immediate reason for the attack and the additional intentions that influenced the decision. Simply put, in the face of the past experience, it will be probably safe to say that without the murderous attack that triggered it, the Gaza raid would not have been carried out. All the additional arguments that supported the decision were insignificant without the one prime cause, the infiltrators' murderous attack. One thing is sure: for Nasser, the timing of the operation was really bad. Entangled in internal and external struggles, the damage caused to the prestige of his power-base, the army, by the Israeli attack, reflected on him, too. In 1954 Nasser was involved in a struggle against General Naguib, whom he was trying to replace, and against the British military presence along the Suez Canal. These struggles put him in a precarious position, and the Israeli attack only aggravated Nasser's position. If that was not enough, in February 1955 the Baghdad Pact was signed, a pact that challenged Nasser's and Egypt's position as the leader of the Arab world. For all of these reasons Nasser's response to the Israeli retaliation attack was different from the Jordanians'. The latter took the attacks for what they were, a tool in the struggle against the infiltrators, and the Jordanian authorities dealt with the Israeli measures by taking steps to remove the cause of friction. Nasser did understand the context of the Israeli actions, but because of his delicate political situation, internally and externally, he was afraid that the Israeli actions, despite their limited purpose, would destabilize his position. For that reason, his response was more aggressive.[54]

Three things happened in the aftermath of the Gaza raid: Nasser established a special military unit, the Fedayeen, whom he threatened to send on terror missions in Israel, where Israeli forces attacked again Egyptian targets, as they did in Gaza; the tension along the Israeli-Egyptian border increased with the intensifying Egyptian military units firing at Israeli patrols across the border; on the other hand, Nasser made it clear to his military men that he had no intention to go to war with Israel over the Gaza Strip. One expression of this trend of Nasser was the resumption of the informal talks between Israeli and Egyptian officers, talks that were carried out until the summer of 1955.[55]

The growing tension along the Israeli-Egyptian border ignited a struggle over Israel's foreign and security policy, in which Moshe Sharett, the prime minister and foreign minister, David Ben-Gurion, the defense minister, and General Moshe

Dayan, the IDF chief of staff, were involved. The struggle evolved over two related questions: how should Israel respond to the border clashes, and what should be the purpose of Israel security and foreign policy on this matter? The struggle is usually depicted as one conducted between Sharett on the one hand and Moshe Dayan and David Ben-Gurion on the other hand, both of the latter wishing to bring a change in the security policy that Sharett led during Ben-Gurion's absence from the government. Sharett, so goes the argument, refrained from authorizing retaliation attacks, preferring instead to use diplomatic means to convince the Jordanian and Egyptian governments to take more vigorous measures in their struggle against the infiltration.[56]

The debate, though, was more complicated than that and it was conducted between Sharett on one side and Ben-Gurion and Dayan on the other side. Ben-Gurion, like Dayan, believed that Israel should respond to the border clashes and the infiltration militarily, that is, through the employment of retaliation attacks. However, unlike Dayan, and concurrently with Sharett, Ben-Gurion thought that the goal of the Israeli retaliation attacks should be forcing Egypt to comply with the armistice regime. Ben-Gurion assumed that adhering to the armistice regime served best Israel's interest, and that it should use any means to enforce its proper implementation on Egypt. Dayan, on the other hand, sought the reprisal attacks as the best means to deal with the violations of the armistice regime. He did not rule out the possibility that it would provoke war with Egypt, and to the contrary, he thought that such an eventuality would be in the best interest of Israel. Ben-Gurion did not approve Dayan's approach, explicitly warning the IDF high command of the danger that the reprisal attacks would slip into war. On one occasion he said: "no one among us considers a war initiated by us." Ben-Gurion disagreed with Sharett over the means that should be used in the struggle against the infiltrators and border clashes, but shared with him the belief that the goal of the Israeli actions should be adherence to the armistice regime. It was on this last point that he disagreed with Dayan, who followed his superior's orders.[57]

Everything had changed on September 27, 1955, when Nasser announced that Egypt concluded a major arms deal with Czechoslovakia. According to the "Arms for Cotton," as the deal was known, Egypt would receive 200 modern tanks and 100 jet combat planes. Nasser explained that he bought the arms since the Gaza raid exposed his army's inferior state compared to the aggressive Israeli army, and his argument was widely accepted by historians.[58] However, as Rami Ginat had shown, the ties between Egypt and the Soviet Union—the deal's true sponsor—antedated February 1955, and it consisted actually of two parts, the first signed in January 1955, a few weeks before Operation Gaza. The context of the deal was Egypt's deteriorating relations with Britain and its and the United States' refusal to equip the Egyptian army with modern arms. The signing of the Baghdad Pact, an act that Nasser regarded—and he was right—as a measure aiming, among other things, to impair his position in the Arab world, further alienated him from the West. The Soviet Union would not miss the opportunity to put a foot in what was traditionally a Western-dominated area.[59]

The deal tilted dramatically the Israeli-Egyptian balance of arms in favor of the latter. Up to that moment, it was assumed that Israel enjoyed a slight military advantage over its neighbors. The deal changed it all, as Israel had nothing that even came close to what the Egyptians were about to receive. But there was more than that. Nasser's pretensions to unify the Arab world under his banner seriously worried Ben-Gurion. Ben-Gurion attributed Israel's success to withstand the Arab assault in 1948 to the disunity of the Arab war effort. The conflicting interests and the internal struggles played to Israel's favor, and prevented a concerted Arab attack, from three fronts, on Israel. The great danger to Israel laid in the emergence of an Ata-Turk-style Arab leader that would unify the Arab world and lead it against Israel. Ben-Gurion identified in Nasser these features in 1954. He became worried, but as long as the Arab world was militarily inferior to Israel, he did not assume that the danger was close. However, now with the arms deal that would give Nasser capabilities far exceeding those in Israel's possession, the threat of the pan-Arab leader leading the Arab world on a crusade against Israel became a threatening possibility.[60]

Nothing in the existing evidence supports Ben-Gurion's conviction that Nasser was planning to use the weapons against Israel. In fact, Nasser did everything he could to impress on his (diplomatic) listeners that he had no such intention.[61] However, for Ben-Gurion, Israel's security conception could not remain the same. He no longer felt obliged to the Armistice Agreements, and was ready to consider the possibility of a preemption war against Egypt. The IDF was preoccupied with the preparations toward such a possibility throughout Autumn 1955, but eventually Ben-Gurion decided to endorse a different path: to balance the Egyptian arms deal with an Israeli arms deal. Following an intensive diplomatic campaign, France agreed to provide Israel with the arms it needed, and with the arrival of the first French tanks to Israel in June 1956, the Israeli-Egyptian arms balance was restored.[62]

CONCLUSION

Technically, Israel went to the war in 1956 in response to the invitation of its strategic ally, France. France sought Israel's participation in the war for reasons that go beyond the current discussion, but it invited Israel to join the war in the aftermath of Nasser's nationalization of the Suez Canal company in July 1956. Would Israel be going to war against Egypt without the French invitation? It is impossible to say. There are those who think that that was possible, as Israel and Egypt were moving along a collision track at least since February 1955, or even earlier, due to the clashes along the two states' border. Indeed, it seemed somewhat artificial to separate the border clashes, the infiltration to Israel, and the reprisal attacks from the 1956 war. However, the distinction is comprehensible when one realizes that Israel's day-to-day security goal, at least until summer 1955, was the preservation of the armistice regime. Its actions, including the retaliation attacks, were all aimed to achieve that goal. Israel let the Jordanian and Egyptian authorities know that this was the rationale behind its aggressive activity, and both the Jordanian and the Egyptian governments understood that, and wanted also to see the armistice regime implemented.

There is another argument that justifies the distinction between the armistice wars and Israel's road to the 1956 war. Tension and violence also prevailed along the Jordanian and (to a lesser extent) the Syrian border, yet war did not erupt there. The critical turning point was Nasser's arms deal and his changing image in Ben-Gurion's eyes. These were unrelated to the border clashes—Israel knew that the Arab governments were neither initiating nor encouraging the infiltrators. It was the regional politics that led to the change, as Nasser got involved in regional and superpower competitions, and his activities in this arena alarmed Israel on the one hand and led him to a clash with France and Britain on the other hand. These events provided Israel with an opportunity that it seized in the summer of 1956, not because of the armistice wars, but because of Ben-Gurion's fears from Nasser. These fears nourished Ben-Gurion's belief that Nasser was the leader who would unify the Arab world and that with the arms he had procured, he would lead the Arab world to a war against Israel.

NOTES

1. David Ben-Gurion, "On the Army Structure and Road," October 27, 1949, in David Ben-Gurion, *Army and Security* (Hebrew), Tel Aviv, 1955, p. 138; David Ben-Gurion Diary, entry for October 23, 1950, Archive of David Ben-Gurion, the Center for David Ben-Gurion Heritage, Sde Boker, Israel (henceforth: BGD); Moshe Sarett in Mapai Political Committee, March 23, 1953, Archives of the Labor Party 26/53 (ALP); Dan Horowitz, "The Permanent and the Changing in Israel's Security Conception," in *War of Choice,* Tel Aviv, 1985, pp. 57–58.

2. Letter of the United States ambassador Riad to the secretary of state, March 25, 1950, *FRUS 1950:V,* p. 718. In a book titled *Arab Attitudes Towards the Arab—Israeli Conflict,* Tel Aviv, 1968, Harkabi presents quotes by Arab leaders in which they made threats against Israel. However the earliest threat is from 1961 (see page 16).

3. BGD, entry for February 23, 1952; Memorandum of Conversation (Moshe Dayan with Henry Byraode), July 16, 1954, NA RG 59, 611/84A/7-1654; Operations Branch: "Review on the Development of IDF Organization from 1949 to 1955," March 16, 1955, Israel Defense Forces Archive (henceforth: IDFA), Givataim Israel, 637/56/1.

4. Memorandum of Conversation (P. Ireland, U.S. Embassy and Colonel Shirin, Egypt Court), May 6, 1950, NA RG 84, Cairo Embassy, General Records, box 4. See also note 2.

5. "Infiltration" (document from the end of 1950), IDFA, 108/52/34; S. Ben-Elkana, head of minorities branch, Israel Police, "Survey on the Infiltration Problem," March 8, 1951, ISA, 2246/51/b. See also BGD, entries for February 3, 1950 and July 5, 1951.

6. "Infiltration" (document from the end of 1950), IDFA, 108/52/34; S. Ben-Elkana, head of minorities branch, Israel Police, "Survey on the Infiltration Problem," March 8, 1951, ISA, 2246/51/b; BGD, entry for September 30, 1949; Baggot J. Glubb, *A Soldier with the Arabs,* New York: Hodder and Stoughton, 1957, pp. 245–246; Ehud Ya'ari, *Egypt and the Fidayun, 1953–1956,* Givat Haviva: The Center of Arabic and Afro-Asian Studies, 1975, p. 9.

7. S. Bruk to Investigation branch, Police HQ, May 4, 1950, ISA, 2181/51/1a; Ya'ari, *Fedayun,* pp. 9–10; Zvi Al-Peleg, *The Grand Mufti,* Tel Aviv, 1989, pp. 126–127.

8. Ben-Gurion's reply to Knesset member Levenstein, September 21, 1949, Ben-Gurion Archives.

9. The foreign minister to the government members, September 10, 1948, ISA, 2348/21; foreign minister lecture before the Knesset Foreign Affairs Committee, May 2, 1949, ISA 2451/18; foreign minister meeting with the members of the Palestine Conciliation Committee, August 17, 1949, ISA 2451/1; Protocol of a meeting in the foreign ministry, January 31, 1950, ISA, 4373/14.

10. *The Knesset Annals* VI, Session 154, June 20, 1950.

11. Count Bernadotte to M. Shertok, 27 June 1948, in Yaov Gedalya, *Political and Diplomantic Documents,* Jerualem, 1980, pages 230–234.

12. "Israel Reply to the United Nations' Mediator Proposals," July 5, 1948, FO/2451/1, ISA; speech of the foreign minister, January 9, 1950, ISA, FO/2380.

13. Letter from Levy Eshkol, director of the settlement division, Jewish Agency to Col. I. Prihar, Commander of the Lowland District, 9 January, 1951, Central Zionist Archives (CZA), S-15/9786; letter from R. Doctory, Kfar Azarya to A. Ikar, Division of Society and Security Affairs, Jewish Agency, 26 January, 1951, *ibid;* letter from Levy Eshkol, director of the settlement division, Jewish Agency, to D. Ben-Gurion, 5 February, 1951, *ibid;* U.S. Embassy, Tel Aviv Telegram to the secretary of state, 31 January, 1953, NA RG 59, 684A85/1-3053.

14. GS/operations cables to fronts commanders, 8 September, 1948, IDFA 2539/50/5; Intelligence Service 1: A Weekly Intelligence Report, 16 September, 1948, IDFA 1041/49/28; 5th Brigade cables to the brigade battalions, 19 September, 1948, IDFA 7011/49/5.

15. Letter of regional assistant inspector to Tel Aviv District HQ, 6 February, 1949, ISA, L/2180 GenCom/51a/1.

16. Ben-Gurion, *War Diary,* pp. 830, 991–992; BGD, entry for December 5, 1952.

17. David Ben-Gurion, "On the Army Structure and Its Way," in *Army and Security,* p. 140.

18. BGD entries for September 30, 1949 and January 24, 1952; letter from Y. Nahmias, deputy general inspector, Israeli police, to the inspector of the southern district, 27 June, 1949.

19. Letter from D. Ben-Gurion to General Avner, 16 August, 1948, Ben-Gurion, *War Diary:* 2, p. 639; letter from Lt. Col. A. Markovski, military commander of the central district, to General Avner, 30 June, 1949, FO/2401/19, ISA; report of the deputy military commander to the military administration, 26 June, 1949, FO/2402/12, ISA.

20. BGD, entry for 21 January, 1951; IDF general staff/intelligence branch: Report on the Fortification of the Border Settlements, 10 February, 1955, FO/2393/22, ISA.

21. Letter from D. Shaltiel to D. Ben-Gurion, September 1949, 580/86, IDFA; BGD, entry for January 1950 (throughout the month); BGD, entry for August 24, 1950, January 11, 1951, and February 17 and 20, 1951.

22. BGD, entry for August 24, 1950.

23. Letter from Ben-Gurion to the government ministers, 24 March, 1953, BGA.

24. Letter of deputy general inspector (Israeli police) to IDF operation branch/commander, 18 June, 1953, ISA L/2301/37/2; letter of operation branch/operations to general staff/personnel, 28 October, 1953, IDFA 63/55/124; letter of operation branch/operations to operation branch/HQ, 3 January, 1954, IDFA 63/55/124; letter of operation branch/operations to the IDF chief of staff, 24 February, 1954, IDFA 8/56/1; letter of S. Tawil to J. Tekoa, 27 July, 1955, ISA 2488/1b.

25. David Tal, "The Local Commanders Agreement (Israel-Jordan): Failure of Direct Negotiations," *Cathedra* (Israel), No. 71, March 1994, pp. 118, 120.

26. See J. Tekoa, Memorandum to the Foreign Minister, 9 March, 1953, ISA, FO2949/2, in the Mixed Armistice Committees, 25 March, 1953, ISA, FO2453/, Telegram from J. Tekoa to various Israeli delegations, 2 June, 1953, ISA, FO2948/17.

27. General Glubb to General Reili, 8 February, 1951, NA RG 59, 684A.85/8-251.

28. Col. Y. Rabin, head of operations division: Operation Order "Cable," May 1951, ISA, L/2251/GI/1/51a.

29. Letters from district inspector R. Lustig (Israeli Policy) to the head of crimes division, 16 May, 6 June, and 1 September, 1949, ISA L/2246/51b; "The Infiltration Prob-

lem" [unsigned and undated documents], *ibid;* letter from A. Katsenlbugen, head of counter-infiltration fight division, to head of organization branch (Israeli police), 21 June, 1953, ISA, L/2257/m.

30. Knesset Session No. 51, July 4, 1949, *The Annals of the Knesset* II, pp. 906–907; M. Hofnung, *Israel: The Security of the State versus the Rule of Law, 1948–1991,* p. 82.

31. Annual Summary of Activity, 1952, ISA FO/2428/10; letter of S. Tawil to J. Tekoa, 27 July, 1955, ISA 2488/1b.

32. Meeting of Mapai secretariat with the party's Knesset members, 18 June, 1950, LPA, 1-11-3.

33. There were cross-border infiltration from Lebanon as well, but these did not generate friction. The Lebanese cooperated with Israel within the framework of the armistice commission.

34. Mordechai Bar-On, *The Gates of Gaza,* Tel Aviv: Am Oved, 1992, pp. 376–377; Kennett Love, *Suez: The Twice Fought War,* London: Longman, 1969, pp. 1–2; Benny Morris, *Israel's Borders War,* Oxford, 1993, p. 428; Michael B. Oren, *The Origins of the Second Arab-Israel War,* London: Frank Cass, 1992, pp. 7–8.

35. Y. Teqoa to Col. Y. Harkabi, head of intelligence branch: "Infiltration casualties," 22 March, 1956. ISA, FO 2404/14.

36. T. Tzvia, central command/intelligence: "Review of Murder Cases in the Command Sector, February–October, 1953," 21 December, 1953, ISA, L/2257/10/m.

37. The Qibiya operation order is quoted in Zeev Drori, *The Reprisal Attacks Policy in the 1950s: The Military and the Escalation Process* (an MA Dissertation, Tel Aviv University, 1988), p. 54.

38. "Jordan's Attitude to the Infiltration," 21 January, 1954, ISA L2257/m/10; letter from Glubb to the police commanders in Nablus, Jerusalem, and Hebron, 11 February, 1954, NA RG 59, 684A.85/2-2254.

39. Letter from Y. Tekoa to Col. Y. Harkaby, 22 March, 1956, ISA FO/2404/14.

40. Moshe Dayan addressing the Mapai secretariat and members of the Knesset, 18 June, 1950, LPA 11-1-3.

41. Quoted in Drori, *The Reprisal Policy,* p. 54.

42. See, for example, Summary of the Government Meeting, 7/314, 19 October, 1953, ISA G/5433/1400/g.

43. Moshe Dayan, *Milestones* (Hebrew), Tel Aviv, 1976, pp. 115, 169.

44. Report of the head of the infantry division, 17 April, 1953, IDFA 63/55/35.

45. Moshe Dayan in a lecture: "Diplomacy and Security, 1953–1957," 7 November, 1963.

46. Sholomo Aharonson and Dan Horowitz, "The Strategy of Controlled Retaliation—The Israeli Experience," *State & Government,* Vol. 1, No. 1, 1971, pp. 77–84; Earl Berger, *The Covenant and the Sword,* London, 1965, p. 96; Fred Khouri, "The Policy of Retaliation in Arab-Israeli Relations," *Middle East Journal,* Vol. 20, No. 4, Autumn 1996, p. 438.

47. David Tal, "The Retaliation Attacks: From Current Security Tool to an Instrument of Basic Security," in Moti Golani, *Black Arrow,* Tel Aviv, 1994, pp. 72–73.

48. Tal, "The Retaliation Attacks," p. 73.

49. Hagai Eshed, *Who Gave the Order?* Jerusalem, 1979, pp. 17–32; Moshe Sharett, *Personal Diary,* Tel Aviv, 1978, Vol. 2, pp. 689, 697, vol. 3, p. 800.

50. Keith Kyle, *Suez,* London, 1991, p. 64; Kenneth Love, *Suez: The Twice Fought War,* London, 1969, p. 83; Michael Oren, *The Origins of the Second Arab-Israeli War* London: Frank Cass, 1992, pp. 7–8.

51. Sharett, *Personal Diary,* 3, p. 800, entry for 27 February, 1955; BGD, entry for 3 March, 1955; IDF Operational Activity 1955–1956 (1), Archives of IDF History Department, 56/27.

52. Sharett, *Personal Diary,* 3, p. 742, entry for 20 February, 1955.

53. Sharett, *Personal Diary,* 3, p. 816, entry for 6 March, 1955; telegram of the American ambassador in Israel to the secretary of state, 4 March, 1955, NA RG 59, 674/84A/3-455.

54. Telegram of the American ambassador in Cairo to the secretary of state, 1 March, 1955, NA RG 59, 674/84A/3-155; Nasser address to the graduates of the Egyptian Military Academy, 3 March, 1955, NA RG 84, CE-GR b/263; Muhamed H. Heikel, *Cutting the Lion's Tail: Suez through Egyptian Eyes,* London, 1986, pp. 66–67.

55. Memorandum by Y. Tekoa to the foreign minister, 12, March, 1955, ISA, FO/2951/3.

56. Benny Morris, *Israel's Border Wars, 1949–1956,* Oxford, 1993, p. 332; Avi Shlaim, "Conflicting Approaches to Israel's Relations with the Arabs: Ben-Gurion and Sharett, 1953–1956," *MEJ,* Vol. 37, No. 2, Spring 1983, p. 189.

57. The whole issue is discussed in David Tal, "Ben-Gurion, Sharett and Dayan: Confrontation over the Issue of Preemptive War, 1955," *Cathedra,* No. 81, September 1996, pp. 109–122.

58. See note 38.

59. Rami Ginat, *The Soviet Union and Egypt,* London: Frank Cass, 1993, pp. 207–219.

60. Ben-Gurion expressed these fears on several occasions: on Oct. 27 1949–*Army and Security,* Tel Aviv: Ma'archot, 1955, p. 138; on Oct. 18 1951—*ibid,* pp. 289–290. See also Sharett, *Personal Diary,* 4: 958, entry for 24 April, 1955; Ben-Gurion's speech in a meeting of the executive committee and the trade unions, 5 January, 1956 in *Ma'arechet Sinai,* pp. 54–55.

61. From Cairo to the secretary of state, 27 November, 1955, NA, 674.84A/ 11-2755.

62. Dayan, *Milestones,* p. 175.

4

The Sinai War, 1956:
Three Partners, Three Wars

Motti Golani

The most recent historical research on the Sinai War—works published in the 1990s—provide telling descriptions of the fact that the war was a coalition endeavor involving Britain, France, and Israel. That basic fact was denied for years by the three governments. There appears to be little to add to the historiographic discussion on the fact of the partnership as such.[1] However, the question of the character borne by the partnership has yet to be fully addressed. Various studies have described and analyzed the vicissitudes of the political-diplomatic process that preceded the final decision for war. Similarly, the different motivation of each of the three partners has been dealt with. In this chapter, I will argue that the application of the "Sèvres agreement" during the war (October 29–November 6, 1956) demonstrated clearly, flagrantly in some cases, the differences of motivation, the divergent interests, and the separate goals of each of the three nations that sent their armed forces into war. From many points of view the military collaboration acted in a moment of truth, when it was no longer possible to hide the fact that each of the three ostensible partners had compartmentalized the other two and that the communications between the three nations that were supposedly fighting shoulder-to-shoulder against Nasser's Egypt were fraught with misunderstandings and half-truths, if not worse. I will indicate the disparities between the three partners; the focus will be on Israel's perception of the military collaboration, though similar problems can be identified also with regard to both Britain and France.

RETROSPECTIVE UNEASE

In the war's aftermath some in Israel sought to downplay the French (not to say the British) assistance that Israel had received. Summing up the war about a year

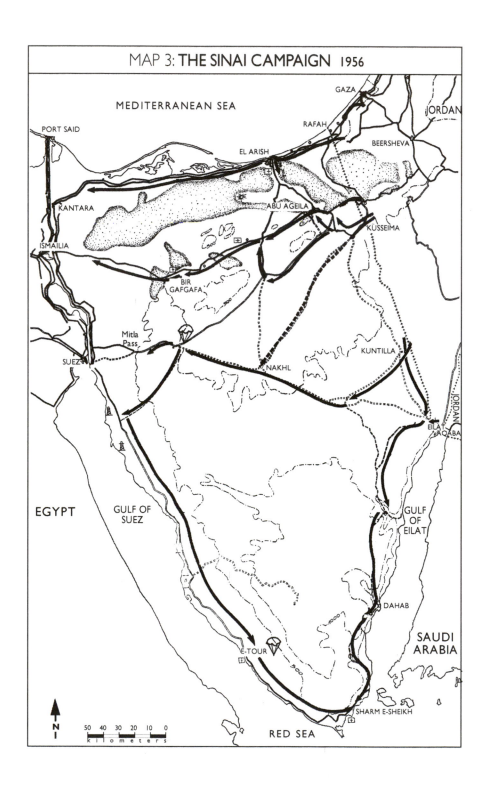

MAP 3: THE SINAI CAMPAIGN 1956

MEDITERRANEAN SEA

PORT SAID

GAZA

JORDAN

RAFAH

BEERSHEVA

EL ARISH

KANTARA

ABU AGEILA

ISMAILIA

KUSSEIMA

BIR
GAFGAFA

Mitla
Pass

KUNTILLA

SUEZ

NAKHL

EILAT
AQABA

JORDAN

EGYPT

GULF OF
SUEZ

GULF
OF
EILAT

DAHAB

SAUDI
ARABIA

E-TOUR

SHARM E-SHEIKH

50 40 30 20 10 0
k i l o m e t e r s

N

RED SEA

afterward, the commander of the Israel Air Force (IAF), Major-General Dan Tolkovsky, wrote:

Although air activity by the enemy was brought to an 'artificial' end by Anglo-French intervention . . . it will be untrue to say that the IDF's [Israel Defense Forces] success was possible because of the active participation of foreign forces in the Suez/Sinai campaigns. There is no doubt, however, that this participation allowed the Air Force to achieve what it did with minimal losses. And this was the real military achievement of these forces.[2]

Many years after the war Major-General Meir Amit, then the IDF's chief of operations—he conducted the war from the Supreme Command Post (SCP) in Ramla—wrote that

collaboration with the French and the British was damaging to the IDF, operatively speaking. The IDF was placed under severe constraints: It was ordered not to cross a line passing 10 kilometers [actually 10 miles, or 16 km.] from the Suez Canal, it was ordered not to use its air force and armoured forces until a certain date. These restrictions tied its hands in a very significant way. I would have thanked God if those restraints had not been put on us. Without them, we would have achieved much better results.[3]

When the war began, on October 29, Israel's military collaboration with France, and through the French with Britain, already bore a blatant operational character. Concretely, the cooperation was effected in part in Israel through the French air squadrons stationed there and by liaison officers (for land and sea forces), and in part through the joint Anglo-French headquarters (HQ) in Cyprus. The French military mission, led by Colonel Jean Simon, was based at the SCP. From time to time General Andre Martin, the personal representative of the French Chief of Staff Paul Ely and of Admiral Pierre Barjot, the senior French officer attached to "Operation Musketeer"(the codename of the Anglo-French invasion of Egypt), flew into Israel from Cyprus.

On the Israeli side the brunt of the liaison work was assigned to Lieutenant-Colonel Shlomo Gazit, formerly the chief of staff's bureau chief, and, in Cyprus, to the deputy director of military intelligence, Colonel Yuval Ne'eman (and afterward to Lieutenant-Colonel Yosef ["Paul"] Kedar from the air force). For all practical purposes, the director-general of the defense ministry, Shimon Peres, was also involved in the liaison activity, as he was responsible for procuring arms supplies, a task that continued during the war, and had excellent ties with the French. Also taking part in the contacts was Colonel Nehemia Argov, Ben-Gurion's personal representative. In Paris, Yosef Nahmias (together with Asher Ben-Nathan, his designated successor as head of the Defense Ministry mission in the French capital) and Colonel Emanuel Nishri, the military attaché, stayed in touch with Major-General Maurice Challe, the French deputy chief of staff for air force affairs, who engineered the triple conspiracy, and with Colonel Louis Mangin, advisor to the French defense minister. These personal relations played an important role in ensuring that wartime collaboration—which was manifested more in coordination and aid, direct or indirect, than in actual joint operations—ran smoothly.[4]

KEEP A LOW PROFILE WITH THE FRENCH, DISAPPEAR
FROM BRITISH VIEW

At the beginning of the war the IDF sent two officers to Cyprus: Yuval Ne'eman representing the General Staff and Yosef Kedar as the representative of the air force. Ne'eman arrived in Israel from France on October 29, the day the war broke out; before proceeding to Cyprus he met with the French and British military attachés in Israel with the aim of expediting the announcement of the Anglo-French ultimatum to Egypt, which Israel was anxiously awaiting. The attachés, who had been victims of the deception campaign conducted by their Israeli hosts and their own governments, now received for the first time, a few hours after hostilities had already begun, an explanation of what was afoot in Sinai.[5]

On October 30 the Israeli chief of staff, Lieutenant-General Moshe Dayan, ordered Yuval Ne'eman to Cyprus, as a liaison with the Anglo-French HQ. Dayan told Ne'eman that he should keep in mind that the IDF's goal was to conquer all of the Sinai peninsula, apart from the Canal Zone, and to try to induce the allies to internationalize the waterway and not to interfere with the Israeli operations. "It is important for us that the French [rather than the British] control the east bank of the Canal," Dayan said. He also authorized Ne'eman to promise the French all the assistance the IDF could render to them east of the canal: "We shall put at their disposal more bases, hospitals, convalescence facilities." Dayan issues no instructions to Ne'eman about working with the British as it was clear that contacts with them would be effected by the French. There was no direct connection during the whole war between the IDF and the British army. Ne'eman's mission was more to observe developments in Cyprus and less to liaise with the allies. Actual coordination was handled by Dayan in Israel, via the French mission in the country.[6]

Ne'eman sent his first report from Cyprus on the afternoon of October 31. No one had expected him, and "in general they are not fighting yet"—whereas for Israel the war had been on for forty-eight hours already. Ne'eman eventually tracked down Martin and Barjot in the joint supreme HQ near Episkopi. Barjot, Ne'eman reported, was "scared stiff of the British—what will he do if they don't want [Israel] in?" The French convinced Ne'eman that he should go into hiding at their Akrotiri base until they could secure British approval for his very presence on the island. The base's location, far from the joint HQ, kept Ne'eman from maintaining regular communications with the French—who obviously found it more convenient to hide their close ties with Israel even if this hindered the joint prosecution of the war.

Finally the French persuaded General Sir Charles Keightley, the commander of Operation Musketeer, that operational and technical coordination with Israel was essential. It was agreed that the British should "know nothing" about the presence of an Israeli mission in Cyprus. Evidently nonplussed by the situation, Ne'eman reported, "All kinds of Englishmen told me (quietly): 'It never crossed my mind that we would be allies, but I must say I'm delighted. As for myself, I was less than delighted about their dubious fair play.' "[7]

On November 2, Ne'eman turned over responsibility for liaison in Cyprus to Yosef Kedar, who was his junior in rank and less informed than Ne'eman about the details of the conspiracy. But in any event the British, and the French for that matter, did not apprise the Israeli liaison officer of their moves. As for the French, they were pleased to keep from their own personnel, and certainly from the British, knowledge of their direct military operations against Egypt that were launched from Israeli soil.

The Israeli liaison mission in Cyprus functioned until the end of the war. It was through the Cyprus station that Operation Tushiya ("resourcefulness") was mounted, in which sixty-five Egyptian Jews were smuggled out of Port Sa'id without British knowledge and with minimal cooperation with French intelligence.[8]

COOPERATION IN THE AIR—"THOSE BASTARDS, NOT EVEN AN APOLOGY"

Israel had pinned high hopes on the allies' intervention in the war, and the greater the expectation, the more intense the disappointment when it was delayed. On the night of October 30, as reports—albeit unreliable—were received that the Egyptians were going to launch a concentrated bombing attack on Israeli cities the following morning, anxiety reached new heights. Still, no one bothered to examine whether the rumors of an attack had any foundation, and Dayan consoled himself with the hope that the Anglo-French bombing campaign, which according to the Sévres plan was supposed to begin that morning (Wednesday, October 31), would prevent an Egyptian attack.[9]

Then came the postponement, and Israel reacted with outrage—and fear. As Dayan summed it up, "Those bastards. They make a political agreement in which one of the main clauses, one we insisted on, was an air strike on Wednesday morning, and here they casually postpone the operation by 12 [hours] with no warning, not even an apology, the bastards."

According to information obtained by Ne'eman from the French (Martin and Barjot in Cyprus), the delay was due to a "rebellion" by the joint forces' commander General Keightley against his own government (they made a mistake, as we will see later). Keightley, who (like the army chiefs in Israel and France) had not been made privy to the Sévres agreement, refused to attack at first light (on October 31), maintaining that the timing was wrong from a military point of view. His plan mandated an evening strike, at last light. Keightley refused to budge, even if it meant his removal. The message from Ne'eman, however, did little to allay the fears of Prime Minister David Ben-Gurion and General Dayan. The latter felt himself constrained, at this stage, to dissuade the prime minister from ordering a general withdrawal of Israeli forces from Sinai, a move that would have spelled the end of the Anglo-French plan: Without an Israeli presence near the Suez Canal the allies would lack any pretext to invade Egypt in order, supposedly, to "restore peace" there.[10]

The French were worried that Israel would react to a delay in the air attack by pulling their forces out of Sinai. On October 31, Mangin arrived in Israel for an unscheduled visit, apparently to reassure the increasingly skeptical Israelis. He told his hosts that over and above the principle of night bombing, which Keightley was insisting on, British concern had also been aroused by a high-altitude reconnaissance flight carried out by a British *Canberra* bomber over Egypt on the first night of the war. It was pursued by an Egyptian *MIG* to an altitude of 50,000 feet, and "the *Canberra* pilot had the feeling that there was a foreign pilot in this *MIG*, not an Egyptian." The British, said Mangin, were upset about the possibility of encountering East European pilots, and perhaps were also concerned that their involvement would be exposed even before the ultimatum was delivered. On this point, at least, Keightley saw eye to eye with his government.[11]

Apparently the information that was made available to the French, and passed on to the Israelis, was far from complete. Had Israel been apprised by the British, through the French, about what really transpired that day in Cyprus, Ben-Gurion might have felt less tense. But the British were too deeply enmeshed in their self-made trap of deniability at all costs; there was absolutely no British-Israeli dialogue on military operations. The entire affair remains difficult to reconstruct, because some of the documents involved were destroyed at the time and others are still classified. To this day, Britain is committed to concealing all evidence of an "Israeli connection." The British historian Keith Kyle, who spent years trying to uncover the documents in question, discovered that an order had been issued to burn any document (and in some cases part of a document) liable to suggest that Britain had known in advance of the Israeli offensive in Sinai on October 29.[12]

As noted, the commanders of the Operation Musketeer task forces, like their IDF counterparts, received no information about the Sèvres agreement. Nevertheless, on October 28 (Sunday) the air squadrons, located in Cyprus and Malta, were ordered to prepare for their first bombing raid on Egypt at 2:15 A.M. local time on October 31. They were not told that the reason for the attack was a political commitment to Israel: Compartmentalization was not only an IDF phenomenon. The next day they were informed that the raid might have to be launched even earlier than that, and preparations were stepped up.

On October 29 there were two *Canberra* squadrons, one in Cyprus and one in Malta, capable of lifting off at six hours' notice; H-hour had not been changed. The operational decision was that the first targets would be the Radio Cairo station and four air bases, including Cairo West, where the (for Israel) fearsome Soviet-made Il-28 bombers were based. Under the pressure of time, Air Marshall Dennis Barnett, commander of the joint air task force, sent reconnaissance missions over Egypt, though these could have sent a clear signal that an attack was imminent. All the same, as of October 31 Musketeer forces were authorized only to continue with the execution of a deception maneuver, codenamed "Boathook," which had begun on the morning of October 29 with naval movements from Malta to the eastern Mediterranean.[13]

Throughout Tuesday, October 30, British pilots remained on alert, though uncertain that the attack order would be given. The only hint that reached Cyprus from London was that the order might be given only after the planes had already lifted off—a scenario not calculated to raise morale. During the day Egyptian radar picked up the British aircraft involved in the photo-reconnaissance missions, and the Egyptian Air Force scrambled jets to intercept them. That afternoon, Keightley was ordered to schedule the first strike, which had been planned as a night raid, to a later, daylight hour on October 31. Apparently London did not want the attack to follow so closely on the heels of the ultimatum, which was issued at 6 P.M. on Tuesday, October 30. Keightley, at Barnett's remonstrations, urged the chiefs of staff in London to avoid a daylight raid, which could be dangerous. Both officers were unaware of the Sèvres agreement.[14]

Keightley's request was addressed in London on the night of October 30 in a meeting of Prime Minister Anthony Eden and his inner cabinet circle and the chiefs of staff. As a matter of fact, since the British government wanted to let as much time as possible elapse between the ultimatum and the allies' intervention, Keightley's request was a godsend—not rebellion, as the French thought. The air strike was put back several hours for political reasons, and then again by several more for operational reasons. Some ministers, says Kyle, noted ironically that there was no sign at that point that Israel had attacked Egypt from the air. The upshot was that Keightley was ordered to prepare for a night strike, but also to be ready for immediate action against Egypt "if Israel suffers serious air attack that morning [by Egyptian Ilyushins]." The start of the bombing campaign was delayed by twelve hours altogether.[15]

"The cover story," Kyle summed up the episode, "had to fit not only here and now, but also the history books of tomorrow." To achieve deniability, Eden was ready to renege on his agreement with Israel, although not totally: Britain would have responded immediately if Israel had been attacked from the air. Ben-Gurion and Dayan were not aware of this, nor were the French, though they must have seen the preparations that were under way in Cyprus. In the final analysis, the Musketeer command structure gave the British the final say in the air as in all spheres of military activity. This episode furnishes additional evidence of the character borne by the cooperation (or noncooperation) between Israel and the allies, and between the allies themselves, in the Sinai War.[16]

Ne'eman, having no direct communication with the British, tried to protest to the French and hold them accountable for the delay. He also insisted that French antiaircraft vessels, which had been ordered to leave Israeli ports that day, be sent back immediately. The French replied that they had left a ship on the Israeli coast but that they could not provide any more, since their ships were required to escort the convoys en route to Egypt. Ne'eman argued that in the present situation it was better to leave the convoys exposed than Israeli cities. Barjot remained unconvinced; he promised to look into the matter, but seems to have done nothing more in practice.[17]

When Ne'eman asked the French for intelligence information, he was told that an Egyptian armored brigade had crossed the Suez Canal eastward. Moreover, the French said that to compensate Israel for the postponement of the air strike they were even ready to consider the possibility of using their squadrons that were secretly based in Israel to attack the Egyptian armor brigade, even before the overt allied assault. But it was clear that within the Sèvres framework, and under the constraints of the Musketeer command structure, this was out of the question—as impossible as it had been to compel General Keightley to attack on the morning of October 31. In any event, using French aircraft based in Israel (even if camouflaged) before Britain and France had officially entered the war might have undone the entire "cover story" of the collusion. How could the Israeli Air Force operate about sixty French *Myste're IV* when it had none only a few months before the war?

The French bent over backward to persuade Israel not to pull out of the agreement because of the delay, but ultimately there was not much they could do. As a conciliatory gesture, Martin placed a special plane at Ne'eman's disposal so that he could fly to Israel whenever he wished.[18]

On the night of October 31, Ne'man informed Dayan that the British did not intend to land at Port Sa'id until November 6. It was Ne'eman's understanding that this issue, too, had generated a sharp dispute between the generals in the field and the government in London, as well as between the British and the French. Ne'eman reported that the French weere pressing for a landing as early as November 3, and "Martin is blowing his top and bombarding Paris with cables." Eden's generals lacked "operational discipline," Ne'eman thought. But the Israeli liaison officer could not have been aware of the seemingly intractable problems faced by the British commanders in view of the ambiguities surrounding Operation Musketeer. By the same token, he had no idea that the British officers knew even less than Martin, or than he himself did, about the underlying causes of the equivocal instructions Eden was strafing them with through the chiefs of staff in London. Ne'eman could never have imagined that the decision to land on November 6 was actually an improvement over the original timetable, which had set November 8 for the landing in Egypt.[19]

Later that evening (October 31) Israeli pressure was turned on the Israel-based French liaison officer for land forces, Colonel Simon. Gazit was sent to impress upon him that Dayan was seriously contemplating the possibility of asking Ben-Gurion's permission to cable French Premier Guy Mollet that the postponement of the air operation was a breach of the agreement. Gazit told Simon that "Even though [Dayan] knows that the liaison officer cannot help, it is important that he know that the delay of the operation is a severe setback for us." The French reported this development immediately, probably to Barjot in Cyprus. Concerned at the Israeli reaction, Barjot ordered his squadrons in Israel to begin providing air support for the IDF in Sinai the next morning. This was, in any event, necessitated by the opening of the British air offensive in Egypt that night. What was most important from Israel's point of view was the goodwill displayed that day by Martin and Barjot. The French began their attacks in Sinai on the morning of November 1 (actually a few hours after the British air attack on Egypt had "officially" begun).

In addition to direct offensive support for the IDF in Sinai, the French also assisted Israel in interdiction, transport, attacking targets in Egypt, and supplying intelligence information collected by their air force. These operations were carried out by planes that lifted off simultaneously from Cyprus and from Israel without knowing about one another's activity.[20]

The disruptions in the communications network between Cyprus and Israel, together with the French insistence on avoiding overt coordination that would expose their collaboration with Israel, resulted in a number of uncoordinated missions, particularly air drops. Tolkovsky later quoted Brigadier General Raymond Brouhon, the deputy commander of Musketeer's air mission, as claiming that the British had deliberately jammed radio communications between French Air Force personnel in Israel and Cyprus. There is no corroborating evidence of this. Israel Air Force historians maintain that the French, with their penchant for secrecy, avoided using their radio links to Cyprus, claiming falsely that their equipment was out of order. Be that as it may, during the war, transport aircraft from Cyprus arrived in Israel without the knowledge of Israeli air control, and it was only by chance that they were not intercepted by Israeli planes. Due to the confusion, a great deal of equipment (in one case even a French paratroopers force, which landed at Lod) ended up at unscheduled destinations where no one knew how to handle it. For example, on November 4 an Israeli paratroop brigade reported unidentified aircraft—apparently Egyptian planes on a bombing run. However, it soon turned out that the French were unexpectedly dropping supplies, including bottles of wine.[21]

It would not be the last time that the French would operate in two channels (Cyprus-Israel and France-Israel) simultaneously but without coordination between them. The desire to placate both Britain and Israel at the same time extracted a price from the French, mainly in the air sphere, though after the war in the political-diplomatic sphere as well.[22]

Some of the problems were resolved thanks to the daily shuttle flight of a Dakota plane that the French operated between Cyprus and Israel. At one point there was talk of canceling the flights, but the French liaison mission in Israel protested and the idea was aborted. It was obvious that the daily flight was the one secure channel of communication that remained between the French missions in Israel and in Cyprus, and between Israel and allied HQ on the neighboring island.[23] The intelligence and other information that the plane brought back to Israel was usually disappointing in both quantity and quality. Mostly it was air intelligence (including aerial photographs) about Egypt, obtained in French and British reconnaissance sorties. The French refused to provide Israel with intelligence about Syria and Saudi Arabia, despite repeated requests.

The IAF was unable to reach an agreement with the allied HQ on Cyprus on setting a shared radio frequency with Musketeer aircraft, or even a common distress frequency. Nor was there an agreed procedure for search and rescue missions in Sinai (though British and French aircraft could land in Israel in emergencies). The result was that Israeli and Musketeer transport planes (including French planes based in Israel) flew missions simultaneously with no communication or coordination.

COOPERATION AT SEA: UNFOUNDED EXPECTATIONS

French naval support to Israel encountered even more hitches and misunderstandings than the situation in the air. Air support had at least involved orderly advance planning, but the joint naval operations suffered from the fact that they were last-minute improvisations. The Israelis found that their expectations were completely unfounded. Compounding the situation, Israel found itself in direct contact with the British in the naval sphere. The chaotic state of affairs caused one direct collision, the combined fault of lack of coordination in the air and the failure of the partners to prepare the naval arena for orderly cooperation between Israeli and Musketeer forces. Small wonder, then, that all the naval operations involving any form of cooperation between Israeli and Anglo-French forces remain controversial to this day.

At around noon on Monday, October 29, Dayan informed the French that Israeli support for their forces at the Suez Canal, if required, would be contingent upon their significant naval support for the IDF. French naval activity was implemented as part of Operation "Archer" (codename for French naval support for Israel), according to which two French destroyers would patrol off Haifa Port and a third destroyer off the coast of Tel Aviv. Israel Navy destroyers were to execute similar missions in coordination with the French. The French informed Israel that on the morning of October 31, with the start of the Anglo-French air offensive against Egypt, two of their destroyers would be diverted to escort the French seaborne convoys making for Egypt, leaving only one destroyer to patrol off the Israeli coast.[24]

However, it soon became apparent that the Sèvres agreement was insufficient for the French naval officers; they said they required additional authorization. The commander of the French flotilla in Israel asked Dayan to issue a formal request to the French Navy for anti-aircraft protection. The bizarre request derived from French reluctance to issue formal orders to their units in Israel, for fear the British would discover their "off-limits" assignment. But there were other factors as well. For reasons of internal compartmentalization between the two French operations, "700" (Musketeer) and "750" (assistance to Israel), the commanding officers of the French naval forces based in Israel (like their air force counterparts) were not briefed on their precise missions in advance. They got their orders only after arriving in Israel, and even then received no explanation of the political background to the mission. At the same time, they were instructed to coordinate naval support (down to the minutest details) and air support (in general terms) with Musketeer HQ in Cyprus, prior to implementation. So in addition to the hitches caused by the compartmentalization between Britain and France, further havoc was caused by internal French compartmentalization.[25]

In the first stage, Israel requested naval support for its operation to conquer Rafah, in northern Sinai. Dayan reminded the French that this was not a case of unplanned assistance: "It was agreed to by Generals Challe and Martin, we were promised execution. . . . The entire operational plan is based on it. . . . We [furthermore] intend to ask for more support as we go along on the Mediterranean coast [eastward along the coast of northern Sinai]." Much to Dayan's surprise, the French had received no prior orders on this point. It was agreed that the French would begin planning their support, and in the meantime one of their officers would fly to Cyprus to get orders from Barjot. It turned out that the French conception called for support on a far smaller scale than Dayan envisioned. In fact, operational expectations of the French naval bombardment itself were never very high: Dayan saw it as more of a test case to discover the extent of French willingness to support Israel, and to create a precedent to be invoked later if needed.[26]

On October 31, Ne'eman discussed this problem in Cyprus with Martin, who was willing to meet any Israeli demand in view of the postponement of the allies' air campaign against Egypt. Martin accepted Dayan's request to intensify the Rafah bombardment, but he also made it clear that subsequently the French might be hard-put to provide additional naval support, once their own sea-borne operations commenced (other than in the Straits of Tiran, should this prove necessary). The French adduced two conditions for providing a more massive bombardment: first, two Israeli destroyers must escort the cruiser that would fire the barrage (as two French destroyers had been diverted to protect Musketeer's maritime convoys); and second, Dayan must withdraw his request for a French bombardment of El Arish (lying west of Rafah, El Arish was the largest town in the Sinai peninsula), even though this had already been agreed on.

The original plan called for a French shelling of Rafah during the night of October 30–31, and of El Arish the next night. But the postponement in the British air offensive against Egypt, and the general delay in the timetable as a result, led the French to conclude that late operation against Rafah and El Arish might interfere with the main operation at the Suez Canal. During the night originally scheduled for the French shelling of Rafah, October 30–31, allied air raids on Egypt were supposed to be in full swing (it happened actually only on November 5). At that stage, Musketeer HQ in Cyprus intended to muster all its available naval forces to support allied troop movements toward Egypt. French Admiral Lancelot, deputy commander of Musketeer's naval task force, after consulting with his British superior (October 31), Admiral Durnford-Slater, agreed to make his cruiser *Georges Leger* available to French-Israeli collaboration for forty hours only.[27]

The *Georges Leger* reached Haifa on October 31 in the afternoon and moved south after dark. Beginning at midnight (October 31–November 1) the French bombarded army bases around Rafah for four hours. Dayan and his aide Mordechai Bar-On, who witnessed the shelling with the forces of the 77th Division, were very impressed, and Bar-On later noted in his diary: "The camps became an inferno. But because of little experience [with international joint operations] there were long pauses between successive barrages, and between the last one (which was rather unimpressive) and the actual assault."[28] Although ultimately ineffective, the French bombardment of Rafah should be judged by its contribution to bolstering Israeli self-confidence by demonstrating French willingness to cooperate with the IDF. It was not a whim of Dayan's to have invested so much time in coordinating this single action. Moreover, the bombardment, however ineffectual, contributed to the rapid collapse (within nine or ten hours) of the Egyptian deployment in and around Rafah.[29]

Admiral Barjot agreed that the barrage was unimpressive but noted that by aiding the IDF to make rapid progress it had effectively supported the Anglo-French move in the northern area of the Suez Canal. Barjot went further, claiming that the shelling had strongly impressed the other Arab nations (meaning Syria and Jordan), who remained on the sidelines despite their mutual defense treaties with Egypt. In general, the senior French officer of Operation Musketeer viewed the Israeli effort in Sinai, particularly along the northern route, as an integral part of the campaign against Port Sa'id, Port Fuad, and indeed the entire Suez Canal. Before the war Dayan, too, had given thought to the military and political benefits, notably in the form of deterrence, that Israel could derive from the spread of rumors about active French support for the Israeli offensive, although such rumors were a rare commodity in the climate of secrecy and intrigue that enveloped the war.[30]

PREPARATIONS FOR A JOINT FRENCH-ISRAELI OPERATION IN THE SUEZ CANAL

The possibility of the IDF's reaching the Suez Canal was discussed on several occasions between Israel and France during October 1956. Although the Israelis made it plain that they had no interest in reaching the canal, and the Sèvres agreement, to which the British were also a signatory, barred Israel from reaching the waterline, the idea constantly recurred, particularly in the discussions between the sides at the military level.

One of Yuval Ne'eman's tasks in Cyprus was to ensure that no clashes occurred between the IDF and French or British forces due to any misunderstanding. Two areas that were blatantly prone to such mishaps were the Suez Canal and the

Straits of Tiran. Anglo-French plans to operate there, and the poor coordination between the IDF and Musketeer HQ—virtually "invited" accidents.

On the morning of Monday, October 29, just hours before the scheduled start of the Israeli sweep into Sinai, Colonel Jean Simon, the French liaison officer to the ground forces, showed Dayan and several senior officers the main points of the Musketeer groundforces' battle plan. Simon told Dayan that General André Beaufre, the deputy commander of the land task force of Operation Musketeer (as in the air and on the sea, the French were subordinate to British commanding officers), was worried about the pace of British preparations, and noted that Israeli pressure could give the British a needed push. Specifically, Beaufre requested that by the time of the French landing at Port Fuad, scheduled for November 6 or 8, the IDF would have decimated the Egyptian forces in Sinai and readied the northern Sinai coast for the landing operation. Beaufre was worried by the fact that the narrow landing site assigned to the forces under his direct command on the east bank of the canal would hinder the effective deployment of his troops. He therefore prepared an alternative invasion plan, without the knowledge of his British superior, involving a joint French-Israeli operation that constituted a sharp deviation from the Sèvres plan.

Beufre's approach was a purely military one and was based on his perception of the military assistance to Israel as part of the general plan for war against Egypt. As he saw it, every operation in support of Israel in the air and on the sea came at the expense of the forces intended for direct action against Egypt; consequently, he, like his colleague Barjot, tended to consider the IDF as part of the French forces operating against Egypt. In his memoirs he maintained that the IDF, which employed three divisions against one Egyptian division (Beaufre exaggerated somewhat, but it was true that the IDF enjoyed overwhelming superiority, qualitatively and quantitatively, against the Egyptians in Sinai), should have been utilized in support of his forces, which faced the bulk of the Egyptian army. He was also concerned that Egyptian troops pushed westward by the IDF would link up with the forces fighting his troops at Ismailiya and Qantara, on the Suez Canal. Anglo-French hopes that the Egyptian army would flee eastward, deeper into Sinai, and become an Israeli problem, were rendered unrealistic once it became clear that the allied landing would occur after the IDF had already conquered most of Sinai.

Still, Beaufre's protestations were not completely off the mark. Beyond the apologetic tone of his memoirs, the truth is that on the eve of the war the French could have justifiably expected much more than they were to get from the IDF, which enjoyed undeniable superiority over the Egyptians in the Sinai and benefited from extensive Anglo-French support. Furthermore, Dayan thought he could turn Beaufre's requests to Israel's advantage. As we saw, for example, he made the pace of IDF progress along the northern route in Sinai contingent on French naval support. Nevertheless, during the first few days of war, there was no reason to expect concrete cooperation in the spirit of these ideas.[31]

In view of the delay in the commencement of the allies' operations, and the presence of IDF units near the Mitla Pass with little capability of defending themselves, the Israeli General Staff decided, on the evening of October 30, to examine the possibility of air strikes against the Canal bridges in order to prevent the Egyptians from moving reinforcements into Sinai. The problem was that this would have meant encroaching on an area slated for Anglo-French operations. The IDF therefore reconsidered Beaufre's offer of cooperation, made a day earlier: IDF assistance for a French landing east of the canal without coordination with the British.

To begin with, Ne'eman tried to sound out the French in Cyprus about an IDF strike against the canal bridges, using French aircraft based in Israel (and still bearing Israeli insignia). The French, who had already expressed their interest in Israeli support in the area of the Suez Canal, did not explicitly object, but explained that the bridges were not on their list of targets. It should be borne in mind that for Britain the main objective was to seize the Suez Canal and reactivate it immediately, without taking action liable to block the waterway—such as knocking the bridges into the water. It is difficult to imagine that the French would have condoned an operation that would undermine a major British objective. Furthermore, they wanted Egyptian forces to cross the canal eastward; if the IDF could draw Egyptian Army into Sinai, this would facilitate Anglo-French activity in Egypt. In short, neither the French nor the British had good reason to prevent the Egyptians from moving east, but they would not have liked to see them retreating back to the west.

The French therefore explained to Ne'eman that close coordination would be required before the IDF could act in their zone of operations along the canal, but in principle, if Israel so desired, it could deal with the canal bridges later on—after the Egyptians were defeated. At this stage, the French did nothing to further the required coordination. Not even the French desire to placate Israel the next day, because of the delay in the start of the British air campaign, induced them to accept Ne'eman's idea; it was put on hold for the time being. Still, Ne'eman found some hope in French willingness to consider the possibility that Israel take control of the harbor at Port Taufiq, at the southern entrance to the canal and well away from the planned Anglo-French combat zone. Ne'eman quoted Martin as saying that "[we may regard] ourselves free to take Port Taufiq as well, if we are interested."[32]

In retrospect, it emerges that what made the French willing to consider a joint operation for the occupation of the entire Canal Zone was not Israel's distress prior to the war—its inability to use the canal—but its success in the first days of the war. Observing the weakness of the Egyptian army in Sinai (in particular the ineffectuality of the Egyptian air force) during four days of allied air strikes and IDF advances, the French decided to reexamine the possibility of making use of the Israeli forces that were near the canal. On Friday, November 2, Martin arrived in Israel with Ne'eman. In a meeting with the senior officers of the IDF General Staff, possible ways of utilizing the IDF presence near the Suez Canal in order to facilitate the French landing there were discussed. Dayan reacted by ordering the IDF not to approach the canal closer than the agreed ten-mile limit; however, he added, when the French reach the canal "we will send out patrols to make contact with them."[33]

Immediately afterward Dayan convened the General Staff and passed on the information that the French would like to see the IDF at the canal by Monday (November 5), so that it could support French operations at Port Sa'id and Qantara. Dayan said that afterward, as far as the French were concerned, Israel could do as it pleased in Sinai. Although it was not clear whether France would provide explicit diplomatic support for an Israeli takeover of part of the canal, "the French are even prepared to see us taking Port Taufiq." The port was important for Israel, Dayan noted, because "we have no other route along the Suez, and we have no water in that area."

Dayan then went with the idea to the prime minister. Ben-Gurion hesitated: He did not want to commit Israel to direct military involvement in the Anglo-French war against Egypt. Israel, he insisted, must do nothing in the Canal Zone that was directly linked to the Suez crisis. In general, Dayan and Ben-Gurion both preferred at this stage to dissociate Israel's operations in the Sinai from the Anglo-French operation. Israel had fulfilled its obligations by giving its allies a pretext for war, and should now concentrate on its own interests in Sinai. Occupying Port Taufiq, though, might be regarded as a move that was not too obviously connected with events in the Canal Zone. Ben-Gurion thus gave Dayan the go-ahead to examine this possibility, and Dayan concluded: "We would prefer it this way: the [UN General] Assembly meets in New York, while Uri [Col. Ben-Ari, commander of the 7th Armored Brigade] and Arik [Lt.-Colonel Ariel Sharon, commander of the 202nd Paratroop Brigade] meet on the Suez Canal."[34]

A renewed French approach on this issue was encouraging. On Saturday night, November 3, Dayan met with Colonel Simon, who elaborated further on Martin's proposal of the previous day. Simon now preferred to talk about Qantara, which was of greater interest to him. In fact, the orders he received from Martin and Barjot left him very little leeway for independent decision-making. The French, it turned out, were in dire straits in view of the UN demand for a cease-fire, on the one hand, and British insistence on sticking to the original plan of a landing only on November 6, on the other hand. The French wanted to attack at once and were even looking into the possibility of doing it alone. As in the previous instances, Israel had a central role in that option, with Martin and Barjot requesting that the IDF support a French landing at Port Sa'id by conquering eastern Qantara and thus creating a concrete threat to the Canal. The French were perfectly aware that this was a major departure from the Sèvres agreement: "Israel has the right to say no," Simon told Dayan.[35]

The French wanted to launch air strikes on Sunday morning (November 4) and effect the landing in the Canal Zone at midday. Simon said his superiors knew that the IDF was reluctant to stage daylight attacks, and were therefore willing to postpone their landing until last light. Without Israel, their operation would be extremely problematic. An embarrassed Simon told Dayan that all this must be kept completely secret: the French government must know nothing about it, to say nothing of the British. As though it were self-evident, he added that the IDF would of course evacuate Qantara as soon as French troops got there. He went on to explain that Barjot himself had conceived the idea of Israeli support for a French landing in order to make it easier for Paris to reach a decision on the matter. Therefore, it was out of the question to appear to depart from Sèvres. Barjot was even willing to lend the IDF French uniforms for the mission, but Dayan rejected the idea as out of hand.[36]

Accepting the French plan would have made the assault on Port Taufiq, already approved by Ben-Gurion, into an Israeli campaign for the entire Canal Zone. Dayan tried to help Simon work out a more realistic plan that might receive Ben-Gurion's approval. First of all, he pointed out, the Anglo-French ultimatum, which required Israel to stay ten miles from the Suez Canal proper, was still in effect. It would be highly embarrassing if the British, who were supposedly intervening to prevent an Israel capture of the canal, should find Israeli troops already dug in there. Second, the French government obviously did not want Israeli participation in the occupation of the east bank of the canal. Consequently, said Dayan, such a move would deeply embarrass the French.

As a more practical solution to the quick conquering of the canal, Dayan asked Simon to consider the possibility of the French (and the British too, if they wished) landing at El Arish, which was already in Israeli hands, and then moving on to the canal. "Anyway, the French may move forces on all our routes, any place they choose." But if they insisted on their plan, Israel would even agree to a daylight attack, though on two conditions: massive air support, and coordination with Britain. Dayan did not want to create a situation in which "the English reach Qantara before the French and open fire on us at 200 meters range, and then claim we did not let them know we were there in the first place."

Dayan insisted on official liaison, including liaison officers on the ground. Simon hesitated. It was finally agreed that the IDF would be ready to assist the French even if they landed on November 6, but under Dayan's two conditions. The French would also be able to evacuate their wounded to Israel, on routes controlled by the IDF. Dayan went to Tel Aviv to obtain Ben-Gurion's approval, while Simon flew back to Cyprus in order get the go-ahead from Barjot.[37]

By this time Ben-Gurion was "in a nitpicking state of mind," according to Dayan. He heard him out on the details of the new French idea, but the discussion revolved around his stay at Qantara with the Jewish Battalion in World War I. Finally Ben-Gurion approved Dayan's plan, with its qualifications. The 202nd Paratroop Brigade was then ordered to prepare for recapturing the Mitla Pass (after the October 31 failure) and move on to Port Taufiq—the "Israeli objective" in the joint operation with France on the Canal.[38]

However, the French decided to avoid taking independent action. Under growing pressure from the United Nations and the United States, France and Britain reached a compromise to attack on November 5 rather than on the November 6. Because of the abbreviated timetable, Musketeer HQ improvised a fast landing plan, called "Telescope." En route to Port Sa'id another improvisation was made, this one codenamed "Omelette," for a "light" landing (infantry and paratroopers, without heavier support). By this stage it was obvious that Egyptian resistance would be minimal.[39]

The French now asked Israel to refrain from any activity at all in the Canal Zone. Without authorization an approach to the canal was ruled out; Dayan was forced to back off. Thus the plan to conquer Port Taufiq was dropped from the IDF agenda.[40]

BRITAIN AND ISRAEL: HOSTILE COLLABORATION

The cancellation of the joint operation in the Canal Zone had repercussions that went beyond the purely military aspect. The British pressure on France to avoid any overt military collaboration with Israel had paid off handsomely for London. With Israel having done its part and the two European powers already at war with Egypt, the British demanded that the French henceforth keep Israel out of their operations. The embarrassed General Martin not only called off the joint French-Israeli action along the canal, on November 3 he sought an understanding with the IDF whereby "the partnership between Israel and the allies is now liquidated, [Israel] having done its part, so that there is no reason now to continue with military coordination."[41]

This was not a major military problem for the IDF, provided the allies continued to fulfill the agreement reached at Sèvres to support the IDF's push to Sharm el Sheikh, which was on the brink of being accomplished. Nor did it represent a significant political problem for Israel. Ben-Gurion and Dayan were willing to end the war even before the Musketeer landing. By pulling out of the conflict, Israel would please the British, who could then proceed without fear of being suspected of collaborating with Israel, while Israel would divest itself of mounting international pressure.[42]

Thus, the IDF was not surprised to hear ambassador Abba Eban announce at the UN on November 4 in the evening (New York time; early morning on November 5 in Israel) that Israel would accept a cease-fire, provided the Egyptians did likewise. There was in fact little coordination between the Israeli military and the diplomats. It was the foreign ministries of the European allies, which remained outside the real decision-making process, that were behind Eban's statement. Eban, who faced heavy pressure in the General Assembly, asked Foreign Minister Golda Meir to sound out her French and British counterparts as to whether their governments would agree to an Israeli declaration of willingness to accept a cease-fire. Meir spoke with the two ambassadors in Israel. She knew the embassies in Israel were unaware of the secret agreements, but it is not clear whether she assumed her question would eventually reach the ambassadors' respective heads of government, who were in the know, or whether she consulted with Ben-Gurion beforehand. Be that as it may, Whitehall and the Quai d'Orsay, which had no knowledge of the military cooperation, responded in the affirmative to her query.

However, a scenario in which Egypt accepted a cease-fire along with Israel was untenable for Britain and France, since their pretext for going to war would disappear even before the first British or French soldier trod on Egyptian soil. The foreign ministries in London and Paris knew nothing of all this.

But when Egypt agreed to a cease-fire, Mollet and Eden found that they still needed Israeli support, after all. Abel Thomas, director-general of the French Ministry of Defense, called his Israeli counterpart Shimon Peres on November 4 to protest Israel's acceptance of a cease-fire. Then the defense minister himself, Maurice Bourges-Maunoury, accused the Israeli government (also in a phone call to Peres) of turning the situation inside out in what was tantamount to a betrayal of France. Britain, though, even at this critical moment, kept mum; the principle of deniability was to be guarded zealously.

Peres defended Israel's agreement to a cease-fire by citing the postponement of the Anglo-French invasion of Egypt, and particularly Martin's declaration of November 3 on terminating military cooperation. Still, it was clear that Eban's statement would damage French interests above all, which was the last thing Ben-Gurion and Dayan wanted. Following a series of diplomatic negotiations involving London, Paris, Jerusalem, and New York, Israel's agreement to a cease-fire was reformulated in a manner that meant a twelve-hour delay in its implementation, giving Musketeer forces time to launch their landing at Port Sa'id and Port Fuad.

So it came about that on November 4 Eban stated at the United Nations that he had been misunderstood—he had only wanted to describe the situation in the war zone. At the same time the British and French governments informed UN Secretary-General Dag Hammarskjöld that they still considered their intervention necessary, in order to prevent the continuation of the Israel-Egypt war. In view of the new military situation in Sinai, they said in their statement, it was essential to ensure the withdrawal of the Israeli troops from Sinai as soon as possible. Ben-Gurion reacted furiously, and the French tried to explain that they meant withdrawal from the Canal Zone. Israeli mistrust, particularly of Britain, was intense even before the war ended.

Hammarskjöld demanded Israel's unconditional agreement to a cease-fire, and meanwhile Britain and France moved up their landing in Egypt by twenty-four hours. Eventually Israel accepted a cease-fire on the evening of November 5, having accomplished all its objectives in Sinai (apart from occupying the tiny islands of Tiran and Sanapir on the approaches to the Straits of Tiran). In addition, the Anglo-French invasion was already under way, so the allies no longer needed the "Israeli pretext." In the final analysis, Israel preferred an Anglo-French force as a buffer between the IDF and the Egyptian army, rather than UN troops (a Canadian proposal, which was adopted that same day by the General Assembly).[43]

Dayan and his aide Bar-On, deeply offended by the British attitude and by French backing for Britain in this episode, noted in conclusion of the cease-fire affair: "What pleas and remonstrations could not accomplish [namely, bringing Musketeer D-day forward], this bold, merciless and impartial diplomatic move did [referring to Israel's unilateral agreement to a cease-fire]. The shameless British's, who stuck by their rigidly frozen plan like a blinker horse, now lost their cool and were forced to bring their landing forward by a whole day, when they suddenly realized they needed Israel even after they thought they could drop it by the sidelines." This was not a completely accurate presentation of the facts, but clearly reflected the feelings about Britain that existed in Israel even in the midst of the joint military move against Egypt.[44]

The disagreements over the Israeli agreement to a cease-fire only heightened Israel's suspicions of Britain. Israel was never able to comprehend British policy in the Suez crisis. For example, even during the war, British propaganda broadcasts to the Middle East remained as blatantly anti-Israel (and anti-Zionist) as ever.[45]

Britain sought to lay the foundations for a new relationship with the Arab world after the war and even to create the impression that Egyptian President Nasser was in collusion with Israel. At the height of the war, the Foreign Office in London vetoed a proposal by Ambassador J. Nicholls, in Tel Aviv, to seize the opportunity for a rapprochement with Israel in order to heighten British influence there. Nicholls was advised not to display too much understanding for Israel's problems. When he tried to explain that Israel was worried about Soviet inroads in Syria, London replied that Israel was "trying to make up a story" and that no movement of troops would be tolerated, even if "intended to save the region from Communism. In such an eventuality, it is better that Iraq [which had the dual advantage of being an Arab state and being loyal to Britain] take action."

The reactions of the British Foreign Office were drawn up by Donald Logan, one of the very few officials who knew about Sèvres (not least because he had been one of the two British signatories on the agreement). Even though Eden himself protested that it was wrong to liken Israeli and communist action—in terms of the ostensible hostility of both—the Foreign Office remained adamant. The looming military fiasco in Egypt, compounded by domestic public pressure, gave Whitehall overriding influence even during the war, and this atmosphere was hardly conducive to British collaboration with Israel. Any such collusion continued to be denied after the war as well. On November 22, 1956, the British government insisted, in response to a query in Parliament, that there had been no contacts, direct or in writing, between Britain and Israel about the situation in the Middle East.[46]

The British-Israeli antipathy also had a military aspect. The agreement reached between the two nations before the war was largely a negative one between adversaries. It held that Britain would not help Jordan if that country initiated a war against Israel, and that Israel would not attack Jordan if Britain agreed not to intervene should Jordan attack Israel. For the British, even during the Sinai War, Israel remained an "enemy by official definition." In the various Musketeer operational orders, and in the intelligence reviews of the operation, both Israel and Egypt were listed under "enemies."[47]

The British received ongoing updates from the French about IDF moves and, equally important, about Israeli intentions. But they wanted more. The Royal Navy monitored Israeli activities by listening and observation. The detailed daily report that the Israeli envoy conveyed daily to Cyprus on the situation of the Israeli forces in Sinai almost certainly reached the British, at least in part. Indeed, it was impossible to keep the French-Israeli collaboration a complete secret. Certainly there was no concealing the fact that two French fighter squadrons had made a brief landing in Cyprus, lifted off again, and never returned; or that a large-scale airlift by French transport planes plied the Cyprus-Israel route daily. Moreover, some French moves—such as the bombardment of Rafah by a French cruiser described earlier—were undertaken only after consultation with British HQ in Cyprus. Still, only a few British officers were in on the secret. Martin told Dayan afterward that "the English [in Cyprus] asked if it was true that Israel was going to take over all of the Sinai, and when he said it was true, general apoplexy broke out there."[48]

Despite the British refusal to communicate with Israel, necessity dictated otherwise. Early in the war, Britain asked Israel for humanitarian assistance in the search for an Egyptian civilian plane which had disappeared over the eastern Mediterranean early on Monday, October 29, not far from the Israeli coast. The request followed an Egyptian approach to Britain itself, also on a humanitarian basis. The Israeli navy joined in the search. The IAF, which knew nothing of the search effort, discovered the search flotilla late Monday night and asked the high command to call in the Navy to engage the ships. That request went unheeded, of course. What neither the British nor the Israel navy nor the IAF—apart from a few top officers—knew was that the missing plane had been shot down by an IAF fighter. On the night of October 28–29, two Egyptian aircraft were on their way to Egypt after having taken off from Syria. One of them carried the Egyptian chief of staff, Field Marshal Amer, who was returning from coordination meetings in Jordan and Syria. Knowing of Amer's presence, the Israelis toppled one of the planes—but the wrong one. Amer reached Cairo safely.[49]

On November 3 the Egyptians shot down a British plane; the pilot bailed out and landed east of Qantara. A unit from the IDF's 27th Brigade in the area tried to assist in the rescue mission, but HQ at Cyprus ordered the rescue force that was dispatched to the site not to draw on Israeli assistance, as this could be misconstrued if reports leaked out. According to Air Marshal Barnett, the commander of the allied air task force, the rescue mission chief needed no such cautioning, since he knew nothing of the collusion and viewed the Israelis as enemies no less than the Egyptians. Nor did Musketeer forces have any liaison arrangements with the Israelis for such eventualities. On top of this, British aircraft circled the area to ward off Israeli troops. The rescue itself was executed by a helicopter—one of the first operations of its kind.[50]

Britain continued to ignore its Israeli ally. In a report on a successful French air strike at Luxor on November 4, the British failed to mention the fact that the attacking aircraft, F-84s, lifted off from and returned to an Israeli air base twice that day. Indeed, the strike itself was an Israeli idea, approved by the joint HQ in Cyprus and carried out by the French. Israel, as already noted, was much concerned about Egyptian Il-28 bombers, which had the range to bomb Israeli cities (the *MIG* G-15 turned out not to have this capability). The bombers had been hastily evacuated from their regular base, Cairo West, to remote Luxor in Upper Egypt. A first raid on Luxor, by British planes, was executed from too great an altitude to be effective. The return raid was carried out by the French following pressure by IAF commander General Dan Tolkovsky, on the basis of intelligence provided by the IAF. But the results of the initial French effort, launched from Lod air base at 6 A.M., did not satisfy Tolkovsky. The French agreed to carry out another strike that same afternoon. Altogether, eighteen Ilyushins were destroyed on the ground, and those that survived were evacuated by the Egyptians to Saudi Arabia.[51]

Several other mishaps occurred during the war due to the absence of direct British-Israeli military liaison. On Saturday, November 3, at about 4 P.M., IAF planes attacked the British frigate HMS *Crane,* inflicting light damage. The incident was hushed up, as neither Israel nor Britain had an interest in making it public, and the details are still a matter of controversy. The IAF version is that the attack on the frigate, which had General Staff authorization, was the result of mistaken identity. The vessel sustained only minor damage because no armor-piercing rockets were used. The frigate immediately left the area.[52] Piecing together the available evidence, we emerge with the following picture: A mixed Anglo-French flotilla, under British command, was operating in the Straits of Tiran within the framework of Operation Toreador, which had been mounted to support the main Musketeer effort from the south, to prevent the Egyptians from sending reinforcements to the straits or north to the Canal Zone. On October 30, the Toreador flotilla, getting to the scene before the Israel Navy, sank an Egyptian ship that was carrying reinforcements from Suez to Sharm el Sheikh. The IDF was concerned about the implications of the incident, and with good reason. At least until November 5, the British—it was one of their ships which had sunk the Egyptian troop carrier—were determined to seize the Straits of Tiran if Israel failed to do so. In this sector, the Israeli advance was far slower than elsewhere.

Once the British discovered that Israel was in control of the straits, Toreador HQ was ordered not to interfere. The Israeli move, they were told, was taking pressure off Musketeer forces. However, Israel knew nothing of this order, and Dayan, as noted, issued orders to prepare for a possible British attack against Sharm el Sheikh. Under these circumstances of unclear intentions, the fog of war, mutual suspicions, and proximity of operations, mistakes were inevitable.

The British version of the *Crane* incident appeared in the summarizing report made by the ship's captain on November 5. He said he was attacked off Ras Nasrani in three sorties, though only minor damage had been caused. The ship had returned fire and shot down one of the attacking planes. He thought his attackers were Egyptians.[53]

On November 2, about twenty-four hours before the air strike against HMS *Crane,* the plane flown by the commander of the IAF's 101st Squadron of *Mystères,* Major Benjamin Peled, was shot down above Ras Nasrani. Tolkovsky claimed that Peled (afterward the commander of the IAF) had been hit by Egyptian antiaircraft fire from Ras Nasrani. Bearing in mind the proximity in time, British identification problems (the British opened fire at Ras Nasrani that day), and Israel's flat denial of any such attack the next day—an attack that could have been taken as retaliation for the downing of the *Mystère*—the possibility cannot be ruled out that the only Israeli *Mystère* lost in the war was actually brought down by the British.[54] In any event, the IAF took precautions to avert similar incidents. No one wanted to engage the British Army. Thus the tangled relations between Israel and Britain that had existed on eve of the Suez crisis and throughout its unfolding continued to manifest themselves even during the course of the war itself.

In conclusion, the different basic motivation of each of the three partners was clearly apparent in the prosecution of the war. The problem was made even more acute by the absence of a joint command. Moreover, the deep compartmentalization and the three-way mutual mistrust made even seemingly simple operations, such as the rescue of a downed pilot, exceedingly difficult. The coalition that attacked Egypt in 1956 was weak and disunited; its existence was heavily conditioned. The speedy collapse of the coalition effort against Egypt was, therefore, due not only to the effective threats issued by the two superpowers; it was also the result of the inherent feebleness of the triple coalition.

NOTES

1. See, for example, K. Kyle, *Suez,* London: St. Martin's Press 1991; M. Bar-On, *The Gates of Gaza,* London: Palgrave Macmillan, 1994; M. Golani, *Israel in a Search of a War,* Brighton: Sussex Academic Press, 1998.

2. D. Tolkovsky, *Operation Kadesh: The Air Force Final Report,* November 1957 (Hebrew), Israel Air Force History Branch Archive.

3. *Ibid.*

4. Chief of Staff Diary (CoSD), IDF Archives (IDFA), Ne'eman's report to Dayan, 31 October, 1956; "Minutes with the French Held on 1 November 1956," CoSD.

5. *Ibid.,* 29 October, 1956; J. Nicholls, (the British ambassador in Israel) to Foreign Office, No. 567, 29 October, 1956, PRO, FO371/121782.

6. Dayan's instructions to Ne'eman are quoted in CoSD, 30 October, 1956.

7. Ne'eman's report to Dayan, CoSD, 31 October, 1956.

8. J. Ne'eman, "Connection with the British and the French during Sinai Campaign," *Marachot,* 306–307, 1986 p. 36 (Hebrew); CoSD, 2–6 November 1956; Tolkovsky 1957, *Ibid.*

9. CoSD, 30 October, 1956.

10. *Ibid.,* 31 October, 1956.

11. *Ibid.,* "Minutes of Meeting with the French Held on 1 November 1956," IDFA 532/73/179.

12. Author's interview with K. Kyle, London, 10 December 1991; see also, Kyle 1991, p. 372.

13. Report of Bomber Wing, Cyprus, on Operation Musketeer, PRO, AIR20/9967.

14. Compartmentalization was not a problem for Israel only. See correspondence between General Keightly (CNC Operation Musketeer) and the military in London: chiefs of staff to Keightly, 30 October, 1956, PRO, AIR8/1490; Keightly to chiefs of staff, 30 October, 1956, PRO, AIR8/2111.

15. *Ibid.,* See note 12; Kyle 1991, pp. 372–375.

16. *Ibid.,* p. 374.

17. CoSD, 31 October, 1956.

18. *Ibid.*

19. *Ibid.* On the uncertainty in planing Operation Musketeer, see M. Golani, *There Will Be War Next Summer . . . , The Road to the Sinai War, 1955–1956,* Marachot, Tel Aviv, 1997, Chapter 20 (Hebrew).

20. Golani, 1997, Chapters 29–33.

21. Tolkovsky, 1957, *Ibid.;* "Tzavta [together] Report" (Hebrew), written by Col. N. Eldar, Israeli liaison officer with the French air force mission in Israel, November 1956, Israel air force branch Archive, File 15.

22. CoSD, 30–31 October, 1956; Report of Lt.-Col Souvier, operation officer of the French air delegation in Israel, Service Historique de L'Arme'e de L'Air (SHAA), Paris, C2496; war diary of the french delegation in Israel, *ibid.,* G5255/Y2.

23. Tolkovsky 1957; "Tzavta [together] Report" 1956; author's interview with Gen. (then Lt. Col.) Souvier, Paris, 18 April, 1991.

24. CoSD, 20 October, 1956; internal report of the French Navy (not in circulation at the time): M. Masson, *La Crise de Suez,* Marine Nationale, Service Historique, Vincennes, 1966, pp. 118–120.

25. CoSD, 29 October, 1956; Masson, 1966, p. 120.

26. CoSD, 29 October, 1956.

27. Masson, 1966, pp. 120–121.

28. CoSD, 1 November, 1956.

29. CoSD, 1 November, 1956; Masson, 1966, p. 121.

30. CoSD, 29 October, 1956; A. Beaufre, *The Suez Expedition 1956,* London, 1969, pp. 64, 74, 79–80.

31. Ne'eman's report to Dayan from Cyprus, CoSD, 31 October, 1956.

32. CoSD, 2 November, 1956.

33. As the Israeli prime minister, David Ben-Gurion made no diary entries while he was ill, this based on CoSD, with obvious limitations.

34. CoSD, 3 November, 1956; for general description of the situation in the French Army at the time, see "Rapport sur L'operation d'Egypt," Force A, Juliet-D'ecembre 1956, SHAA, C2307.

35. CoSD, 3 November, 1956.

36. IDF General Staff Branch, "War Diary," operative order "Advance to the Canal and Deployment," 3 November, 1956, IDFA; DoSD, 3 November, 1956.

37. *Ibid.*

38. *Ibid.*

39. Final report by Air Marshal D. Barnett, the Musketeer aerial task force commander, 27 November, 1956, PRO, ADM116/6133.

40. CoSD, 3 November, 1956; Moshe Dayan, *Yoman maarekhet Sinai* (Diary of the Sinai Campaign), Tel Aviv: Am ha-sefer, 1965, pp. 142–144; discussion of the entire affair (possible French-Israeli collaboration at the Suez Canal) can be found in M. Bar-On, *Etgar Vetigra* (Challenge and Quarrel), *Bear Sieva*, 1991, (Hebrew), pp. 318–320.

41. CoSD, 4 November, 1956.

42. The background to the British role at the Sinai campaign, Golani, 1998 (see note 1).

43. *Ibid.*; concerning international developments, see report by ambassador Aba Eban, "The Political Campaign in the UN and the U.S. following the Sinai Operation, October 1956–March 1957," Washington, June 1957, Ben-Gurion Archive at Sde Boker, Israel (BGA); See also Bar-On, 1991, pp. 321–325.

44. CoSD, 4 November, 1956.

45. Kyle 1991, pp. 238–240.

46. Correspondence between Nicholls in Tel Aviv and Logan in London and final report by Ross, head of Levant Department at the Foreign Office, PRO, F0371/121696, 3 November, 1956; background material for Foreign Office responses to questions in Parliament, PRO, F0371/121706.

47. See for example, "Military Intelligence about the Enemy," PRO, AIR20/9677, 30 October, 1956.

48. CoSD, 2 November, 1956; report by chief of naval intelligence to the admiralty, 30 October, 1956, PRO, ADM/205/19. On this subject, see also a paper by the head of history branch, French air force, L. Robineau, "Les Port-a-faux de L'affaire de Suez," *Revue Historique des Armm'ees, 4,* 1986, pp. 44–46.

49. CoSD, 28–29 October, 1956.

50. Bar-On 1991, p. 320; Barnett's final report (see note 35); "Tzavta [together] Report," 1956.

51. Daily report by the Musketeer aerial task force HQ, 4 November, 1956, PRO, AIR/9675; Tolkovsky 1957.

52. Daily report by the Musketeer aerial task force HQ, 3 November, 1956, *ibid.*

53. CoSD, 30 October, 4 November, 1956. On Operation Toreador, see PRO, ADM116/6103 vol. VII in ten-volume report by the Royal Navy; Masson, 1966, pp. 121–124; M. Dayan, *Story of My Life,* Jerusalem, 1976, p. 307.

54. Report to the admiralty and commander, Mediterranean theatre, PRO, ADM205/141, 6 November, 1956.

5

"The War over the Water" during the 1960s

Ami Gluska

"The war over the water" is an accepted idiom in Israel used to describe the battle over the Jordan River water between Israel and the Arab world during the 1960s—the period preceding the Six-Day War. Israel, despite Arab resistance, initiated and carried out a large national enterprise to divert water from the Jordan and the Kinneret Lake in the north to the arid areas in the south. The Arabs, in response, decided to redirect the flow of Jordan River water originating in Arab countries, with the aim of sabotaging the Israeli water venture. Israel employed military means against Syria, thereby foiling the Arab diversion plan. The battle over the water was determined in 1965, when the Arabs, in the absence of an effective response to Israel's military operations, abandoned the diversion plan and the Jordan River water flowed uninterrupted in Israel's national water conduit. The "war over water" was a preliminary phase in the escalation that led to the all-out war between Israel and its neighbors in June 1967.[1]

First, it must be said: the definition of "war" does not befit the battle over the water. The military operations directly related to the water issue were isolated, pinpointed, and very brief. They were part of the usual border conflicts between Israel and Syria over the pasture and cultivation of land in the demilitarized zones, and fishing rights in the northeast of the Kinneret. The term "war over the water" possibly reflects the importance of the subject under contention, but not necessarily its manifestations in the battlefield.

Water is the source of life for people everywhere, and in the Middle East it is not in abundance. The approach toward the issue of water is therefore emotionally charged, and the preservation of the valuable resource of water is considered a supreme interest.[2] It is only natural that water became a subject of extreme confrontation in the Israeli-Arab conflict, in which emotions and interests often overshadow rational judgment. In the early 1950s, when Israel began carrying out its water plans, the Syrians demonstrated their objection, thereby leading to border-firing incidents. In the late 1950s, when the issue of water was back on the agenda, Syria was part of the "United Arab Republic" (UAR), headed by Egyptian President Gamal Abd el-Nasser, who strove for an all-Arab leadership. The issue of water therefore exceeded the boundaries of the Israeli-Syrian context and became a pivotal regional issue.

THE SOURCES OF CONFLICT OVER THE WATER

The roots of the conflict over the Jordan River water emanate from a series of historic, geographic, ideological, political, and strategic factors. We will elucidate three of these factors in this section.

The International Border between the Land of Israel (Palestine) and Syria was determined in 1923, after lengthy negotiations between Britain—which was granted the mandate on Palestine by the League of Nations—and France, which won the mandate over Syria. Britain insisted on including the Jordan River and the Kinneret Lake inside the boundaries of their mandate, and succeeded. At a peace conference in the aftermath of World War I, British Prime Minister Lloyd George explained to his French colleague, Georges Clemenceau, that without control over the Jordan River anyone in the north could reduce the land to the level of arid wilderness.[3] In the sections bordering the waterline, the international border was drawn on the map 100 meters east of the Jordan River and 10 meters from the shore on the northeast of the Kinneret.[4] To this day, Syria does not recognize the legitimacy of this border.[5]

At the conclusion of Israel's War of Independence in 1949, the Syrian army controlled small territories inside the boundaries of the Jewish State as marked in the 1947 UN Partition Plan. In the negotiations on the armistice agreement, Israel demanded the withdrawal of the Syrian forces to beyond the boundaries of the international border, and even considered applying force to compel the Syrians to withdraw. Syria, which remained isolated in its confrontation with Israel after the latter had already signed armistice agreements with Egypt, Lebanon, and Jordan, was forced to retract. The two countries accepted the compromise settlement submitted by Dr. Ralph Bunche, the UN arbitrator, according to which Syria would withdraw its forces from the territories it conquered west of the International Border, and those territories would be demilitarized. The result was that most of the east bank of the upper Jordan River, as well as certain territories west of the Jordan River, and the northeastern bank of the Kinneret, were included in the demilitarized zones. The armistice agreement between Israel and Syria, signed on July 20, 1949, left vague the question of sovereignty in the demilitarized zones. Israel considered them an inseparable part of its territory, to which all sovereign authorities, not specifically limited by the armistice agreement, applied. Syria claimed that they were disputed territories—to which it had claims—and that no party had the authority to change the status quo without the other party's consent. The UN was inclined toward the Syrian interpretation.[6]

The dearth of Israel's water sources and the disproportional allocation of water resources between the north of the country and its arid south resulted in numerous plans for the efficient use of water, dating back to the period of the British mandate. The Zionist ethos of the "blooming of the desert" found particular expression in the vision of populating the Negev, where the leader and first prime minister of Israel, David Ben-Gurion, envisioned the future of the State. The fulfillment of this vision was conditional on diverting large quantities of water from the Jordan and Lake Kinneret to the Negev. Israel's national water enterprise—the National Water Conduit—was intended for this purpose. Throughout the years, Syria, the most immediate interested party, was Israel's most radical adversary in the battle over water. But Israel's vision of developing the Negev was perceived as a threat also in wider Arab circles: the Egyptians believed that Israel's control over the Negev constituted a buffer between them and the Arab lands in the Fertile Crescent and hindered Egypt's aspirations of hegemony; the hypothetical possibility of populating millions of Jews in the Negev was perceived as a basis for Israel's aspirations of expansion. Israel's consolidation through the "blooming of the desert," mass-immigration, and widespread Jewish settlement stood in direct contradiction to the Arab desire to wipe out the existence of the Jewish State in the Arab lands, and their commitment to restore the Palestinians' rights.[7]

The Jordan River is formed by the joining together of three primary tributaries approximately twenty-eight kilometers south of the Israel-Lebanon border: the Hatzbani, originating in Lebanon, with an average annual capacity of approximately 150 million cubic meters; the Banias, originating in Syria (in its pre-June 1967 borders), with a similar capacity; and the Dan, originating in Israel, with an annual capacity of approximately 260 million cubic meters. From here, the Jordan River flows south on the western side of the international border and into Lake Kinneret. From the Kinneret, the river flows into the Jordan Valley, on Israeli soil, to Naharayim, and from there to the Beit-She'an valley, where it forms a border between Israel and the Kingdom of Jordan. The most important additional tributary south of the Lake is the Yarmuk River—originating primarily in Syria—and its most southern part constitutes the border between Israel and Jordan. The annual capacity of the Yarmuk is approximately 450 million cubic meters. These geographical facts mean that a substantial portion of the Jordan River and Kinneret water originates in Arab countries, which have the ability to deprive Israel of this water by diverting the streams and preventing them from flowing into the Jordan River and the Kinneret.

THE BATTLE OVER THE WATER IN THE 1950s: THE FIRST ROUND

The Hula was a small and shallow lake north of the Kinneret, covering an area of approximately fourteen square kilometers, surrounded by swamps of some thirty-one square kilometers. The first phase in Israel's national water plan was to drain the lake and swamps in order to conserve water and expand the territory of agricultural cultivation. The work to lower the bed of the Jordan River and drain the swamps was launched at the beginning of 1951 in the demilitarized zone, sections of which were Arab-owned lands. Syria filed a complaint with the Armistice Committee, and threatened to open fire. The Chief of Staff of the UN Truce Supervision Organization (UNTSO), American General William Riley, ruled that since no party had sovereignty over the territory, Israel had no right to expropriate land in the demilitarized zone. Israel rejected Riley's stand on the issue of sovereignty and continued the work. The Syrians opened fire against the Israeli bulldozers, killing an Israeli worker on March 25. The government of Israel decided, in response, to exercise its sovereignty over the demilitarized territory by providing Israeli ID cards to Arab residents, severing their ties with Syria, and even transferring them from their villages. On April 4, an Israeli police patrol was sent to Hamat Gader, a site of hot springs on the Yarmuk that had been captured by the Syrians, ran into fire and seven of its people were killed. Israel responded with aerial bombings against the police structure on the premises. Another severe incident occurred a month later, when a Syrian force seized a strategic hill, Tel-Mutilla, on Israeli soil, and was warded off after a ferocious battle. The Security Council denounced Israel for its use of aircraft in the Hamat Gader incident and instructed that the draining of the Hula be forestalled until an agreement was reached in the framework of the Armistice Committee. Eventually, Israel found a way to carry out its plan to drain the Hula without encroaching on Arab-owned lands, and the work was completed, with Syrian acquiescence. By the summer of 1958, the lake and swamps were completely drained.[8]

SECOND ROUND: RESISTANCE WITHOUT FIRE

Between the fall of 1952 and the spring of 1953, the Israelis and the Syrians conducted serious and direct negotiations, in the framework of the Armistice Committee, on the allotment of the demilitarized zones and practical arrangements relating to the use of water. The negotiations did not yield fruit, and in September 1953, Israel decided to proceed to the next stage in its national water plan. The plan was to divert part of the Jordan River water south of the Hula, near the Bnot-Ya'akov bridge, and channel it through a canal to the Kinneret, taking advantage of the height differences between the upper Jordan (approximately 70 meters above sea level) and the Kinneret (some 210 meters below sea level) to produce electricity. Another portion of the water was to be diverted south through the Valley of Beit-Netofa. Syria voiced extreme objection to the plan, and filed a complaint with the Security Council. The United States exerted heavy pressure on Israel to cease the work and announced the suspension of economic aid to Israel. On October 28, Israel declared a cessation of the work. A suggested resolution by the Security Council, intended to enable the continuation of the work under certain conditions, encountered a Soviet veto. Israel subsequently decided to abandon the Bnot-Ya'akov Bridge plan, alter the plan from scratch, and pump water from the Kinneret. The work for the construction of the "National Conduit" commenced in 1956 and was completed in 1964.

THE JOHNSTON PLAN

The water conflict between Israel and Syria motivated the U.S. government to take the initiative in order to settle the conflict and prevent the Soviet Union from reaping the fruits of the confrontation. Several months earlier, U.S. Secretary of State John Foster Dulles embarked on a comprehensive tour of the Middle East, and his conclusion was that a more evenhanded and less pro-Israel American policy was needed in the region. In October 1953, President Eisenhower appointed Eric Johnston, chairman of the Advisory Board for International Development, as his personal representative, with the rank of ambassador, to formulate an overall plan for joint and agreed-upon use of the Jordan River water, with American financial aid. In October 1955, after two years of activity in the region, including shuttle tours and meetings with leaders and water experts in the region, the submission of offers and counteroffers, Johnston concluded his plan—"the Jordan Valley Plan." The plan included a distribution of water quotas from the Jordan River and the Yarmuk to Lebanon (3.1 percent), Syria (11.7 percent), Jordan (46.7 percent) and Israel (38.5 percent), and determined that no country would intervene in the manner in which the program would be carried out in another country. Israel signed a memorandum with Johnston and approved the plan. The technical committee of the Arab League also gave its consent. On the other hand, the League's Political Committee, which convened in October 1955, rejected the plan, lest its approval implied indirect recognition of the State of Israel and because of principle objection to any right and any means that would provide for the strengthening and consolidation of the Jewish State.[9]

The Johnston plan reflected a fair compromise, which might have settled the conflict over water had it been concluded earlier, but it was too late. 1954–1955 were marked by radicalization in the Arab world, particularly in Egypt and Syria, and exacerbation of the Arab-Israeli conflict. There was deep polarization in the Arab world over the "Baghdad Pact," struggle for hegemony, and the Arab world's stand in the inter-bloc cold war. At the Bandung Conference in April 1955, Nasser became an international figure and one of the prominent leaders of the Bloc of Nonaligned Countries, and shortly afterwards signed a large arms transaction with Czechoslovakia. In the fall of that year, following the publication of the "Czech transaction" and the deteriorating security situation, Israel considered waging a preventive war against Egypt, and in December the IDF carried out a large-scale retaliatory operation against the Syrian posts east of the Kinneret. The general atmosphere in the region was one of noncompromise and the clouds of the war that would break out a year later were appearing. Under those conditions, the Johnston plan had no chance.[10]

THE LEGAL SITUATION

International law for the use of international waters sets forth a number of principles, including:

. . . Except as otherwise provided by treaty or other instruments or customs binding upon the parties, each co-reparian State is entitled to a reasonable and equitable share in the beneficial uses of the waters of the drainage basin. What amounts to a reasonable and equitable share is a question to be determined in the light of all the relevant factors in each particular case. . . .

International law further stipulates:

. . . Co-reparian States should refrain from unilateral acts that affect adversely the legal rights of a co-reparian State in the drainage basin so long as such co-reparian State is willing to resolve differences as to their legal rights within a reasonable time by consultation. . . .[11]

Syria and the other Arab states did not recognize the State of Israel or its legal rights as a legitimate partner to the drainage basin of the Jordan River, and were not prepared to negotiate with it. Their stand was weakly anchored in international law. Their arguments were mainly political, making use of certain clauses in the Armistice Agreements. Article 2 in the Israeli-Syrian armistice agreement stipulates: "The principle that no military or political advantage should be gained under the truce ordered by the Security Council is recognized."

Syria claimed, for instance, that the draining of the Hula provided Israel with a military edge, and must therefore be viewed as a violation of the agreement.

The armistice agreement further determines:

It is also recognized that no provision of this agreement shall in any way prejudge the rights, claims and position of either Party hereto in the ultimate peaceful settlement of the Palestine question. . . .

And also (in article 5):

. . . arrangements for the Armistice Demarcation Line between the Israeli and Syrian armed forces and for the Demilitarized Zone are not to be interpreted as having any relation whatsoever to ultimate territorial agreements affecting the two Parties. . . .

The Arab assertion was that Israel's water enterprise was likely to predetermine or affect the nature of the agreements and borders.[12] Israel, of course, rejected these arguments and based its own claims on international law and on Israeli consent to use the water within the constraints stipulated by the Johnston water distribution plan.

COMPLETION OF THE "NATIONAL CONDUIT"

The absence of Arab consent did not forestall the realization of Israel's water plans, and the water enterprise, based on pumping water from the Kinneret, began operating in 1964. While diverting water from a location outside the demilitarized area allayed concerns of political obstacles to the water plan, pumping from the Kinneret, approximately 210 meters below sea level, increased the cost of the enterprise. The idea of diverting water through gravitation and producing electricity was rejected, and instead, electric energy was to be invested for the purpose of pumping water and raising it to a level from which water could be redirected south. The pumping of water from the Kinneret adversely affected the quality of water channeled through the conduit. The Kinneret waters are saltier (an average of some 300 milligrams of chlorine per liter) than the upper Jordan waters, due to salty fountains originating from the bottom of the lake and its western coast. It also entailed the construction of a canal to divert part of the salty fountains, in order to minimize any detrimental affect on the quality of water.

The system of channeling the water from the Kinneret included pumping stations, canals, reservoirs, tunnels, and pipes along some 130 kilometers to the fountains area at Rosh Ha'ayin in the center of the country. At this point, the conduit merged with the Yarkon-Negev waterline, which was constructed a few years earlier. On June 10, 1964, the conduit began operating and the Kinneret waters were channeled to the water network in the south of Israel.[13] At the government's request, the Israeli press played down the news of the operation of the conduit, so as not to inflame tension with the Arabs.[14]

Simultaneously, Jordan carried out irrigation enterprises and developed the water infrastructure in its territory, particularly on the eastern side of the Jordan Valley. The Jordanian plan included the Ghor Canal, transferring water from Adassiya on the Yarmuk, along seventy kilometers, to Wadi Zarqa in the south of the Jordan Valley. Furthermore, Jordan continued the construction of the Muheiba dam on the Yarmuk in order to accumulate water for the purpose of irrigating the Jordan Valley and enriching the Jordanian water infrastructure. Israel did not oppose these enterprises, since Jordan undertook the project, though not publicly and formally, to refrain from deviating from the water quotas allocated by the American arbitrator.[15]

CRYSTALLIZATION OF ARAB RESISTANCE
TO THE ISRAELI WATER VENTURE

At first, the implementation of the Israeli water plan did not attract particular attention. Arab countries were preoccupied with other issues during 1957–1958. The political defeat of Britain and France in the Suez War marked the zenith of Gamal Abd el-Nasser's prestige, who decided to temporarily freeze the conflict with Israel and give priority to his vision of unifying the Arab world under Egypt's leadership. The first step came in February 1958, with the declaration of the unification of Egypt and Syria in the framework of the "United Arab Republic." The dormant water conflict between Israel and Syria was now under the responsibility of the UAR president, Nasser. In July 1958, the pro-Western Hashemite Kingdom in Iraq was toppled, and American and British troops were dispatched to Lebanon and Jordan in order to curb the revolutionary vortex which threatened their regimes. In the late 1950s, following a rift between Egypt and the new republican regime in Iraq, a triple rivalry was created in the Arab world: UAR versus Iraq versus the conservative regimes. In 1961, Syria departed unilaterally from the union with Egypt in frustration over its relegation to an Egyptian protégé and losing its independence. Following that, inter-Arab feuding was expanded as a result of the powerful campaign conducted by Abd el-Nasser against the Syrian government, which had turned its back on the unification with Egypt. The issue of the Jordan water became a pawn in these rivalries, when both conservative and revolutionary regimes attempted to embarrass their adversaries by taking extreme nationalist stands, while accusing other regimes of forsaking the national Arab interest.[16]

The issue of Israel "diverting" the Jordan water was raised in September 1959 by the Saudi representatives at the Arab League Council convention in Casablanca, *for the first time* as an all-Arab problem (as opposed to the 1951 and 1953 crises which focused on the Israeli-Syrian context). The Council decided to establish a technical committee to study the issue and submit recommendations. The committee concluded its discussions in December 1959, with a recommendation to take steps to prevent Israel from continuing its "aggressive plans." From this point on, attention towards this issue was accelerated at the political level and through the Arab media to a point where the atmosphere of crisis reached almost hysterical proportions. The Arabs' impression in the fall of 1959 was that Israel was on the brink of completing the "National Conduit" and that the flow of water was close to being operational. One of the reasons for this impression and the sense of urgency was the renewed activity by Eric Johnston, who met, at his own initiative, with Egyptian Foreign Minister Mahmud Fauzi, in an attempt to renew the negotiations over a regional water settlement, with American mediation. At the same time, the Israeli finance minister, Levi Eshkol, visited Washington in an attempt to mobilize American aid for Israel's water enterprise. Another possible reason was statements made by Israeli officials, against the backdrop and in the aftermath of Knesset elections in November 1959, regarding Israel's determination to realize its water plans and the priority that would be given to the subject.[17]

The tension over the water issue faded after a while as a result of widespread diplomatic activity on the part of the Western states, particularly the United States, after the Arabs had become convinced that the flow of Jordan River water in the Israeli enterprise would not commence before 1963–1964. At the same time, the subject was not removed from the Arab agenda and a declarative all-Arab commitment to prevent Israel from realizing its water plans had begun to formulate. Due to the centrality of this matter, Nasser took it upon himself to coordinate all aspects of this issue, in line with his commitment at the time to "revive the Palestinian entity" as a tool for strengthening his leadership in the Arab world.

The Syrian leadership was the most radical in demanding to forcibly prevent Israel from diverting water from the Jordan. Arab chiefs of staff who convened in Cairo in April 1961 explored the possibilities of foiling Israel's plans through military means, and determined that the Arab states must be ready to take action to terminate Israel's military capability before the end of 1963. Two months later, the Defense Council of the Arab League (comprised of foreign ministers, defense ministers, and chiefs of staff) convened in Cairo to discuss the preparations to divert the Jordan sources and the establishment of a joint command for Arab armies. This was a signal of the future to come in less than three years.

Syria's withdrawal in September 1961 from the unification with Egypt was the first incident to undermine Gamal Abd el-Nasser's leadership and symbolized its decline. Nasser responded by radicalizing Egypt's domestic and foreign policy, and in September 1962, he dispatched his army to Yemen to support the rebels against the Imam. Egypt's long and inextricable involvement in Yemen (1962–1967) severely undermined Nasser's standing. As we shall see, the Egyptian army's involvement in Yemen hindered Nasser's ability to act against Israel in the water conflict.

In April 1963, following coups which brought to power the Ba'ath ("Revival") party in Syria and Iraq, a triumvirate unity was heralded in the Arab world—Egypt-Syria-Iraq. This unification never materialized and its rapid disintegration further exacerbated polarization in the Arab world. In the interim, Israel's water enterprise was close to completion, and the Syrian threat to go to war presented the Egyptian president with a challenge. The rift and mutual accusations between Syria and Egypt were of a virulent nature.

In December 23, 1963, Nasser surprised the Arab world when, in a speech at Port Said he called for the convening of an Arab summit "to address the problem of the Jordan River, which is part of the problem of Palestine." Nasser was concerned that matters may get out of hand as a result of Syrian moves which could involve Egypt in a premature war with Israel. His initiative was therefore intended to regain control and formulate a coordinated Arab strategy to confront the challenge presented to the Arabs by Israel's water venture. He declared: "in order to confront Israel, which is threatening us, we have no choice but to convene the Kings and Heads of Arab states as soon as possible, putting aside any disagreements or disputes between them."[18]

In January 1964, all heads of Arab states convened in Cairo for a summit meeting. In September of that same year, a second summit was convened in Alexandria, Egypt, and a third was convened in September 1965 in Casablanca, Morocco. The main theme of these conventions was the Jordan water and the military confrontation with the State of Israel.

The first summit in Cairo made three important decisions:

1. To divert the Jordan River tributaries originating in Arab countries
2. To establish a joint military command to protect the diversion and strengthen the armies of Syria, Jordan, and Lebanon
3. To take concrete steps to organize the "Palestinian entity" (a decision followed by the founding of the "Palestine Liberation Organization," the PLO, four months later)

THE ARAB PLAN TO DIVERT THE JORDAN STREAMS

The main points of the Arab diversion plan were as follows:

• In Lebanon—The Upper Hatzbani water would be diverted through a canal from the Hatzbaya and Wadi Shab'a area into the Litani, which spills into the Mediterranean Sea. The Central Hatzbani water would be redirected through a canal to the Banias, and from there—through the Syrian water diversion project—to the Yarmuk. The water from the Wazani fountain in the lower bed of the Hatzbani would be used for irrigation of lands in Syria and Lebanon.

• In Syria—The Banias water (and the Hatzbani water that would be diverted there from Lebanon) would be redirected through a canal, seventy-three kilometers long. A portion would be used for irrigation in Syria and the remainder would spill into the Yarmuk. The Syrian part of the plan also included the pumping of water from the Kinneret for use by the villages in the Bteiha Valley, northeast of the Kinneret.

• In Jordan—A dam would be constructed on the Yarmuk (the Mucheiba dam), with the capacity to impound 200 million cubic meters of water, in order that the diverted water be used in large-scale irrigation plans in the Jordan Valley and for the development of the water infrastructure.

The second Arab summit (September 1964) approved the operational plans and decided to begin the work immediately. Dr. Ahmed Salim, chairman of the "Authority for the Use of the Jordan Water," established at the first summit, estimated the time needed to complete the plan to be at least eight years. The head of the joint military command, Egyptian General Ali Amer, estimated that Israel might initiate military action shortly before or immediately upon completion of the work.[19]

ISRAEL'S RESPONSE TO THE WATER-DIVERSION PLAN

Initially, Israel did not take the Arab water-diversion plan seriously. The decisions of the first Arab summit were believed to be a leadership maneuver on the part of Nasser and an attempt to spread responsibility for the Arab failure to prevent the realization of Israel's water plan. The Israeli intelligence questioned the feasibility of the diversion plan, and the subject was not high on Israel's public agenda.

The decisions of the second Arab summit in September 1964 to begin the water-diversion work were probably what motivated Israel to put on a show of force, the purpose of which was to signal to the Arabs that Israel was determined to protect its water sources. Even before the Syrians and Lebanese began the work in their territories, Israel deviated from its routine operational mode in border incidents with Syria, and made powerful use of its air force.

THE TEL DAN INCIDENT: NOVEMBER 13, 1964

The Dan, the most important of the three Jordan tributaries, originates in Israeli territory and abuts the Syrian border. The IDF patrolling route, leading to the Dan fountains, included a disputed area, which the Syrians claimed was theirs. The Syrians enjoyed a topographical edge and for a long period of time, the IDF refrained from patrolling that route. A decision was then made to refurbish that route and use it in order to illustrate Israel's control over the Dan fountains. It was predictable, of course, that the Syrians would open fire.

The first firing incident occurred on November 3, after the Syrians fired from the post in Nuheila, overlooking Tel Dan, toward an IDF patrol. In the exchange of fire, Israeli tanks failed to hit the Syrian tanks. Ten days later, on November 13, an IDF patrol was again dispatched to the Dan route. As expected, the Syrians opened fire, and this time, the Israeli tanks successfully destroyed three Syrian tanks. The Syrians responded by artillery fire from Nuheila toward the adjacent Kibbutz Dan. Chief of Staff Yitzhak Rabin received Prime Minister and Minister of Defense Levi Eshkol's approval to silence the Syrian fire using the air force. Approximately twenty fighter aircraft attacked the Syrian artillery posts. In the border clashes and incidents, the scope of the air force attack was unprecedented, and was clearly meant to deliver a message to the Arab side.[20]

PRESSURE ON LEBANON

Lebanon's part in the Arab diversion plan was the simplest one, and able to produce results in a short space of time. Thus, in December 1964, Egypt began exerting pressure on Lebanon to begin the work. Lebanon was fearful of Israel's response, particularly after the Israeli "signal" in the Tel Dan incident and warnings delivered by Israel through secret channels. On the other hand, the Lebanese leadership feared that the Muslim population would be incited against its government if it failed to implement the summit resolutions. In an editorial in the semiformal Egyptian newspaper *El-Ahram,* Hasnin Heikal accused Lebanon of failing to comply with its commitments.[21] The Lebanese, who were dragging their feet, were compelled to begin diverting water from the central Hatzbani, yet without deviating from the Johnston plan. Israel's military responses to the diversion work that commenced in Syria (see following discussion), motivated Lebanese President Charle Hilu to rush to Cairo in May 1965 and meet with Nasser. Hilu requested the Egyptian president's consent to cease the diversion project in Lebanon until the United Arab Command completed its preparations to defend the water venture. Nasser became convinced that Lebanon should not be expected to carry out the impossible, and that as long as the Arab states were unable to withstand Israel's attacks, there was no choice but to postpone the diversion.[22]

At the beginning of July 1965, the diversion work in Lebanon was suspended, and the third Arab summit, which convened in September, gave it the official seal. Therefore, the "war over the water" on the Lebanese front ended before it even began, without one shot being fired.

UNDERSTANDING WITH JORDAN

The water-diversion plan in Jordanian territory was in fact integrated in a previous Jordanian plan to irrigate large areas in the Jordan Valley. The original "Yarmuk plan" included the construction of dams (the Muheiba and Makarin dams) on the Yarmuk river and the streams spilling into the Jordan river, for the purpose of impounding and accumulating the water designated for the irrigation project. Back in 1958, the Jordanians began digging a seventy-kilometer canal along the eastern bank of the Jordan. The Jordanian water plan in itself did not deviate from the framework of the Johnston plan. In fact, only after completion of the diversion plan in Lebanon and Syria was Jordan slated to receive substantial quantities of water from the diverted Banias and Hatzbani, which would be channeled into the Yarmuk. While Jordan enjoyed generous Arab funding for the implementation of its water plan—as part of the Arab diversion plan—Israel saw no reason to object to the Jordanian plan. Israel and Jordan enjoyed a quiet understanding that Jordan would not deviate from the Johnston plan and Israel would not take action against the Jordanian water project. Jordan was also, therefore, outside the "war."[23]

CONFRONTATION WITH SYRIA

The "war over the water," even if it can be defined as such, was in fact only between Israel and Syria. To be precise, Syria attempted to implement the water-diversion plan in its territory, and Israel prevented it from doing so through military means. Syria remained isolated and with no military means to confront Israel. Egypt, which championed the diversion plan in the first two summits as an alternative for a premature military confrontation with Israel, changed its stand. Nasser remained committed to Israel's destruction, but claimed that the

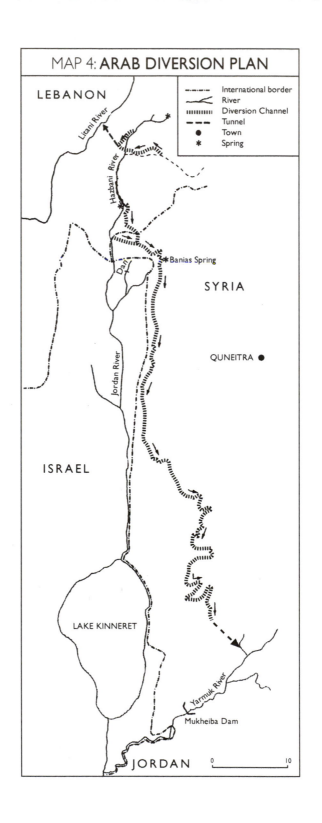

MAP 4: ARAB DIVERSION PLAN

International border
River
Diversion Channel
Tunnel
● Town
✳ Spring

LEBANON

Litani River

Hazbani River

Dam

✳ Banias Spring

SYRIA

QUNEITRA ●

Jordan River

ISRAEL

LAKE KINNERET

Yarmuk River

Mukheiba Dam

JORDAN

0   10

showdown with Israel required fundamental preparation, the uniting of forces in the Arab world, and the right timing to guarantee Arab victory. As Israel, unexpectedly, employed military forces in a preliminary stage of the diversion project, Nasser preferred to withdraw his support for the diversion, so as not to become embroiled in a war with Israel before the Arab armies were prepared. The third summit confirmed the suspension of the diversion project and concentrated on the approval of a coordinated Arab military plan for war against Israel, with the aim of eradicating it. Syria, which, from the beginning, demanded an immediate war against Israel over the issue of water, defiantly continued the diversion work alone, despite Israel's military actions. However, the scope of work in Syria was merely symbolic, and the June 1967 Six-Day War put an end to this also.[24]

ISRAEL'S STAND ON THE DIVERSION PROJECT

At the beginning of 1965, the military and political leadership in Israel came to realize that the Arab plan to divert the Jordan River sources was more serious than initially estimated. On January 1, concurrently with the commencement of the project in Syria, an unknown Palestinian organization named "al-Fatah" began carrying out acts of sabotage, initially against water facilities (the Fatah's first action was actually aimed at a tunnel of the water conduit in the Beit Neqofa valley). After eight years of relative calm following the Sinai War, the security situation suddenly deteriorated and a military confrontation over the issue of water lurked closer than ever.

The government of Israel, headed by Levi Eshkol, who succeeded David Ben-Gurion in 1963, was a moderate one that did not want war. Nevertheless, there was full governmental consensus that Israel could not forfeit its water rights. From Israel's standpoint, the "National Conduit" was a constructive venture that did not affect the Arabs at all. Israel believed that its stated willingness to use the water only in the framework of the quota stipulated by the Johnston plan pulled the rug from under the Arab resistance to the Israeli water project. Levi Eshkol announced that the water was vital to Israel "like the blood in our veins."[25] Knesset member Moshe Dayan, who had recently resigned from the Eshkol government, expressed his opinion that if the IDF's deterrence capability did not prevent the diversion project, the IDF would be forced to employ operational capability. Capitulation on this subject embodied a two-fold risk. On the one hand, subtract over 100 million cubic meters of water annually from the Jordan, salinize the Kinneret, and cast doubt over the entire water venture. And on the other hand, violation of the status quo with no Israeli response would escalate the situation and lead to the renewal of the hostilities which had ceased since 1957.[26]

The IDF General Command formulated various operational plans to confront the diversion challenge, reflecting four possible modes of operation:

- Limited deterrent military action, through incursion or firing at mechanical and engineering equipment
- Attacking the weak spots of the diversion project (pumps, decks, dams, etc.) through large-scale incursion

- Seizing and holding demilitarized zones controlling the diversion areas—referring particularly to Ramat Banias and Tel-Azaziat
- Conquering the demilitarized areas and sovereign Syrian territories in the Golan Heights, controlling the diversion areas—Tel-Hamra, Tel-Azaziat, and Ramat Banias to Birkat Ram.

Each possibility had pros and cons. The first possibility could become operational immediately; it was easier and more convenient politically and militarily, and left the IDF with the possibility of taking more comprehensive action in the future. However, the General Command questioned whether such limited action would deter the Syrians. Moreover, such an action was liable to trigger a counterresponse, validate the joint Arab command, provide the Egyptians with an excuse to withdraw its army from Yemen, and perhaps motivate the Arabs to slow down the pace of the diversion until they were militarily prepared. The primary advantage of the second option was a much stronger effect. Its obvious disadvantage was the need to wait a year or more until the targets were actually present, while in the interim, public opinion could "get used" to the reality of the diversion project. The third option could provide the IDF with effective control of the territory to prevent the diversion, and even enable it to determine the timing of the operation. On the other hand, it would put the Arab unification to the ultimate test, and the risk was that Egypt might use the opportunity to extract itself from Yemen and initiate indirect aggression against Israel, such as the blocking of the Straits of Tiran. The main concern was that this option would expose Israel to political pressure, which would undermine the military achievements. The pros and cons of the fourth option were similar to those of the third, but greater. At the same time, it could provide Israel with a political bargaining chip, to prevent blocking the Straits, for instance.[27]

The possibility of escalation to an all-out war in each of the four operational modes was taken into consideration, but it was clear to General Yitzhak Rabin, the chief of staff, that the government would prefer means that would minimize the risk of war. The government of Israel was facing a dilemma: the Arabs began diverting the Jordan sources, but it was a long-term plan (eight to twelve years, according to estimates by the professional echelons). This time frame left room for diplomatic activity, and as long as Arab states carried out infrastructure work in their sovereign territory and did not divert water, and as long as it had not been proven that they exceeded the quotas provided by the Johnston plan, Israel had no real excuse for military operation. Prime Minister Eshkol himself stated more than once that Israel should wait and see whether the diversion work did indeed deviate from the Johnston plan.[28] Moshe Dayan, on the other hand, demanded an immediate response. In reply to the question of what he intended, Dayan responded: ". . . do not let their tractors, bulldozers, or surveyors pass. We cannot postpone the operation, not even by one hour! We must not let them work!"[29] The United States exerted pressure on Israel to refrain from the use of force. From the summer of 1964, Washington even seriously considered the possibility of assisting with the establishment of a large facility for the desalination of seawater through nuclear energy to solve Israel's water problem.[30]

At the end of February 1965, President Lyndon Johnson of the United States dispatched two high-ranking envoys to Israel—former Under-Secretary of State

Averell Harriman and National Security Council official Robert Komer—to discuss Israel's requests to purchase American tanks and fighter aircraft, as well as other security issues, including Israel's nuclear development. One of the demands presented by the American envoys to Israeli leaders was an Israeli commitment to exhaust every possible avenue, including approaching the UN, to resolve the water conflict with the Arabs, without the use of fire. The Israelis agreed. At the same time, Chief of Staff Rabin gave Komer and Harriman a helicopter tour along the border with Syria and pointed out the diversion sites. He explained that the IDF could disrupt the diversion work on the Syrian side through a direct hit to the engineering machinery operating along the route, without crossing the border. The two envoys listened without responding. Rabin deduced from their silence that a pinpointed military action (option A) would not encounter American objection, and he discussed it with Eshkol. The prime minister sought approval from the Ministerial Committee for Security, and it was decided that the IDF would take advantage of one of the frequent border incidents to strike the heavy-duty equipment along the diversion route in Syria.[31]

IDF OPERATIONS TO FOIL THE DIVERSION

On March 17, 1965, only a week after the American envoys' visit, Israel launched the first military action to disrupt the water-diversion project in Syria. There was no difficulty in finding the opportunity. The border clashes and firing incidents between the IDF and the Syrian army over the cultivation of disputed fields in the demilitarized zones were a matter of routine. On March 16, an Israeli tractor driver who was ploughing a field in the central demilitarized zone was killed by Syrian fire. The next day, the IDF initiated another incident. A patrol was sent to the patrolling route leading to the Dan fountain, and the Syrians, predictably, opened fire from the Nuheila post. Two IDF tank platoons, which were prepared in advance, returned fire, also against the Syrian diversion equipment at the Banias section over two kilometers away. Eight tractors were hit; the Syrians were taken by surprise and failed to respond. Until that point, the Syrians managed to pave a route of approximately fifteen kilometers west and south of the Banias village. As a result of the damage caused to the diversion equipment, the Syrians terminated the work at the area close to the border on the Banias section. Syria demanded that the joint Arab command launch a "decisive" response to the Israeli operation, but was dismissed. Four weeks later, the Syrians renewed the diversion work on another section, the central part of the Golan Heights, some five kilometers from the border, opposite the Bnot Ya'akov bridge.

For political reasons, particularly the establishing of diplomatic relations with West Germany, Israel did not initiate an immediate military response to the renewal of the diversion work in Syria. Only on May 13, after government deliberations and preparations on the ground, did the IDF initiate a firing incident in the central demilitarized zone, south of Mishmar HaYarden. In the exchange, Israeli tanks fired against the diversion equipment and succeeded, despite the vast distance (over five kilometers), in hitting two or three Syrian tractors. During that entire time, Israeli air force planes circled the area, but the Syrians did not respond, and the planes were not put into action. The Syrians had managed to pave a route of approximately five kilometers in that area. Following the incident, the diversion work was also terminated in that section.[32]

THE RESOLUTION OF THE BATTLE OVER THE WATER

Israel's two military actions to disrupt the water-diversion work in Syria presented Arab leaders with a difficult challenge. Contrary to all expectations, Israel had no intention of waiting until the completion of the diversion project in order to respond. On the other hand, the Arabs were not yet prepared for a military show-down with Israel, as Syria had vehemently demanded. Everyone waited for the central figure in the Arab world—Gamal Abd el-Nasser—to speak up.

On May 31, 1965, Nasser spoke. At a Cairo convention of the Palestinian National Council, the Egyptian president stated that he had no intention of becoming embroiled in a premature war with Israel because of a Syrian tractor. He declared: "50,000 of our soldiers are in Yemen. How will I attack Israel? First, I must bring the 50,000 back. We do not want to repeat [the defeat] of [19]48." Nasser rejected the demand to launch an immediate attack against Israel, which he construed as playing into Israel's hands: "What next? If Syria is attacked, then I should attack Israel. The result is that the Israelis can dictate to me when I must hit them. They will destroy a tractor in Syria and I shall be forced to attack. It is unhealthy. We alone will determine the date. . . ." Nasser confessed: "We cannot divert the Jordan streams unless we have ground and aerial defense . . . if we cannot divert them today, let us say that we will postpone the diversion until we are able to defend it . . . we must be candid and decide that we must first guarantee defense, and at the same time, prepare to achieve our primary goal."[33]

Nasser's public withdrawal of his support for the continuation of the diversion work took IDF Central Command by complete surprise. No one expected that two minor and local IDF actions, in which several tractors were hit, would lead to the abandonment of the entire diversion plan. No one estimated that this plan, which was at the center of the Arab agenda for years, which was the subject of summits and countless discussions in political, military, and technical forums, and whose implementation had commenced, would be suddenly abandoned. Chief of Staff Yitzhak Rabin expressed great surprise: "The results are totally disproportional to our actions . . . after two [small] IDF actions, Nasser will make such a public statement? I did not believe that would happen!" Rabin concluded that the IDF had the "ultimate solution" for eliminating the Arab diversion plan.[34]

Despite the setbacks they had suffered and Nasser's retraction, the Syrians stubbornly continued the diversion work. They moved the diversion work to a section located approximately ten kilometers from the border with Israel, at the center of the Golan, opposite the northern shores of Lake Kinneret. The government of Israel consequently approved another action. On August 12, 1965, an Israel tractor was dispatched to cultivate disputed land in the central demilitarized zone at Hirbat Kara, north of the Kinneret. When it appeared that the Syrians were aiming the barrels of their tanks at the tractor, the IDF opened fire from tanks and cannons against the diversion equipment. Despite the vast distance, the Israeli fire struck two Syrian tractors.[35]

At the third Arab summit, convened in Casablanca in September 1965, the heads of Arab states acknowledged that Israel had succeeded in sabotaging the Arab plans to divert the Jordan water. The chief of the United Arab Command, General Ali Amer, determined that "continuing the technical work, knowing the substantial lag in our military preparations . . . does not correspond with common sense. The assumption was that the diversion work in progress [before completion] would not generate an attack by Israel. But in fact the opposite happened." The summit provided a seal of approval for the termination of the diversion work and devoted its main discussions to a three-year plan for Arab military armament toward the showdown for achieving "the final Arab national goal," namely, the extermination of Israel. In Nasser's words: "elimination of the Israeli imperialism and the recovery of the lands of Palestine."[36] The Arab plan to divert the Jordan water was waning. Moreover, the pretentious all-Arab plan for the annihilation of the State of Israel, sanctioned by Arab leaders at the third summit, remained on paper only. Within several months, the "summit climate" faded and the inter-Arab rift deepened significantly. An additional summit scheduled for 1966 was called off after Egypt cancelled its participation. The inter-Arab rivalry between the conservative, pro-Western states, and the "progressive" states supported by the Soviet Union, turned into a venomous war of propaganda and mutual slander. Nasser's status as the leader of the Arab world was on the decline and his involvement in the war in Yemen intensified. The Arab world had never looked so divided and helpless.[37]

We can draw a line at this point and conclude that the "war over the water" ended with a smooth and easy Israeli victory. The "National Conduit" continued to divert water from the Kinneret south to the Negev, and the Arabs could do nothing to prevent it. The "war" was therefore concluded in three local military actions—on March 17, May 13, and August 12, 1965—and damage to a number of Syrian tractors along the diversion route. The victory was achieved both through the deprivation of the Arab ability to realize the diversion plan, and by the acknowledgement that they had to abandon the plan.

REPERCUSSIONS OF THE DIVERSION (JULY–AUGUST 1966)

Although the diversion plan had become unfeasible, the Syrians did not completely forfeit the continuation of the work, for reasons of prestige and a show of defiance. The pace of work became very slow, its scope symbolic, and did not concern Israel. Nevertheless, a year later, Israel delivered another blow to the Syrian diversion plan, this time from the air. The background for that action, on July 14, 1966, was not so much the actual diversion work, but another dimension that had begun to evolve in the conflict, and which ultimately became a major factor in the escalation leading to the June 1967 war. I am referring to the guerrilla warfare on the part of Palestinian organizations, primarily el-Fatah, against Israel, with Syrian support. In February 1966, a radical sect of the Syrian Ba'ath Party seized power in Damascus, through a military coup. Syria's new leadership[38] championed a continuous fight against Israel in the form of a "popular liberation war." Syria gave patronage to the Fatah, provided it with bases, equipment, and training for terror acts against Israel, and orchestrated its activities.[39] Most of the Fatah attacks, under Syrian inspiration, were launched from Lebanese and Jordanian soil, and only isolated attacks emanated from Syria. On July 14, following two such attacks on May 16 and July 13, 1966, which claimed the lives of four Israelis, the IDF initiated an aerial retaliatory attack, in which Israeli aircraft destroyed five heavy machines working along the diversion route at Ein-Sufira, in the southern Golan Heights, approximately twelve kilometers inside Syrian territory.[40] This action almost completely paralyzed the continuation of the diversion work.

A month after the Israeli aerial attack at Ein-Sufira, the Syrians seized an opportunity to respond with an aerial assault of their own. At 3:30 in the morning of August 15, 1966, an Israeli navy patrol boat ran aground near the northeastern coast of the Kinneret, approximately eighty meters from the shore, opposite the Syrian posts. While the Kinneret lake in its entirety was in Israeli territory, the Syrian army controlled its northeastern coast, and Israeli navy boats were mindful of keeping a distance of 250 meters from the shore.[41] Close to 9:00 A.M., four Syrian MIG 17's attacked the grounded boat. One of the attacking airplanes was hit by antiaircraft fire from the boat and crashed into the water.[42]

A notification of the attack was delivered to Yitzhak Rabin, the IDF chief of staff, who ordered an immediate "unlimited pursuit" of the Syrian aircraft. Two *Mirage* planes, which were launched earlier, identified two Syrian MIG 21's approaching the area. One of the MIGs was shot down by Israeli *Mirage* cannons. The chief of staff also ordered the air force to launch an aerial strike against targets on the Syrian coast, but to refrain from hitting houses in the adjacent Massadia village. The bombing, which occurred at 10:00 A.M., employing *Vautour* light bombers, missed the Syrian post, and several bombs hit houses in the village, causing casualties. Attempts to rescue the boat were unsuccessfully carried out with UN mediation on that same day and the following day. Israel rejected the Syrian demands to permit them to extricate the airplane and the pilot's body from the water, on the grounds that as it was sovereign Israeli territory, Israel would extract the airplane and the body, and would be willing to transfer them to the Syrians later. Israel also rejected the request to extricate the airplane and body in the presence of UN observers and to deliver them immediately to the Syrians on the eastern coast of the Kinneret. The Syrians therefore announced that they would prevent the rescue of the boat.

Following a meeting between Prime Minister Eshkol and the head of the UN observers, Norwegian General Odd Bull, an agreement was reached that the rescue of the boat and the extrication of the plane would be conducted simultaneously, in the presence of UN observers. On the morning of August 17, the IDF made preparations to renew the rescue attempts, but the Syrians, which had, in the interim, concentrated large forces on the shore, announced that they would object to the rescue of the boat as long as their conditions for the extrication of the plane and the pilot's body were not met.

IDF Navy submariners and the engineering corps unit spent the next several nights attempting to rescue the boat, grounded "right under the nose" of the Syrian posts. They succeeded only after eleven days.

DETERIORATION TO WAR

The incidents at Ein-Sufira and the Kinneret during July–August 1966 were not part of the "war over the water," which, as mentioned, had been determined a year earlier. They reflected the exacerbation of the Israeli-Syrian conflict, which emanated partly from Israel's success in foiling the Arab diversion plan, and primarily from Syria's support of the "popular war" against Israel. Since 1951, as a result of the dispute over the demilitarized areas, the situation along the Israeli-Syrian border was tense and fraught with incidents. The water conflict significantly heightened the tension, but Syria's backing of the Palestinian guerrilla warfare against Israel, which was partly the result of the Syrian frustration over its failure in the water campaign, was the primary factor in the deterioration to war. In November 1966, Egypt and Syria signed a mutual defense pact, which enhanced the Egyptian commitment to defend Syria against an Israeli attack. During January–February 1967, the Mixed Armistice Committee (MAC), under the auspices of the UN, conducted Israeli-Syrian talks aimed at reaching agreement on the demilitarized areas. The talks failed due to a complete lack of confidence between the parties and the Syrian refusal to discuss the overall problem of security.[43] The continuation and intensification of attacks against Israel led the IDF General Staff to the conclusion that a powerful military strike against Syria was inevitable. For a long period of time, the government rejected the army's recommendation for fear of becoming embroiled in a war against Egypt also. On April 7, 1967, due to the continued attacks, Prime Minister and Minister of Defense Levi Eshkol authorized the full use of the air force in a previously unplanned border incident that evolved on that same day. Israel's fighter planes penetrated Damascus air space and brought down six Syrian MIGs. Even after the incident, Syria did not suspend its support for the "popular war," and Israel's warnings gave the clear impression that a large IDF operation against Syria was imminent. On May 12, 1967, the Soviet Union delivered false information to Egypt regarding the concentration of massive IDF forces on the Syrian border. Nasser decided to move Egypt's forces to the Sinai in order to deter Israel, and subsequently expelled the UN Emergency Force, stationed along the border with Israel in 1957, following the Sinai War. Nasser's crucial decision on May 22 to block the Straits of Tiran to Israeli vessels brought the parties to the brink of war. Israel made futile attempts to find a diplomatic solution to the crisis, and the siege tightening around Israel intensified its sense of apprehension. The continued concentration of Arab forces along Israel's borders, Nasser's statements that the goal was the elimination of Israel, and Jordan's inclusion on May 30 in the alliance with Egypt finally convinced the government of Israel (which, on June 1, became a wide National Unity government, with Moshe Dayan as minister of defense) to give the IDF the green light to launch a preemptive strike. On June 5, 1967, Israel went to a war which would change the face of the region and the face of the State of Israel.[44]

CONCLUSION

The battle over the Jordan waters was a result of the Arab-Israeli conflict, predicated on the Arab refusal to recognize the State of Israel, accept the outcome of the 1948 war, or acknowledge the armistice lines as the permanent borders. The Arab objection to Israel's water plans was not the result of unjustified distribution of the Jordan waters. The Johnston plan for the distribution of the Jordan waters—in the framework of which Israel agreed to operate—did not neglect the Arab states, and the technical committee of the Arab League even acknowledged it. The Arab resistance emanated from their perception of the State of Israel as an illegitimate entity, the very existence of which was based on injustice, and whose fate was to cease to exist. The water enterprise, aimed at contributing to the development of the Jewish state and populating the Negev, stood in stark contrast with the Arab desire to weaken Israel and wipe out its existence.

At the beginning of the 1950s, Israel's initial implementation of the first stage of the water enterprise, through the draining of the Hula, led to a brief confrontation with Syria. The draining of the Hula was ultimately completed, but Israel's plan to divert water from the upper Jordan River in the demilitarized area near the Bnot-Ya'akov bridge and channel the water south was foiled due to Syrian objection and pressure from the UN and the United States. Israel was compelled to alter its plan and pump water from the Kinneret, significantly increasing the cost of the water venture and adversely affecting the quality of water channeled through the National Conduit. At the end of that decade, the dispute surfaced again. Syria was then unified with Egypt in the framework of the "United Arab Republic," and the UAR president, Gamal Abd el-Nasser, placed the subject at the top of the Arab agenda. After Syria's secession from the unification, the inter-Arab rift deepened and the water conflict with Israel became the subject of inter-Arab discord, its importance being accentuated to the point of creating a declarative all-Arab commitment to foil Israel's water plan, whether forcibly or through technical means. At the end of 1963, close to the completion of the Israeli "National Conduit," Nasser called for the convening of Arab leaders in order to coordinate a joint strategy aimed at preventing a premature military venture. At the first summit (Cairo, January 1964), a decision was taken to divert the Jordan waters originating in Syria and Lebanon, and the second summit (Alexandria, September 1964) authorized the operational plans. The Israeli government decided not to wait until the completion of the diversion work, and the IDF took advantage of one of the frequent border conflicts in the demilitarized areas with Syria in order to strike against the engineering equipment along the diversion route in Syria. After merely two incidents—in March and May 1965—Nasser withdrew his support of the diversion plan. The third summit (Casablanca, September 1965) affirmed the cessation of the diversion work and concentrated on a coordinated three-year military plan toward an all-out war with Israel, for the purpose of eradicating it. Syria, for reasons of prestige and national honor, continued the diversion work in areas distant from the Israeli border, and the IDF initiated two additional actions to hit the diversion equipment and torpedo the work.

Israel enjoyed a clear victory in the battle over the water. In June 1964, the "National Conduit" began operating, and the water flowed uninterrupted. The Arab diversion plan, on the other hand, waned as a result of IDF operations. Even the all-Arab plan for an overall military confrontation with Israel, ratified at the Casablanca summit, quickly disintegrated as a result of the deep rift in the Arab world.

On June 5, 1967, two years after the battle over the Jordan water was determined, an all-out war between Israel and the Arab states broke out. Was the Six-Day War the continuation of the "war over the water"? The Arab failure in the battle over the Jordan water undoubtedly made an impact, and it may have contributed to the escalation leading to the war in June 1967. At the same time, the water conflict was not a direct cause of the war, which was mainly the result of guerrilla warfare by Palestinian organizations, primarily the Fatah, against Israel. The exacerbation of the hostilities, with Syria's support, and Israel's retaliatory military operations, brought the tension to a climax in the spring of 1967. Egyptian steps, encouraged by the Soviet Union, to deter Israel from initiating military action against Syria, triggered the crisis that ended in war. The conquering of the Golan Heights by the IDF was intended, *inter alia,* to provide Israel with control over the water sources. The "war over the water" remained no more than an historic episode.

NOTES

1. See Y. Rabin, *Service File* (Hebrew), Tel Aviv, 1979, pp. 119–125; H. Bartov, *Daddo* (Hebrew), Tel Aviv, 1978, pp. 106–113.

2. On water conflicts in the region, see A. Sofer, *Rivers of Fire: The Battle over the Water in the Middle East* (Hebrew), Tel Aviv, 1992.

3. See A. Even, *Life Chapters* (autobiography, Hebrew), Tel Aviv, 1978, p. 186.

4. See H. P. Frischwasser-Raanan, *The Frontiers of a Nation,* London, 1955, pp. 87, 91, 130–139

5. In early Israeli-Syrian contacts for the settling of the conflict, the Syrians demanded that the border run through the center of the Kinneret, the Hula Lake, and the Jordan River. See Husni Zaim's peace initiative, in I. Rabinovich, *The Road Not Taken: Early Arab-Israeli Negotiations* (Hebrew), Keter, Jerusalem, 1991, pp. 60–97. See also Syrian President Adib Shishakli's position, *FRUS 1952–1954, Vol. 9,* pp. 1042–1044. Syria's demand that Israel withdraw beyond the international border, and its insistance to regain control over the northeast shore of the Kinneret, was an important cause for the failure of U.S. President Bill Clinton's effort to reach an Israeli-Syrian peace agreement in the years 1999–2000.

6. On the armistice agreement between Israel and Syria, see A. Shalev, *Cooperation under the Shadow of Conflict* (Hebrew), Tel Aviv, 1989, pp. 15–146.

7. For a thorough and comprehensive survey of the Arab stand on the water conflict with Israel, see M. Shemesh, "The Arab Battle with Israel over Water," *Studies in the Establishment of Israel* (Hebrew), 7, 1997, pp. 103–168.

8. Shalev, *ibid.,* pp. 149–184; S. Golan, *Hot Border, Cold War,* Tel Aviv, 2000, pp. 301–334.

9. President Eisenhower appointed Eric Johnston on October 7, 1953. The goals of his mission were outlined in an October 13 letter by Secretary of State Dulles. The first: to secure the agreement of the states of Lebanon, Syria, Jordan, and Israel to the division and use of the waters of the Jordan River basin. The second goal was to secure agreement between Israel and Jordan on the internationalization of Jerusalem, should the State Department decide to hold a discussion on the subject. *FRUS, 1952–1954,* Vol. 9, pp. 1345–1348. On the Arab response to the Johnston plan, see Shemesh, *ibid.,* pp. 103–114; A. Rabinovich, "The Battle over the Jordan River Waters as a Component in the Israeli-Arab Conflict," in A. Shmueli, A. Sofer, N. Cliot (eds), *Lands of Galilee* (Hebrew), Ministry of Defense and Haifa University, 1983, pp. 863–868.

10. On the rising tension in the Israeli-Egyptian relations in 1955, see M. Bar-On, *The Gates of Gaza,* New York, 1994. On the general background in the Middle East during that period, see M. Shemesh, "The Kadesh Operation and the Suez Campaign: The Political Background in the Middle East 1949–1956," *Studies in the Establishment of Israel* (Hebrew), 4, 1994, pp. 66–97.

11. *Helsinki Rules on the Uses of the Waters of International Rivers,* The International Law Association, London, 1966, p. 3.

12. Shemesh, *The Arab Battle over the Water,* pp. 138–139.

13. On the implementation of the National Conduit plan, see E. Kalee, *The Struggle for the Water,* Tel Aviv, 1965, pp. 7–107. The most comprehensive description appears in S. Blass' book *Waters of Conflict and Enterprise* (Hebrew), Ramat Gan, 1973.

14. See report (page 8) in *Ha'aretz,* June 12, 1964, "The Conduit Waters Reached Rosh Ha'ayin."

15. Shemesh, *The Arab Battle over the Water,* pp. 164–166.

16. Rabinovich, *ibid.;* M. Kerr, *The Arab Cold War,* Oxford, 1967; P. Seale, *The Struggle for Syria,* London, 1964.

17. Major-General (res.) Moshe Dayan, who was appointed minister of agriculture after the elections, announced on the eve of the elections that the new government would divert the Jordan waters to the Negev, with or without Arab consent (*Ha'aretz,* October 5, 1959). And in another speech: "if the Arabs do not cooperate . . . we will take the water by force" (*Ha'aretz,* October 17, 1959). Finance Minister Eshkol announced after the elections that "the plan to divert the Jordan waters has become top priority" (*Ha'aretz,* November 19, 1959).

18. Shemesh, *The Arab Battle over Water,* pp. 133–134.

19. Shemesh, *ibid.,* pp. 129–141.

20. Shemesh, *ibid.,* pp. 149–151; A. Gluska, *Israel's Army Command and Political Leadership in the Face of the Security Problems, 1963–1967* (dissertation, Hebrew), The Hebrew University, Jerusalem, 2000, pp. 64–69.

21. *El-Ahram,* March 19, 1965.

22. Shemesh, *ibid.,* pp. 144–146.

23. Shemesh, *ibid.,* pp. 164–166.

24. *Ibid.,* pp. 148–164; Gluska, *ibid.,* pp. 70–84.

25. *Ha'aretz,* January 2, 1965.

26. M. Dayan, "Diverting the Jordan Sources," *Ha'aretz,* January 29, 1965.

27. Gluska, *ibid.*

28. *Ma'ariv,* January 17, 1965; *Yediot Aharonot,* March 5, 1965.

29. *Yediot Aharonot,* April 9, 1965.

30. A. Cohen, *Israel and the Bomb,* Shoken, Tel Aviv, 2000, pp. 276–281. After two years of inspections, the enterprise turned out to be economically unfeasible and was dismissed.

31. Rabin, *Service File,* a, p. 124.

32. Shemesh, *ibid.,* pp. 151–156. Golan, *ibid.,* pp. 857–858. Gluska, *ibid.,* pp. 78–80.

33. Shemesh, *ibid.,* p. 158. By "our primary goal," Nasser meant the elimination of the State of Israel.

34. Gluska, *ibid.,* pp. 80–83.

35. Shemesh, *ibid.,* pp. 161–163.

36. Shemesh, *ibid.,* pp. 137–138.

37. On relations and rivalries in the Arab world at that period, see M. Kerr, *The Arab Cold War 1958–1967,* Oxford University Press, 1967.

38. The new government in Syria was labeled "the doctors' government," due to the fact that three of its leading figures were physicians who served in the past as volunteers in the National Liberation Front revolt against the French, which led to Algeria's independence in 1962: Dr. Nur al-Din al-Atasi was the president, Dr. Yusuf Zuein served as prime minister, and Dr. Ibrahim Mahus was foreign minister. At the same time, the real power remained in the hands of the army officers, particularly the "strong man" Tzalah Jadid, minister of defense, air force Commander Hafez Asad, and Chief of Staff Muhammad Swidani. See P. Seale, *Asad of Syria* (Hebrew edition), Maarakhot, Tel Aviv, 1993, pp. 110–147.

39. Gluska, *ibid.*, pp. 85–150.

40. A. Cohen, *Defending Water Resources* (Hebrew), Tel Aviv, 1992, pp. 139–148.

41. Already in 1956, Israel agreed, following mediation efforts by UN Secretary-General Dag Hammarskjöld aimed at thawing the tension along the borders, to keep its patrol boats away from the Kinneret coast, which was under Syrian control. Bar-On, *ibid.*, p. 154.

42. For a detailed description of the incident, including background, maps, and sketches, as well as details of the investigation conducted by the General Command, see IDF Archive files 192/74/1378 and 192/74/1390. See also A. Cohen, *ibid.*, pp. 149–156; E. Weitzman, *Yours Is the Sky, Yours Is the Earth* (Hebrew), Tel Aviv, 1975, pp. 252–253.

43. Gluska, *ibid.*, p. 139.

44. On the escalation leading to the Six-Day War, see *ibid.*, pp. 153–291.

6

The Six-Day War

Michael Oren

At 7:10 in the morning Israel time, on June 5, 1967, some 200 Israeli fighter jets took off and flew south and southwest. Their targets were nineteen airfields in the Sinai peninsula and across the Suez Canal where Egypt had stationed the bulk of its air force. Thus began the third Arab-Israeli war, a conflict that was to change the course of the Middle East conflict and to alter the region's politics irrevocably.

The war had broken out within a "context of conflict" in the Middle East, an environment in which conflict was occurring on virtually every possible level—international, regional, and domestic. That context had generated an atmosphere in which the slightest spark could ignite a regional conflagration. This is precisely what happened in the months leading up to the major clash later known to the Arabs as the June War, or more commonly, the Six-Day War.

THE ORIGINS OF THE CONFLICT

On the international plane, the war was precipitated in part by escalating cold war tensions between the United States and the Soviet Union. The year 1967 saw the worsening of the war in Vietnam and the intensification of American airstrikes against Hanoi. These attacks deeply disturbed the Soviet Union, North Vietnam's staunchest ally. The Kremlin at the time was ruled by a troika consisting of Premier Alexi Kosygin, Communist Party leader Leonid Brezhnev, and President Nikolai Podgorny. Of the three, Brezhnev, with close ties to the Soviet military establishment, was particularly anxious to relieve the pressure on North Vietnam by fomenting minor crises elsewhere in the world—in the Middle East, for example.

The United States, for its part, was virtually powerless to avert such a crisis or to cope with it once it broke out. The administration of President Lyndon Baines

Johnson had come under increasing domestic criticism for its escalation of the Vietnam War, and was swiftly losing influence in Congress. With its forces and political capital so fully invested in Southeast Asia, the United States had few resources available for handling upheavals in the Middle East.

In the regional sphere, the 1960s gave rise to an Arab cold war every bit as vicious as that between the superpowers. The Arab World was bitterly divided between the conservative monarchies of Jordan, Saudi Arabia, Morocco, the sheikhdoms of the Persian Gulf, and the radical regimes of Egypt, Syria, and Iraq. The conflict found expression in a protracted civil war in Yemen, in repeated assassination attempts against Arab leaders, and propaganda campaigns in which Arab regimes relentlessly vilified one another.

Among the charges regularly exchanged between rival Arab regimes was that of pro-Zionism. Since the defeat of Arab forces in Israel's War of Independence in 1948, and in the aftermath of Israel's cooperation with Britain and France in the 1956 Suez War, opposition to Israel (or, as most Arabs preferred, "the Zionist entity") became integral to Arab identity. Consequently, the worst aspersion that one Arab leader could cast on another was to call him either a Zionist sympathizer or a collaborator with Israel. Fearing such allegations, the leaders of the Arab states bordering Israel, in particular Egypt and Syria, sought to prove their steadfastness on the Palestine issue by maintaining high levels of belligerency with Israel, sometimes to the point of provoking violence.

Israel, however, did not sit passively in the face of these provocations. Endowed with an activist and dynamic spirit, determined to maintain its deterrence power at all costs, Israel retaliated heavily against Arab displays of aggression. These reprisals in turn humiliated Arab regimes and increased the pressures on them to respond with even greater ferocity.

Finally, in the domestic dimension, the 1960s was a period of marked political and social instability in all the Arab countries and, to a significant degree, in Israel as well. Lacking roots in democratic institutions, Arab rulers were perennially forced to prove their legitimacy vis-à-vis rivals both in the region and at home. Opposition to Israel provided a convenient vehicle for establishing this legitimacy. In Israel, meanwhile, the end of the long premiership of David Ben-Gurion gave rise to new leaders who had yet to entirely prove themselves to the public. Demonstrating truculence against the Arabs was a prime means of establishing political bona fides in Israel.

All of these factors converged to create a "context of conflict" that was highly unpredictable, unstable, and potentially explosive. Though neither the superpowers nor most of the parties to the Arab-Israeli conflict wanted or even anticipated the outbreak of war, events would soon converge in an inexorable process leading ultimately to collision.

THE PATH TO WAR

Though no single event can be said to have sparked the Six-Day War, it is possible to trace the evolution of that conflict to November 1966. That month, tensions between Israel and Syria reached a climax. The Ba'thist regime in Damascus, eager to establish its primacy over domestic rivals and to arrogate the leadership of the Arab world, had launched a series of markedly aggressive actions against Israel.

These included attempts to divert the Jordan River, Israel's main supply of fresh water, and efforts to support Palestinian guerrillas of the al-Fatah organization under Yasser Arafat. Armed clashes also broke out along the Israel-Syrian border over various demilitarized zones separating the two countries. While Israeli forces succeeded in destroying Syria's diversion project and in gaining dominance over the demilitarized zones, they proved unsuccessful in stemming the guerrilla attacks, many of which were launched from Lebanon and Jordan.

In response to al-Fatah incursions, IDF Chief of Staff Yitzhak Rabin proposed mounting a major retaliation raid against Syria, but Levi Eshkol, Israel's prime minister and defense minister, feared that such an attack would provoke Soviet intervention against the Jewish State. It was therefore decided to strike back at a Palestinian stronghold in the West Bank village of Samu'a.

The operation, Israel's largest since the 1956 war, was conducted on November 13 and resulted in unexpected bloodshed. In addition to destroying much of the village, the Israelis also killed a number of Jordanian soldiers and so embarrassed Hussein, the king of Jordan. Hussein sought to regain his honor by blaming Egyptian President Gamal Abdul Nasser for failing to defend the West Bank and for "hiding behind the skirts of UNEF"—the UN peacekeeping force that had been placed in Sinai and the Gaza Strip at the end of the 1956 war. Nasser, the preeminent political figure in the Arab world, a man of prodigious pride, was deeply insulted by this charge, and searched for a means of ridding himself of United Nations Emergency Force (UNEF). That pretext was furnished to him on May 12, 1967, when the Soviet Union, still interested in igniting low-level crises in the Middle East, informed Egypt that it had uncovered a secret Israeli plan to invade Syria.

Though Nasser quickly ascertained that the Soviet warning was baseless—Israeli forces were not, as claimed, massed on the Syrian border—he saw it as the opportunity to evict UNEF. He issued orders to concentrate the force in Gaza and at Sharm al Sheikh, the Sinai promontory overlooking the Straits of Tiran, thereby exposing Israel's border to tens of thousands of Egyptian troops who then paraded into the peninsula. Nasser's aim was to win a bloodless political victory over Israel, and not to initiate a war by opening fire on Israeli forces or by blockading shipping through Tiran to Israel's vital southern port of Eilat. The de facto commander of Egypt's armed forces, however, Field Marshal 'Abd Hakim 'Amr, who had performed poorly in both the 1956 and Yemen wars, was eager to prove his mettle against Israel. He was also Nasser's principal contender for power. 'Amr revised the orders to UNEF, instructing the unit to exit the region entirely, and sent paratroopers to occupy Sharm al Sheikh. Thus positioned, Egypt had little choice but to close the Straits on May 22, thus providing Israel with a *casus belli,* a justification for waging war. Israel, however, did not want a war. Israeli leaders appealed to UN Secretary General U Thant to preserve UNEF's mandate, and to President Johnson to publicly declare America's support for Israel's defense. Rather than resist the Egyptian evacuation order, U Thant quickly capitulated to it, and advised UNEF to withdraw. Johnson, though bound by previous presidential pledges to protect Israel's rights in Tiran, explained that the Vietnam controversy precluded robust American intervention in the Middle East. Repeatedly warning Israeli foreign minister Abba Eban that "Israel will not be alone unless it decides to be alone," in going to war, the President proposed recruiting an international maritime convoy to break the Tiran blockade, by force, if necessary.

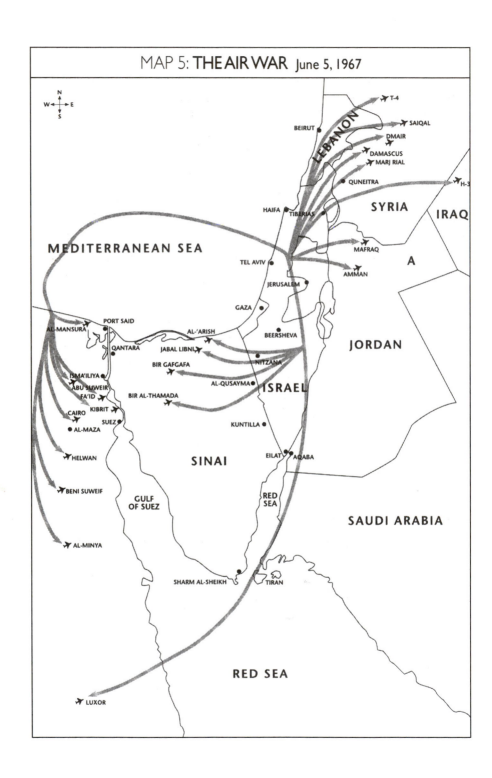

MAP 5: THE AIR WAR June 5, 1967

The worsening crisis presented the Israeli government with a number of dilemmas. The steady buildup of Egyptian forces in the south—100,000 men, 1,000 tanks, 400 warplanes—required the prolonged mobilization of Israeli reserves at a crippling cost to the national economy. There was also the danger posed by the blockade, which not only curtailed Israel's oil supplies but also impaired the country's ability to deter future bellicose acts. IDF commanders expressed deep fears—in fact unfounded— that Egypt planned to bomb Israel's most sensitive strategic site, the Dimona nuclear reactor. Though confronted with rising domestic criticism of his policy of restraint, Eshkol elected to wait and see whether Johnson could rally the maritime convoy. Israel was not alone in facing dilemmas, however. As public opinion in the Arab world reached an almost frenzied pitch at the prospect of Israel's demise, Hussein realized that he could no longer remain out of the fray. Nasser could defeat Israel and then turn his forces against Hussein, or lose and blame Hussein for his failure— either way the king would die. Hussein resolved to escape his predicament by signing a defense pact with Egypt and placing his army under direct Egyptian command. In a dramatic move on May 31, he flew to Cairo and met with his arch-nemesis, Nasser, and returned to Jordan later that day as a hero.

The conclusion of the Egyptian-Jordanian treaty, together with the previously signed Egyptian-Syrian and Egyptian-Iraqi pacts, meant that Israel was effectively surrounded on all sides by massing, hostile armies. Arab leaders proclaimed their intention to "meet in Tel Aviv" and to "drive the Jews into the sea." As its regional situation deteriorated, so too did Israel's international standing. France, once Israel's closest ally and principle supplier of arms, announced its intention to switch sides and support the Arabs. The Soviet Union, though opposed to starting a war, would not rein-in its Arab client-states. Most disturbingly for the Israelis, however, was the realization that Johnson had failed to rally support in Congress and among the maritime nations for his international convoy. On June 1, Eshkol was forced to relinquish his defense portfolio and to appoint in his place Moshe Dayan, the enigmatic and highly popular former chief of staff during the 1956 war.

Still, Dayan's nomination as defense minister did not mean that Israel went immediately to war. Many other ministers still doubted Israel's ability to win a multifront battle and to survive possible Soviet intervention. The U.S. position on the impending war also remained a mystery, and one that was scarcely clarified by Meir Amit, chief of the Mossad, who met with senior administration officials in Washington. It was only on June 4, after many pained and acrimonious debates, that the government finally decided on action. Even then, the operational plans were severely limited in scope. Israeli planes were to neutralize the Egyptian air force, while IDF tanks destroyed the first of three Egyptian defense lines in the Sinai. The entire campaign was to last no longer than forty-eight hours.

THE WAR: DAY ONE

Israeli planes struck the Egyptian airfields at 8:30 A.M., Egypt time, just as Egyptian pilots were sitting down for breakfast. Exploiting excellent intelligence regarding the position of Egyptian jets, and the fact that the Egyptians had left their planes unsheltered, the Israelis succeeded in bombing runways and strafing enemy jets before they could take off. The results shocked Israeli leaders. In just over an hour

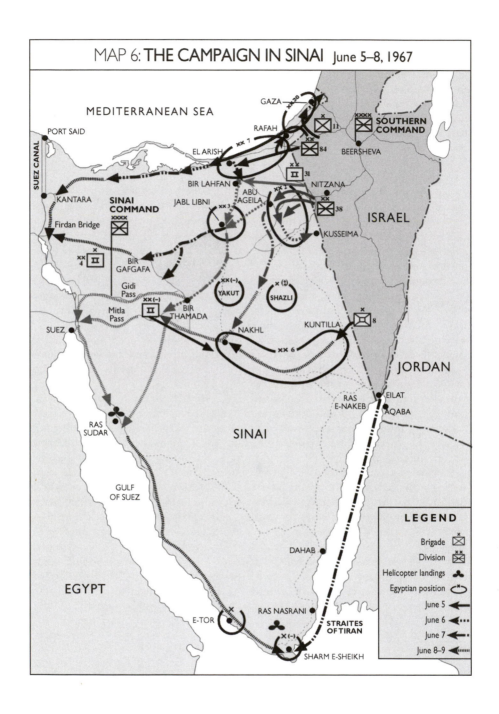

MAP 6: **THE CAMPAIGN IN SINAI** June 5–8, 1967

MEDITERRANEAN SEA

GAZA
PORT SAID
RAFAH
EL ARISH
SOUTHERN COMMAND
BEERSHEVA
BIR LAHFAN
NITZANA
KANTARA
SINAI COMMAND
JABL LIBNI
ABU AGEILA
ISRAEL
Firdan Bridge
KUSSEIMA
BIR GAFGAFA
Gidi Pass
YAKUT
SHAZLI
Mitla Pass
BIR THAMADA
SUEZ
NAKHL
KUNTILLA
JORDAN
RAS E-NAKEB
EILAT
AQABA
RAS SUDAR
SINAI
GULF OF SUEZ
DAHAB
EGYPT
E-TOR
RAS NASRANI
STRAITES OF TIRAN
SHARM E-SHEIKH

LEGEND

Brigade
Division
Helicopter landings
Egyptian position
June 5
June 6
June 7
June 8–9

and a half, the Israeli operation—code-named "Focus"—destroyed 286 Egyptian aircraft in one of the most audacious maneuvers in aviation history.

While Israeli planes were returning from their sorties, three Israeli armored divisions broke through Egyptian defenses in north, central, and southern Sinai. Significantly outnumbering the Israelis, the Egyptians were poorly led and haphazardly deployed. Scattered units did, however, put up a spirited defense, though not for long. Israeli forces generally progressed ahead of schedule, overcoming redoubts and crossing deserts once thought impassable. Some momentum was lost when the paratroopers, responding to fire from Palestinian gunmen, entered the Gaza Strip, a battle that Israel had hoped to avoid.

Learning of the attack, Egyptian military leaders appealed to their Syrian, Jordanian, and Iraqi allies to join in the conflict. After many delays, all three begrudgingly sent jets to strafe and bomb targets in northern Israel. These operations caused relatively little damage, and in counterstrikes launched that afternoon, the Israeli air force destroyed most of the Jordanian and Syrian air forces on the ground. Syrian troops positioned atop the Golan Heights proceeded to shell Israeli settlements in Northern Galilee, while Jordanian artillery situated in the West Bank and in East Jerusalem opened fire on Jewish Jerusalem and on the outskirts of Tel Aviv. Israel, however, reluctant to open additional fronts in the north and the east, refrained from crossing either border.

By midday on June 5, the Israeli war plans were proceeding excellently, but events on the ground soon outpaced them. Jordanian infantry, acting on false Egyptian reports of victories in the south, invaded a sensitive demilitarized zone in Jerusalem and prepared to assault the Israeli enclave on Mount Scopus. Fearing a pincer movement to encircle west (Jewish) Jerusalem, the Israelis ousted the Jordanians from the demilitarized zone and dispatched paratroopers to link up with Mount Scopus. Full-scale fighting in Jerusalem was accompanied by an armored thrust into the West Bank to silence the guns shelling Tel Aviv. An Eastern Front had been opened.

The diplomatic front, meanwhile, was no less confused. The Johnson administration had learned of the war at dawn but was unsure which side had started the fighting and which was winning it. Generally, the Americans were inclined to let Israel humble Nasser, but not at the price of a regional conflict that could escalate into a global showdown. The Israelis were interested in delaying a cease-fire resolution in the Security Council—an objective that was ironically shared by Arab representatives who, misinformed by their leaders back home, believed the Israelis were losing. The Soviets, although aware of the true situation on the battlefield, were reluctant to pressure the Arabs to accept a cease-fire in place.

By the end of the first day of fighting, Israel had freed itself from any serious aerial threat, and had made impressive ground gains in Sinai, Jerusalem, and the West Bank. An intelligence report received at the White House that evening described the war as a "turkey shoot."

THE WAR: DAY TWO

The second day of the war opened with an intense artillery barrage from the Golan Heights and an easily repulsed assault by Syrian ground troops against Israeli

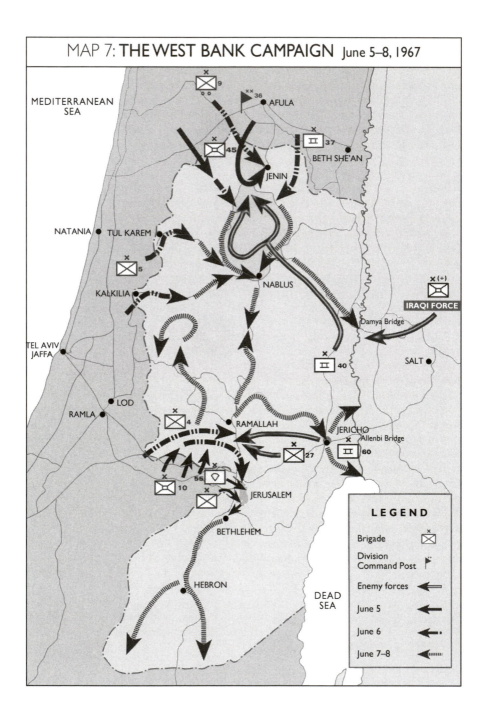

MAP 7: THE WEST BANK CAMPAIGN June 5–8, 1967

MEDITERRANEAN
SEA

AFULA

BETH SHE'AN

JENIN

NATANIA
TUL KAREM

KALKILIA

NABLUS

IRAQI FORCE

Damya Bridge

SALT

TEL AVIV
JAFFA

LOD

RAMLA

RAMALLAH

JERICHO
Allenbi Bridge

JERUSALEM

BETHLEHEM

HEBRON

DEAD
SEA

LEGEND

Brigade

Division
Command Post

Enemy forces

June 5

June 6

June 7–8

farms in the Galilee. While Israeli generals in the north pressed for permission to invade the Golan and silence the Syrian guns, Moshe Dayan, still wary of Soviet intervention, vetoed the idea. In contrast to the relatively static situation in the north, however, circumstances in the east and the south remained extremely fluid.

Jordanian forces in the West Bank fiercely resisted and inflicted heavy casualties on the Israeli invaders, but were slowly driven from their positions. By the end of the day, most were following Hussein's instructions to retreat across the Jordan, though the king later that night tried to reverse the order and to rally his men back to battle. In Jerusalem, too, the fighting raged at close quarters, often hand-to-hand, but there as well, Israeli troops gradually routed the Jordanians and nearly surrounded the Old City.

In the south Israeli forces advanced against dogged opposition in many parts of Sinai, and especially in Gaza. Yet the most dramatic development occurred around midday, when Nasser and 'Amr issued orders for a general retreat. The reasons for this decision remain obscure. Tactically, even without air cover, Egyptian forces, most of which had not fired a shot, could well have dug in and fought for days. Apparently, unnerved by the loss of their air force, and believing they could repeat the successful retreat of the 1956 war, Egypt's leaders told their troops to withdrawal beyond the Suez Canal. The disorganized evacuation of thousands of soldiers resulted in utter chaos. Many were left stranded in the desert, there to die of thirst, or trapped in massive traffic jams that provided easy targets for Israeli jets.

Pursuing the retreating Egyptians, the IDF quickly advanced beyond its maximum objectives, and its commanders thereafter had to improvise their war plans. These called for bypassing the Egyptians columns and blocking the entrance to the Gidi and Mitla Passes, the gateways to the Suez Canal. Dayan was adamant, however, that the Israelis were not to advance to the canal itself as they had in 1956, when the international community condemned Israel for the action.

In spite of the growing U.S. apprehensions over the fate of Hussein, a long-standing ally, the United States made no major effort to push through a cease-fire resolution of the Security Council. Neither did any of the other parties—Israeli, Arab, or Soviet. Within the White House, however, administration officials were already examining ways of translating Israel's anticipated military victory into a diplomatic breakthrough for peace. Many of the principles of future U.S. Middle East policy—the need for defensible borders, the right of all states to live in security, and the notion of land for peace—were forged on this day.

THE WAR: DAY THREE

Perhaps the most memorable moment of the war occurred at 11:30 in the morning on June 7, when Israeli paratroopers broke through the Lion's gate and entered the Old City of Jerusalem. The attack followed hours of intense diplomacy during which the United States pressured Israel to accept an undeclared cease-fire with Jordan, and Israel insisted on receiving an open cease-fire as well as a pledge for future peace talks with Jordan. Several ministers within Israeli government, Dayan among them, were also reluctant to capture Christian holy places, for fear of an international backlash. In the end, Hussein made the crucial decision by rejecting Israel's demands. With his army shattered and in full retreat, the king had little

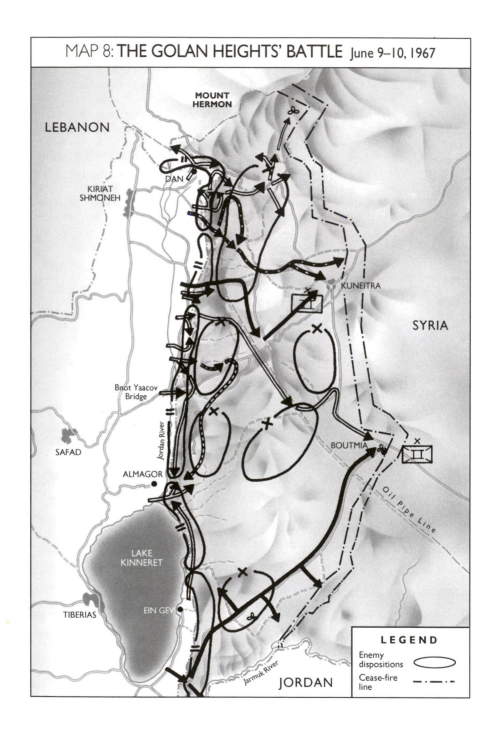

MAP 8: THE GOLAN HEIGHTS' BATTLE June 9–10, 1967

LEBANON

MOUNT HERMON

KIRIAT SHMONEH

DAN

KUNEITRA

SYRIA

Bnot Yaacov Bridge

SAFAD

Jordan River

BOUTMIA

ALMAGOR

Oil Pipe Line

LAKE KINNERET

TIBERIAS

EIN GEV

Jarmuk River

JORDAN

LEGEND

Enemy dispositions

Cease-fire line

choice but to concede the city. Just after 12:00, the paratroopers reached the Western Wall, the holiest site to Judaism, inspiring Jews and non-Jews worldwide.

While Israeli forces accepted the surrender of major West Bank cities—Nablus,
Hebron, Bethlehem—in Sinai, they closed the trap on Egyptian columns in the
Passes. For miles, the desert was strewn with the burnt-out wrecks of vehicles and
with the abandoned boots of fleeing soldiers. Elements of the Egyptian army managed to escape across the canal, but even that venue was rapidly closing as Israeli
units, in violation of Dayan's orders, reached the banks of Suez. At the same time,
a combined air-and-sea operation resulted in the capture, after scant resistance, of
Sharm al Sheikh. An Israeli flag now flew over the Straits of Tiran.

The bombardment of Israeli villages in the north continued, meanwhile, but IDF
commanders, backed by Eshkol, could not persuade Dayan to approve a counterattack. At most, Israeli jets were allowed to pummel Syrian positions, softening them
in case of a change of policy.

THE WAR: DAY FOUR

June 8 was a bitter day for Egypt, as its UN representative, Muhamed El Kony,
with tears in his eyes, announced his country's acceptance of an unconditional
cease-fire in place. Though sporadic fighting continued in Sinai and in Gaza, the
war in the south was effectively concluded. The remnants of the Egyptian army
streamed back to Cairo in shame.

Nevertheless, one of the most violent and disturbing events of the war occurred
on the afternoon of June 8, when Israeli jets and torpedo boats attacked an American spy ship, the USS *Liberty*. The boat had been sent to eavesdrop on Egyptian
troops and their Soviet advisors south of Gaza—neither were still in the vicinity—
but without informing the Israelis. Sighting an unidentified naval vessel in an active
war zone, the Israelis swiftly struck. Though greater caution might have been exercised by both the U.S. and the Israeli military, thus averting the tragedy, in the end,
the *Liberty* became the victim of a type of friendly fire accident that is all too common in battle. A total of 34 American servicemen were killed in the incident and
171 wounded.

Israel's artillery and aerial strikes against the Syrians in the Golan had begun to
take their toll by the evening of June 8, and in the Security Council, the Syrians
were indicating their willingness to accept the cease-fire. Aware of this, and sensing
that the Soviets would no longer intervene on the Syrians' behalf, Dayan reversed
his earlier opposition to attacking the Golan Heights, and ordered Israel's Northern Command into action.

THE WAR: DAY FIVE

Israel's assault on the Golan Heights began at dawn, and in spite of heavy air
and artillery cover, Israeli forces encountered stiff resistance. Progress up the steep
and heavily mined Golan escarpment was excruciatingly slow. Learning of Dayan's
unilateral decision to sanction the invasion, the Israeli cabinet criticized the defense
minister, and reviewed the possibility of stopping the action. Permission was eventually given for twenty-four hours of battle, to end at noon on June 10.

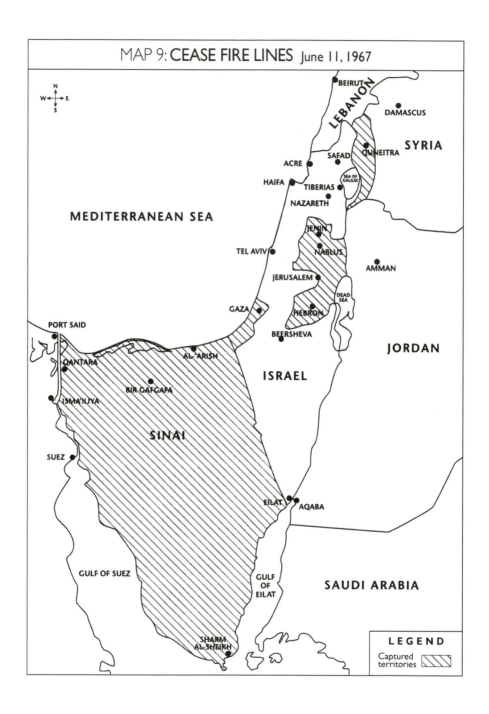

MAP 9: CEASE FIRE LINES June 11, 1967

LEGEND
Captured territories

News of the Israeli incursion also set tempers flaring in the Security Council, where the Soviet representative Nikolai Federenko accused the Israelis of plotting to take Damascus and likened them to Nazis. The United States, though eager to see a Syrian defeat, began to show concern over the Soviets' willingness to intercede to save Syria, and began to urge the Israelis to conclude their action as soon as possible.

THE WAR: DAY SIX

Under mounting pressure both from Washington and from cabinet ministers in Jerusalem, and in the face of withering Syrian fire, Israeli forces advanced eastward across the Golan plateau. The noon deadline passed and still the attack continued. Dayan tried to buy time by engaging in cease-fire talks with UN representatives, but the Soviets would not be put off.

On the morning of June 10, Kosygin hot-lined Johnson in the White House, to the effect that the Soviet Union would soon adopt "an independent position," and "undertake military action," if Israel did not cease its aggression. President Johnson refused to buckle to this threat, and ordered the U.S. Sixth Fleet to block any possible move by Soviet forces in the Mediterranean. Simultaneously, however, he informed the Israelis in no uncertain terms that they would have to stop fighting at once. The battle indeed stopped at 6 P.M. that evening. The Six-Day War was over.

THE ENDURING LEGACY

History holds few examples of events so limited in their duration and geographical scope but which have had such long-term regional and even global ramifications. The Six-Day War was such an event. On a purely military plane, the war resulted in one of the most startling and lopsided victories in the annals of modern warfare. Israel destroyed over 600 enemy warplanes, thousands of tanks and armored vehicles, and inflicted tens of thousands of casualties. The price of this victory was also high, however, especially for a small country like Israel: 20 percent of the air force lost, over 700 soldiers killed.

The strategic and political impact of the war, no less than its military outcome, was immense. From a situation in which of all its major population and industrial centers were within range of Arab artillery, Israel had literally turned the guns on the Arabs, and now threatened all of their capitals. In six short days, the Jewish State had captured the entire Sinai peninsula, the Gaza Strip, the West Bank, and the Golan Heights, almost quadrupling the territory under its control. It had dealt a severe blow to Soviet prestige in the Middle East, and gained a new superpower ally, the United States.

The war also changed Israel culturally and demographically. Reunited with their historical, Biblical homeland, the Jews of Israel became less Israeli and more Jewish—a development rife with ramifications for Israeli politics. A year after the war, Israeli religious activists established the first settlement in the West Bank, in Hebron. Israel's victory also reunited the Palestinians of the West Bank and Gaza who, since 1948, had been divided by the Jewish State, and who now were joined with their Israeli Arab compatriots under a single rule—Israel's.

The Arab world was also radically altered by the war. The age of Nasserism and secular pan-Arabism had come to an end. In their place arose new ideologies, in particular Islamic extremism, which claimed to remedy the ills that had brought on the Arabs' defeat. No less significant was the rise of Palestinian nationalism, and of the Palestine Liberation Organization, a movement originally founded by Nasser for propaganda purposes. By 1968, the PLO, under the leadership of Yasser Arafat, had become a prominent force in inter-Arab politics.

Thirty-six years later, the Middle East is still grappling with the results of the Six-Day War. Israel and the Palestinians have yet to agree on the final status of the West Bank, Jerusalem, and Gaza, and many Arab states remain in a de facto state of war with Israel. The United States, still striving to apply UN Resolution 242 enacted immediately after the war, continues to play a central role in efforts to reach an Arab-Israel peace. Yet, in addition to opening opportunities for diplomacy, the Six-Day War also laid the groundwork for future hostilities, beginning with the Yom Kippur War of October 1973. It is perhaps too early to reach a conclusion on the impact of 1967 on the Middle East, only to say that it has indeed been profound.

7

The Israeli-Egyptian "War of Attrition," 1969–1970

Dan Schueftan

Between the drama of the 1967 war and the trauma of the 1973 war, the 1969–1970 Israeli-Egyptian "War of Attrition" is all but forgotten. An in-depth study of that war is not only interesting as an epilogue of the Six-Day War and the prologue of the Yom Kippur War. It is important not only because it became a political-military laboratory that exposed the structural flaws of Nasser's grand strategy of the 1950s and 1960s, but also because Sadat formulated his own grand strategy primarily on the basis of the lessons learned from these structural flaws. In more ways than one, this was "Nasser's last stand"; like General Custer's almost a century earlier, it was doomed because it was based on a profound misperception of the balance of power.

In one very important sense, the Arab-Israeli conflict should be studied in three different contexts: the pre-Nasser era (1947/8–1954), Nasser's era (1955–1970), and the post-Nasser era (from 1970 on). Nasser is so crucially important, even in a perspective of one third of a century after his death, because he is the only one that offered the Arabs a real hope of fundamentally changing their standing in the world and "liberating Palestine" in the process. The Six-Day War may have been his last monumental failure, but the strategic impasse represented by the War of Attrition was the ultimate proof that the hopes he raised could no longer be resurrected. Whatever the medical reason for his premature death at the end of this war, politically, he died of a broken heart.

To understand the full significance of the War of Attrition, one needs to go back to Nasser's dramatic impact on the Arab world, to identify what hung in the balance in that war, and to evaluate the impact of its outcome on the political and strategic reality in the region in the last three decades of the previous century.

The pre-Nasser period of the Arab-Israeli conflict was characterized by a confused Arab world, confronted with the challenge of the Jewish State, completely
unprepared and surprisingly defeated in the 1947–1949 war, mainly because of its
internal divisions, its social weaknesses, and its corrupt regimes and state structures. Not only was there no all-Arab strategy for the struggle against Israel, there
was hardly anything beyond empty rhetoric and no operative concept anywhere of
how to go about it.

NASSER'S ERA AND HIS POST-1967 DILEMMA

The early stage of Nasser's era was not much different, as far as strategy and
operative measures were concerned, but something fundamental had changed in
the broader regional and global context that presented a grave, even existential,
challenge to Israel. Within a very short time, Nasser managed to inspire millions of
Arabs to underwrite a radical policy that produced enormous and immediate political and strategic dividends. He masterminded an ingenious concept that allowed
Egypt (and other "nonaligned" states) to benefit from the cold war by undermining
vital Western strategic interests, and threatening the United States with an even further damage to its global position.

For almost a decade, from the mid-1950s to the mid-1960s, Nasser managed to
secure, at the same time, massive support from the Soviet Union, as well as major
assistance from the Eisenhower and Kennedy administrations. The success of this policy catapulted Nasser, Egypt, and the Arabs to a position of regional and global significance unknown in modern times. Nasser's impressive gains on the international
scene were rivaled only by his messianic position among the Arabs. His leadership
and achievements were widely perceived as the ultimate answer to the generations-
long Arab quest for power and respect, reflected in such perceived victories as the
1956 Suez crisis and the 1958 Egyptian-Syrian union in the United Arab Republic.

Unlike other would-be messiahs, Nasser seemed to deliver even more than he
promised. Millions, "from the [Atlantic] Ocean to the [Persian or 'Arab'] Gulf,"
were convinced that Arab unity, international glory, and the consequent "liberation of Palestine" were at hand. Even when miraculous successes could no longer
be delivered, and the first cracks in the glorious picture began to show (the breakdown of the union with Syria, the dead-end in the Yemen War), these were first
perceived as temporary setbacks that could still be rectified. Even the significance
of the crucial change in U.S. policy when President Johnson came to power was
gravely underestimated. Most Arabs initially considered the May–June 1967 crisis
before the war erupted as Nasser's comeback, rather than as the final indication of
the demise of his power.

The colossal defeat of 1967 was so traumatic to the Arabs because they assumed
even in the late 1960s that Nasser's success story, diluted as it may have been, was
largely intact and reflected the "real" regional and global balance of power. This
defeat had shaken the very foundations of their self-image, not only because it
could no longer be blamed on corrupt regimes or lack of all-Arab coordination; the
defeat was traumatic also because it challenged the pervasive belief that the Arabs
had finally found the political recipe and charismatic leadership that would reflect,
in the modern era, the greatness the Arabs had manifested in the distant past, a
greatness that they inherently possessed and richly deserved.

Nasser's dilemma following the 1967 defeat was, therefore, not only political and strategic, but, to some extent, even cultural. His messianic movement produced the ultimate test to prove what the Arabs were worth, and it ended in a humiliating debacle: The Arabs as a civilization, not only their 1967 armies and specific strategies, were weighed in the balance and found wanting. The challenge on the seventh day of the Six-Day War was not merely to proceed in the most effective way in the conflict with Israel, or to restore the territories that were occupied; the challenge was to salvage the greatest hope the Arab nation had ever possessed in modern times, and resurrect its chance to play a respected role in the world that Nasser secured for the Arabs for the first time since they were humiliated in the encounter with the West, more than a century and a half earlier.

This required, above all else, a rejection of the meta-political defeat, even in the face of military failure and major negative changes in the balance of political power. The armies may have lost on the battlefield; Egypt, Syria, and Jordan may have lost precious land including Jerusalem to Israel; and the "cause of Palestine" may have suffered a temporary setback, but the Arab nation did not lose its well-justified claim for a role in the world befitting its great heritage. Nasser had to prove that he was not transformed by the defeat to become a domesticated minor Arab despot of the kind Washington sought to deal with.

Whereas the Arabs insisted that what they had lost in 1967 must be restored to its rightful owners, Nasser could not come to the negotiating table as a beggar, exchanging the fruits of Israel's 1967 "aggression" for "peace" that would legitimize the original 1948 "aggression" that created Israel. By the same token, he could not be perceived as the Arab leader who was compelled, in the shadow of defeat and helplessness, to have accepted the American dominance in the Middle East. To acquiesce with these two would have meant that the Arabs struggled in vain for decades and that Nasser, his generation, and millions of Arabs had surrendered their lives' hopes and ambitions.

Nasser's post-1967 dilemma was that on the one hand, he was far too weak to pursue his pre-1967 strategy and, on the other hand, could not possibly afford to abandon his quest for Arab power and dignity, betraying everything he believed in and symbolized to his people. Dictating his terms to Israel (let alone defeating it) was beyond his power, while "peace" that accepted and legitimized Israel's existence was perceived as the worst possible humiliation. Nasser had to do something dramatic to change the post-1967 reality, but there was almost nothing he could do that would produce the dramatic effect he needed.

THE CONCEPT OF THE WAR OF ATTRITION

This predicament produced, in time, more as a trial-and-error policy than as a carefully crafted and meticulously orchestrated master plan, the political-military strategy that came to be known as "The War of Attrition." Rather than Nasser's weapon of choice, it represented his "instrument of no choice" or strategy of last resort. Acutely aware of its flaws, dangers, and shortcomings, he was forced to pursue it only because the alternatives would have produced immediate disaster.

Nasser's point of departure was the need to elevate the conflict from the bilateral Israeli-Arab level to the global level. On the bilateral and regional level, Israel obviously had the upper hand, hence Israel's insistence on direct face-to-face negotiations without preconditions. On the global level, however, Nasser's position may have been very difficult, but not altogether hopeless. It was difficult because the Soviet Union could not deliver the goods he needed and the United States did not want to. The Russians could (and very quickly and effectively did) rebuild his armed forces, but could not "deliver" one-sided Israeli concessions. The United States, on the other hand, could break Israel and force it to unilaterally abandon its territorial acquisitions, as it did in 1957, but the Johnson administration, unlike the Eisenhower administration a decade earlier, did not want to reward Arab radicalism and Soviet adventurism by doing so.

President Johnson was determined to learn from past mistakes and force the radical anti-American forces in the Middle East to pay the price of the dangerous policies they had pursued in the 1960s. He presented Nasser with a choice: either abandon these policies, demonstrate to would-be radicals that they do not pay by yielding to the American "rules of the game," or be stuck with the consequences of this radicalism, exposing Egypt's impotence, as well as the inability of its Soviet supporters to extract the Arabs from their predicament.

With the Soviet Union unable and the United States unwilling to help him, Nasser was left, even on the global level, with not much hope, let alone a solution to his problem. Acutely aware of his military inadequacies and the insignificance of any measure other than American political pressure on Israel, Nasser was desperate to find a way to force the United States into a course of action that the president was determined not to pursue.

With Egypt and the Arabs weaker than ever before, and the order taller than ever presented to the administration in Washington, a desperate measure was called for. This desperate measure was "The War of Attrition." It was desperate because it called for an exhausted Egypt that just suffered a humiliating defeat to embark on another war that it would inevitably lose. Nasser knew he could not win it militarily, but concluded that the spectacle of yet another Egyptian debacle would draw the Soviet Union in, to maintain its credibility as a superpower. He hoped that such involvement would present the United States with a choice between letting Israel be defeated by the Soviet Union, on the one hand, and major American involvement that could deteriorate into global confrontation, on the other.

Nasser assumed that, faced with such an impossible choice, the United States would go out of its way to stop the war. Since Nasser started it, and since the danger of losing it militarily did not deter Egypt from continuing the war, Nasser would have to be politically motivated by American inducements to put an end to the war. This inducement could only be pressure on Israel to yield the territories occupied in 1967 without Egypt and the Arabs having to make, in return, any real political concessions that would legitimize the Jewish State in their midst.

Having presented this elaborate concept, it is important to repeat that is merely a stream-lined reconstruction of Nasser's de-facto strategy, rather than an A-priory, meticulously calculated master plan. Nasser started the War of Attrition in the early spring of 1969 (after a short prelude in the autumn of 1968), hoping to confront Israel with a new kind of war, which Israel could not possibly win.[1] He knew Israel needed its wars to be decided quickly by the kind of superior initiative, maneuverability, accurate firepower, ingenuity, technology, and organization that only a modern society and a sophisticated military machine could provide. Nasser designed this war in a way that prevented these advantages of Israel from coming to the fore;

his version emphasized the Egyptian advantages—low regard for casualties, massive firepower with random consequences, and proven absorption capability both in the battlefield and on the home front.

Having been defeated in the worst possible way in 1967, all Nasser expected now was to deny Israel a quick and decisive victory, while claiming hundreds of Israeli lives and draining Israel's limited resources. At this early stage, he wanted the war to threaten the stability of the Middle East, thereby convincing the United States of the need to stop the war at the political expense of Israel. When he still believed he could determine the nature of the war, Nasser probably did not expect the Soviet involvement to become half as direct and massive as it eventually did, to the point in which it could produce a major and immediate threat of global confrontation. It was only when Nasser was defeated at his own game that a much more dangerous version of his original strategy became necessary.

A WAR GONE SOUR

By the autumn of 1969, Israel adapted to the new military challenge. Resorting to her advanced air power, Israel took the war gradually into Egypt. The first phase started in July 1969 and focused on the systematic destruction of Egypt's massive air-defense system, built to cope with Israel's air superiority, which the Arabs were unable to challenge. By the winter of 1969/70, this Israeli campaign was so successful that Egypt was completely helpless, with its cities and infrastructure at the mercy of Israeli jets. This was not only the failure of the Egyptian military, the massive air-defense system was state-of-the-art Soviet equipment and strategy. If Israel could circumvent and subsequently destroy the defenses of Cairo and bomb infrastructure at the outskirts of the city at-will with American planes, the defense of Moscow could hardly be considered dependable.

In late 1969 to early 1970, Nasser's war was getting out of hand. The challenge to Egypt was not only in the air, and far beyond military: When an Israeli armored column proved in September 1969 that it could operate freely on the African shore of the Gulf of Suez under an effective air umbrella, without Nasser even knowing what was happening or what to do, this was no longer a war in which Israel was attritioned and Nasser determined "the rules of the game."

In January 1970, after Israel started to make careful and selective use of the new freedom of action over Egypt, with "deep penetration air raids" against military and infrastructure targets even in the outskirts of Cairo, in the Nile Valley, and in the Delta, the rules of the game changed. At this point Brezhnev realized no less than Nasser that the Soviet patron, as well as the Egyptian client, was about to be compromised; it was here that he was forced to embark on the final state of the war— "the superpower gambit." On the one hand, this chapter in the war demonstrated to Israel the limits of its military potential and its self-evident inability to play in the "big league" of major powers. On the other hand, it forced Nasser to accept that even his most desperate measures and his willingness to make enormous sacrifices could only produce meager political progress towards his desired objective.

Israel's bitter lesson came in the spring and the early summer of 1970. The Soviet Union introduced into Egypt not only its most sophisticated equipment and its own organic units, but also the massive, practically unlimited resources a superpower can commit when its global prestige is at stake. Israel could defeat the individual

Soviet pilot or missile, and the electronic warfare or air-control systems, but could not cope with the massive deployment of inexhaustible resources. When the Soviet air-defense system fired against a single Israeli plane as many surface-to-air missiles as a medium-size country would stock, Israel was simply "outgunned" (or "outmissiled"). Elementary extrapolation told the IDF that it would be banging its head against the Soviet missile war.[2]

But the Egyptian political predicament was even more frustrating than the Israeli military impasse. Nasser came to Moscow in January 1970 as a defeated head of state, seeking to convince his global patron to prevent another collapse of an important client. He had to threaten Brezhnev, Kosygin, and Podgornyi with resignation, imply replacement with a pro-American leader in Egypt, and explicitly mention embracing exposure of the uselessness of the Soviet superpower umbrella to convince his host to send its own armed forces to protect Egypt from Israel's superior power. The Russians understood that they had no choice but major involvement. They may have decided to save the credibility of their global position and arms systems even before Nasser made his desperate plea, but preferred to come to Egypt at the request of its distraught president.

By now it was a different ballgame altogether: No longer an Egyptian attempt to force on the United States a change of policy vis-à-vis Israel that would satisfy Nasser's needs, but an urgent and vital need of the Soviet leadership, as well as the American administration, to stop the Egyptian-Israeli War of Attrition before it escalated into global confrontation. At this point, Nasser no longer had the choice of stopping the war only if his political demands were met in Washington, or protracting it if they were rejected.

Not only was Nasser himself totally and hopelessly defeated and helpless; the Soviets that came to his rescue were eager and determined to stop the war no less than the Americans, regardless of Nasser's preferences. Egypt was unable to pursue the war as a political instrument; the Soviet's were running the show and Egypt was not even a major player anymore. The Soviets only wanted to make the point to the Americans that Israel could not, again, with impunity defeat Egypt and demonstrate the impotence of Egypt's patron. When they accomplished this limited objective, they were ready to stop the war and eager to do so in the earliest practicable moment.

Nasser's strategic objective was far more ambitious: to use the American fear of global confrontation in order to convince the United States to force Israel out of the territories occupied in 1967, without a major political quid-pro-quo. The broader context of this objective was no less important: to prevent the institutionalization of the major negative change in the balance of power produced by the 1967 war and restore the bulk of his bargaining power of the 1950s and the 1960s. All Nasser could get, after almost two years of pain and defeat, was a mild and ambiguous formula ("the Rogers initiative") that proved to be politically hollow.[3]

While Israel was licking its wounds, it still managed to make its most important point: If the Arabs wanted what they had lost in 1967, they would have to legitimize what Israel had captured and maintained since 1948. This, in fact, happened on the Egyptian front only some seven lean years and a major war (1973) later, but it was made possible by Nasser's defeat in his 1969–1970 "last stand" in the War of Attrition.

SADAT'S LESSONS OF THE WAR IN THE POST-NASSER ERA

Sadat's lessons of the War of Attrition are crucially important for the post-factum evaluation of the war in its full historical context. Two lessons stand out—one military, and the other political.

The military lesson concerned the evaluation of the essential balance of power between Israel and Egypt. Sadat's conclusion determined not only his 1973 strategy, but also his subsequent 1977 initiative, and was reflected in Mubarak's policy after Sadat's assassination. It was not only the IDF's performance in the 1967 war, but also its overwhelming and sustainable air dominance in the War of Attrition that convinced Sadat of Israel's strategic predominance as a lasting feature of its relations with the Arab world. What left its mark on Sadat's assessment was not only the fact that it took a superpower to suppress this dominance at the end of the war in 1970, but also the acknowledgment that even a superpower had to resort to massive employment of unsophisticated systems to cope with the advanced challenge of the Israeli air force.

The combined outcomes of the Six-Day War and the War of Attrition convinced Sadat, a decade or two before the rest of the Arab world came to the same conclusion, that in a conventional war the Arabs could prevail over a modern and technologically advanced Israeli society. The 1967 victory could be perceived as a one-time surprise achievement against unprepared Arab armies; the War of Attrition demonstrated that Israel could present a challenge that even a superpower did not find easy to meet.

These conclusions were reflected in the 1973 war. On the one hand, the Soviet Union prepared a massive surface-to-air missile system that effectively suppressed the Israeli air superiority for the crucially important first days of the war, on the other hand, as Sadat expected, this could only detain Israel for a very short time from manifesting its overwhelming strategic predominance. Sadat knew even better than his generals that, militarily, Israel could have decisively defeated Egypt three weeks after the war had started.

Based on the lessons of the War of Attrition, Sadat designed the 1973 war as a short period of intense fighting of controlled and limited scope, to be immediately followed by a meticulously preplanned political move (see following discussion) designed to stop Israel before it could bring to bear this strategic preponderance. The military action was not designed to break Israel's back or attrition it to submission, but to shake it, not to reconstruct the pre-1967 reality, but to find for Egypt a less painful and humiliating way to adapt to the changed balance of power and make the best of it.

The political lessons of the War of Attrition were even more far-reaching and long-lasting than the military. Sadat's most important lesson from the Nasser era in general, and from his predecessors' last three years in particular, concerned the futility and the prohibitive costs of Nasser's defiant policy vis-à-vis the United States. Nasser's grand strategy rested on the assumption that the United States could afford a confrontation with the radical leadership of the Arab world, particularly when it played a major role in the "nonaligned" (or "Third-World") movement. While this apprehension indeed dictated American policy in the mid-1950s and prevailed in the early 1960s, President Johnson, nevertheless, pursued a different approach after the mid-1960s. Sadat understood that Nasser underestimated the determination of Presidents Johnson and Nixon not to save the still-defiant-but-beaten Egyptian ruler after 1967 from the consequences of his radical anti-American policy, the way President Eisenhower had a decade earlier.

The War of Attrition represented a major effort by Nasser to force on the United States a counterproductive and dangerous policy in the shadow of a threat of global confrontation. President Nixon and his national security advisor Kissinger were even more determined than other American leaders to deny minor "Third-World" despots the option of threatening the United States and forcing a policy on it that would encourage radicalism and extortion. In the case of Egypt, this determination had an additional dimension, because the defeat of Nasser's radicalism and the demonstration of Soviet impotence to extricate a major client from a dire predicament were expected to send the desired message to many others and produce positive effects on the global balance of power of the cold war.

Both Kissinger and Nixon considered the region to be a volatile "powder keg" and were fully aware of the unique danger of global confrontation in the Israeli-Egyptian War of Attrition. They knew that direct and massive Soviet involvement made this danger immeasurably more acute, and were determined to stop the war every bit as much as Nasser hoped and expected them to be. They were even prepared to make Israel carry the brunt of the political costs for a speedy termination of the war and the removal of that threat. But they would have been prepared to do so only if Nasser would have contributed his share by a major shift from Soviet client to a more cooperative, not to say domesticated, leader and abandon his active policy of undermining of American interests in the Arab world and far beyond.

With Nasser militarily defeated to the point of impotence, the Soviet Union, every bit as apprehensive as the United States of global confrontation, and a defiant Nasser refusing to know his place, Nixon had no motivation to award the radical Egyptian despot with yet another 1957-style strategic victory by forcing Israel to yield to his terms. Sadat's 1973 political strategy proved that he understood only too well that the meager 1970 political returns for the enormous effort and sacrifice of the War of Attrition could be traced to Nasser's unrealistic expectations of the United States, even more than to the military defeat vis-à-vis Israel. Sadat's strategy, on the other hand, was built in advance on a major, even historic shift in Egypt's global orientation. While Nasser tried to coerce the United States by inducing deeper and deeper Soviet involvement, Sadat attempted to win the Americans over by bringing them in, at the expense of his previous patron.

Sadat's military and the political lessons converged on October 16, 1973, when he realized that Israel's strategic predominance was beginning to show and he called on Kissinger to save Egypt from another defeat. This time Kissinger did play one part of the role Nasser has expected him to, because he realized that this would be the first step in Egypt's abandonment of its intimate ties with the Soviet Union, opening the door for American hegemony in this crucial region.

The War of Attrition was a hopeless attempt by a defeated leader of an exhausted underdeveloped ("developing") country, to dictate his terms to a modern regional power and to the most important global power, while "The Arab World" he claimed to speak for was far less united or potent than he believed it to be. The 1973 war was, by contrast, a successful attempt to reestablish the Egyptian prominence in the Arab world on a different basis and to improve its bargaining position vis-à-vis Israel by accepting the predominant role of the United States. The difference between the unmitigated failure of the first and the relative success of the second reflects the distinction between Nasser's quest for Arab greatness and glory, on the one hand, and Sadat's resignation to a more realistic assessment of the regional and global balance of power, on the other.

"THE FORGOTTEN WAR" IN HISTORIC PERSPECTIVE

The War of Attrition is all but forgotten on both sides. In Egypt and in the Arab world, nobody can forget the 1967 defeat and everybody wants to remember only the first few glorious days of the 1973 War of Ramadan, conveniently suppressing the rest. On the Israeli side, the 1967 Six-Day War is well remembered as Israel's one and only ultimate and clear-cut victory. Concerning the 1973 Yom Kippur War, Israelis strangely share the Arab perception, remembering only the initial traumatic phase and forgetting the impressive achievements against impossible odds that brought Egypt to the brink of collapse, to be saved only by the American intercession.

Both sides prefer to forget the 1969–1970 War of Attrition, not only because both had very little tangible achievements to show for it, but also because it was so difficult to comprehend. In the Six-Day War, Israel could point at salvation from an existential threat, a fundamental change, very positive even if problematic, in Israel's standing in the regional and global arenas, an improved strategic position, and tangible territorial games, including Jerusalem. In the 1973 war, the Arabs could claim a victory of sorts, salvage their dignity, and demonstrate that they had considerably improved their bargaining position vis-à-vis Israel.

In the War of Attrition no side could claim an achievement that people could relate to. Militarily, Nasser never had far-reaching objectives; even the little he expected came to naught. His only consolation could have been that his defeat and humiliation were not as bad and visible as they were in 1967 and that he caused Israel some pointless suffering, too. Politically, Nasser could not point at one single, meaningful achievement, except having caused Israel to pay for the perpetuation of its occupation.

The Israeli achievements were preventive in nature or long-term and too complicated to leave a mark on the perception of Israelis and others. There is no way Israel could have celebrated the prevention of the massive negative impact that the war could have had on the American global and regional strategy, dictating Nasser's terms to Israel. Israelis were understandably more impressed with the IDF's inability to cope with the massive Soviet presence in Egypt than with the fact that it took such a massive involvement, in the first place, for the Soviet Union to deal with the Israeli air force. The outcome and impact of the 1973 war were traumatic enough, without introducing into the Israeli public debate the argument that Sadat's lessons from the War of Attrition helped him shape the strategy that actually worked a few years later.

It is, thus, left to the historians to set a complex event like the War of Attrition in its proper perspective. It seems that the major macrolesson this perspective can offer goes back to the unique phenomenon of Nasser's messianic movement: This war was the ultimate test to the limits of Arab radicalism; it proved, to the extent that such proof is possible, that under the terms that prevailed at the time (and still prevail one generation later) the Arabs could not play a major role in world affairs to the extent of dictating a major change in American foreign policy.

The second half of the twentieth century witnessed two major changes in international norms. The first was the product of the final disintegration of the old colonial order and the emergence of an unprecedented number of new sovereign states. In the middle of the century, this newly established sovereignty of these nations was perceived as absolute and widely considered as a desirable contrast to the denial of basic national rights in the colonial era. The cold war strengthened this tendency by providing a Soviet shield to new nations that pursued violent and radical policies of undermining American interests. In 1956, this new norm became institutionalized, when the United States itself saved Nasser from paying the price of his radical, anti-American practices.

The second and countervailing change in international norms came a few decades later. The first indication of change appeared in the late 1960s, following the Six-Day War. The old norms were completely reversed in the 1990s, following the collapse of the Soviet Union and in the beginning of the millennium, following September 11 and the subsequent American "War on Terrorism." In the year 2003, the circle was closed with the occupation of Iraq and the capture of Sadam Hussein. The essence of this change is that "Third World" countries no longer enjoy the immunity of their sovereign status or the shield of another superpower when they provoke the United States.

Nasser's historic mistake in the War of Attrition was that he grossly underestimated the slow but very consistent shift in the *zeitgeist,* assuming that the Arabs had much more political clout left even after the 1967 defeat. The shift was not as profound as it became at the end of the century, but Nasser did not realize how far it had already gone and paid the price of being out of step.

Sadat's lessons from the War of Attrition—military and political—were not only on the operative level. He understood the essence of the new and much less favorable era immeasurably better than his predecessor and adjusted Egypt to the new circumstances. The mainstream in the Arab world were almost as unwilling as Nasser was during the War of Attrition to accept the new constraints. It took decades longer than Sadat's rule for most of the Arab world to abandon Nasser's fantasies. A few Arab regimes persisted with similar fantasies of grandeur and policies of defiance even in the new millennium.

NOTES

1. Clashes along the Suez Canal had been a permanent feature since July 1967. In September and October 1968, Egypt initiated massive artillery barrages along the Canal front, killing twenty-five Israelis and wounding fifty-two. Israel responded with commando raids deep in the Nile Valley, hitting bridges and a transformation station. Israel used the relative lull in military activities between November 1968 and February 1969, when Egypt was preoccupied with putting its home front in order, to build fortified strongholds along the Canal that came to be called "The Bar-Lev Line" (after Israel's chief of the general staff at the time). Major artillery barrages were renewed in early March 1969. In late April–early May 1969, Egypt announced its departure of the ceasefire that ended the Six-Day War. After that, "The War of Attrition" raged continuously until August 1970.

2. Throughout the war Israel lost fourteen aircrafts, five of them in June–August 1970.

3. The different components of "The Rogers plan" (for the Egyptian and the Jordanian fronts) that was issued at the end of 1969, determined the *substance* of the deal between the Arabs and Israel, bypassing the need for a negotiated settlement, by prejudging their outcome, based practically on an Israeli withdrawal to the pre-1967 lines. On the one hand, the plan was much less than Egypt hoped for and did not have the personal weight of the president behind it; but on the other, at least it implied total withdrawal on all fronts, it was imposed rather than negotiated and Israel considered it a calamity (PM Golda Meir said its acceptance would be tantamount to "treason").

The "Rogers initiative" of June–July 1970, by contrast, was procedural rather than substantive, focused on the establishment of a limited cease-fire, and called for negotiations. On the one hand the terms of reference for these negotiations were somewhat difficult for Israel to digest (and caused the departure of Menachem Begin's Gahal party from the "National Unity" government established in 1967), but on the other, the president explicitly assured Israel that the United States would not pressure for withdrawal to the pre-1967 lines, that the final borders would be determined by negotiations between the parties, and that no Israeli soldier would withdraw from the occupied territories until a just and lasting peace was established, that would satisfy Israel.

8

The Yom Kippur War

Shimon Golan

BACKGROUND

The Yom Kippur War broke out on Yom Kippur, October 6, 1973 on the initiative of Egypt and Syria. The geostrategic situation that prevailed in 1973 was to Israel's advantage. In the Six-Day War, Israel took over all of the West bank, the Sinai peninsula, and the Golan Heights. Control of these areas moved the enemy threat further from civilian centers and increased overall alert time. It did not bring the anticipated peace but the resulting security was to Israel's benefit. The fact that it continued to control the territories captured during the Six-Day War enhanced Israel's interests as conceived at that time by the makers of policy.

In the spring of 1973 rumors accrued indicating that Egypt and Syria were planning to go to war with Israel within a short time. This information caused the Israel Defense Force (hereinafter "IDF") to review its operational plans and to take steps to improve its strength and upgrade its readiness. Amongst these steps was the speeding up of the creation of a number of units and formations, including a division that was added to the five that existed previously; emergency supply units were brought forward to the front lines; roads were readied as was a canal crossing system; methods and means for crossing water obstacles such as the Suez Canal were developed and acquired and units were trained in operating these measures. When war did not break out and the validity of this information was upset, the state of alert in the IDF returned to its previous level.

The accepted evaluation of the decision makers in Israel was that Syria would not go to war on its own—but only simultaneously with, or after, Egypt, whilst Egypt would not make war until it acquired the means for striking deep into Israel's territory so as to deter Israel from striking the heart of Egypt in response to its starting the war. It was estimated that Egypt would not possess these means—operative long-range aircraft and long-range ground-to-ground missiles—before 1975.

EGYPT'S WAR AIMS

In retrospect it turns out that at the end of August 1973, the presidents of Egypt and Syria, Anwar Sadat and Hafez Assad, decided on going to war at the beginning of October that year. Both countries sought to recapture the territories they lost in the Six-Day War as well as to solve the Palestinian problem in a way that would serve Palestinian interests. Gamal Abdul Nasser, the previous president of Egypt, contended that "what was lost by force would be regained by force" and launched a war of attrition to attain this objective. This war ended on the night of August 7–8, 1970, without Egypt obtaining its objectives: the IDF did not retreat from any part of the areas that it conquered in the Six-Day War. Sadat, who took over from Nasser after his death in September 1970, sought to get Egypt's objective by diplomatic means, hoping that the major powers would pressure Israel to retreat from these areas. In 1973 Sadat arrived at the conclusion that diplomatic means were not sufficient and that to break the impasse and to get Israel to retreat, war had to be initiated.

Sadat writes in his book that on October 1, he issued an order to the Minister of Defense in which he wrote that the strategic objective of the armed forces of Egypt was "to undermine Israel's security doctrine by executing military activities within the capabilities of the armed forces that would cause the enemy the heaviest possible losses and convince them that, in the short run, to continue occupying Egyptian territory would be too costly and would undermine Israel's security while, in the long run, it would enable the Middle East conflict to be settled honorably."

Four days later, on October 5, Sadat sent a strategic directive in the following words:

1) Further to the military/political directive which I gave you on October 1st, and based upon the current political and strategical situation, I have decided to fulfill the following strategic objectives:

To put an end to the current military deadlock by disrupting the ceasefire as of October 6th 1973

To cause the enemy maximum damage and loss of personnel and equipment

To enable the freedom of occupied territory in continuous stages, in accordance with and related to the ability of our armed forces

These objectives will be achieved solely by Egyptian military forces or in conjunction with Syrian military forces.

Thus, inevitably, the following day saw the launching of war by Egypt and Syria.

ISRAEL ON THE EVE OF WAR

Israel was not aware at the end of August 1973 of the decision of the two presidents, but prior to this, in the middle of August, the IDF became aware of the widening of the surface-to-air missile capability facing the Golan Heights. From the beginning of September, the reinforcement of Syrian ground troops at the battlefront was noted. On September 13, in the Tartus area in northern Syria, aerial combat took place between IDF aircraft returning from a photo-reconnaissance mission and Syrian planes. In this battle, twelve Syrian aircraft were downed for the loss of one Israeli plane. This incident gave, as it were, an explanation of the continuing Syrian reinforcement.

On September 24, Major-General Yitzhak Hoffi, northern front commander, warned of the IDF's limitations in knowing what was happening on the Syrian front: Syrian forces had recently detached themselves from the front and then returned without the IDF's knowledge. Additionally, there is no land barrier in the Golan Heights which could prevent Syrian forces from penetrating the area in which settlements are threatened and air force capabilities are limited by the dominant surface-to-air missile batteries. Therefore, the chief of staff, Lieutenant-General David El'azar, decided to reinforce the IDF on this front to preempt any Syrian reaction to the downing of their aircraft which could take the form of an attack on a settlement or stronghold.

On September 25, Egyptian forces were noted to be moving towards the front. At the end of the month it became known that the Egyptian army was planning to hold a large-scale exercise spreading troops in the area. On the night of October 4–5, it became known that the Soviets were removing their advisors' families from Egypt and Syria. This step, for which there was no explanation, raised doubts as to the assumption that the two nations were not planning to go to war, and in its wake the chief of staff decided to reinforce both fronts by adding regular forces of armor and artillery.

On Yom Kippur morning, October 6, word was received to the effect that Egypt and Syria intended to launch war that very day, before darkness fell. Prime Minister Golda Meir authorized the call-up of reserves as requested by Lieutenant-General David El'azar, but did not authorize his request for a preemptive air strike. The IDF began to prepare for war. War broke out at 1400 hours, about four hours earlier than expected.

THE GROUND SITUATION AND RELATIVE STRENGTHS

On the Egyptian front, the Suez Canal separated IDF forces from those of Egypt. The canal connects the Mediterranean Sea and the Red Sea, is 160–180 meters wide, and is 160 kilometers long. Prior to the Six-Day War, the Sinai peninsula that, at its narrowest point—the Northern section—was about 200-kilometers wide, separated Israel from Egypt, and after that war it remained in Israel's hands. During the War of Attrition referred to earlier, Israel built the "Bar-Lev Line," consisting of strongholds on the banks of the Suez Canal and second-line forts. The strongholds were basically intended to be look-out posts and their fortifications were intended to withstand bombardments and infiltrations. Some of them were intended to protect major routes and control those which were considered crossing points for Egyptian troops. Armored forces patrolled the length of the canal and were meant to prevent incursions and destroy the enemy. Ten kilometers east of the canal, a road known as "Artillery Road" was laid down to enable the movement of artillery and vehicles from along the north-south axis. Another north-south lateral road called the "Width Road" was laid down some thirty kilometers from the Suez Canal.

At the outbreak of the war the Egyptian forces were deployed on the canal front in two armies comprising two armored divisions, two mechanized divisions, and five infantry divisions. These forces numbered 1,700 tanks and about 250 artillery batteries. There was also a dense concentration of surface-to-air missiles. At the start of the war, one regular division of about 300 tanks and twelve artillery batteries commanded by Major-General Albert Mandler faced them. Only one of the three armored brigades of these forces was deployed on the front with the other two in the rear. An infantry unit manned the forts along the canal. Two additional brigades commanded by Major-Generals Ariel Sharon and Avraham Adan arrived in Sinai on October 7.

As opposed to the Egyptian front, where the frontline was far from inhabited areas, the Golan cease-fire line, at the end of the Six-Day War, was only eighteen to twenty-two kilometers forward from the Armistice Line before the Six-Day War. Furthermore, although civilian settlements had been established on the Golan Heights, as has been stated no real land barrier existed to separate Syrian forces from the Golan Heights. At the outbreak of the war, the Syrian force on that front consisted of three infantry divisions and two armored divisions embracing 750 tanks and 300 artillery batteries. As mentioned, there was also a dense concentration of surface-to-air missiles. Against this force Israel fielded, at the beginning of hostilities, 177 tanks and eleven artillery batteries while two infantry battalions held the frontline.

THE PHASES OF THE WAR

The war can be divided into a number of phases according to the initiators and nature of fighting.

> **PHASE ONE**—The IDF on the defensive
>
> *First Stage:* Holding ground by regular forces while reserves are mobilized (October 6–7)
>
> *Second Stage:* Counterattacking enemy forces penetrating both fronts (October 8)
>
> *Third Stage:* Continuing counterattacks on enemy forces that penetrated in the north, defending but not counterattacking in the south (October 9–10)
>
> **PHASE TWO**—Attacking in the North, continuing to defend in the South (October 11–15)
>
> **PHASE THREE**—Attacking on both fronts
>
> *First Stage:* Establishing and consolidating a beachhead on the west bank of the Suez Canal (October 16–18)
>
> *Second Stage:* Breaking through to areas west of the canal and capturing Mount Hermon in the North (October 19–22)
>
> *Third Stage:* Surrounding Egypt's third army (October 22–24)

DESCRIPTION OF THE WAR IN ITS VARIOUS STAGES

Holding by Regular Forces and Enlisting Reserves (October 6–7, 1973)

The Egyptian Front

At the start of the war, five Egyptian infantry divisions crossed the Suez Canal. Initially the Egyptians started bombarding Israel's line and their aircraft attacked targets in Sinai. Under cover of this fire their infantry crossed the canal at all points, using streams of water from high-pressure hoses to burst through the sand dikes that the IDF had constructed. Simultaneously, their commando forces, using boats and helicopters, penetrated into south and north Sinai. After capturing footholds on the west bank, these forces built bridges over which the tanks from their armored and infantry divisions began to cross the canal.

The plan of Israel's Sinai divisions called for spreading two of its three brigades over the frontline. One of these brigades was already there when the war broke out, the second was to have been sent forward when the war was about to begin, but since the war began earlier than anticipated, this brigade was still in the rear. When the war broke out, this brigade was sent forward to the frontline south of the Bitter Lakes district and came into contact with the enemy within three hours of the war's commencement. The fighters of both armored brigades encountered antitank ambushes and suffered heavy losses.

The IDF maintained about twenty forts along the banks of the canal in which, when war started, there were approximately 450 combatants. In most cases the Egyptian forces surrounded the forts. The southernmost fort, on the Suez seafront bay, was evacuated on October 6. On the following day orders were issued to evacuate the remaining forts but these were, by then, surrounded by enemy troops. Armored forces fought to reach them and evacuate them. Eleven forts were evacuated between October 9 and October 11. Some of their soldiers fell into captivity while some escaped. Six forts surrendered and their soldiers were taken into captivity. The last of these, the "Pier" fort, located opposite the Port Taufik bay in the south of this area, continued fighting until October 13 and then surrendered under the auspices of the International Red Cross. The only fort that did not fall into the hands of the Egyptians, despite the fact that it was cut off from the rear, was the "Budapest" fort on the northern coast of Sinai, some fifteen kilometers east of Port Fuad.

On October 7, the Egyptians continued to move troops to the east bank, and held a three to four kilometer stretch of this bank whilst continuing to attack the forts. The Sinai division forces continued their efforts to join up with the forts to prevent the enemy's advance and during the first thirty hours of battle, until the reserves arrived, they lost two-thirds of their strength.

On the eve and the night of October 6, the air force was planning to attack next morning the Egyptian front, first the artillery that protected their surface-to-air missiles and certain Egyptian air bases, and thereafter to destroy their missile formations, but the situation as perceived in Northern Command headquarters regarding the difficulties of the groundforces facing the Syrians on the northern front motivated Israel's GHQ to divert the air force from the Egyptian missile sites on the Suez Canal front to the Syrian missile sites opposite the Golan.

For this reason, on the missile-infested Egyptian front, the air force was only employed to back up the groundforces. They also attacked enemy forces and bridges over the Suez Canal to slow down the passage of Egyptian forces to the west bank.

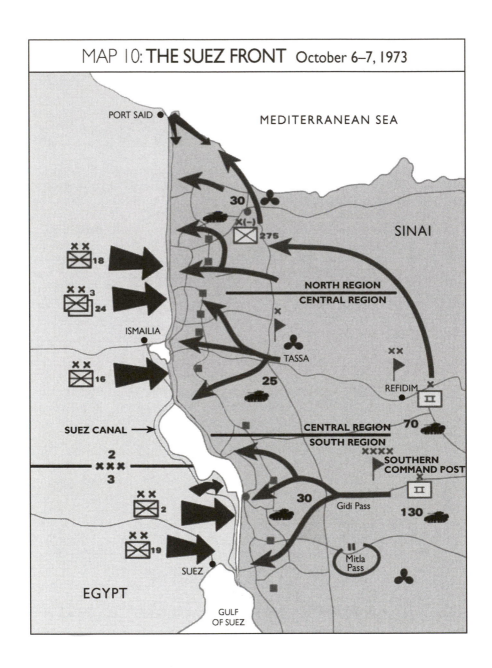

MAP 10: **THE SUEZ FRONT** October 6–7, 1973

PORT SAID

MEDITERRANEAN SEA

SINAI

30

X(−)
275

18

3
24

NORTH REGION
CENTRAL REGION

ISMAILIA

TASSA

16

25

REFIDIM

II

SUEZ CANAL

CENTRAL REGION
SOUTH REGION

70

2
3

SOUTHERN
COMMAND POST

II

2

30

Gidi Pass

130

19

Mitla
Pass

SUEZ

EGYPT

GULF
OF SUEZ

During the noon hours of October 7—earlier than planned or intended—two reserve divisions reached the canal and joined the fighting. The division commanded by Major-General Adan reached the northern sector after overcoming an Egyptian commando ambush. The Sinai divisions of Major-General Sharon and Major-General Mandler took responsibility for the central sector and the southern sector, respectively. They were able to stabilize a line along the "Artillery Road."

The Syrian Front

The Syrians opened their attack simultaneously with the Egyptian attack on October 6 at 1400 hours. It commenced with an artillery barrage and sorties by Syrian aircraft on targets on the Golan Heights. Under cover of this fire, three infantry divisions made an attempt to cross the minefields and pass through the antitank ditches and to capture the IDF posts on this front so that the Syrian armored formations could make inroads into the territory held by Israel. In view of the assessment that the main Syrian effort would be at the entrance to the Kuneitra area, in the middle of the northern sector, Northern Command diverted to this sector the bulk of the armored brigade that was in the command's reserve, and, in fact, repulsed the Syrians and maintained their own positions.

In the southern sector, on the other hand, Syrian forces succeeded in breaching the lines and three armored brigades penetrated IDF positions. Towards dawn these outposts were evacuated, as were the civilian settlements on the heights. The Syrians achieved further successes in the Hermon area. Their helicopter-borne commando troops, assisted by a force that arrived on foot, captured the outpost that the IDF had held there until then.

During this same period, reserve forces whose organization had been completed, and those that were ready previously, began moving to the front. The first reserves arrived at the Golan close to midnight between October 6 and 7, and joined battle with the Syrian forces on the oil route near Nafach in central Golan. On the morning of October 7, additional reserve forces arrived and went up the heights on all routes. In view of the grim situation as seen in headquarters in the early hours of October 7, the chief of staff decided to activate the headquarters reserve division commanded by Major-General Moshe Peled and to deploy it on the Syrian front. This division began to move from its location in the center of the country and arrived at the Golan that same evening. The chief of staff also decided to activate the air force that morning to destroy the surface-to-air missiles in that region. By noon, the Golan was divided into two fronts: the northern front was the responsibility of Major-General Rafael Eitan's division, and the southern front was in the hands of Major-General Dan Laner.

That morning, the Syrians threw their 1st Armored Division into the fray. It succeeded in penetrating the Kudne area in central Golan and advanced northwards towards the Kudne camp, considered to be the "heart of the Golan." Its forces reached the fences of the camps, where the IDF forces repulsed them and they began retreating southwards. Additional Syrian forces advanced in the southern sector with the intention of reaching the River Jordan. They got to the Katzbiyeh area—midway between the 1967 cease-fire line and north Kinneret—in the west, as far as the Nov village (midway between the 1967 cease-fire line and south Kinneret) in the south. The reserve forces that went up to the Heights managed to repulse the Syrians on the banks going down to the Jordan and the Sea of Galilee, assisted by the air force, whose aircraft were active in the missile-infested area. At noon, the air force attacked the surface-to-air missile concentration on the Syrian front, but this attack failed and the air force continued its missions in the missile-infested areas.

Counterattacks on Enemy Forces That Had Penetrated Both Fronts (October 8)

Egyptian Front

In the night of October 7, the political leadership empowered the chief of staff to weigh the chances of counterattacking, on the following morning, the Egyptian forces that had entered the eastern bank of the Suez Canal, and in the light of his assessment authorized him to attack them. The purpose of the counterattack was to repulse the Egyptian attack, to prevent the Egyptians from setting up beachheads, to destroy them, and to create the conditions for moving the battle into their territory, which in fact, meant crossing the Suez Canal.

Towards evening of that same day, Chief of Staff Lieutenant-General David El'azar flew southwards and met with the division commanders and command staff in the war rooms of Southern Command. Based on these consultations and assessments, he concluded that the time for action was ripe and he established the plan to be followed. His plan required Major-General Adan's division to attack, in the first instance, the Egyptian forces in the central sector and when this was completed, the chief of staff would decide whether to initiate phase two, whereby Sharon's division would attack the Egyptian forces in the southern sector. Responsibility for the area from Kantara in the center of the canal and northwards was transferred to the special force that had been set up under the command of Major-General Kalman Magen. This force, together with the Sinai division commanded by Major-General Mandler, was to defend the areas under their control. In addition, their attacks were to take place outside the range of the Egyptian infantry on the dike near the east side of the Suez Canal since these forces were equipped with antitank weapons including "Sagger" missiles that were causing heavy losses to the IDF troops. As for crossing the canal, this did not seem to be possible to his thinking until the bridgeheads on the east bank were destroyed.

The counterattack began on the morning of October 8. Adan's division attacked and advanced to within three kilometers of the canal, but instead of advancing southwards, opened two attacks westward. Major-General Shmuel Gonen, commanding officer (C.O.), Southern Command, was under the impression that the attack was progressing favorably, and, at his recommendation, the chief of staff authorized the use of Sharon's division to attack the Egyptian forces on the south sector even before Adan's division finished its attack on the central zone. More so, he even agreed to authorize the request of the major-general in command to implement this in variance with the plan he had previously concluded. Major-General Gonen had requested permission to advance, on a circuitous route, to the southern end of the sector, to then cross the canal in the Suez city area and to attack the Egyptian forces in the southern sector, moving from south to north. The chief of staff authorized this request and forward forces of the division began to move southwards with this intention.

In the afternoon hours, it became apparent that Adan's counterattack had failed. Its forces entered battle in disarray, suffered heavy losses, and were obliged to retreat. The Egyptians wanted to exploit their success and attacked the division's forces. In view of this, Sharon's forces, which were moving southward, were returned to the central sector and by a combined effort the two divisions repulsed the Egyptian attack. The counterattack on the Egyptians was thus repulsed and this slowed down their thrust, leaving in the IDF's control bases for launching attacks on the west coast of the canal.

The Syrian Front

Along with the decision to counterattack in the South, the high command, on the eve of October 7, decided to counterattack the following morning in the north as well. The attack in this sector was led by the high command's reserve division, which, as stated, reached the Golan Heights on the eve of October 7. According to plan, this division was to attack from the South, Lanner's division would attack the central Golan Heights from the west, and Eitan's division would hold its own sector against the Syrians northern sector while, at the same time, directing its efforts to attacking from Nafach southward. Contrary to the southern front, where the counterattack failed, on the northern front it succeeded. IDF forces advanced and repulsed the Syrian troops. On the same day, an attempt was made to capture the Hermon outpost but this did not succeed and IDF forces retreated.

Continuing to Counterattack in the North, Defensive Action without Counterattacking in the South (October 9–10)

Egyptian Front

In view of the failure of the counterattack on the Egyptian front, the minister of defense, Moshe Dayan, and the chief of staff, Major-General David El'azar, arrived at the conclusion that under the present circumstances, the IDF could not fight an attacking war on two fronts simultaneously, and so decided to concentrate the IDF's attack effort on one front—the Syrian front—in order to remove Syria from the conflict as soon as possible, thus enabling the IDF to concentrate on the Egyptian front in the following phase. The forces in the southern front were instructed to maintain a defensive stand in the areas east of the "Artillery Road" about ten kilometers from the Suez Canal, to resist being drawn into battle with Egyptian forces, and to prepare for the next attack phase. The Egyptians kept up the pressure on the "Artillery Road" and even attempted to advance southward along the Suez coast towards Ras Sudar, but halted south of Ayun Mussa.

The events of October 8 and October 9 led the minister of defense and the chief of staff to the conclusion that the major general in command, Major-General Shmuel Gonen, was not in control of his divisions nor was he managing the battle suitably. Major-General Gonen was appointed to his post on June 15, 1973—less than three months before the start of the war—and they considered him not ripe for controlling a central command. As part of the trend to improve control of the southern front, Lieutenant-General Chaim Barlev, previously chief of staff, was

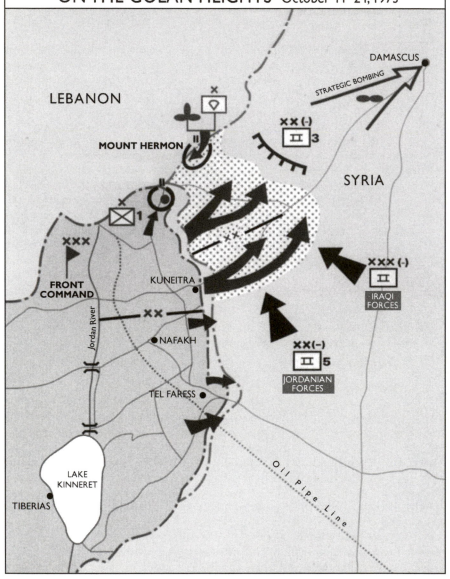

MAP 11: ISRAELI COUNTER OFFENSIVE ON THE GOLAN HEIGHTS October 11–24, 1973

DAMASCUS

STRATEGIC BOMBING

LEBANON

SYRIA

MOUNT HERMON

XX (-)
3

X

XXX (-)
IRAQI
FORCES

XXX

FRONT
COMMAND

KUNEITRA

XX

Jordan River

NAFAKH

XX (-)
5
JORDANIAN
FORCES

TEL FARESS

LAKE
KINNERET

Oil Pipe Line

TIBERIAS

appointed commander of the front. Barlev was at that time minister of commerce and industry, and with the consent of the government was drafted to the war effort and the major general in command of Southern Command was subordinated to him. On the previous day, the Shlomo Bay area had been dissociated from Southern Command and became an independent command under Major-General (reserve) Yeshayahu Gavish, major-general in command of the southern front during the Six-Day's War. This new command became responsible for southern Sinai including Ras Sudar on the Suez Bay. Gavish repulsed the attempts of the Egyptian forces in his sector to advance, destroyed Egyptian commandos dropped in his region and, with the aid of the navy that struck at Egyptian anchorages on the west bank of the Suez Bay, foiled attempts at invasion from the sea.

The Syrian Front

The IDF's attack at this time was concentrated, as stated, in the Northern Command. As part of the effort to remove Syria from the war, the air force bombed strategic targets in Syria, military headquarters in Damascus, power stations, refineries, and fuel dumps. The Peled and Lanner divisions continued their counterattacks and by October 10, Syrian troops were expelled from all the areas they had previously captured. Eitan's command repulsed Syrian efforts in his sector, the pinnacle being the "Valley of Tears Battle." This was fought on the plains north of Kuneitra and southeast of the Hermon rise. About 160 Syrian tanks swarmed over the few score tanks of the 7th Brigade and threatened to penetrate deep into the sector. In a moment of desperation, whilst considering retreating, eleven tanks that arrived at the critical moment and managed to repel the enemy attack while inflicting heavy losses on them reinforced the 7th Brigade.

The IDF forces regrouped on the armistice line established by the Six-Day War. The only place remaining under Syrian control was the Hermon stronghold.

Attacking in the North, Holding in the South (October 11–15)

The Syrian Front

When assembling its forces on the 1967 cease-fire line at the Syrian front, the IDF was faced with a dilemma as to what would create a better situation for it at the war's end—would it be better to continue attacking into Syria or rather to hold the Syrian position and to divert the attack to the Egyptian front with the intention of removing Egyptian forces from the forts and strong points they had captured on the east side of the canal? This dilemma was solved when it became known that the USSR had started a move at the United Nations to initiate a cease-fire wherever the troops were when the cease-fire began. Assuming that only a few days were left until the Soviet proposal became a fact, meaning the end of hostilities, it was decided to prefer an attack into Syrian territory, which could be undertaken immediately, whereas an attack in the south would necessitate moving a division from the north. Transferring a division would take a number of days and would leave the IDF without any actual gains.

The tendency on the Syrian front was to advance far enough to bring Damascus within range of Israel's artillery. In the early hours of October 11, the Eitan and Lanner divisions broke through the northern sector of the Golan Heights following aerial and artillery softening-up. Eitan's division advanced in the direction of Mazra'at-bet-Jan and Chalas to a depth of about eight to ten kilometers while threatening to cut off the Syrian forces that blocked the main road to Damascus at Chan Arnabe about three kilometers from the 1967 cease-fire line. Lanner's division met strong resistance at the break-through and suffered badly. On the night of October 11–12, both divisions were reinforced and continued their advance twenty-five kilometers into Syrian territory while approaching Tel Shams and Kenaker.

The momentum of the attack slowed when, unexpectedly, an Iraqi force entered the battle zone. The forerunner of this force, about one brigade strong, appeared in the afternoon hours of October 12 on the flank of Lanner's division towards Kafr Nashaj and Tel Shaar on the way to Kenaker.

On October 13, the IDF struck from an ambush they had laid at the Iraqi force that had meanwhile been reinforced by another brigade. Renewing its forward thrust, the Israeli force regained its previous positions in the expanse between Tel Maschara and Tel Mar'ee, about eighteen kilometers beyond the cease-fire line. On the night of October 13–14, paratroopers from Eitans's division operating on foot took Tel Shams and long-range artillery bombarded the El-Mazeh airport in the southern suburbs of Damascus. October 14 saw the end of the IDF's progress on this front. Additional Iraqi and Jordanian troops arrived in Syria with about 500 Iraqi and about 170 Jordanian tanks. Opposing all the enemy forces stood 300 IDF tanks which lined up to hold on to what they had taken.

The Political Front

The Yom Kippur War was waged between Syria and Egypt, who were under Soviet influence, and Israel in the American orbit. Both those major powers wanted their satellites to finish winners. The United States had the additional objective of wishing to obtain influence over Egypt. With this in mind, it was important that Israel's superiority be established on the one hand, while the United States was to be seen as having saved Egypt from defeat on the other hand.

In the early stages, thanks to the element of surprise, the armies of Egypt and Syria had certain gains, and the major powers did not intervene. Israel and America assumed that, given enough time, Israel would be able to turn the tables, remove the enemy forces that had penetrated, and cause them a crushing defeat.

In view of the deterioration of the situation of the Syrian forces during the counterattack, which enabled the IDF to expel the Syrian forces that had penetrated past the cease-fire line, the USSR began, on October 10, sending a massive airlift, which, amongst other items, included surface-to-air missiles. On the morrow it began an airlift to Egypt as well. Fearing a further deterioration of the Syrian position, the Soviets began a move towards a cease-fire at the positions occupied by the forces. The two superpowers organized a scenario whereby Britain would bring a cease-fire resolution before the Security Council, and the United States and the USSR would both abstain from voting, thus ensuring the passage of the resolution. The United States agreed to this initiative on the understanding that Israel would achieve a rapid victory without requiring military aid during the war. However, in view of the massive support that the Soviet Union was providing its allies, Egypt and Syria, the United States decided to operate an airlift to supply Israel with weapons and ammunition if a cease-fire was not obtained in the near future.

The United States encouraged Israel to flog the Syrians and even asked, on October 11, how much time was needed for this. Israel's answer was that forty-eight hours were required in order to complete the moves on the Syrian front, and that to achieve a serious victory in the Egyptian front an additional week was needed. Secretary of State Henry Kissinger, promised to delay the Security Council meeting for a period of forty-eight hours. There are those who claim that there is a connection between the moves for a cease-fire and for the airlift, and that the United States delayed the airlift because Kissinger wanted to exploit the war to obtain influence in Egypt, and he preferred not to supply Israel with massive aid unless there was no other choice. He pinned his hopes on the Russian move for a cease-fire, hoping that if it would be implemented rapidly there would not be a need for an airlift to Israel. The Egyptians torpedoed this move when the British, who were due to move the resolution in the Security Council, asked them if they agreed to the move. The Egyptians answered in the negative since they planned to make their next attack the following day. When it came to Kissinger's knowledge that no cease-fire could be expected in the near future, he was afraid that the Soviet airlift could weigh the scales against Israel. In view of this and in view of the fact that Egypt had torpedoed the initiative for a cease-fire, he decided to send the airlift that was destined to replace the arms and ammunition that Israel had lost in the war, so that it could continue fighting on a parity basis. President Richard Nixon gave orders to expedite the airlift and on October 14, the first *Galaxy* aircraft bringing military supplies to Israel landed.

Against the background of the intention to bring the Security Council to debate a cease-fire, the chief of staff examined the question of IDF's need for a cease-fire and arrived at the conclusion that this was necessary. When examining the means of expediting the proposed cease-fire, he came to the conclusion that a hostile crossing at the Egyptian front was the best way. While Israel was deliberating on a joint military and political level whether to undertake a hostile crossing of the Suez Canal, word arrived that the Egyptians intended to start the next phase of their attack that included the transfer of armored divisions from the west side to the east side of the canal. In view of this, Israel's chief of staff preferred to wait for their crossing and to pummel them east of the canal, thus creating the conditions for moving the war to Egyptian territory on the west side of the canal where there were only sparse Egyptian forces.

As for the cease-fire, Minister of Defense Moshe Dayan assumed—retrospectively shown to be correct in this assumption—that Egypt would reject the proposed cease-fire because of its plan to begin the next phase of its attack. Retrospectively, this assumption was shown to have been correct. Dayan assumed, in view of Egypt's expected refusal, that there would not be a debate in the Security Council nor would a cease-fire be imposed. And Israel, seeming to have answered the American suggestion positively, could then continue its attack on the Syrian front, and could even begin an attack on the Egyptian front with the United States supporting and supplying the necessary weaponry. Thus, Prime Minister Golda Meir accepted Dayan's suggestion to give a positive answer to the United States' proposed scenario, which, in any case, would not prove fruitful. In the new situation developing, the chief of staff did not see a need for an immediate cease-fire, on the contrary, the longer the war continued the wider could the IDF extend its gains.

The Egyptian Front

Between October 9–11, the Egyptians strengthened their bases east of the Suez Canal and Southern Command's forces deployed to prevent them from widening their holdings. On October 13, the commander of the Sinai division, Major-General Albert Mandler, was killed and Major-General Kalman Magen was appointed in his place as division commander, with General Sasson Yitschak assuming command of the force that had been, until then, under Major-General Magen's command and was then relegated to the northern sector. When the Egyptian intention to start the next phase in their attack became known, the Southern Command forces stood by to meet them.

Egypt's President Anwar Sadat decided to start the next phase in his attack to meet, among other reasons, Syria's request to Egypt to act in order to decrease Israel's pressure on them. It would seem that Sadat wanted to widen his hold on the Egyptian sector before the defeat of Syria which would enable the IDF to concentrate its efforts on the Egyptian front. The heads of his army did not see any logic in making an additional attack. The Egyptian chief of staff, Saad-a-din Shazli, claims in his book that the reason for the Egyptian plan (including an attack towards the Gidi and Mitla passes thirty miles east of the Suez Canal), was to appease the Syrians who, without this move, would refuse to go to war. Military commanders pressured President Sadat to avoid this step but the political considerations prevailed and the attack was not cancelled but merely postponed for one day, from October 13 to October 14.

On October 14, the Egyptians began their attack whilst moving to the east bank of the Suez Canal part of their forces that had remained on the west bank. IDF forces repelled the attackers, causing them heavy losses. During the fighting on that day the Egyptians lost no less than 200 tanks and the IDF lost about 25 tanks. These developments enabled the war to be transferred to the enemy's territory.

Creating and Stabilizing a Bridgehead on the West Bank of the Suez Canal (October 16–18)

The Egyptian Front

On the night of October 15–16, the IDF began the crossing of the Suez Canal. The IDF had prepared for this crossing for years and had acquired and prepared equipment for this purpose. They exercised and prepared for the crossing with troops deployed on the water's edge, but now they had first to open a way to the banks of the Canal that Egyptian forces controlled. The location selected for the crossing was Dveir Suar, north of the Great Bitter Lakes. This area had been planned as such before the war and a large, open assembly area had been prepared for the forces that would be crossing. This spot was chosen at that stage of the war since it was at the boundary between the two Egyptian armies, a boundary that had been discovered by Sharon's division prior to the crossing. It thus proved reasonably easy to get to the waterfront without heavy fighting, particularly as the Great Bitter Lake provided a secure flank against attacks from the south.

For the mission of crossing that was assigned to his division, Sharon received a variety of specialized equipment for crossing water obstacles: rafts, from which a bridge could be built once they were afloat; a "rolling bridge"—an Israeli invention—elements made of flat, metal plates linked longitudinally and rolled up for transport to the crossing site; and "crocodiles," vehicles with inflatable floats on their sides enabling them to float so that they could move both on land and on water. The rafts and the rolling bridge elements were not mobile and had to be transported or towed to the canal bank.

According to the plan authorized, an armored brigade from Sharon's division, reinforced by infantry, was to have penetrated the boundary between the two Egyptian armies and to have reached the Canal bank; a brigade of paratroopers was to have crossed in assault combat boats while the armor brigade held the corridor and opened two routes—one for pulling the rolling bridge and the second for rafts. Following this, Sharon's division would widen the beachhead northwards on both banks—as far as Lake Timsach and the Ismaliya Canal, with Adan's division crossing the canal and advancing southwards with the intention of surrounding the third Egyptian army in the southern sector east of the canal.

The paratrooper brigade crossed the canal on the night of October 15–16, held and took over the strip known as the "Agricultural Barrier"—a strip with much foliage, small fields, and water canals linked to the Canal—established a beachhead, and waited for the armored forces which were also due to reach the west bank. These forces, however, struck an Egyptian demarcated area at the crossroad of the route leading to the east canal code named "Tirtur" and the route linked to the Canal known as "Lexicon." They fought hard battles but could not clear the route. A serious breakdown of the rolling bridge took a long time to repair and the rafts could not pass along the routes clogged with vehicles that they tried to pass by moving off the road, only to sink in the sand. Only the "crocodiles" reached the canal and moved seventeen tanks to the west bank on the morning of October 16.

The paratroopers dug in on their beachhead on the morning of October 16, and a tank force moved in against surface-to-air batteries and destroyed them, thus enabling the air force to help the ground forces efficiently. On the east bank, after a fierce battle, the armored troops captured the Tirtur-Lexicon junction, but did not manage to open the Tirtur axis. The routes remained blocked and no bridge was established. In light of this, the commander of the front ordered that no more troops were to be moved over the canal lest they become stranded there.

In these circumstances, Adan's division that was to have crossed after Sharon's division's first troops was prevented from doing so and was therefore required to open the blocked axis and to bring the rafts forward to the canal. Their efforts to do so during the day were not successful and on the night of October 16–17, they were reinforced by a battalion of regular paratroopers on whose shoulders fell the onus of opening the axis. A heavy battle took place in the "Chinese Farm" area. This was the spot opposite Dveir Suar where, prior to the Six-Day War, Japanese experts built an agricultural farm that was not completed. Because of the signs in Japanese, the IDF incorrectly named it "the Chinese Farm." The Israeli paratrooper battalion encountered an Egyptian unit and in attempting to avoid them kept bumping into new posts and suffered heavy losses. They were evacuated from the area without having opened the Tirtur axis, but this fighting tied the Egyptians down and made it possible to bring the rafts forward on the more southerly Akavish

(Spider) axis. They arrived at the mouth of the canal on the morning of October 17, and towards evening on the same day the engineering force completed the building of the raft bridge.

It would seem that on that day the Egyptians realized the significance of the crossing. They carried out heavy bombardments on the crossing area and the beachhead, and even brought forces forward from the east side of the canal. They tried to attack, from both the north and the south, the narrow corridor that led to the point of crossing. IDF forces repelled the attacks from the north and in the south; Adan's division laid an ambush for the Egyptian brigade that was approaching the area and wiped them out east of the Great Bitter Lake.

When the building of the bridge was completed on the night of October 17–18, Adan's division began crossing the canal. On the dawn of October 18, they advanced from the bridgehead, captured a number of Egyptian positions, destroyed batteries of surface-to-air missiles, and reached the "Road of Treaty," a wide road eight kilometers west of the canal. On the same day troops from Sharon's division captured "the Chinese Farm" on the east bank and opened the Tirtur axis while the barrel bridge was brought to the canal, launched and positioned across the width of the canal after midnight on October 18–19.

Breakthrough to Expanses West of the Canal and the Capture of the Hermon Strongpoint (October 19–22)

The Political Front

On October 16, Prime Minster Alexei Kosygin of the USSR arrived in Egypt and tried to convince President Sadat to agree to an immediate cease-fire, but the Egyptian president did not bow to Kosygin's pleas. On October 19, Kosygin returned to Russia and on the morrow Sadat, realizing that the Egyptian forces could not halt the IDF's advance, agreed to Brezniyev's suggestion to obtain a rapid cease-fire. The Soviets invited the American secretary of state to Moscow to coordinate a cease-fire. In the evening hours of October 21, the United States and the USSR arrived at an agreed text and the Security Council decided by Resolution 338 that a cease-fire would come into effect the following day, October 22, at 17:52 Israel time.

The Syrian Front

Until that time fighting continued on both fronts. After their forward momentum was checked, the Northern Command forces regrouped to withstand attacks by the various forces in the area. On October 15, a force from Lanner's division struck eastward and hit an Iraqi force. October 16 saw the IDF attacked by three armies, Syrian, Iraqi, and Jordanian. These attacks were successfully repelled. On October 19, the IDF forces repulsed attacks from the various enemy forces. Because of a lack of coordination between the three enemy armies, the IDF was able to move armored troops forward, reinforce vital areas, and repulse the attacks. From that day on the pressure on the IDF on the Syrian front lessened, which enabled the IDF to send an armored brigade smaller than those that fought on the Golan to the canal front, where they managed to participate in the battles on that front. The Hermon stronghold had remained in Syrian hands from the first day of the war and the attempt to recapture it on October 8 had not succeeded. Now, with the cease-fire imminent, it was decided to try again to capture it. On the night of October 21–22, a brigade of reserve paratroopers that was landed by helicopter captured the Syrian Hermon stronghold, taking the Hermon peak as well. The armored Golani brigade climbed to the top of the mountain and after a fierce battle captured Israel's Hermon stronghold. So ended the fighting on the Syrian front—of all the positions taken on the first day of war, not a single one remained under Syrian control and the IDF forces were holding a deep wedge into the Syrian Golan.

The Egyptian Front

On October 19, Southern Command forces broke out of the bridgehead. Sharon's division protected the corridor east of the canal and the bridgehead on the west and pushed the Egyptian forces northwards in an effort to put their artillery that had continued to shell the bridgehead out of range. Some of their troops crossed the canal and advanced northwards on both banks, arriving at the outskirts of Ismalyia.

Adan's division burst into the plains opening souththward and advanced in the Jebel Jenifa sector, the mountainous area parallel to the canal and about ten kilometers south and along the west coast of the Great Bitter Lake, destroying enemy forces on the way. Magen's division crossed the canal on the morning of October 19 and moved after, and west of, Adan's division. When, on October 21, it became clear that the encirclement of the Egyptian third army would not be completed by the time the cease-fire came into being, Adan's division was diverted to the south of the Great Bitter Lake to strengthen the IDF wedge. On October 22, they descended the Jenifeh rises and set up a post on the west bank of the canal. A unit of Magen's division arrived on the same day at kilometer 101 on the Suez-Cairo road, and blocked it before the cease-fire came into effect.

Encircling the Third Army (October 22–24)

The IDF did not manage to surround the third army in time, but since the UN did not then control the frontline, battles continued even after the time that had been set for the cease-fire. Already on the night of October 22–23, the Egyptian forces opened up attacks on the IDF troops in the wedge that was created south of the canal, in what appeared to be an attempt to improve their situation and to escape westwards. When it became clear that Egypt was not honoring the cease-fire, the government of Israel authorized the IDF to advance and complete the encirclement. On October 23, Magen's division captured Adabiye on the Suez Bay shore and completed the encirclement of the third army. Adan's division arrived the same day at the outskirts of the city of Suez and entered the city on the following day, intending to capture it and thus fasten the encirclement of the Egyptian third army. These forces met fierce resistance and suffered heavy casualties. Some of them were left, cut off, in the city and were rescued at night. This attempt to capture the city of Suez failed and the forces of the division remained on the outskirts. The Security Council, convening again, adopted Resolution 339, which called upon both countries to honor the cease-fire and to return to the posts they occupied when Resolution 338 was slated to come into effect.

POLITICAL SETTLEMENTS

On the morning of October 24, Resolution 339 took effect and the political struggle began—initially on applying Resolution 339 and subsequently on lifting the siege of the third army, which was left east of the canal on its southern sector, or supplying it. On October 27, Egypt agreed to Israel's suggestion regarding a meeting of the representatives of both armies to discuss outstanding matters, and on that same day the first meeting was held at kilometer 101 on the Suez-Cairo road, following which further meetings were held. Through U.S. mediation, agreements were arrived at in January 1974 and in May 1974 to separate forces on the Egyptian and the Syrian front, respectively. September 1975 saw the beginning of a process, which Anwar Sadat saw subsequently as leading him to Jerusalem in November of 1977, in order to reach peace with Israel.

SUMMARY

The armies of Egypt and Syria surprised the IDF when they opened war on the afternoon of Yom Kippur in 1973. It was only on that morning that word was received of their intention to attack in the evening hours. The IDF's disadvantage lay in the belief in the widely held concept that Egypt would not attack until such time that it had the means for striking deep into Israel's territory and by an additional belief that if there was to be war, Israel would be warned in good time. But the surprise was not only due to a lack of good intelligence. It would seem that the IDF's complacency regarding the formations that the Syrian and Egyptian armies had built up on the fronts prior to the war resulted from the assumption, amongst others, that the enemy armies would not succeed in making any significant gains and that Israel would regain any lost ground in a very short time and cause the enemy a crushing defeat.

The IDF was surprised on the tactical level as well. For example, the IDF was aware of the many "Sagger" missiles in enemy hands, but did not estimate correctly the significance of the concentrated use of these missiles that caused many casualties. Nor did the IDF estimate correctly the significance of a major crossing of the canal by Egyptian troops. The effect of the surprise attack was that the IDF, which until then had been the initiator and attacker, was forced to react and defend itself. The IDF had not built itself properly for defense and paid the price in this war. One of the results of the surprise was that the operation of the air force was not conducted in accordance with existing plans. According to the IDF's plans, the air force was to have obtained at the beginning of the war aerial supremacy with control over the battlefields by wiping out the enemy surface-to-air missile batteries as well as its airplanes. The surprise element forced the air force to alternate between the two fronts. Its attack on the Syrian missiles on October 7 was a dismal failure and on the following days it had to support ground troops while operating in a missile-infested enemy theater which caused the IDF heavy losses and lessened their support of the ground troops. A result of the air forces's vulnerability to the enemy's missile system was a dependence on the American airlift, which, in turn, increased Israel's dependence on the United States.

The IDF entered the war in the worst possible state and did not manage to reverse the initial setbacks as anticipated before the war. But it overcame the shock in a matter of days, and succeeded in repulsing the Syrian forces completely and capturing a considerable area of Syrian territory, reaching a position from where its artillery could threaten the suburbs of Damascus. On the southern front, however, a large part of the territory which the Egyptians had taken at the beginning of the war, remained in their hands. But here, too, the IDF broke into Egyptian territory on the west side of the Suez Canal and reached a point 101 kilometers from Egypt's capital. The IDF even encircled one of the two armies on the east bank, and only American intervention saved it from destruction. Militarily, then, the IDF won a big victory. Nevertheless, the Yom Kippur War was perceived by the public, the political community, the Arab world, and internationally as a war in which the IDF failed. It would seem that the cause of Israel's initial failure springs from the war between anticipations and what actually took place. Everyone was used to the IDF's coming out on the upper side of any confrontation with an Arab force, with its hand on the upper side and winning a resounding victory. It would seem that the opening events caused the feeling of defeat. This was the first war in which the IDF was taken by surprise, sustained heavy losses, and enemy forces captured and held territory. The Agranat committee that investigated the era preceding war and its three first days recommended removing the chief of staff and a number of commanders from their posts, but declined to recommend steps to be taken against the political leaders. But the Israeli public felt that the political leadership was also guilty and as a result of the growing public pressure, the government, headed by Golda Meir after the 1973 elections, was forced to resign. There are those that see this resignation as the end of the Yom Kippur War. Nevertheless, it would seem that this war prepared the way and the series of events that came in its wake led to the signing of a peace treaty with Egypt, the initiator of the war and the largest and most important of the Arab countries.

BIBLIOGRAPHY

Hebrew Sources

Bar-Joseph, Uri, *The Watchman Fell Asleep—The Surprise of Yom Kippur and Its Sources,* Zmora-Bitan, 2001.

Bartov, Chanoch, *Dado—48 years and 20 more days—An Enlarged and Illustrated Edition,* Dvir, 2002.

Braun, Aryeh, *Moshe Dayan and the Yom Kippur War,* Idanim, 1993.

Cordova, Yishai, "The Political Background to the American Airlift in the Yom Kippur War," *Maarachot, 256,* 1977.

Cordova, Yishai, "The Soviet Nuclear Threat at the Height of the Six Day War," *Maarachot, 266,* 1978.

Cordova, Yishai, "The USA Stance on a Pre-Emptive Strike" *Maarachot, 276,* 1980.

Cordova, Yishai, "The American Effort for a Ceasefire during the First Week of the Yom Kippur War," *Maarachot, 289,* 1983.

Cordova, Yishai, *American Policy in the Yom Kippur War,* Ministry of Defense Publications, 1987.

Dayan, Moshe, *The Story of My Life,* Iydanim, 1976.

Golan, Shimon, "12th October 1973—The Stance of the Chief of Staff and the Political Level towards the Ceasefire and Crossing the Suez Canal," *Maarachot, 327,* 1992.

Golan, Shimon, "Army as Instrument in Foreign Policy: Egypt in the Yom Kippur War," *Maarachot, 338,* Oct–Nov, 1994.

Greenberg, Mattie (Editor), *Beoz Rucham,* IDF Manpower Division/Ministry of Defense Publications, 1998.

Kahalani, Avigdor, *Oz 77,* Shoken, 1975.

Meier, Golda, *My Life,* Maariv Library, 1975.

Meier, Shmuel, "Nuclear Stand-by October 24—An Intelligence Failure," *Maarachot 289,* 1983.

Nakdimon, Shlomo, *Slight Possibility,* Revivim, 1982.

Oren, Elchanan, "The Yom Kippur War," in Bennie Michelson, Avraham Zohar, and Effie Meltzer, *The Struggle for Israel's Security,* Kal Press, 1999.

Pail, Meier, "The Yom Kippur War—An Historical Look at a Strategic Level," *Maarachot, 276,* 1980.

Sadat, Anwar, *The Story of My Life,* Iydanim, 1978.

Shai, Avi, "The Yom Kippur War as Seen by the Egyptians," *Maarachot, 245,* 1975.

Shai, Avi, "Egypt Facing the Yom Kippur War—The War's Targets and the Plan of Attack," *Maarachot, 250,* July 1976.

Shazli, Farik Sa'ad Adin, *Crossing the Canal, Recollections of the Egyptian C-in-C during the Yom Kippur War,* Maarachot, Ministry of Defense Publications, 1987.

Shiff Zeev, *An Earthquake in October,* Zmora, Bitan, Modan, 1975.

Zeira Elie, *The October 73 War—Myth against Reality,* Yediot Achronot, 1993.

English Sources

Handel, Michael, *Perception, Deception, and Surprise—the Case of Yom Kippur War,* the Hebrew University, Jerusalem, 1976.

Heikal, Mohamed, *The Road to Ramadan,* Collins, London, 1975.

Herzog, Chaim, *War of Atonement,* Steimatzky, Jerusalem, 1975.

Israelian, Victor, *Inside the Kremlin During the Yom Kippur War,* Park Uni, 1995.

Kissinger, Henry, *Years of Upheaval,* Little, Brown and Company, Boston, Toronto, 1982.

O'balance, Edgar, *No Victory No Vanquished—the Yom Kippur War,* San Rafael, 1978.

Quandt, William, *Soviet Policy in Oct 73' War,* Santa Monica, 1976.

9

Insurgency and Counterinsurgency in Israel, 1965–1985

Benny Michelsohn

INTRODUCTION

Israel, confronted by the PLO during thirty years of insurgent conflict, found that its sovereignty was constantly challenged. The aim of the Palestinian revolutionary movement was consistent over all those years: to establish an Arab-Palestinian state in place of Israel. Arab states such as Egypt, Syria, Jordan, Lebanon, Iraq, Libya, Saudi-Arabia, and Yemen provided all kinds of assistance to the Palestinian armed groups and often built-up their power on their own initiative. Such a goal required continued offensive action against the Israeli territory and Israel interests and representatives around the world. To execute that campaign, the PLO, who lead other groups, choose the Maoist model with some adaptations to conditions in the Middle East and changed frequently the tactical concepts of operations with a tremendous flexibility and skill. They created a good intelligence network, terrorists groups, guerrilla forces, and an army-in-exile, and used those tools interchangeably according to changing circumstances and political opportunities. In addition, they built a powerful diplomatic and propaganda network around the world to keep their case alive on the international agenda. That effort was assisted extensively by the Eastern bloc in general and Soviet Union in particular. The "Third World" states such as Yugoslavia and India also provided support and sympathy to the Palestinian struggle. Other "liberation movements" such as the African National Congress (ANC) in South Africa, Front for the Liberation of Mozambique (FRELIMO) in Mozambique, South West African Peoples Organization (SWAPO) in South West Africa, Bader Mainhoff in Germany, the Red Brigades in Italy, the Japanese Red Army, and many others were "sister organizations" who supported each other against the legitimate governments of their respective countries.

The Israeli aim was to deny the Palestinians the opportunity to achieve their goals. Its basic policy was based on self-defense. To confront that huge effort to destroy and eliminate the state of Israel, IDF had to develop a unique force capable to win any conventional attack from the Arab states and at the same time to fight efficiently the Palestinian guerrilla and terror war.

This chapter is a short description of this struggle during the first twenty years. We divide those years in four periods:

1965–1967, the rising of the Fatah.

1967–1973, the War of Attrition.

1973–1982, the war on the northern frontier.

1982–1985, counterguerrilla warfare inside Lebanon.

THE RISING OF THE FATAH, 1965–1967

Fatah is a reverse acronym of the Arabic "*Hareqat at-Ttahrir al-Watanyye al-Falastinyye*" (The Movement for the National Liberation of Palestine). The Fatah organization was established in October 1959 in Kuwait. At the beginning, its number of members was very small, it wasn't supported by any Arab state, and its influence was very limited. The growing extremism of the Syrian regime during the 1960s and its rivalry with Egypt, together with the search for ways to attack Israel, created the environment for the Syrian assistance to the Fatah. At the beginning the assistance was confined to consultancy and propaganda. At the middle of 1965 the Fatah leadership transferred its HQ to Damascus. The Syrian government began to support the Fatah by recruiting personnel, training personnel, and supplying weapons. Their only condition was that the guerrilla's raids against Israel would not be launched from Syrian territory. The first Fatah operation against an Israeli target happened on January 1, 1965, when the Fatah group laid an explosive charge (that didn't explode) on the canal of the National Water Carrier. During that first year, however, Fatah executed thirty-five attacks against Israel, which were mainly directed to water installations but also against civilian houses and laying mines. Twenty-eight of these attacks came from Jordanian territory and the rest from Lebanon.

IDF response was, at first, defensive in principle: increasing patrols and ambushes along the border areas and fencing water installations. The overall IDF strategy was to put the responsibility on the Arab neighboring state for each of the violent actions originating from their territory. That strategy led to several warning/retaliation raids against Jordan and Lebanon. The largest one was launched against the Arab-Jordanian village of Samoa south of Hebron on November 1966. As a result of that activity, Jordan and Lebanon increased their efforts to stop Fatah activity. IDF retaliation operations and the obstacles put to Fatah activity in Jordan and Lebanon changed the Syrian attitude and the Fatah was permitted to act also from Syrian territory under close supervision. Among more than seventy terrorist attacks launched by Fatah against Israel in the years 1966–1967, about one third (30 percent) came from Syria.

To conclude that period, the main effort of terrorist activity against Israel before the Six-Day War came from Syria, who led the struggle against Israel by utilizing the young Fatah organization as a tool to bring forward Syrian policy and interests. The increasing tension between Israel and Syria and the IDF strategy against terrorist originator countries triggered the Soviet Union warning to Egypt—as if IDF had concentrated forces to attack Syria. That information convinced Egyptian president Nasser to deploy troops into the Sinai peninsula, a move that lead to the Six-Day War.

THE WAR OF ATTRITION, 1967–1973

Following the Six-Day War, IDF conquests created a new situation. The new cease-fire lines changed the Middle East maps completely. While the length of the Israeli land border shrank to 650 kilometers and the naval border extended to 1,000 kilometers, those lines that were now a distance from Israeli's cities entailed the deployment of the IDF further away from its population. In addition, the Arab population of the newly occupied territories numbered one million inhabitants. A military government was established to control the Sinai peninsula, the Gaza Strip, and the West Bank.

In September 1967, three months after the Six-Day War, the Arab summit was assembled in Khartoum (the capital of Sudan) to discuss the Israeli government's offer to withdraw from occupied territories in exchange for peace agreement with all Arab states. The resolution of that summit was "the three famous No's": No peace, No recognition (to the state of Israel), and No negotiation. Immediately after that summit the Egyptian army began to provoke incidents along the Suez Canal, and soon this frontier become the arena for a continuous "War of Attrition."

In the Jordan valley and along the Jordan River, on its eastern frontier, and west of the river Jordan many IDF and border police camps were moved to new sites inside Judea and Samaria territory. During the years 1967–1969, twenty-five strongholds were built along the west bank of the Jordan River. Eighteen of them were manned continuously. A double security fence was built along eighty kilometers with mines in between. Two roads were constructed west of the fence, one covered with asphalt, the other with dust to allow patrols to detect steps of crossing. Many new, special weapons were developed and deployed along the border.

After the Six-Day War, the Palestinian organizations made an attempt to start a "Popular Liberation War" into the occupied territories of Judea and Samaria. The organizations' HQ was transferred to inside that area, in order to encourage a revolt among the population, gain mass recruitment and contraband weapons, and execute the struggle against Israel into the occupied territories. At the beginning they achieved assistance and cooperation from the local population by providing shelters and supplying food.

IDF strategy was to separate between the terrorists and the entire population. The security forces acted offensively and aggressively against the insurgents and their supporters while the military government provided the means to the local population to manage their normal daily lives. Also, the connection with the Hashemite Kingdom of Jordan through "the open bridges" policy was maintained. The effort to incite a liberation-revolutionary war failed, although many terrorist attacks were launched successfully against Israeli targets in Judea and Samaria, the Gaza Strip, and inside the State of Israel.

After that failure inside the occupied territories, the revolutionary organizations moved their base of operations to the east of the river Jordan, close to the cease-fire line. Their activity at this stage included infiltrations over the Jordan, laying mines, and cross-border fire. During that period, hundreds of incidents were counted. Most of the incidents were initiated by the terrorists but the Jordanian army was also often involved, especially when it tried to provide assistance to the terrorists or its own positions were hit by Israeli counterfire. The Iraqi units who remained in Jordan after the Six-Day War also participated in those incidents. During these confrontations the Israeli civilian villages and settlements in the Beit Shan Valley suffered tremendous destruction and many casualties. The terrorist activities lead to hard retaliation by IDF, sometimes against civilian targets as well. The peak of IDF activity was marked by the raid operations "Inferno" and "Assouta" in March 1968. The IDF occupied a large part of the eastern side of the Jordan Valley, including the town of Karame and a piece of Jordanian territory south to the Dead Sea. Those "search-and-destroy" operations inside Jordan forced the terrorist organizations to remove their bases from the Jordan Valley eastwards to the mountain area of Gilad and Moab and later to the Jordanian heartland.

The guerrilla groups that succeeded to penetrate over the Jordan River into Judea and Samaria territory had to face a new form of battle—"The Pursuit." This involved highly mobile IDF infantry and reconnaissance troops carried by vehicles and helicopters. Those units would follow any infiltration that was detected by pathfinders on the dirt road, cutting across the terrain along the appreciated line-of-advance of the terrorists, until the final interception.

The Palestinian guerrilla organizations that were pushed to the Gillad Heights in Jordan began to establish "safe havens" inside the urban centers and the adjusted refugee camps in the Jordanian Kingdom, creating a "state within a state" since the Jordanians lost the ability to control them—this situation created more and more friction with the Jordanian authorities during the years to come. IDF operated against those bases mainly by airstrikes.

Another course of action initiated at that time by the revolutionary organizations was to attack Israeli targets outside Israel. During that period three terrorist attacks were launched against El-Al aircrafts abroad. In response, IDF launched operation "GIFT," a raid on a Beirut airport, blowing up fifteen Arab airline aircrafts.

March 1969–August 1970

This period was dominated by the War of Attrition along the Suez Canal, carried out by the Egyptian army, which attracted IDF's main efforts and attention. Nevertheless, the counterinsurgency fighting along the eastern and northern borders and inside the occupied territories continued and even intensified. The Syrians and Palestinians tried to assist the Egyptian struggle.

Along the Jordan Valley the attacks on IDF positions and cross-border artillery shelling become a daily routine. Mortar and rocket fire continued to harass the Beit Shan settlements. IDF's operational success in the Jordan Valley pushed the terrorists to move their activities south of the Dead Sea and along Wadi Arava. The IDF responded by creating a "prohibited area" closed to civilian movement and a network of long-range observation posts, intensifying the patrols and ambushes. On the Dead Sea, the Israeli navy took the responsibility, organizing a special reconnaissance force to survey systematically the sea and its banks and initiate raids to search on the eastern beaches.

By February 1970, the first crisis between the Palestinian revolutionary movement and the Jordan army took place. On April 1970, King Hussein was forced by Palestinian terrorist pressure to appoint a new pro-Palestinian government, but the incidents between the Jordanian army and the terrorists increased and the general relationship deteriorated. The tension reached its peak in September 1970.

The Syrian border, which was relatively calm during the first two years after the Six-Day War, became very active in order to support the Egyptian effort along the Suez Canal. The volume of incidents along that border rose to forty per month during that period. Shelling and airstrikes on IDF strongholds and observation posts, ambushes, and terrorist operations also characterized the Syrian army activity.

The Syrian army allowed terrorist organizations, especially the El-Zaika, their own loyal guerrilla group to enlarge their cross-border activities, including ambushes, attacks on vehicles, and laying of mines.

Thus the IDF constructed fifteen strongholds along the cease-fire line and an antitank ditch, fences, and minefields protected some parts of that frontier. The IDF's offensive activity along the Syrian line was characterized by "battle days," including artillery and tank fire, air force strikes, and helliborne raids into the Syrian rear. The peak of this offensive activity was three "Battle Days" initiated by IDF and code-named "Kiton-10." In June 1970, IDF armor units broke through the Syrian line of fortifications at the rapid district with close support of the air force. The Syrians lost hundreds of men, and IDF forces came back with three Syrian tanks in captivity, rolling into Israel.

During 1968 the terrorist organizations also began to build area bases on the southwestern slopes of the Hermon Mountain on the northwest corner of the Golan Heights, these bases were used for cross-border terrorist raids. During 1969, some eighty attacks were launched from this base area nicknamed "Fatah-Land," and during 1970, 200 attacks were launched. The terrorists' intention was to operate from Lebanon territory west to the Hatsbani River as well, but the Lebanese authorities didn't allow terrorist activity against Israel during that initial period. However, in November 1969, the Cairo Agreement was signed between the terrorist organizations and the government of Lebanon, in which permission was given for terrorist attacks launched from the "Fatah-land." These activities now extended further along the Israeli northern border. The terrorist activity along the Lebanon border was characterized by cross-border rocket fire against Israeli settlements, cross-border fire on vehicles traveling along the "north-road," and infiltrations for terrorist attacks inside Israeli territory. The most famous incident was the shooting at a children's bus at Avivim village in May 1970. In that incident, twelve children were killed and twenty-nine wounded.

Construction of a "fence system" also began. This manmade obstacle was very much the same as along Jordan Valley and on the Golan Heights and included fences with mines in between and pathfinder's roads. An intensive engineering work was undertaken to construct new roads, including a paved road overlooking the Fatah-land (the Hermon Mountain's western elbow), where a fortified stronghold was built. Later on, some roads were opened into the "Fatah-land," affording more flexibility for counteroperations. IDF operations along the Lebanese border were characterized by cross-border ambushes, patrols along the "fence system," and observation posts (OPs).

Until June 1970, air force strikes and artillery fire were the main offensive activities. That year also witnessed an operational change in the counterinsurgency concept of the IDF/Northern Command, which initiated many raids against terrorist bases inside Lebanon. The largest one was on May 12, 1970—"Kalahat (Cauldron) 2"—an armored raid against several villages in south Lebanon.

During that period terrorist attacks in the Gaza Strip increased tremendously. They were characterized by hand-grenade drops, short-range fire, and mine-laying. A dominant feature was killing Arabs who were suspected of collaborating with Israel.

The international terrorist activity was directed mainly against air traffic to Israel and against Israel's embassies abroad. The largest attack was the blowing up of a *Swissair* airplane during its flight to Israel from Zurich. Forty-seven passengers were killed, among them thirteen Israelis.

September 1970–October 1973

During this period the border with Lebanon became the main IDF front combating Palestinian terrorism. In the aftermath of the Jordanian civilian war ("Black September") and the expulsion of the terrorist organizations from that country, about 6,000 Palestinian terrorists were concentrated in several locations in Lebanon: in the east, at the Fatah-Land region and its rear around the villages Kuc, Ianta, and Reshaia-el-Wadi; in the central region; and inside the cities of Tire and Beirut. Their activity was characterized by infiltrations across Israeli border, seaborne attempts, cross-border fire against IDF patrols and Israeli vehicles along the northern border, and cross-border rocket launching on civilian targets.

The IDF completed the construction of the "fence system" and a road complex on the slopes of the Hermon, bypassing asphalt roads were also constructed around Israeli settlements, and new path roads were broken. Day and night patrols were carried out along the "fence system"; special weapons ambushes combined with radar activities operated behind the Lebanese border. Sometimes sectors of that front were declared as prohibited areas.

At the beginning of 1972, the terrorist attacks from the northern border intensified and the State of Israel presented an ultimatum to Lebanon to stop the terrorist attacks or Israel would enter into southern Lebanon. The situation calmed down only for a short period. In February 1972, IDF changed once more its operational concept and began to launch raids with large forces and air force strikes on deep targets. In the same month, an armor raid was executed against Einata village. Those raids into Lebanon drove the terrorists to abandon the towns and the villages and to create operational bases on the fields and mountain areas; as a result the volume of terrorist attacks decreased. In September 1972, following a deterioration along the Syrian front and Palestinian attacks abroad, the IDF opened a mini-offensive against terrorist bases in Lebanon as well. During that offensive, three major raids were launched: "Cauldron 4 Extended," a multibrigade armor raid against terrorist concentrations in south Lebanon—twenty-two villages were

occupied and during forty-eight hours the taskforce cleared that area from terrorists in close cooperation with the air force, who struck terrorist targets all over
Lebanon (September 1972); "Hood 54–55" an helliborne/seaborne raid against a
huge terrorist camp in Tripoli, deep in north Lebanon, launched by the paratroopers (February 1973); and "Spring of Youth" against the terrorist organizations'
leadership in Beirut, a combined operation against PLO HQ and the residence of
their leaders. During that operation, the entire leadership of the Black September
organization was executed (April 1973).

September 1972 was a watershed in the IDF's operational concept on the Syrian
front. That month witnessed a peak of incidents along the line and the IDF
launched a mini-offensive against terrorist targets and concentrations in Syria and
Lebanon. That offensive began with air force strikes and artillery fire against the
Syrian army and terrorist bases deep in Syrian territory up to north of Damascus.
By October 1972, four battle-days were initiated under the code name operation
"Capital." Operations of this kind become a constant reality in the Golan Heights.
After January 1973, the situation at the Syrian frontier calmed down.

During 1971, IDF operations in the Gaza Strip passed through a radical change.
IDF's Southern Command concentrated its main effort to assure full control of the
district. That change occurred after a period of many terrorist attacks culminating
with the murder of two children during a walk with their parents. A civil administration tended to the general public while a new territorial brigade was formed to
deal with military affairs. The brigade order of battle included two or three regular
elite infantry battalions, a border-guard company, and a special reconnaissance
unit. Those counterinsurgency forces were deployed in the Gaza Strip for a long
period in order to allow the unit to become familiar with the details of the terrain
and the population. Curfew and search operations were performed very often,
sometimes several hours after the previous one. The refugee camps were reorganized. Part of the population was deported from this area and wide roads were constructed inside the camps to facilitate IDF troops' rapid movement. The Israeli
navy controlled the sea and a new road was constructed along the seashore. These
military activities created a radical change, the majority of the terrorists and insurgent's cells were destroyed, many of their leaders were killed, captured, ran-away,
or surrendered to the Israeli security forces, and Gaza Strip relaxed.

By March 1972, Southern Command succeeded in creating a secure setting in
which the military government agencies could reconstruct the environment and
infrastructure and allow the orderly withdrawal of most of the IDF forces from
Gaza Strip that were placed under the Central Command.

The failure of the Palestinian national movement to develop a revolutionary
uprising in the West Bank (1967–1968) and Gaza Strip (1970–1971) and to use
the Hashemite Kingdom of Jordan as a "Safe Haven" for attacks against Israel
(1968–1970), and because they could not see much progress in their efforts along
the Syrian and Lebanese borders (1971–1972), a process in which IDF had beaten
the revolutionary-terrorist organizations on all fronts, caused them to look for a
new Israeli vulnerability. They decided to concentrate their efforts, attacking Israeli
and Jewish interests and targets all over the world in cooperation with "sister terrorist organizations" from other nations. That terrorist offensive abroad was
aimed to attract international public opinion in favor of their cause. The terrorist
organizations used a variety of techniques and methods: airplane highjacking,

attacks on international airports, sending blast envelopes to Israel, and VIP assassination. The most serious attacks were: (a) The highjacking of "Sabena" airplane by four Black September terrorists and its subsequent landing in Lod airport May 8, 1972 (the hostages were released by an elite IDF unit who stormed the airplane the day after); (b) The massacre at Lod airport that was carried out by three Japanese terrorists in service with the Palestinian Popular Front Organization (May 1972), killing twenty-six and wounding seventy-six innocent civilians; (c) The massacre of eleven Israeli athletes at the Munich Olympic Games (September 1972)—when eight Black September terrorists occupied the Israeli athletes' residence at the Olympic village. The Israeli defense establishment reorganized in order to counter the new challenge. Clear division of responsibility was marked between IDF, Mossad, and Shabac. The Shabac (the national security service) undertook the responsibility for protection and precaution guidelines for all Israeli installations and air traffic around the world. The Mossad (the intelligence and special operations organization) received an offensive mission to identify and eliminate the terrorist leaders and saboteurs in Europe and other parts of the world. IDF's mission was to attack the terrorist bases in Lebanon who manufactured weapons and charge-blasts and trained terrorists for attacks abroad.

1973–1982: THE WAR MOVES TO THE NORTH

During the early months after the end of the "War of Atonement" (October War), as long as the new lines were not firmly established, a mini-attrition campaign took place on both the Syrian and the Egyptian fronts. Although the terrorists continued their cross-border fire along the Lebanese border, the IDF's main efforts were concentrated in the mini-attrition campaign. However, after achieving a final cease-fire in the conventional war with Egypt and Syria, the fight with the Palestinian terrorist organizations came once more to the foreground.

From the Disengagement Agreement with Syria (June 1974) to Operation Litany (March 1978)

The only neighboring country that remained to provide "Safe Haven" for the Palestinian guerrilla movement was Lebanon. IDF had the possibility during that period to concentrate its main effort to the counterguerrilla and counterterrorism struggle. In the north, since April 1974, the terrorists had focused their "modus-operandi" on two things: (a) attacks in order to take hostages and achieve mass-killing, and (b) seaborne operations in order to penetrate deep into Israel. During the years 1974–1975, seven mass-killing/hostages terrorist attacks were performed against Israel: Kiryat Shmona (eighteen killed, sixteen wounded), Maalot (thirty killed, seventy-nine wounded), Kibutz Shamir (three killed, one wounded), Naharia (four killed, five wounded), Beit Shan (four killed, twenty-two wounded), Savoy Hotel (eleven killed, twenty wounded), Kefar Yuval (three killed, six wounded). Two of the these attacks came from the sea (Naharia and Savoy). The seriousness of the terrorist attacks was because of the heavy casualties they inflicted and the international attention they attracted.

After the first mass-killing attacks, the IDF drew some lessons, and during 1974 the "fence system" was upgraded by electronic devices, more fences, more strongholds and OPs, and more mines. And some reshuffling of the command structure was also introduced. In order to improve combat against the seaborne attacks, a number of shore-to-sea radars were operated by the Navy, and sea patrols were employed. The defensive activity also included patrols and ambushes on both sides of the Lebanese border.

The IDF's offensive campaign against the terrorist organizations during this period became very intensive and included many search operations in Lebanese villages near the border (so called "Knock-on-the-Door" operations), raids, shelling of terrorist targets by missile boats along Lebanon beaches, destruction of fishery boats inside Lebanon harbors and anchorages, massive artillery fire, and many airstrikes against targets deep inside Lebanon.

In 1975, a civil war broke out in Lebanon (as in Jordan five years prior and for similar reasons), but the state wasn't strong enough to suppress the rebels led by the Palestinian movement or control the country. That situation pushed the Syrian army to invade Lebanon, answering to the request of the Christian minority and fighting against the Palestinians. After the Syrian army offensive achieved its goals and the Palestinians were beaten, the Syrians allowed some 3,500 terrorists to deploy into southern Lebanon on the Israeli border.

Israel began to provide assistance for organizing a Christian army in south Lebanon by training that army and providing artillery fire support. At the same time the "good fence" was opened to provide humanitarian assistance to south Lebanon inhabitants.

At this stage the PLO decide to cease the terrorist attacks abroad, but the "refusal front," a coalition of dissident Palestinian terrorist organizations who refused to abide by this decision, continued to carry out attacks against Israeli and Jewish targets all over the world. The most well-known attack was the highjacking of an *Air France* airliner to Entebbe-Uganda in July 1976 and the successful rescue operation of the IDF.

On March 11, 1978, the most murderous terrorist attack from the sea occurred on the beach-road near Tel Aviv. Eleven terrorists who belonged to the Fatah organization landed at Maagan Michael beach, killed a female tourist, captured a cab and then a bus and drove to Tel Aviv. On their way they captured another bus. That bus stopped near the country-club junction. During the fight between the Israeli forces and the terrorists, the bus burned. In that attack, thirty-five were killed and seventy-one wounded. Nine terrorists were killed, two were captured, and two drowned on their way to the shore. This cruel assault triggered the March 14, 1978, "Operation Litany." During this operation, the IDF occupied all of south Lebanon to the Litany River, excluding a small perimeter around the Tyre and Rashadia refugee camps. Terrorist casualties reached 300 killed and 300 wounded. The IDF evacuated its forces gradually, stage-by-stage, and on June 13 the last withdrawing troops left southern Lebanon.

At this stage the situation on the Jordanian border was stabilized as well. Some street demonstrations, which occasionally became violent, occurred in the West Bank from time to time as a reaction to political events such as the Lebanon civil war or Arafat's speech at the UN. Also, some attacks were penetrated inside Israeli territory. The terrorist organizations directed their attacks on crowded areas in urban centers, and some were quite sophisticated, such as the blasted refrigerator in Jerusalem (fifteen killed, seventy-six wounded) and rocket launching against Jerusalem (April–May 1976). However, these were, at that time, sporadic operations only.

From Operation Litany to the Peace-for-Galilee War (1978–1982)

The peace agreement with Egypt was signed on March 1979 and the IDF gradually withdrew from Sinai peninsula (except Taba) and redeployed along new lines on April 1982.

However, the deterioration of the situation in Lebanon affected the increase of terrorist attacks in Judea and Samaria. The most spectacular attack took place near the Hadasa House in Hebron, with six killed and sixteen wounded (May 1980).

An attempt was also made to hit Israeli soldiers "accidentally, by car." Most of the activity was performed in crowded locations such as the Carmel Market in Tel Aviv. The IDF's retreat from southern Lebanon after Operation Litany was complete came only after the border area (to the north) was under full control of the Christian militias. The three Christian perimeters were merged into one belt, from Shuba village at the east, westwards to the Mediterranean Sea. The length of this belt was eighty kilometers and the width five to fifteen kilometers. The size of the population inside this area was about 100,000. The belt was now called South Lebanon Area (SLA) Belt. On April 1979, the Lebanese central government made an attempt to impose its sovereignty on the SLA but major Saad Hadad, the commander of these Christian militias, reacted by declaring independence, creating the "Independent State of Lebanon." Under his command were 1,300 soldiers and about 700 civil guardmen.

The UN Interim Force in Lebanon (UNIFIL) deployed its seven infantry battalions along the area between SLA and the Litany River. This 6,000-soldier-strong force was created by the UN after Operation Litany in order to keep the peace in south Lebanon and to fill the gap created by the IDF's retreat, but its inefficiency allowed the terrorist organizations to reestablish strongholds inside UNIFIL's area of responsibility. Until the Peace-for-Galilee War, twenty-five subpositions were created under the "nose" of UNIFIL to be used by the terrorists as "Safe Haven" to shell and launch rockets against Israeli northern settlements as well as for cross-border infiltrations. All of these came under the control of UNIFIL.

After Operation Litany the terrorist organizations redeployed and reorganized north to the Litany River, and rebuilt their logistic infrastructure. That operation, in any case, didn't affect their seaborne capability because of their continued presence along Lebanon shores.

During that period the terrorist organizations also continued their land attacks, but the two belts guarded by UNIFIL and the SLA and the upgraded "fence system" along the border had created for them many operational obstacles, so they decided to increase their attempts from the sea and succeeded in this way to hit, once more, Naharia (April 1979). Other forms of seaborne attacks were tested as well but the Israeli navy succeeded in destroying a rocket-launcher boat north of Nabaq (at the Red Sea) on its way to attack the city of Eilat (September 1978). The Palestinians experimented also with airborne attacks; they tried to fly over the belts of defense by gliders and balloons. Guerrilla warfare was also launched against the SLA to an extent of an "Attrition War." More and more attacks were directed by the Palestinian terrorist organizations against the Christian entity in south Lebanon in order to try to deter it from cooperation with the IDF and out of frustration caused by their inability to attack effectively Israeli soil.

The IDF increased its initiative activity against Lebanon during that period. Combined raids were launched against terrorist targets in the Lebanese rear. The Israeli navy shelled selected targets along Lebanon's shores, artillery fire and airstrikes were executed against terrorist targets, and many seaborne raids were carried out.

In June 1979, the Syrian army deployed in Lebanon began to react against the intensive IDF activity in this area and made several attempts to provide support to the terrorist organizations by intercepting IAF fighting aircrafts. The confrontation between Syria and Israel over Lebanon reached its peak in April 1981 when Syria deployed surface to air missiles in the Beq'a Valley as a reaction to IAF interception of two Syrian helicopters.

The Palestinian organizations in Lebanon, which encountered more and more difficulties to achieving any progress in developing an effective guerrilla war against Israel, were left with the only way of action—rocket-launcher cross-border fire against Israeli villages and towns in the north. Since January 1981, the fire had escalated until July 1981, when ten days of missile and artillery shelling took place between the IDF and the terrorist organizations. The number of shells and rockets shot during this month on Israeli territory reached 1,870. Six people were killed and 122 wounded. In retaliation, the IAF attacked terrorist camps and bridges all over Lebanon and the Israeli navy shelled terrorist bases at the Zaharani and Kasmia districts. Intervention of the United States as a mediator succeeded to reach a cease-fire on July 24, 1981. Relative calm was maintained but the terrorist organizations interpreted from the cease-fire agreement that they still had the right to attack Israeli targets from Jordanian territory and abroad. On June 3, 1982 an assassination attempt was perpetrated against the Israeli ambassador in the UK. In retaliation, the IAF attacked terrorist bases in Lebanon. The terrorist organizations responded with cross-border artillery and rocket fire. One soldier was killed and eleven people were wounded. On June 6, 1982, the Peace-for-Galilee War began.

IDF PRESENCE IN LEBANON (AUGUST 1982–JUNE 1985)

The IDF's presence in Lebanon, from the end of the Peace-for-Galilee War (August 1982) until its final withdrawal and its redeployment along the security zone (June 1982) in the south, took three long years. Terrorist attacks against the IDF numbered 2,914 during these three years, inflicting 1,106 casualties, including 187 killed and 919 wounded.

At the end of that period the Israeli government decided unilaterally on the IDF's retreat and its redeployment along the security zone. IDF presence in Lebanon could be described as another "Attrition War" characterized by guerrilla and counterguerrilla warfare from both sides.

September 1982–August 1983

This time period covers the expulsion of the terrorist organizations and the Syrians from Beirut until the IDF's retreat from the Shouf Mountains and its redeployment along the Awalli River. This period witnesses a clear increase of the guerrilla and insurgency activity against the IDF. Terrorist attacks, 652 in number, were executed against the IDF in Lebanon, inflicting 469 casualties including 77 killed and 392 wounded. The guerrilla activity was characterized by attacks against patrols, HQs, and roadblocks; attacks on vehicles, rocket-launchers; soldiers' assassination; and exploding blast-cars. The most lethal attacks were against patrols and vehicles.

The insurgents were, in general, Palestinian members of the "refusal front" who remained behind in Lebanon after the expulsion of PLO and Yasser Arafat from Beirut. Since the spring of 1983, attacks by Shiaa terrorists had begun and became more and more significant. That phenomenon was a result of the IDF's retreat from the Shuff Mountains, which caused the deterioration of Shiaa-Israel relations. Nabiah Berri, the Shiaa leader, estimated that the retreat was the first step in a division of Lebanon between Israel, who would receive the south, and the Christians, who would control the rest. That estimate lead the Shiaas in Lebanon to tighten their relations with Syria and convert their political movement, Amal, into a Syrian ally.

That retreat from the mountain had strong influence on the Israeli relations with other ethnic groups in Lebanon as well. When the first information about the IDF's intention to retreat, the Druze, too, began escalating their struggle to fortify their position in Lebanon; their fear was that the Christians would be allowed to replace the retreating IDF. The Druze protested against the peace agreement that was signed between Israel and Lebanon on May 17, 1983, and increased their attacks against the IDF and the Christians in the Shuff Mountains. Immediately after the IDF's retreat, the Druze forces succeed to defeat the Lebanon army forces and to exile them from the Shuff Mountains. In February 1984, Amal members took control of west Beirut (Syria exploit the strengthening of Amal by supplying arms to the Shiaas and the Druze in order to weaken the Lebanon Christian government and to cancel the peace agreement with Israel that was signed on May 17, 1983).

September 1963–August 1984

Three main developments tightly linked to each other characterized the political aspects of the 1963–1984 period:

1. The diminishing of the Christians' position in Lebanon
2. Fortification of Nabbiah Berri's position and the escalation of the Israeli-Shiaa tension
3. The rise of the Syrian position and its influence in Lebanon

The terrorist attacks against the IDF during this period increased in number but were less effective. The 915 attacks inflicted 322 casualties, including 60 killed and 262 wounded. The fiercest attacks were by small-arms fire (25 percent) and side-charges (20 percent). Although only six blast-car attacks were performed, they inflicted much damage and many casualties (twenty-nine killed and twenty-eight wounded).

It seems that Shiaa terrorists at that stage were less trained and organized than the Palestinians, and the IDF began to draw lessons and gain more control over the occupied territory in Lebanon.

September 1984–June 1985

This period covers the beginning of the retreat negotiations until the retreat from Lebanon. Terrorist attacks increased during this period to 1,191, but the casualties inflicted by them decreased significantly—255 (versus 322 at the previous period and 469 at the first period), including 50 killed and 205 wounded. The nature of the attacks remained almost the same by percentage. The blast-cars were once again a way to achieve mass-killing and mass-destruction. The most significant blast-car attack was on March 10, 1985 when a Shiaa suicide terrorist exploded with a blast-car near an IDF convoy, inflicting twelve deaths and fifteen wounded.

However, the relations between Israel and the Shiaa ethnic group deteriorated rapidly. The alliance between the Shiaa, the Druze, and the leftists in Lebanon led to an increase in terrorist attacks against Israel. The situation required some change of the IDF's strategy, and an "iron fist" against the Shiaa ethnic group and the villages that provided shelter to the terrorists was implemented.

On December 14, 1984, the Israeli government decided on a gradual general retreat from Lebanon. On April 21, 1985, the Israeli government approved a retreat to be completed by June 10, 1985 of the Israeli troops that remained in the "security belt," in support of the Christian South Lebanon Army.

During these years of IDF presence in Lebanon, the forces of Order of Battle included two divisional HQs. The eastern one was deployed mainly against the Syrian threat in the Beq'a Valley and along the anti-Lebanon mountain ridge and the western one was a Co-Ordinator of Intelligence division dedicated to the guerrilla fight against the terror organizations. IDF established the Lebanon Liaison Unit, responsible for coordinating operations with SLA. A special operations branch of the Israeli General Security Service (the Shabac) executed the counterintelligence tasks in Lebanon.

10

The 1982 "Peace for Galilee" War: Looking Back in Anger— Between an Option of a War and a War of No Option

Eyal Zisser

The Lebanese War, also known as the "Peace for Galilee" war or campaign, is undoubtedly worthy of the title the "Repressed War." Despite the loss of over one thousand Israeli lives in this war from its outbreak until May 2000, when Israel withdrew from Lebanon, there has not been any real public or academic debate in Israel of the reasons behind the decision to go to war or on the conduct of that war. It is therefore no wonder that the courtroom, rather than the public arena, became the venue for this discussion in the wake of lawsuits brought Ariel Sharon, the man who led Israel to the war, against those journalists who criticized him in the Israeli and foreign press, accusing him more or less of luring Israel into Lebanon.

There will most certainly be those who will argue that there is no reason to conduct a public debate of this kind since all the information about the war is well known to all. One event of the war, beyond a doubt one of the most important and best known of its events, the massacre in the Sabra and Shatila Palestinian refugee camps in Beirut in September 1982, was the subject of a State Commission of Investigation (the Kahan Commission). Alongside this Commission's comprehensive report, several books, few in number, but piercing in their criticism, were published on the subject. These include *Israel's Lebanon War* by Ze'ev Schiff and Ehud Ya'ari, published in 1984 under the Hebrew title "The War of Deception"[1] and the memoirs of Mordecai Zipori, *Bekav Yashar* ("In a Straight Line"), published in 1997.[2] Zipori had been the minister of communications in the Israeli government at the time of the war, and was well known for his opposition to the war in Lebanon. However, this cannot suffice to excuse, and certainly not to explain, the absence of debate on, or even public interest in, Israel in this war. One possible explanation for this is the fact that the issue quickly acquired a political tinge and became part of the never-ending debate between the right and the left in Israel.

This can also be explained by the fact that some of its heroes, most notably then-Minister of Defense Ariel Sharon and then-Chief of the General Staff Raphael Eytan, enjoyed something of a subsequent rejuvenation (Raphael Eytan served as a minister in several Israeli governments in the mid 1990s and in February 2001 Ariel Sharon was elected prime minister of Israel). It may also be necessary to wait for the opening of the Israeli archives, which could provide new insights that could explain the conduct of this war. Finally, it may be necessary to wait for some time until Israeli society can take the necessarily more mature and sober backward look in order to examine this war, and actually itself. After all, the Peace for Galilee War, like the Yom Kippur War, was a war that reflected not only the decisions and worldview of the Israeli leaders, but also the national mood of a people that still adhered, despite the trauma of the Yom Kippur War, to the belief that Israel could change the regional set-up and create a more favorable strategic environment by means of using its military might.

From its beginning, Israel's Lebanon War was the subject of controversy, and did not enjoy broad support among the Israeli public. This was augmented by the fact that there were many in Israel who felt that this was not a "war of no option" forced upon Israel, its back to the wall, needing to defend its very existence, but an ambitious military move by Israel designed to promote long-term strategies. Indeed, it was the then-prime minister of Israel, the late Menachem Begin, who stated in the early days of the war that though the Peace for Galilee War was a "war of option" initiated by Israel, there was nothing wrong with this. After all, even a "war of option" is still a worthy, justified, and sometimes even unavoidable war, which a state should initiate in order to promote its vital interests.[3]

This discussion was quickly joined by Ariel Sharon, the minister of defense at the time, still considered to have been the one who initiated that war. Sharon expressed his surprise that there was even any public debate of the essence of the war, and stated that in several ways it was similar to the Sinai campaign of 1956, which was also a kind of Israeli-initiated move. This move, according to Sharon, had its roots in Israel's opting for war as a means of promoting Israel's national security and interests at that time. While according to Sharon the Sinai campaign did not arouse public criticism, many have targeted the Peace for Galilee War in their gun sights. Sharon argued that this was because a Likud government, headed by Menachem Begin, was the one to decide to initiate the war, and in the eyes of the leftist camp in Israel, this government lacked any legitimacy.[4] These statements by Sharon aroused sharp criticism within the Israeli Labor Party. Particularly prominent in his criticism was Shimon Peres, the leader of the Labor Party and one of Ben-Gurion's closest aides at the time of the Sinai campaign. Peres accused Sharon of besmirching Israeli history in order to gain legitimacy for his moves.[5]

It seems, however, that there was considerable truth in what Sharon had said. After all, the Sinai campaign and the Lebanese War ("Peace for Galilee") have surprising similarities. First, the seemingly insignificant but important aspect of the terminology used by official Israel in connection with those wars: the Lebanese War was given the name "Peace for Galilee" by the Israeli government—an indication that it was to be limited in time, scope, and space. This was also true of the Sinai campaign. However, the apparently innocuous names in both cases hid moves that were broad and deep in scope with far-reaching political goals. Second, it is interesting to discover that a similar worldview guided the planners and executors of both campaigns—the concept that Israel has the power to bring about a radical change in the Middle East designed to create new regional realities more advantageous to Israel. Toward this end, Israel joined, in October 1956, Britain and France in a move designed in the first stage to bring down the regime of Jamal 'Abd-al Nasir and remove the threat Israel perceived to exist. In the Lebanese case, Israel's aim was the establishment of a government in Lebanon friendly to Israel as the first stage in the creation of a regional ambience convenient for and friendly toward Israel. Third, these identical concepts had their roots to a great extent in the fact that the personalities and worldviews of the initiators of the "Peace for Galilee War" were fashioned in the 1950s, the time of the Sinai campaign, during which they served in various key positions in the Israeli defense system. This is particularly true of the minister of defense in the Peace for Galilee War, Ariel Sharon, commanding officer of the Paratroop Brigade in the Sinai campaign, but is true of others as well.[6]

There are also, however, substantial differences between these two wars. For example in the Sinai campaign, Israel's illusions were dashed within one week because of international pressure, which lead to Prime Minister David Ben-Gurion's decision to pull the Israeli army out of Sinai. On the other hand, the Israel that initiated the Peace for Galilee War was much stronger and more self-confident than in the earlier campaign, and therefore neither international pressure nor criticism could divert it from its goal. Moreover, pressure of that kind was almost imperceptible. On the contrary, Israel even gained the backing and support of the United States, which, as will be recalled, had to a great extent been behind the failure of the French-British-Israeli venture. The result was that not only was Israel's ambitious move in Lebanon not nipped in the bud, but rather grew into a prolonged and bloody Israeli presence in that country that lasted for years. Israel's delusions about Lebanon were destroyed mainly by the heavy price in losses it was forced to pay for its presence there.

It might quite possibly be that Ben-Gurion's courage—his daring to give in to international pressure, especially from the United States and the Soviet Union, despite stiff opposition at home—allowed Israel to reap strategic gains from the Sinai campaign for years, especially its deterrent capability against the Arab states, mainly Egypt. As is known, this did not happen in the Lebanese context. This despite the fact that Menachem Begin explained in an interview on Israeli television in the course of the war that one of the objectives, albeit indirect, of this war was to cure Israel of the trauma of the Yom Kippur War. However, the trauma of the Yom Kippur War was merely replaced by another trauma.[7]

Israel's prolonged stay of almost two decades in Lebanon makes it difficult to define the Lebanese War in terms of time and space. While the generally accepted date of its beginning is June 6, 1982, the day that the Peace for Galilee Campaign began following the decision taken by the Israeli government on the previous day; the question of when it ended has remained unanswered. Was it on June 11, 1982, the day that the cease-fire between the forces came into effect, a date that Israel completely disregarded? Perhaps it was on June 23, 1982, the day that Israel completed its encirclement of the Lebanese capital, Beirut, and the fighting against the Syrian forces ended? Could the date have been August 23, 1982, when the PLO and Syrian military personnel began evacuating Beirut? Another possibility is September 14, 1982, the day the president-elect of Lebanon, Bashir Jumayyil, was assassinated. Or could the dates be September 16–17, 1982, the dates of the massacres at the Sabra and Shatila refugee camps, in the wake of Jumayyil's assassination, which in turn led to the beginnings of Israel's separation from Lebanon? Another, much later, date could be May 2000, when the last of Israel's soldiers left Lebanon, at least for the time being. We have chosen, for the purposes of this article, to focus on the period from June 6, 1982 to the summer of 1985, when Israel's forces retreated from most of Lebanon's territory. This retreat symbolizes, more than anything else, the final shattering of Israel's delusions regarding what was possible and desirable for Israel to achieve in that country, and more than that, the internalization by many Israelis of the need for separation from Lebanon.[8]

THE ROOTS OF THE PEACE FOR GALILEE WAR

We have already mentioned that the initiation of the Peace for Galilee War was a carefully thought-out move. It resulted in the pinnacle of the implementation of the process of deepening Israel's involvement in Lebanon. This involvement had started out as a constraint and a solution to the complicated realities that Israel faced along its northern border, but with the passage of years it became more and more institutionalized with more far-reaching goals.

It was toward the end of the 1960s when Palestinians began attacking Israel along the Israeli-Lebanese border, or carrying out terrorist activities against Israel while depending on Lebanon as a territorial base for them. This practice increased in 1970 when the PLO arrived in Lebanon, turning that country into its base for its military activities against Israel. From a situation in which Israel's northern border had been completely tranquil, it became a very active line along which hundreds of terrorist activities were carried out every year, most of them directed against Israeli civilians. Israel then adopted a policy of retaliation for these attacks, the same policy it was enforcing against Jordan. Israel was hugely successful in the case of Jordan, since the fact remains that ultimately it was the Hashemite regime in Jordan that brought about the expulsion of the PLO from Jordan to Lebanon.[9]

In the Lebanese instance, however, Israel failed. The PLO had nothing to lose, and it would appear that the bitter war that Israel had declared against it only strengthened it and served its purposes. On the other hand, unlike the case in Jordan, the Lebanese State proved to be too weak to reach the necessary conclusions from the Israeli threat arising from Israel's retaliatory action. According to the threat, Lebanon had to take action against the PLO or leave itself open to the serious damage that might lead to the collapse of its economy as well as to its political apparatus. Indeed, Lebanon refrained from confronting the PLO and stopping its activities. Thus the cycle of violence along the Israeli-Lebanese border exacerbated: a terrorist attack against Israel, followed by Israeli retaliatory action causing severe damage to the Lebanese infrastructure and army, the lack of any Lebanese action against the PLO, continued PLO terrorist attacks, increased Israeli retaliation and then more of the same. Instead of making Beirut change its policy, increased Israeli strikes along Lebanon's border, they had the opposite affect. They accelerated the process of the collapse of the Lebanese apparatus and finally lead to its total collapse.

One must admit, however, that in view of the ongoing and bloody terrorist activity emanating from Lebanon, causing considerable casualties in settlements in northern Israel, and in view of the international terrorism originating in Lebanon, Israel could not refrain from retaliating. Israel may not have been sufficiently aware of or sensitive to the implications of its activities in Lebanon, but as already mentioned, its options of how to retaliate were limited in any case. Moreover, it should be emphasized that the collapse of the Lebanese system was not the result of Israel's actions, but was entirely the result of the internal dynamics of the system itself against the background of the changes in the delicate balance of power—political, economic, as well as demographic—between the Maronites, the largest and most important Christian community in Lebanon, and the Muslim communities headed by the Sunnis. In the wake of these changes, the Muslim communities desired to challenge the seniority, not to say the hegemony, that the Maronites enjoyed in Lebanon, and thus, the deterioration to a state of a violent confrontation and anarchy was not long in coming. Alongside this, one must also mention the PLO's entrenching itself in Lebanon as a power factor competing with the Lebanese State, and the regional and inter-Arab dynamics as contributing factors making the burden on the Lebanese unbearable. Finally, also worthy of mention is the growing strength of Lebanon's Syrian neighbor to the east, which was also showing a growing interest in increasing its influence over what was happening in Lebanon.[10]

However, the constantly increasing friction between Israel and Lebanon did not bring about any real attempt on the part of Israel in the early 1970s to interfere in Lebanese internal affairs and it certainly did not try to establish a new Lebanese political order. However, the signs of the complete collapse of the Lebanese apparatus, which ultimately became a fact in the mid-1970s, created new realities, and one might say a window of opportunity, that pushed Israel towards increasing involvement in Lebanese affairs.

On the one hand, PLO's control over certain parts of Lebanon and its turning South Lebanon into "Fatah-land" forced Israel to consider the threat of the creation of a terrorist entity along its northern border. Syria's entry into Lebanon in 1976 in the wake of the outbreak of civil war in Lebanon, bringing with it the threat of Syrian control over Lebanon, also required that Israel formulate a new policy on the Lebanese issue, mainly how to grapple with the vacuum being created along its northern border and the possibility that at a later date Syria would try to establish an eastern front against Israel.

On the other hand, certain Christian elements developed an interest in dragging Israel into increased involvement in Lebanese affairs. Prominent among them was the Jumayyil family, especially its most prominent son, Bashir Jumayyil. Towards the end of the 1970s, Bashir became a key figure within the Maronite community. He used the Phalangist movement, established by his father, Pierre, in 1936, as a power base on which he established the "Lebanese Forces" as a militia in every sense of the word. Jumayyil wanted to forge a path to the senior leadership of the Maronite community and even hoped to become the Maronite president of Lebanon. Towards this end, he wanted Israel's help with the rival Maronites and the other ethnic communities in Lebanon. Moreover, he expected Israel to fight for him against the PLO, which controlled parts of Lebanon, and ultimately against Syria. Jumayyil's stratagem was simple. He provoked the Syrians who opposed his forces and quickly exploited the confrontation with the Syrians as proof of their wanting to annihilate the Christians in Lebanon. This narrative found an attentive and sympathetic ear in Menachem Begin, then-prime minister, who came into office in 1977. Begin became enamored of his image as the son of the Jewish people, who had been allowed by the nations of the world to suffer their own fate in World War II, now coming to the aid of the tiny Maronite people about to suffer a similar fate.[11] Thus, at a meeting of the Israeli cabinet held in April 1981, during which it was decided to increase Israel's involvement in events in Lebanon and to attack the Syrian forces acting against the Phalangist fighters, Begin bluntly told those opposing the decision: "Israel will not allow genocide to happen."[12]

Israel's policy in the first years following the outbreak of the Lebanese crisis and in view of the escalation of terrorist acts along its northern border was cautious and balanced and saw as its main and, essentially, its only objective ensuring quiet along the Israeli-Lebanese border. Indeed, when Maronites leaders approached Israel in 1976 with a request for assistance in dealing with their enemies—a coalition of the PLO, the Lebanese left-wing, and the Sunni Muslim community—the prime minister of Israel until 1977, the late Yitzhak Rabin, replied that "Israel will help the Christians to help themselves." In other words Israel would assist with weapons and good advice to the Christian forces, which had found themselves fighting to maintain their status in that country, but would be careful not to actually fight their war.[13] The Maronite leaders approached Syria and requested its intervention on their behalf. The Syrians acceded to their request and in June 1976, Syrian forces penetrated Lebanese territory in order to strike the Maronites' enemies, and most certainly to entrench Syria's position in that country.[14] Israel, under Rabin, quite surprisingly lent its tacit agreement to the entry of Syrian forces into Lebanon on the premise that the Syrian presence in Syria was a factor that would actually assist in stabilizing in that country, a situation enduring quiet along Israel's northern border. During this period a kind of tacit understanding existed between Israel and the Syrians on what was and was not permissible in Lebanon for each of the countries.[15]

The change in regime in Israel and the rise of the Likud Party brought about increased Israeli involvement in Lebanon. The main figure behind this was Prime Minister Menachem Begin, who believed, as already mentioned, that the Maronites in Lebanon were a minority in danger of extinction. There is no doubt that Chief of Staff Raphael Eytan, who was appointed to this job in April 1978, was also one of those who pushed to further Israeli involvement in Lebanon. Nevertheless, it is clear that the appointment in July 1981 of Ariel Sharon to the post of defense minister added further impetus to increased Israeli involvement in Lebanon. Sharon formulated an assertive worldview designed to establish Israel's standing as a leading regional power in the Middle East, comparable in its ability in this part of the world to the U.S. or the Soviet Union. Indeed, in a number of his speeches in the early 1980s, and certainly after his appointment as defense minister, Sharon defined Israel's sphere of interests as stretching from Pakistan in the east through the Soviet Central Asian Republics to Chad and Niger in the west. In Israel at that time there was even talk of coming to the aid of the United States if necessary, in case Kuwait, for example, were attacked and the United States would need allies that could assist it.[16]

It seems, however, that the drive to become involved in Lebanon was too deep and too strong for it to be put down solely to the interface between the two personalities constituting the senior Israeli leadership since the early 1980s: Menachem Begin and Ariel Sharon. Worthy of mention is the fact that many in the Israeli security establishment seriously urged greater Israeli involvement in Lebanon. First and foremost, there were the Israeli Mosad people who were charged with fostering relations with the Maronites. It would appear that for these people the investment and preservation of Israeli involvement in Lebanon had become a goal in its own, to the point where they had lost sight of Israel's basic objectives in that country. However, it must also be emphasized that alongside the Mosad people, there were those in the security apparatus, and it seems even among the Israeli public, who felt that the Maronites were Israel's natural allies, and with a little help and effort it would be possible, with their assistance, for Israel to lead a move with strategic implications that could change the face of Lebanon.[17] It may be assumed that without that deeply entrenched belief in the chances of an Israeli move in Lebanon, the Peace for Galilee War would not have broken out or have been conducted in the manner in which it was conducted. Thus, the Peace for Galilee War was the result of the link between this faith and a deeply rooted worldview among major components among the Israeli public of the chances of establishing an Israeli-Maronite alliance; the interest and even the desire of bureaucratic elements (the Mosad, for example) in deepening Israel's involvement in Lebanon; and finally the political will of Menachem Begin and Ariel Sharon in deepening Israel's involvement in Lebanon.

Before Ariel Sharon's appointment to the post of minister of defense, the groundwork had already been laid for a comprehensive Israeli move in Lebanon. In the course of 1980, Israel's ally in Lebanon, Bashir Jumayyil, succeeded, by means of an iron-fisted and bloody move including the liquidation of many of his opponents, in gaining control of the leadership of the Maronite community in Lebanon. After he had become the senior leader in the community, Bashir turned against the Syrians, escalating the confrontation with them with the clear aim of drawing Israel into involvement in Lebanon. Thus, in April 1981, following a Syrian-Maronite confrontation in the town of Zahla in the Beq'a Valley, the Israeli government decided to come to the aid of the Maronites, and Israeli planes downed two Syrian transport helicopters. In response, Syrian President Hafiz al-Asad ordered to deploy inside Lebanon surface-to-air missile batteries, which Israeli threatened to attack. Immediate exacerbation was avoided through American mediation, but the crisis was not resolved. Later, in July 1981, the Israel-Lebanese border heated up, this time involving the PLO and Israel. This time, too, a ceasefire was achieved and lasted until the Peace for Galilee War broke out, again through American intervention, and again it appeared that this was not a basic resolution of the explosive realities along the Israeli-Lebanese border, and that it was only a matter of time until the explosives would be detonated.[18]

In any event, from the moment that Ariel Sharon was appointed minister of defense, it was only a question of time until war broke out. Sharon began promoting his "Big Pines" plan, which replaced the "Little Pines" plan, whose purpose was dealing with the security threats Israel was facing along its northern border. The "Little Pines" plan called for the broadening of the security zone that Israel had established with local Maronite elements under the leadership of Major Sa'd Haddad, along the Lebanese-Israeli border to a range of forty kilometers from the border, designed to prevent katyusha rocket fire on Israeli settlements. One the other hand, the "Big Pines" plan comprised four objectives: first, the physical destruction of the terrorists in Lebanon, both their political and military arms; second, forcing

Syria out of the southern Lebanese Beq'a and the region between Beirut and Zahla; third, the establishment of a sovereign government in Lebanon that would be part of the free world and would sign a peace agreement with Israel or would at least live in peace with it; and fourth, the complete end to the bombardment of Israeli settlements along Israel's northern border.[19]

However, Begin and Sharon needed an excuse to execute such a move, which would include the introduction of massive Israeli army forces deep into Lebanon. The attempt on the life of Israel's ambassador to Britain, Shlomo Argov, on June 3, 1982 provided the excuse. On June 4, 1982, in response to this assassination attempt, Israeli planes attacked PLO targets in Lebanon; the PLO retaliated with attacks on Israeli targets, and this led to the introduction of Israeli army forces into Lebanon.

When the decision was taken to react to the assassination attempt on Ambassador Argov, it was already clear that the PLO was not behind that attempt. The attackers had apparently come from the ranks of Abu Nidal's organization in Baghdad, operating under the aegis of Iraqi leader Saddam Hussein. However, the Israeli government decided to use the attempt on the life of the ambassador in London as the excuse for the execution of its large and ambitious plan. Those who participated in the meeting at which the decision was taken later related that military intelligence personnel explained to Begin that Argov's attackers were Abu Nidal's people, but he fobbed them off with a wave of his hand and said: "They're all Abus, and it doesn't matter which Abu it is" (Hinting to the fact that Yasser Arafat is called Abu 'Ammar).[20]

THE AIMS OF THE PEACE FOR GALILEE WAR

Any attempt to acquire a deeper understanding of the objectives of the entry into Lebanon in June 1982 reveals several motives. First was the desire to remove the threat that the PLO posed to the Israeli settlements along Israel's northern border. Although an American-brokered cease-fire agreement between Israel and the PLO had been achieved in July 1981, the assessment in Israel was that it was a rather weak agreement that would probably not hold up. In any event Israel wanted once and for all to strike a blow to the PLO's military strength, that is, the organization's disposition threatening Israel's northern border.

Second was the desire to establish a new order in Lebanon based on a Maronite, pro-Israel regime that would create an Israeli-Maronite alliance. A step of this kind would create much broader implications than ensuring quiet along Israel's border with Lebanon. Reference would have been to a substantial regional move designed to strengthen Israel's standing as well as that of the Israeli-Egyptian axis, the axis of peace, as countries that had reached peace accords between them and had hitched themselves to the American wagon.

Third was the desire to strike out at Syria, which Israel considered at that stage to be its main threat following Egypt's exit from the confrontational front following the Israeli-Egyptian peace accord reached in March 1979. At that time, Syria was in the midst of an arms race with Israel and in the process of building up its army. However one must admit that it was also in the throes of an acute domestic crisis in the wake of the rebellion of the Muslim Brotherhood against the Ba'ath regime, which had reached its peak at that time. It would appear that there were those in Israel who wanted to exploit this opportunity in order to strike at Syria, Israel's bitter enemy, in order to weaken it and ensure Israel's dominance in that part of the Middle East.[21]

Fourth and finally was the desire to reduce the weight of the Palestinian problem. It seems that one of Israel's objectives was to somewhat blunt the sting of the Palestinian issue. The thinking in Israel was that if the PLO lost its territorial foothold in Lebanon, in which it had established a state within a state, it would be considerably weakened and the Palestinian nationalist idea would die down—both its ability to take terrorist action against Israel, which had served as a means of strengthening and encouraging its sense of Palestinian nationhood, and what was no less important, the PLO's ability to promote this idea by means of its information, propaganda, and educational and cultural apparatuses operating in Beirut at that time. In the past several years, information has been published, according to which Ariel Sharon had planned in the advanced stages of the war to strike at Jordan, if that country were to join the Israel-Syrian confrontation. If this is true, then the intention behind it was to bring down the Hashemite regime and to establish a Palestinian state in that country, thus providing a solution to the Palestinian problem without its being incumbent on Israel to resolve it.[22]

THE PEACE FOR GALILEE WAR—MAIN MOVES

On June 6, 1982, the government of Israel ordered the Israeli army to mount a campaign aimed at "getting the settlements in the north out of the range of fire of the terrorist deployed—them, their commanders and their bases—in Lebanon." At that session it was decided to call the operation the "Peace for Galilee Operation." An announcement published by the government concerning the operation and its objectives stated that the Israeli army had been directed "not to attack the Syrian army unless it attacks our forces." Finally, the government of Israel stated that "The State of Israel continues to strive for the signing of a peace agreement with independent Lebanon while preserving territorial integrity."[23] This decision by the Israeli government was taken, as already mentioned, following the attempt on the life of the Israeli ambassador to Britain, Shlomo Argov, on June 3, 1982, by a member of the Abu Nidal Palestinian terrorist organization. The immediate reaction to this was an attack by Israeli planes on PLO targets in Beirut and its environs. Following the Israeli air attack, the PLO retaliated with katyusha and artillery fire on Israel settlements along the northern border. In reaction to that, as already mentioned, the Israeli government ordered the Israeli army to mount the "Peace for Galilee Operation."

The plan for the operation approved by the government called, as mentioned, for a short action designed to clean out the "terrorist nests" along the northern border and to remove the threat they posed to the Israeli settlements in the north. At the meeting of the government that approved the plan, the participants heard that reference was to a short operation designed to last from twenty-four to forty-eight hours and that its operative aim was to reach a distance of forty kilometers from the Israeli-Lebanese border, the range of the katyusha rockets hitting the settlements in northern Israel that the government wanted to stop. At that same meeting, the ministers were told that Israel had no intention of reaching Beirut since, as explained by Defense Minister Ariel Sharon, "Beirut is out of the picture. There are foreign embassies there, and we must keep away from there. The 'Peace for Galilee Operation' is not designed to bring about the conquest of Beirut, but rather to distance the katyushas and the artillery from our settlements. We are speaking today of a range of 40 km, and that is what has been approved by the Government."[24]

This statement was repeated by Prime Minister Menachem Begin in his announcement to the Knesset on June 8, 1982. In this announcement he addressed his words to the Syrians, urging them not to intervene in the battles between the Israeli army and the PLO combatants since Israel had no intention of attacking them. Begin said, *inter alia,* that:

I once again state that we do not want war with Syria. From this platform I call on President Asad to instruct the Syrian army not to harm Israeli soldiers and then nothing bad will happen to [Syrian soldiers]. We desire no clashes with the Syrian army, if we reach the line 40km from our northern border the work will have been done, all fighting will end. I am directing my words to the ears of the President of Syria. He knows how to keep an agreement. He signed a cease-fire agreement with us and kept it. He did not allow the terrorists to act. If he behaves in this manner now in Lebanon, no Syrian soldier will be harmed by our soldiers.[25]

This statement by Begin was made even as Israeli forces began attacking Syrian forward positions in the area of Jizin on Mt. Lebanon.

At first, the operation enjoyed broad support in the Israeli public, especially in view of its aim as presented to the public, on which there was a broad consensus in Israel—the removal of threat from the terrorist organizations to the settlements in northern Israel. For example, most of the members of the Labor Party supported the operation, at least at first, and at the session of the Knesset at which it was discussed, most of the Labor members voted in support of the prime minister's statement, despite the reservations and warnings about it that several of its leaders expressed to Begin. Incidentally, the United States, Israel's strongest ally, did not at first hide its support of the operation, and there are those who claim that the Secretary of State at the time, Alexander Haig, was even said to give Sharon the green light to go ahead with the operation. However, at the end of June 1982, Haig resigned from the post of secretary of state, thus Sharon lost one of his most important supporters in Ronald Reagan's administration.[26]

However, it quickly became clear that the limited operation was gaining in scope well beyond it original aims, as presented to the government of Israel which approved them. First, Syria's involvement in the war—despite the fact that Israeli spokesmen made sure to stress that Israel had no desire for a confrontation with Syria, the two countries rapidly came into direct confrontation in Lebanon. The confrontation with Syria was solely the product of a move initiated by Israel designed to involve Syria in the war in order to strike at its army and remove it from any position of influence in Lebanon. Already at the meeting of the government that approved the operation, there were ministers, for example Minister of Communications Mordecai Zipori, who pointed out the contradiction between the intention to reach the line forty kilometers from the border and the declaration that Israel was not interested in a confrontation with the Syrians. Zipori explained to his fellow ministers that in view of the fact that Syrian forces were deployed in eastern Lebanon in areas less than forty kilometers from the Israeli border, any Israeli effort to stabilize the line forty kilometers from the border would involve a confrontation with the Syrians; and that is indeed what happened. Israeli army forces attacked Syrian forces deployed in the Jizin area, which is within the forty-kilometer range from Israeli territory. The friction between the Syrian and Israeli forces was exploited for a comprehensive Israeli move against the Syrians in Lebanon. The Israeli army attacked Syrian forces in the Lebanese Beq'a, and even began advancing in the Mt. Lebanon area in the direction of the Beirut-Damascus road with the aim of gaining control over it. It became clear to the Israeli government and public that the aim of this move was a breakthrough in the direction of this strategic road designed to outflank the Syrian forces from the west and force them to abandon their positions in the southern Beq'a without a confrontation with Israeli forces. Menachem Begin was absolutely thrilled with this move and even said that it was reminiscent of Hannibal's brilliant moves. The results, however, were a full-scale confrontation with the Syrians and everything that entailed, certainly in complete contradiction to the operation's aims as they had been presented to the government. At the same time, Syrian missile batteries that had been set up the previous summer in the Beq'a were attacked and destroyed, and the ministers were told that because of the threat that these missiles posed, the Israeli air force could not provide assistance to the fighting forces. Senior Israeli commanders subsequently said that the operation's objectives could have been reached without a confrontation with the Syrians; but that is not what happened.[27]

Second, the Israeli army had begun advancing towards Beirut and joined the Christian forces there. The army rapidly laid siege to the PLO forces as well as to the Syrian forces deployed in western Beirut. The result of that prolonged siege, which seriously damaged Israel's image in world public opinion, was the removal of the PLO and the Syrian forces from Beirut in August 1982.

Finally, Israeli soldiers effected the election of Bashir Jumayyil as president of Lebanon on August 23, 1982. Israeli soldiers forced the members of the legislature to get to the House of Representatives to vote for Bashir Jumayyil or secured their arrival. Jumayyil was indeed elected with a majority of 57 of the 62 members of the House who had arrived or had been brought there. The election of Jumayyil was to have been the beginning of the path towards establishing a new Lebanese order.[28]

THE ALLIANCE WITH THE MARONITES—A BROKEN REED

Thus, the beginning of the war was marked by stunning military success. The Israeli forces pushed rapidly on towards Beirut, reaching it very quickly. Then, Israelis succeeded in effecting the election of Bashir Jumayyil to the presidency of Lebanon. However, several days later, on September 14, 1982, Jumayyil was blown up by Habib Tanyus al-Shartuni, a Greek Orthodox member of the Syrian Nationalist Party (P.P.S.), who carried out the assassination at the behest of the Syrians. He was the son of the landlord of the building that housed the Phalangists' headquarters. Thus, the Syrians succeeded in bringing down a hard-won achievement, a house of cards. The death of Bashir Jumayyil marked the beginning of Israel's sinking into the Lebanese quagmire and the first stages of Israel's painful and prolonged awakening from the illusion of establishing a new order in Lebanon, beneficial for Israel.[29]

However, even before Jumayyil's assassination, Israel was able to understand his limits and even more the limits of his commitment to the Israeli-Maronite alliance. At a meeting between Menachem Begin and Bashir Jumayyil shortly after the latter's election to the presidency of Lebanon, it became clear to the Israeli prime minister that the Lebanese leader was far from ready to commit himself to ties with Israel. Begin insisted that Jumayyil commit himself to the peace process, but instead he was surprised to hear that Jumayyil would be happy to maintain under-the-table relations with Israel, but that he viewed himself as committed to maintaining his ties with the Muslim communities in Lebanon and with Syria.[30]

Indeed, all Jumayyil wanted from Israel was to help him gain the upper hand in the dialogue he planned on holding with the Syrians and with the Muslim communities in Lebanon. It was quite clear to him as one who had lived and grown up in Lebanon, that it was *sine qua non* that he maintain a dialogue with these factors if he wanted to rule Lebanon, since it is a country of all its ethnic communities (comprising a mosaic of communities, none of which can prevail over the others). Jumayyil also understood that it was essential for him to maintain a dialogue with the Syrians because he wanted Syria to continue keeping its borders open to Lebanese trade with the Arab countries, since the Lebanese economy was, and still is, dependent on this trade.

Nevertheless, the belief that the Maronites are Israel's natural allies did not arise *ex nihilo* among the decision makers in Israel. As already mentioned, there is reference to a concept extant in Israel for years rooted in contacts maintained between the Zionist representatives with the Maronites in the 1930s and 1940s. In these talks the Maronites promised their friendship to the Jewish partners to the talks, but in practice at the moment of truth they refrained from any public expressions of that friendship, to say nothing of deeds.

One must also recall that in 1954, David Ben-Gurion, then in exile in his home in Sde Boker in the Negev after resigning as prime minister of Israel, approached the then-Prime Minister Moshe Sharett with a proposal to take the steps designed to introduce radical reforms in Lebanon. Sharett turned down the suggestion in a long and detailed letter to Ben-Gurion in which he numbered one by one the reasons why Israel should not initiate such an invasive move in Lebanon. Among the reasons Sharett mentioned was the fact that the Maronites were no longer a majority in Lebanon, that they were no true friends of Israel whose concern was the promotion of their own interests, and finally that even among the Maronites themselves there was disagreement regarding ties with Israel and they were not a united community. Incidentally, this letter was included in Sharett's diaries, published in 1978. However, it seems that no one read these diaries or fully grasped what was written in them.[31]

Following the death of Jumayyil, Israel gained control over western Beirut. It gave control over the Palestinian refugee camps to Bashir Jumayyil's Phalangist forces, which on September 16 and 17, 1982, carried out a horrendous massacre in the Sabra and Shatila refugee camps. In the wake of this massacre, Israel was forced to leave its strongholds in Beirut, thus beginning the long journey of retreat back to the border, leaving behind strongholds, allies, as doubtful as they were, and finally a worldview as well.[32] The Israeli Army forces initially retreated in August 1983 from the Shouf Mountains where a mini-civil war had broken out between the Phalangist forces and Druze inhabitants of the area. On more than one occasion the Israeli army suffered casualties when it tried to mediate and reach a cease-fire. The Israeli forces pulled back to the Awali River.

A substantial change in Israel's policy came after the establishment of a National Unity Government headed by Shimon Peres in July 1984. In June 1985, this government, in which Yitzhak Rabin served as minister of defense, pulled the Israeli forces out of most the Lebanese territory. This decision enjoyed a majority of one vote after the minister of housing from the Likud Party decided to join the Labor Party ministers in this vote. The Israeli army held on to a narrow security zone in South Lebanon, and in order to bolster its position it created the South Lebanese Army (SLA) based on Christian elements, but only those with whom Israel had cooperated since the beginning of the civil war in Lebanon in 1975. Of note is the fact that the main consideration in establishing that security zone was the defense of Israel's northern border from terrorist attacks. In any event, the withdrawal in the summer of 1985 was the precursor to the end of Israel's Lebanese adventure, at least from Israel's point of view.

It was only in May 2000 that Israel pulled out of the security zone, thus writing the final chapter in Israel's years-long involvement in Lebanon. Ehud Barak, then-prime minister of Israel, wished to view this act on the part of Israel and the end of the "Lebanese tragedy," in which, according to him, Israel found itself immersed up to its neck from 1982 until 2000. However, that removing of Israel from Lebanon was not enough; Lebanon must be removed from Israel. As it transpired, Hezbollah was quick to renew its activities against Israel along the Israeli-Lebanese border, and just as quickly there were those in the Israeli public who renewed their call for Israel's return to Lebanon, this time to clean out the "Hizbollah cells," thus removing the threat they posed to Israel's north.[33]

CONCLUSION—THE LEGACY OF THE WAR

In the book *The War of Deception,* by Ze'ev Schiff and Ehud Ya'ari, published in 1984, the authors summed up the war, and mainly Israel's entanglement in it, in the following words:

The war in Lebanon—born in the wild spirit of one man, determined and with no limits, sweeping along an entire nation in a hopeless race after objectives—some of them imaginary; a war founded on illusions, full of deceptive stratagems whose inevitable end was disappointment. It was a war for whose weak achievements we have paid a tremendous price which has not as yet been finally determined; a war in the course of which whose defensive justifications were pushed aside in the face of far-reaching ambitions of a short-sighted policy. Thus Israel was swept into an adventure which cut deep scars into its internal strength in shallow mission, and the Israeli army was sent into foreign fields, paying with the lives of more than 500 of its best fighters, in a futile attempt to fill tasks they were not supposed to fill.[34]

It seems from the material available to us, everywhere, that most of the government ministers and some of the senior military officers were not aware of the grandiose plan behind the move led by Ariel Sharon. They believed that they were approving, in the case of the ministers, or preparing for, in the case of the military officers, a limited operation both in time and territory, and found themselves dragged phase after phase into a comprehensive and ambitious move, whose end could not be foreseen. Nevertheless, reference was, after all, to high-ranking military commanders and seasoned politicians, and one cannot shake off the impression that those who had been misled had fallen willingly into the trap. Moreover, one can also not shake off the impression that Sharon's hawkish position had many supporters within the entire chain of command in Israel's security apparatuses.

Since the move ultimately failed, it is no wonder that many began to ask themselves how such a move by Israel in Lebanon had been approved in the first place. Parallel to this, there began to be a campaign of denials and shrugging off of any responsibility for it. As already noted, most of the government ministers claimed that they had not been aware of the larger plan on which the operation was based, and the military commanders claimed that the orders that had been handed down to them had to do with limited and disconnected moves and not with a comprehensive move that had a beginning and an end. Particularly prominent were the words of the then-commander of the Northern Command, Amir Drori, that if he had known that it was the aim of the Israeli army from the start to reach Beirut, he would have deployed and operated his forces differently.[35]

It is no wonder, then, that the differences over the question of the Peace for Galilee War ultimately reached the courts, mainly in the wake of Prime Minister Sharon's suits for libel against anyone who tried to accuse him of taking in the Israeli government and its prime minister. For instance, Sharon sued *Time* magazine for publishing an article stating that he had known about the intentions of the Phalangists to carry out the massacre at Sabra and Shatila, and two decades later he sued Ha'aretz journalist Uzi Benziman for an article he had published according to which Sharon had lied to Begin on the matter of the Israeli Army's entry into Beirut. Sharon, for his part, claimed that all his moves in Lebanon, including the army's entry into Beirut, had been carried with Begin's knowledge and approval. The court decided in favor of the journalist, with the assistance of testimony by Menachem Begin's son, Benny Begin, who testified that Sharon had not made his father partner to his grandiose plans.[36]

One may argue over the long-term implications of the war, nevertheless, the following paragraphs discuss the issues that are worthy of mention.

On the one hand, the war provided proof of Israel's total technological-military superiority over any possible Arab coalition against it. On the other hand, it became clear that military strength of that kind is not enough to impose Israel's will on its neighbors, and that the use of force also has its limitations. These limitations relate to the need to operate in the framework of a broad coalition in Israel, the need to acquire an international umbrella and gain the support of world public opinion, and finally in the light of these limitations the need to use force proportionate to the threat confronting Israel.

As already mentioned, Israel's military superiority over the Arabs was once more proven in the course of the Peace for Galilee War. In that war, the Israeli air force downed over 100 Syrian planes and destroyed about twenty Syrian missile batteries without Israel's losing even one plane. It should, however, be mentioned that the successes of the Israeli army land battles were far more limited. The Syrian commandos succeeded for some time in holding off Israel's attempts to advance in the direction of the Beirut-Damascus road, and in armored battles between Israeli and Syrian forces, the Syrians were successful in a number of instances, for example in the battle at Sultan Ya'qub. Once again it became clear to Israel that striking a military blow on its enemies was not enough to remove the threat they posed to it. Indeed, if Israel chose as one of the war's objectives to strike a blow to Syria and harm the process of its growing in strength, the result was exactly the opposite. As a result of lessons learned from this war, Syria mounted an accelerated campaign of military build-up as part of its adopting a worldview aiming for "strategic parity" with Israel. While serious economic and political problems did eventually prevent Syria from achieving this parity, the fact remains that throughout the 1980s, Syria was considered a palpable threat to Israel's existence.[37]

Moreover, Israel failed in its efforts to oust Syria from all its positions of influence in Lebanon. In fact, in the Peace for Galilee War, Israel rescued Syria from the strategic bind in which Damascus had been in the years before the war. Syria returned to Lebanon after Israel had left as a stronger Syria than it had been before. Also in the course of the war, Israel dealt a death blow to the Maronites' ability to stand on their feet in the Lebanese arena. Until that time, the Maronites had been aided and supported by the masked Israeli threat to act in their favor in Lebanon if things developed not as Israel wanted and against Maronite interests. However, after Israel had already entered Lebanon and become enmeshed in it, that threat was no longer effective.

Israel's hope of striking a blow at the PLO and reducing the acuteness of the Palestinian problem also remained fulfilled. While Israel did succeed in sending the PLO into exile in Tunisia, this exile led to a process of moderation in the organization, even if only in lip service, after the organization had lost its territorial foothold. This moderation was expressed already in 1988 when Arafat declared his recognition of Israel and later his intention to reach the Oslo Accords with Israel. If there were those in Israel who had hoped to put an end to the Palestinian problem, the Peace for Galilee War, paradoxically, accelerated the adoption of the political path as a mode of action by the PLO.

Finally, there was the Shi'ite aspect. It seems that the most prominent of Israel's lost opportunities in Lebanon was its failure to acquire the friendship of the Shi'ite residents of South Lebanon, turning them into its bitter enemies. As will be recalled, Israel entered the Peace for Galilee War completely depending on its Maronite allies while totally ignoring the Shi'ites, who made up the majority of the population, and constituted a community whose status was rising. Parts of the Shi'ite community had actually been prepared to cooperate with Israel. For example, several senior members of the Shi'ite community had approached the Israeli forces with an offer to cooperate with them and to assume the administrative tasks they had previously held. The Amal leader Nabih Berri was prepared already in June 1982 to join the "National Salvation Front" headed by Bashir Jumayyil, thus implicitly cooperating with Israel. However, the Israeli side preferred to ignore the Shi'ites completely. Subsequently, there were those who claimed that Israel had, for all intents and purposes, established Hizballah through its own doing. Thus a tactical threat in the form of the PLO was replaced by a strategic threat in the form of a radical Lebanese Shi'ite organization, armed from head to foot and supported by Iran. There is something to this claim: after all it was Israel that forced the PLO out of its strongholds in South Lebanon, abandoning this region to the Hizbollah. It also pushed the Shi'ites into the arms of Hezbollah through its policy of ignoring them completely. However, one could argue the point that Hezbollah grew out of the internal processes going on within the Lebanese Shi'ite community at the time and it was certainly influenced by the Islamic Revolution, over which Israel obviously had very little influence.[38]

There can be no doubt that the Peace for Galilee War taught Israel the limitations of power. It became clear that conventional military power is not enough to promote far reaching political moves, and that the challenges facing Israel from the Arabs is not expressed solely in a highly powerful army but also in a stone and in an explosives charge. The war also revealed the Achilles heel of Israeli society—sensitivity to victims, certainly in a war in which the consensus regarding it was somewhat in doubt from the start. The lessons of the Lebanese events were also learned by Israel's neighbors. The fact is that a straight line leads from Israel's experiences in South Lebanon to the outbreak of the first Intifadah, through Israel's unilateral withdrawal from Lebanon in May 2000 to the outbreak of the second Intifada.

On the margins, one can not refrain from mentioning the argument regarding the research of Israel's history that erupted with all its might in the wake of the Peace for Galilee War, although signs of it were also apparent previously. Israel of the 1980s was already a satisfied and self-confident society, and therefore more open to criticism and the raising of questions and even to the slaughter of sacred cows, including issues involving security and the army. It would, however, appear that these trends grew even stronger in the wake of this war, since it raised among some people doubts as to the logic, morality, and justice of Israel's moves. There were, of course, those who justified the war and what happened after it, and others who blamed the failure on Israel's leaders in those years, who had come from the ranks of the Likud. But there were also those who wanted to go backwards in the claim that the roots of the Peace for Galilee War lay in the basic concept of Israel's policy towards the Arabs already at the beginning of the conflict in the days just prior to the establishment of the State of Israel. From this point, it was only a short road to the appearance of "New Historians," who exploited for their own purposes the Israeli archives that had recently been opened to them for the first time (approximately thirty years after the establishment of the State). The historiographic debate is destined to be a focal point in the Israeli dialogue from this time forward.[39]

It is ultimately possible under duress to place boundaries of time and space on this war. However, it would seem that for many Israelis, it has not ended and will never end. First and foremost for the families of the fallen, for the many casualties, and for those who, with disillusioned eyes, saw how their country was becoming embroiled in a hopeless and senseless adventure. There can be no doubt that for most of the Israelis the war in Lebanon was a traumatic experience, and at this point they prefer to deal with it by suppressing it and forgetting it.

NOTES

1. See Ze'ev Schiff and Ehud Ya'ari, *Milhemet Sholal* ("Israel's Lebanon War"), Tel Aviv: Schoken Publishing House, 1984. For the English version see Ze'ev Schiff and Ehud Ya'ari, *Israel's Lebanon War,* New York: Simon and Schuster, 1994.

2. See Mordechai Zipori, *Bekav Yashar* ("In a Straight Line"), Tel Aviv: Yedi'ot Aharonot, 1997.

3. See Menachem Begin, interview to the Israeli TV, 9, 14 June, 1982. See also *Ma'ariv, 11,* 18 June, 1982; Yehushafat Harkabi, *Hachra'ut Goraliyut* ("Fateful Decisions"), Tel Aviv: 'Am Oved, 1986, p. 130.

4. *Ha'aretz, 11,* 18 June, 1982.

5. *Ibid.*

6. See Ariel Sharon with David Chanoff, *Warrior: The Autobiography of Ariel Sharon,* New York: Simon and Schuster, 2001; see also Yehushafat Harkabi, *Hachra'ut Goraliyut* ("Fateful Decisions"), pp. 130–136.

7. See Menachem Begin, interview to the Israeli TV, 9, 14 June, 1982. See also *Ma'ariv, 11,* 18 June, 1982.

8. For more on the question of periodization, see Aharon Klieman, "Israel," in Haim Shaked and Daniel Dishon (eds.), *MECS (Middle East Contemporary Survey),* Vol. VI (1981–1982), New York: Holmes and Meier Publishers, 1984, pp. 641–650; Schiff and Ya'ari, *Milhemet Sholal,* pp. 380–388; Itamar Rabinovich, *The War for Lebanon, 1970–1985,* Ithaca: Cornell University Press, 1985.

9. See Yazid Saigh, *Armed Struggle and the Search for a State: The Palestinians National Movement, 1949–1993,* Oxford: Oxford University Press, 1997; see also Marius Deeb, *Syria's Terrorist War on Lebanon and the Peace Process,* New York: Palgrave, 2003, pp. 5–38; Robert G. Rabil, *Embattled Neighbors, Syria, Israel and Lebanon,* Boulder, CO: Lynne Rienner Publishers, 2003, pp. 5–84.

10. For more see Farid el Khazen, *The Breakdown of the State in Lebanon, 1967–1976,* London: I. B. Tauris, 2000; Itamar Rabinovich, *The War of Lebanon, 1970–1985;* Marius Deeb, *Syria's Terrorist War on Lebanon and the Peace Process,* New York: Palgrave, 2003; Kamal Salibi, *Cross Roads to Civil War, Lebanon: 1958–1976,* Delmar, New York: Caravan, 1976.

11. See Mordechai Zipory, *Bekav Yashar,* p. 267, Ze'ev Schiff and Ehud Ya'ari, *Milhemet Sholal,* pp. 56–57. See also Robert M. Hatem, *From Israel to Damascus,* New York: Pride International Publications, 1999. Mordechai Zipory, *Bekav Yashar,* p. 268.

12. See Yitzhak Rabin, *Pinkas Sherut* ("Rabin's Memoirs"), Tel Aviv: Ma'ariv, 1979, pp. 502–507.

13. *Ibid.,* pp. 502–503.

14. Moshe Ma'oz, *Syria and Israel, from War to Peace-Making,* Oxford: Oxford University Press, 1995, pp. 144–152.

15. See Mordechai Zipory, *Bekav Yashar,* p. 314; Ze'ev Schiff and Ehud Ya'ari, *Milhemet Sholal,* p. 38; an interview by the author with Yehoshua Sagi, former head of the Israeli Military Intelligence in June 1981, Bat Yam, 17 April, 1994.

16. Raphael Eytan, *Rafol, Sipuru shel Hayal* ("Raful, the Story of a Soldier"), Tel Aviv: Ma'ariv, 1985, p. 307. See also Mordechai Zipory, *Bekav Yashar,* p. 299; Ze'ev Schieff and Ehud Ya'ari, *Milhemet Sholal,* pp. 110–111.

17. See Aharon Klieman, "Israel," in Haim Shaked and Daniel Dishon (eds.), *MECS (Middle East Contemporary Survey),* Vol. VI (1981–1982), pp. 641–650; Ze'ev Schiff and Ehud Ya'arif, *Milhemet Sholal,* pp. 28–31.

18. Ze'ev Schiff and Ehud Ya'ari, *Milhemet Sholal,* pp. 31–32.

19. *Ibid.,* pp. 11–13.

20. See Raphael Eytan, *Rafol,* p. 310; Ze'ev Schiff and Ehud Ya'arif, *Milhemet Sholal,* pp. 28–31.

21. See Mordechai Zipori, *Bekav Yashar,* p. 314; Ze'ev Schiff and Ehud Ya'ari, *Milhemet Sholal,* p. 38; an interview by the author with Yehoshua Sagi, former head of the Israeli Military Intelligence in June 1981, Bat Yam, 17 April, 1994.

22. *Ha'aretz, 7,* 8 June, 1982.

23. Mordechai Zipori, *Bekav Yashar,* p. 279.

24. *Ha'aretz, 9* June, 1982.

25. Richard B. Parker, *The Politics of Miscalculation in the Middle East,* Bloomington: Indiana University Press, 1993, pp. 167–178; see also Mordechai Zipori, *Bekav Yashar,* p. 266; Ze'ev Schiff and Ehud Ya'ari, *Milhemet Sholal,* p. 183.

26. Mordechai Zipori, *Bekav Yashar,* p. 297; an interview by the author with Amir Drori, former commander of the Northern Command, Tel Aviv, 7 June, 1997.

27. *Al-Nahar* (Beirut), *24,* 25 August, 1982.

28. *Ha'aretz,* 15 September, 1982; see also Raphael Eytan, *Rafol,* pp. 218–220.

29. See Ze'ev Schiff and Ehud Ya'arif, *Milhemet Sholal,* pp. 289–291.

30. Moshe Sharet, *Yoman Ishi* ("Personal Diary"), Tel Aviv: Ma'ariv, 1978, Vol. 8, pp. 2397–2400. See also Eyal Zisser, "The Maronites, Lebanon and the State of Israel: Early Contacts," *Middle Eastern Studies,* Vol. 31, No. 4 (October 1995) pp. 889–918.

31. See Aharon Klieman, "Israel," in Haim Shaked and Daniel Dishon (eds.), *MECS (Middle East Contemporary Survey),* Vol. VI (1981–1982), pp. 641–650.

32. For more see Eyal Zisser, "Is Any One Afraid of Israel?" *MEQ (Middle East Quarterly),* Vol. VIII, No. 2 (Spring 2001), pp. 3–11; "The Return of Hizballah," *MEQ,* Vol. IX, No. 4 (Fall 2002), pp. 3–11.

33. See Ze'ev Schiff and Ehud Ya'ari, *Milhemet Sholal,* p. 380.

34. See *Ha'aretz,* 17 June, 2001.

35. See 'Uzi Benziman, *Emet Dibarti* ("I Spoke the Truth"), Jerusalem: Keter, 2002; see also by 'Uzi Benziman, *Sharon, an Israeli Ceasar,* New York: Adama books, 1985.

36. See Mustafa Talas, *Al-Ghazw al-Israeli liLubnan* ("The Israeli Invasion to Lebanon"), Damascus: Mu'assisat Tishrin lilSahafa wal-Nashr, 1983; Eyal Zisser, *Asad's Legacy: Syria in Transition,* New York: New York University Press, 2000, pp. 11–23.

37. See Fouad Ajami, *The Vanished Imam, Musa al-Sadr and the Shia in Lebanon,* Ithaca: Cornell University Press, 1984.

38. Magnus Ranstrop, *Hizballah in Lebanon, the Politics of the Western Hostage Crisis,* New York: St. Martin's Press, 1997; Hala Jaber, *Hezbollah, Born with a Vengeance,* New York: Columbia University Press, 1992.

39. See Anita Shapira, "Politics and Collective Memory: The Debate over the New Historians in Israel," pp. 9–40; Baruch Kimmerling, "Academic History Caught in the Cross-Fire: The Case of Israeli-Jewish Historiography," pp. 41–65; Ilan Pappe, "Critique and Agenda: The Post-Zionist Scholars in Israel," pp. 66–90, *History and Memory,* Vol. 7, No. 1 (Spring/Summer 1995).

11

The Palestinian Intifada, 1987–1991

Reuven Aharoni

Despite the fact that the Palestine Liberation Organization (PLO) had encountered difficulties in its desire to establish pivots of control in the West Bank and Gaza Strip, and in its ability to recruit supporters, finally an uprising broke out in December 1987. It was a massive act of resistance, which had gained the title "Intifada" (in Arabic, a "shaking off").

The popular uprising of 1987 was part of a struggle waged for almost a century between two peoples—Zionist Jews and Arab Palestinians—over the same piece of land. It was the third outbreak of the Jewish-Palestinian intercommunal conflict. The first two outbreaks took place in the Mandatory period—in its midst (1936) and in its end (1947–1948). The conflicts had a character of a classical intercommunal struggle, and the two groups fought in relatively equal conditions, meaning that both of them had to rely on illegal militias, without having the advantages provided by controlling the enforcement apparatus of the government.

This latest case was quite different. It was essentially asymmetric since the Israelis by then had at their disposal all the paraphernalia of a sovereign state, which the Palestinians totally lacked.

The uprooting of the PLO from Lebanon and its scattering in the periphery of the Arab world dismissed the option of the Palestinian "armed struggle,"—the dream that Israel could be suppressed by terror, guerilla war, or even a conventional war. Since 1982, violent demonstrations and violations of order in the "territories" (the West Bank and Gaza Strip occupied by Israel in 1967) had increased six times and a tremendous change happened in the ratio between spontaneous violations of order and initiated terror activities: In 1984 only one terror action emerged, compared with eleven violations of order, in 1987, one terror action compared with eighteen violations of order.

In their book *Trouble in Utopia,* Dan Horowitz and Moshe Lissak defined the differences in perceptions between the Likud and the Labor Parties, regarding the nature of the Israeli-Arab conflict as "fundamental attitudes": whether it is a conflict between countries, as it was seen after the birth of Israel, or a conflict between communities, as it was regarded at the time of the *Yishuv* (in Hebrew, "the [Jewish] population" of the Land of Israel before 1948). The Labor holds the idea that the conflict is between states while the Likud "tended to emphasize the inter-communal aspects of the conflict." The opposed perceptions were actually operational guidelines. The Camp David Accord, the peace treaty with Egypt, and the Lebanese war caused the Palestinization of the conflict. Not only did the conflict become intercommunal at the end of the Lebanese war, it also focused on the borders of the Mandatory Land of Israel. The debate between the "fundamental attitudes" continued as if it had not been resolved. That is the reason why the Labor government and the defense authorities (which continued to act according to the inter-state model) did not understand the meaning of the Intifada. The PLO, which truly perceived the conflict as an Israeli-Palestinian confrontation, did not understand that in its new stage (after the Lebanese war) the intercommunal conflict returned to its original territorial limits, meaning the Mandatory Land of Israel. Therefore the Palestinian "inside" will dictate its dynamics. Not only did the PLO not initiate the Intifada, as it pretended afterwards, but it even did not realize the Intifada's implication for a long time.

The Intifada broke out at the time when political, social, cultural, and economic processes had matured in Israel and had changed Israel from a Jewish-Israeli nation-state to a de-facto binational state. From that aspect, December 9, 1987, is the day of the symbolic announcement of the intercommunal conflict, the barrier of the conceptions collapsed in the face of the reality. When the violent confrontation erupted in its full scale, a new chapter in the history of the Jewish-Arab conflict had opened. Although the Intifada was the fourth outbreak of this old dispute, its uniqueness was being the first general uprising against a Jewish-Israeli rule.

The Palestinian Intifada should be examined in a wide context that includes the Israeli policy toward the PLO, Jordan, the local Palestinian leadership, and the territories. A review of the Israeli internal political arena, the attitudes of the major parties, and the reactions of the Israeli society enable one to draw a better picture of the road to the Intifada.

ISRAEL, THE TERRITORIES, AND THE PALESTINIAN SOCIETY

The declared aim of the Intifada was to put an end to the governmental status quo in the Land of Israel and to the monopoly of the Jewish-Israeli community on public and government resources. But, paradoxically, the Intifada could begin only because this status quo became established and reciprocal relations were created between the two communities in the fields of politics, society, economy, and culture. The publicist Meron Benvenisti defined the pattern of relationship between the two communities in conflict as "intimate hostility." Relations of confrontation and hostility procreate not only alienation and separation, they create intercommunal interactions, which are stronger than peace relationships.

Two processes were underway. Among Palestinians, a rebuilding effort (called "restructuring") began. The other process, initiated by Israelis, was a gradual encroachment upon Palestinian resources, manifested in the seizure of land and the establishment of Jewish settlements in Gaza Strip and the West Bank.

Israel went on immersing into the occupation and had deepened its grip in the territories already after 1967. In October of that year, "The Land of Israel" movement was established, asserting the right of Israel to rule all of the historical Mandatory Palestine. Issues of the political agenda and contents of the collective and historical memory had changed rapidly. Questions such as defensible borders, the historical rights of the Jews, which were regarded as already solved, became the core of the public debate. The public discourse was about the possibilities of land for peace agreements and the settlement of Jews in the new territories of the Land of Israel.

Behind the settlement project was a new social movement—Gush Emunim ("the Bloc of the Faithful"), founded after the 1973 war. By 1977, over eighty settlements existed in the territories. It was the year Israelis voted the Labor government out of office, in favor of the Likud nationalist right-wing party, under the leadership of Menachem Begin. Under the new Likud regime, about 100,000 Jewish settlers took up residence in the territories by the end of the 1980s. However, the territories of the West Bank and the Gaza Strip were never annexed to Israel, but remained within the scope of the Israeli rule and control.

Lacking the possibility to implement the options of annexation, or withdrawal in return for peace, or transferring Arabs, the status quo continued and turned into a slow-progressing annexation of the territories by laying down the fact of Jewish settlement in the territories. By the early 1980s, the Jewish presence gradually intensified. Many unsettled lands were announced as state lands and were opened for founding Jewish settlements, even adjacent to Palestinian-populated areas. The Israeli occupation had turned into hardened military rule—a stick far more than a carrot, because of the fear that the Palestinian nationalism was accelerating. In 1985, the Defense Minister Yitzhak Rabin introduced the term "iron fist," while international initiatives failed to bring a solution to the dispute, and among the Palestinians a young generation of leadership began to develop, a generation which was growing from the "inside" and the "bottom."

AN INSIDE VIEW—DEMOGRAPHY OF FRUSTRATIONS AND HARDSHIP

Palestinians in the West Bank and Gaza Strip were largely a young people. In the first decade of Israeli rule in the territories, the population increased by almost 19 percent, and from 1967 until 1986, by 20 percent. In absolute figures, this means that until 1986, more than 140,000 persons were added to the population of the West Bank (from 696,000 to 836,000) and more than 94,000 in the Gaza Strip (from 451,000 to 545,000).

The increase in the young population was paralleled by impressive strides in education. In 1970, about half the population aged fourteen and above lacked formal education, and by 1986 this figure had shrunk to less than half. The spread of higher education was an outcome of the establishment of academic institutions after 1967. At the time Israel entered the territories, no single university existed. By 1982, eight academic institutions opened their doors in the West Bank and Gaza Strip. The growth in the student population was unprecedented. In the mid-1970s, there were 1,086 students in the West Bank. By the mid-1980s, there were 10,000 students.

Probably no structures played a more important role in this regard than the new universities. Jordanian authorities did not allow opening institutions for high education in the West Bank, fearful of the emergence of an independent political center there. It was Moshe Dayan who approved creation of three universities as part of his "liberal policy." Also six other colleges now functioned. These institutions became centers of thought and a greenhouse for a new potential leadership. The universities' students and graduates hoped to achieve appropriate jobs, but integration either in the Israeli or in the Palestinian labor market was hopeless and useless. Many of them had to be content with blue-collar simple and even sleazy jobs in the Israeli towns, which caused growing frustration. Thus, the university and college students were determined to broaden their social and political activities outside the campuses, looking to form an alternative social, institutional network.

The social volatility generated by the radical thrust was fueled by a growing gap between the more extended education available to the young generation and the limited availability of jobs commensurate with that education and the expectations it generated. There was a striking disparity between the increase in the number of university graduates and their inability to find suitable jobs in either the local or the Israeli labor markets. True, in the first decade of Israeli rule in the territories, both the West Bank and Gaza experienced high growth rates in terms of GNP and per capita consumption, thanks in large measure to the opening of the Israeli economy to workers from the territories. However, the local employment market relied predominantly on agriculture and menial labor. Israeli policy since 1967 was to avoid investments in infrastructures and industry in the territories. In the absence of changes in the economic infrastructure, employment opportunities commensurate with the education of the young generation did not develop. Israeli society could not endure Palestinians having jobs in Israel, other than those that were menial and of the lowest level.

Only 15 percent of university graduates were able to find work suited to their qualifications. Others continued their studies or took blue-collar jobs that were far below their level of expectations and were irreconcilable with their self-image. Some drifted to Arab oil-exporting countries in search of employment, but the economic slowdown in those countries, beginning in 1983, reduced this form of emigration. According to Israeli military government figures for 1985, there were 4,000 unemployed university graduates in the West Bank. By the time the Intifada erupted, their number had risen to 8,000.

High school graduates found themselves in the same situation. The majority remained unemployed or took jobs in Israel, usually in construction or the service sector. Both possibilities were incommensurate with their education and totally at variance with their expectations.

The broadening of education among the Palestinian younger generation and the absence of suitable employment nourished a climate of political radicalism. The resultant gap—what sociologists call a disparity between high personal expectations in the employment sphere, generated by education and opportunities in the economic market—fomented a desire for action geared to alter the existing order. In a situation in which the potential and economic loss was negligible, the benefit to be derived from changing this situation was perceived to be promising and attractive.

Union activity increased dramatically after the 1967 war. Growth was most rapid after 1975, especially in the West Bank, although the unions did not incorporate that half of the workforce commuting daily to Israel, where they were not recognized. Like the student-led groups, the unions were part of an intense effort by leftist organizations to mobilize the population. Political radicalism was always at the top of their agenda. The trade unions were models for a common effort transcending family and other ties. They also served as excellent schools for local and regional leadership, most union leaders eventually being detained or deported by the Israelis.

Student groups and labor unions constituted only a small portion of the institutional network that existed at the outbreak of the Intifada in 1987. Charities, branches of the Red Crescent Society, the Palestinian Physicians', Pharmacists', and Lawyers' Association, and other professional organizations, all thrived—especially when compared to the period of the Jordanian rule—helping build a viable infrastructure under prolonged occupation.

Equally important was the deteriorating standard of economic life in the territories during the 1980s, a major factor in the semblance of normality during the occupation's first fifteen years as a burgeoning economy. Three sources of prosperity had fueled this economy—Israel itself, with its developed, labor-intensive market; Jordan, with its strong agriculture build-up; and the Persian Gulf states, with their seemingly endless supply of petro-dollars. By the early 1980s, each had entered a prolonged crisis, in turn choking the West Bank and Gaza. A sense of economic hopelessness now combined with flagging hopes that international diplomacy, the PLO, or outside Arab military forces would bring an end to the Israeli occupation.

The contrast between the pre- and post-1980 economy in the West Bank and Gaza Strip was dramatic. With overall economic growth in the period from 1967 to 1980 averaging over 5 percent annually, the territories had witnessed an easing of the harsh material conditions the Palestinians had endured under Jordanian and Egyptian rule. The people of Gaza, in particular, had entered the era of occupation with annual per capita incomes averaging $80. By the beginning of the Intifada, the figure had reached $1,700. Even in the West Bank, which had been part of Jordan's rapidly growing economy—over 8 percent annual economic growth between 1954 and 1967—personal consumption was far greater than at the beginning of Israeli rule, the gross domestic product more than tripling between 1968 and 1980, an extraordinarily high rate of growth by world standards. Those economies had made life materially pleasurable for most of the population.

During the late 1970s, worrisome economic signs were seen. Israeli economy slipped into a long period of slow growth and stagnation, with extremely high rates of inflation. For Palestinians, now deeply integrated into the Israeli economy, stagnation had dire consequences. By 1985, it was evident that the wages for those working in Israel were eroding impressively. Unemployment began to hit the territories seriously in the early 1980s. The young and the educated particularly were affected harshly. The resulting economic discontent, combined with the occupation, formed the basis for easy nationalist fervor.

Complicating the situation in Israel was that in outside economies. Through the 1970s, Palestinians had left the West Bank and Gaza in large numbers for opportunities elsewhere. However, during the 1980s, Jordan's absorptive capacity dried up in the wake of the larger Middle Eastern economic crisis. The oil-producing states were also facing severe contraction. Palestinian Arabs in the West Bank and Gaza were thrown back on the local economy and that of Israel at precisely the wrong time. The Israeli policy of carrots and economic opportunities—something for

Palestinians to contemplate losing when the thought of resistance crossed their minds—meant little to a generation raised and educated under occupation, many of whose members were now unemployed and held little economic hope for the future.

The activities initiated by the Palestinian youth had at least two immediate results. For the population at large, participating in community activities heightened the sense of self-reliance. For the young activists, direct contact with the population supplied experience in dealing with daily problems. In the long run, the sustained interaction between the youngsters and the local population would erode the authority of local leaders, such as the *mukhtars,* who had acted as "go-betweens" for the population and the Israeli authorities. It would also undermine the effectiveness of the military government and the civil administration, providing the organizational basis for the Intifada.

The ability of Palestinian youth to gain the cooperation of broad sectors of the population, to the point of disrupting the day-to-day activities of the Israeli authorities, was not an inevitable outcome. It is difficult to imagine the Intifada without the youngsters first laying the groundwork among the local population. But it is equally insufficient to explain the sustainability and duration of the Intifada solely in terms of the youngsters' community activity. The key to the Intifada's resilience lies in the participation of the merchants and the white-collar groups.

Occupation had made it more likely that such voices would be heard, and that enough cohesion existed for a collective response to be effective. The occupation had substantially weakened the group of landowners and merchants, what ordinarily would have been the most prominent and influential social class. The new institutional activities, led by the university and high school graduates, served as meeting grounds for diverse groups of the Palestinian society. The occupation thus resulted in the first steps toward a political leveling of the society. The revolutionary fervor and style of action of the youngsters may have been in tune with the inner feelings of this class, but hardly with their wallets, their worldview, or their way of life. They preferred caution to daring, measured steps over dramatic acts.

So, at the outbreak of the Intifada, the Palestinian society already incorporated student groups, labor unions, women's associations and other professional, welfare, and cultural organizations. All thrived to build a well-developed civil society, helping make life under prolonged occupation viable. They all were ready to take an active part in the uprising.

Moreover, the Intifada was not only a manifestation of a resistance against the Israeli rule but also an expression of dissatisfaction from the Palestinian politics and leadership outside the territories. Thousands of young Palestinians, who resisted actively to the Israeli rule, were arrested. In the Israeli prisons and in the refugee camps their national consciousness and political identity had become crystallized. Young activists became local leaders.

JORDAN AND THE PLO IN THE POLITICAL GAME

If, nevertheless, the middle class became a full partner in the Intifada, the causes were twofold: One was the absence of an effective local leadership to shield them from the pressures exerted by the young radicals, and the second was the growing erosion in Jordan's standing in the West Bank, weakening its ability to offset radical influences. Their disappearance created an institutional vacuum through which latent radicalism erupted in a manner that left both Israel and Jordan at a loss to contain or control events. As a result, what had seemed improbable from the point of view of the middle class in the pre-Intifada period assumed an aura of inevitability in the course of the uprising.

The conditions that prevailed in the West Bank left the local leadership no real choice but to seek support from both Jordan and the PLO. The absence of a tradition of political independence in the West Bank, combined with the lack of a distinctive ideology and a self-sustaining economy, and the fact that the only common border with the Arab world was with Jordan, precluded the creation of an autonomous power base that might have impelled the West Bank leadership to pursue political initiatives beyond the parameters of Jordanian-PLO coexistence. An Israeli approach to the local leadership as a political partner for negotiations on a permanent settlement, if accompanied by far-reaching territorial concessions, might have created a convenient political climate to build such a power base. Without that willingness, it was unrealistic to expect the emergence of an independent power base in the West Bank.

As the local leadership became more aware that both Jordan and the PLO buttered its bread, it was increasingly disinclined to embark on a new path that could be perceived as a threat to either side's vital interests. The leadership scrupulously refrained from initiating or taking part in political activity beyond the day-to-day level—be it negotiations on a political settlement detached from the PLO, from Jordan, or from both; or full-scale civil disobedience, entailing a severance of contact with the Israelis, would lead to a forceful Israeli reaction. This, in turn, could harm the local institutions that assisted both Jordan and the PLO to tighten their grip on the Palestinian population. By the same token, talks by the local leadership with Israel on a political settlement would undercut the demand of both Jordan and the PLO to play a dominant role in decisions concerning the future of the territories.

The emerging coexistence between Jordan and the PLO encouraged the Palestinian leadership in the West Bank to move toward what can be termed *controlled radicalism*. The ensuing activity was characterized by no acceptance of the Israeli occupation, but at the same time, avoidance of a direct clash with the Israeli authorities. It did entail readiness for cooperation with Israel on daily matters. Radical leaders organized strikes and mass-demonstrations and voiced publicly their unequivocal support for the PLO as their sole representative in any political settlement. Nevertheless, the radicals and certainly the more moderates were careful not to strain their relations with Israel irrevocably. They maintained constant contact with the military government in order to ensure the continued operation of the local governments and of essential services in the realms of health, welfare, education, and commerce.

Local activity associated with controlled radicalism gained Jordan's acquiescence as well as PLO support. PLO backing for such activity was not self-evident. Although activity in the spirit of controlled radicalism helped the PLO maintain a political and economic infrastructure in the West Bank, it also entailed dependence on local institutions that derived their legitimacy from Israel. Against this background, one might argue that the PLO was willing to acquiesce in Israel's continued presence in the territories, assisting it to ensure normalization in day-to-day life.

The mainstream headed by the Fatah preferred to support the pattern of controlled radicalism rather than back what it considered irresponsible radical activities against Israel. Arafat summoned all the rhetorical ability at his command to justify calculated radical actions: "The most important element in the Palestinian program is holding on to the land and not warfare alone. If you only fight—that is a tragedy. The important thing is that you hold on to the land, and afterwards—combat" (*Al-Fikr* [Paris], June 1985).

The practice of controlled radicalism involved formidable difficulties. Yet local leaders continued to see in controlled radicalism an optional mode of behavior. As long as Jordanian-PLO coexistence prevailed, and as long as Israel continued to pin its hopes on political settlements with Arab partners outside the territories, simultaneous reliance on the PLO and Jordan, followed by cooperative relations with Israel, remained the West Bank's preferred mode of action.

It was the stance of controlled radicalism that helped the local leadership retain its standing among the population and repulse pressures toward extremism from the youth. As a result, the middle class—merchants, officials, and other white-collar employees—were able to pursue their quotidian activity in the presence of a prolonged occupation.

ISRAELI SOCIETY AND POLITICS AND THE INTIFADA

In Israel, political stands regarding the territories derived primarily from two simultaneous yet contradictory political conceptions: the Greater Israel vision associated with the right-wing Likud (meaning "uniting"), and the territorial compromise approach espoused by the Labor alignment.

The Labor, which was in power until 1977, viewed the West Bank and Gaza Strip in terms of security considerations, whereas the Likud, which succeeded the Labor, spoke in terms of historic rights as well. The Labor, fearful of what demography portended, sought a political settlement that would enable Israel to rid itself of densely populated Arab areas, while the Likud, with an eye on geography—the whole land of Israel—urged a permanent Israeli presence throughout the West Bank and Gaza. While the Labor advocated selective settlement, chiefly in the Jordan Rift Valley and the Etzion bloc south of Jerusalem, whereas for the Likud the entire West Bank was a legitimate, indeed vital, target for Jewish settlement. Under the Likud government, the pace of settlement in the West Bank intensified, the settler population increased, and budgetary allocations for the physical infrastructure in the West Bank were multiplied.

During the entire first year of the Intifada the Israeli government did not advance a single plan or policy for dealing with it politically. There were three reasons for this. First, the cabinet was deadlocked on the question of the territories, and any political initiative risked a collapse of the government coalition, which included both Likud and Labor and forcing new elections. Second, the Likud bloc was not enthusiastic for a negotiated settlement with the Palestinians. Third, the Israeli electorate was not sufficiently exercised or united to push the government toward a political resolution of the dispute. It seems that Israelis could not accept another independent nationality that had claims to the same land, since this would imply renouncing their own exclusive claims. Only in 2003, after three years of the bloody second Intifada, Prime Minister Ariel Sharon declared for the first time his agreement for a Palestinian State in the West Bank and Gaza. Nevertheless, according to an opinion poll taken in March 1988, 39 percent of Israelis desired the immediate opening of negotiations and 58 percent believed that their government should make a positive response to the American Shultz plan, which was based upon the principle of "land for peace." Many Israelis did not define *Eretz Yisrael* as encompassing the entirety of the West Bank and Gaza Strip.

Two constraints on the way should be examined. The 1984 election had produced a situation in which neither bloc could form a coalition without the other. A government of "national unity," as such cabinets were called, was formed that included six other small coalition partners drawn from the political left, the right, and the ultra-orthodox religious bloc. The 1984 coalition agreement also provided for a rotation of the office of prime minister. Simon Peres, head of the Labor, served the first two years, with Yitzhak Shamir, leader of the Likud, succeeding him. Thus the existence of a government in which power was divided between two rival political blocs, the Likud and the Labor, representing different constituencies and holding divergent views on how to deal with the territories. Within the cabinet a rule of parity also existed, which meant that the government could act only when a consensus was obtained. One side, then, could block the other. Deadlock on the Palestinian question was guaranteed.

The National Unity government had been brought into existence in 1984 with a mandate to solve two short-term but pressing problems: rampant inflation and the withdrawal of Israeli troops from Lebanon. These, it was thought, could be better achieved by the Labor and the Likud governing jointly. The second and more basic reason for the two main parties to collaborate in one government was a badly fragmented political system. Beginning in the 1970s, a shift occurred within the political order, manifested in the decline of the Labor Party, the rise of the Likud, and in the 1980s, the proliferation of small parties of all kinds on the right and left of the political spectrum. These parties gained influence at the expense of the major blocs, and this eventually produced a stalemated political situation in which the Labor and the Likud had little alternative but to join together.

The development was largely the result of a mutation in the basic structure of society, which became much less European (Ashkenazi) and more Oriental (Sephardi) in composition and culture. This, added to already existing tensions and divisions, brought the society to a point where no basic agreement was possible on solutions to the fundamental problems facing the country. The stalemated political system was thus the result of a divided electorate.

The second constraint upon a political initiative was ideology, in particular, the beliefs of one man—Prime Minister Shamir—and their concrete expression in the policies and program of the Likud Bloc, which he headed. Shamir was a true believer in the doctrine of Greater Israel. It was the Likud that translated the ideology of "Greater Israel" into a practical program and built a huge constituency to support it. In Israel a hard-line position on the Palestinian question was one way to win votes, especially from Oriental Jews. Inside Israel the settlement movement became a sacred cow, receiving disproportionate favor in budgetary allocations and enjoying priority in almost every sector.

There was yet another reason why the government did not rush to advance any political proposals during the first year of the Intifada. This was the general acceptance of the awakening by Israeli society, which became resigned to it. After the initial months of excitement, debate, and increased polarization, Israelis learned to live with the Intifada. The absence of strong pressure upon the government was thus a significant negative factor.

The most important impact of the Intifada upon society was psychological. The awakening took away the justification of the occupation. Israelis were used to believing that the occupation was improving the standard of life for Palestinians. Now Israelis did not believe anymore that their government had any positive role to play there. The occupation could not be justified.

The second effect was political. The Intifada stimulated a tremendous amount of discussion among all sections of the general population, and helped polarize society even more. Prior to the Intifada, the Palestinian question had objectively been the most important political issue, but the majority of Israelis had succeeded in blocking it out of their daily lives. After the eruption of the Intifada, Israelis were obliged to talk about the Palestinians. Should the government recognize and negotiate with the PLO? Should part of or all of the territories be given up? And if so, under what conditions? The right questions had finally emerged and were being discussed as part of ordinary political discourse. The Intifada also gave a stimulus to the Israeli left, especially the Peace Now movement, moribund since Peres had brought the Labor Party into coalition with the Likud. The conscience of the Israeli left was pricked by the IDF's harsh response to the Palestinian demonstrations. Some widely publicized instances of IDF brutality—the burial alive of four Palestinian youths and some deaths of Palestinian infants following their exposure to tear gas, for example. The Israeli right was also prompted to take action, for the Intifada posed a grave threat to the realization of its program. The right thus became more right, and the left more left.

As time passed, however, the Israeli society began to move ever so slightly to the right. As late as November 1987, opinion polls showed the Labor with a 10 percent lead over the Likud; by the following June, there was parity. The "transfer" idea also began to gain acceptance. In a poll conducted in June 1988, almost half of the Israelis questioned supported the mass-expulsion of Palestinians from the West Bank and Gaza Strip. Yet in the same poll, 50 percent of people supported a redivision of the territories between Israelis and Palestinians even before negotiations had begun. Many polls exhibited contradictory results. It seems that Israelis were basically confused and held contradictory views on the same subject.

By early autumn 1988, many Israelis had begun to tire of the steady stream of news emanating from the territories. People continued to talk about the problem, but most learned to live with the Intifada by blocking it out. One explanation to such reaction is what the publicist Tom Segev saw as a phenomenon of escapism from politics coming from the Lebanon war and the establishment of the National Unity government, which turned all real debate meaningless.

A more comprehensive explanation is that an entire generation of Israelis, that of military age, had grown up to think of the West Bank and Gaza as part of Israel—a perception insufficiently challenged by teachers in the classrooms where maps of Israel often did not even show the "green line" (the pre-1967 border of Israel). Moreover, Israelis who heard interviews with Palestinians and watched on television demonstrators clashing with security forces saw the bitterness and hatred accumulated over the last twenty years being unleashed. Under such circumstances, Israelis were not likely to make fine distinctions between resistance to occupation and repudiation of the State of Israel itself.

Most Israelis were not directly affected by the uprising. Israelis did not demand that the government find a political solution because they could not see any pressing need to do so. Israelis will only get excited if other Israelis are killed and this was rarely the case in the Intifada. After ten months, only five Israelis had died as a result of it. The liberal-left discussed the conflict, but its members rarely visited the West Bank or Gaza. For Israelis the Intifada was not a major issue and most continued to support the status quo in the territories.

Ironically, however, it was the political establishment that had been most affected by the Intifada. Israel's leaders had to plan and conduct the "war," face the frustration of seeing the Palestinian revolt spiral out of control, deal with settlers' accusations of lack of governmental protection, and parry international criticism and attacks in the press.

An important distinction, however, must be made between the period from December 9, 1987 (the start of the Intifada) to November 15, 1988, on the one hand, and the period following the mid-November 1988 Palestinian National Council (PNC) declaration, on the other. The Proclamation of Palestine statehood, the PLO's recognition of Israel, and Arafat's speech and the Geneva press conference had marked a major propaganda victory for the Palestinians internationally. In Europe, governments opened official dialogues with the PLO, issued formal invitations to Arafat to visit, and generally upgraded the Palestinian issue. In addition, the U.S. administration's decision to begin talks with the PLO suggested a shift in policy that had grave implications for U.S.-Israeli relations. In late December 1988, some political analysts in Israel estimated that the government had a very short time to state a policy before the Americans began submitting their own proposals. Under these new circumstances, no Israeli government could ignore the pressure that was building up.

To a certain extent, the formation on December 22, 1988, of a new National Unity government was a response to this state of affairs. Elections held on November 1 had confirmed the earlier trend toward political polarization and the weakening of the political center. The Likud gained forty Knesset seats (30.8 percent of the vote) and the Labor thirty-nine seats (30 percent), but parties on the left and the right and especially those in the ultra-orthodox religious bloc made the real gains. It was argued, then, that another National Unity government, however weak, would at least be stronger than a narrow right-wing government of the Likud and the religious parties. As a result of the election, the Likud strengthened. Shamir would now be prime minister for a full four-year term. Rabin returned to his former post as defense minister. However, the reconstitution of the National Unity government reestablished the same basic constraints that had previously existed. In the inner cabinet, divided equally between the Labor and the Likud, a tied vote automatically defeated any proposal under consideration. Any initiative would have to be supported by both factions of the coalition.

Following the PNC 1988 declaration, Peres and Shamir declared that it had not changed the PLO's hostility to Israel. There would be no Palestinian state and no negotiations with the PLO. This, however, did not imply an identity of policies. Peres and the Labor still favored territorial compromise, while Shamir was opposed to the convening of an international conference to talk with Palestinians. The Labor, on the other hand, saw an advantage in making contacts with Palestinian public personalities in East Jerusalem who, its leaders believed, were more moderate and flexible.

In January 1989, Rabin proposed that elections be held in the territories to choose Palestinians who would administer them for an interim period of "autonomy." Rabin may have hoped to divide Palestinians and thereby weaken the Intifada. Shamir was uncomfortable with the notion of any peace proposal. He was concerned that the new Bush administration in the United States might have a change of heart, compared to its predecessor Ronald Reagan. The United States criticized the IDF policy of opening fire upon Palestinian civilians. Bush invited Shamir to Washington, spurring him to bring a definite proposal.

The real question was how to satisfy the United States jeopardizing the Likud's longstanding position of not ceding an inch of land to the Palestinians. Rabin's idea of elections, therefore, was tailored to Likud needs at that stage. Shamir offered a proposal providing for the election by Palestinians in the territories of representatives who would negotiate with Israel for a five-year period of autonomy. At some point, but not later than three years, negotiations would begin for a permanent solution. Each side could than introduce whatever proposals it wished. However, the Likud's basic position was also reaffirmed. A section of the document entitled "Basic Premises" stated that Israel would not talk with the PLO, would not accept the establishment of a Palestinian state in the West Bank and Gaza, and would not agree to any change in the status of the territories. In April 1989, Shamir officially presented the general details of his plan to President Bush, who accepted it, though cautiously. He was pleased that a link had been established between autonomy and final status negotiations. The bottom line was that the Shamir plan, after all, became the basis of U.S.-Middle East diplomacy.

Too many questions remained unanswered. For example, the nature of the final settlement was left entirely open. As for the elections, would the Intifada have to come to an end before they could be held? Would the inhabitants of East Jerusalem be able to vote? For Shamir, ambiguity was an advantage, a key to short-term success. The postponement of discussion of the terms of the final settlement had averted a clash between the Labor and the Likud, enabling the two to unite in support of the plan. By not dealing with issues on which there was disagreement, the government could exploit the potentialities of the initiative and improve its international standing.

This plan stood little chance of being accepted by Palestinians. After more than a year of Intifada, after having recognized Israel and accepted a two-state solution, Palestinians were being asked to postpone consideration of the most important issues for several years. Shamir was fond of saying that during final status talks all options would be open, that any subject could be raised, but the document itself made it clear that a Palestinian state was not an acceptable option. The United States hoped that it could entice Palestinians at least to begin some kind of negotiating process, but Shamir himself made this difficult.

Shamir's basic assumption was that Israel would have to talk to the leadership in the territories, so elections were not needed to identify those leaders. Israel knew who they were and had been talking to them all alone. The Shamir plan was an attempt to undermine the PLO's public relations successes. Israel's leadership chose to dig in and play for time.

Indeed, for a short duration Shamir succeeded. The Bush-Baker team gave him six to twelve months to find Palestinian interlocutors. The implication was clear. Israel's government had already achieved its main aim. Shamir had regained the initiative in the United States. Approved by the entire cabinet on May 14, 1989, Shamir's plan became the official policy of Israel. It was now up to the Palestinians, and especially the PLO, to deal with this new situation.

ISRAEL AND THE LOCAL PALESTINIAN LEADERSHIP

Israeli policy toward the local leadership and the Palestinian population as a whole remained unchanged. Hand in hand with further intensification of the settlement in the West Bank, the Likud government behaved as if this leadership was capable of functioning under such circumstances and pleasing the Israeli authorities. Israel gave priority to securing calm in the territories through cooperation with the local leadership on day-to-day matters. At the same time, Israel refused to consider these leaders as potential partners for talks on a permanent settlement. Two repercussions followed from the Israeli policy. First, the disinclination to conduct political negotiations with the local leadership encouraged that leadership's continued cultivation of political and economic ties with Jordan and later on with the PLO; and second, Israel's desire to maintain calm relations with the Palestinian population through cooperation with the local leadership meant Israel's acquiescence in the continued influence of Jordan and the PLO and in consequence, the affinity of Palestinians in the territories for both alike.

Indeed, Israel continued to acquiesce in the local leadership's affiliation with both the PLO and Jordan even after the 1976 West Bank municipal elections. The victory of pro-PLO candidates did not prevent the military government from appointing them as mayors. Furthermore, Israel allowed the mayors to visit Amman and other Arab capitals for meetings with Jordanian personalities and senior PLO officials. Israel took no steps to block the continued transfer of funds by Jordan and the PLO to local authorities and other institutions. The National Guidance Committee (NGC), formed in October 1978, benefited from the same Israeli policy. The committee included mayors as well as representatives from trade unions, charitable societies, women's organizations, student associations, and the religious establishment. The NGC was established with PLO's encouragement to help in the political struggle against the autonomy plan contained in the Camp David Accords.

Israel continued to tolerate the local leadership's dual PLO and Jordan affiliation, despite the escalation of anti-Israeli activities in the territories, after Anwar al-Sadat's visit to Jerusalem in November 1977 and the signing of the Camp David Accords. There were more demonstrations, more school and commercial strikes, more petitions, and a growing readiness to challenge law and order. Heightened cooperation between the local leadership and the PLO was undeniable fact. Yet, as long as the local leadership did not press its anti-Israeli activity to the point of discarding the pattern of controlled radicalism and as long as the PLO and Jordan continued to operate within that framework, Israel tended to accept the population's simultaneous reliance on both parties.

Israel's stand was an outgrowth of the autonomy talks between Israel, the United States, and Egypt pursuing the peace agreement with Egypt. The Israeli interest was to conduct negotiations on the autonomy plan with a delegation comprised of Jordanian representatives and Palestinian leaders from the territories now identified with the PLO. But Israel was unwilling to pay the price demanded by

Jordan and Palestinian leaders to make their participation more feasible. Both Jordan and West Bank Palestinian leaders considered favorably the idea of entering negotiations with Israel on an interim agreement in the spirit of the autonomy plan, provided Israel showed a willingness to stop settlement activity in the territories and commit itself to the character of the future permanent agreement. For Palestinian leaders, a permanent settlement meant the creation of an independent Palestinian state at the end of the autonomy period.

In the absence of an affirmative Israeli response to such conditions, a head-on clash with the local leadership would have inevitably triggered an Israeli showdown also with Egypt and the United States.

FLARE-UP IN THE TERRITORIES—THE COURSE OF EVENTS

The Intifada changed the state of affairs more than anything else. Protests by civilian Palestinians, in the form of an uprising, were ignited in December 1987 in every remote corner of the territories. The symbol of this Intifada was fearless stone-throwing youths facing heavily armed Israeli soldiers. Evidence of the youngsters' volatility was visible as early as December 1986, a year before the start of the Intifada. When two students were killed in a clash at Bir-Zeit University, the West Bank and Gaza Strip riots erupted for ten days, with youth and students leading the demonstrations. This incident was a watershed. Two developments poured oil on the flames: the dcision of the PLO's Executive Committee, on the eve of the meeting of Eighteenth Palestinian National Council in April 1987, to annul its agreement with Jordan, and the attempt of Jordan and Syria, during the Arab summit conference held in Amman in November 1987, to undercut the PLO's standing as the sole representative of the Palestinian cause. The West Bank and Gaza experienced more disturbances, more clashes with the army, more petrol bombs, and more stone throwing. The initiative passed into the hands of the youngsters, and no one, not Israel, not Jordan, and not the PLO, could control the unfolding events.

Eruption and Popular Confrontation, December 1987–July 1988

It was Gaza that gave the signal—and set the tone. On May 18, 1987, six members of the Islamic Jihad movement *(al-Jihad al-Islami)* escaped from the Gaza central prison. On August 8, they assassinated an officer of the military police in Gaza. On October 1 and 6, bloody confrontations took place between members of the group and Israeli security forces, resulting in the death of four Palestinians and one Israeli. On December 8, an Israeli citizen was stabbed to death in the Gaza market. On December 9, rioting broke out in Jabalya refuge camp north of Gaza after four camp residents were killed and seven injured in a road accident near Erez checkpoint at the northern entrance to the Gaza Strip. It was rumored that the road accident had been deliberate and was meant to avenge the death of the Israeli who had been stabbed in the market. On December 10, the flames spread to the other Gaza refugee camps and engulfed the West Bank as well. Since 1967, Gaza had always known more violence than the West Bank. Gaza, more than the West Bank, is economically pinched, demographically saturated, dense with refugees, and consumed by the fervor of religious faith. These characteristics set the stage for a violent eruption. But this time, the West Bank was ripe to join. The Intifada primarily expressed itself through stone throwing and petrol bombs but also verbalized its message through poems, extensive wall graffiti, and underground leaflets. Over the next six months, there were 42,355 recorded incidents. During December, the confrontations between Palestinian civilians and Israeli soldiers occurred largely in the camps—the sites of the most extreme misery as well as the centers of radicalism over the previous decades. Between mid-January and mid-February 1988, villages and towns also became actively involved in the resistance.

Getting Organized and Institutionalized, April–July 1988

In spring 1988, a shift in focus was taking place. While the uprising had begun as a spontaneous movement, consisting of mainly large-scale demonstrations and strikes in dozens of localities, and having an emphasis on street confrontation, now a process of getting organized and institutionalized had begun. A boycott of Israeli products coupled with efforts to increase Palestinian self-reliance. By March, Palestinians en masse were now ready to carry out the acts of civil disobedience. People began to organize themselves in their neighborhoods, towns, villages, and camps for the purpose of achieving self-sufficiency. In July, Jordan announced its juridical and administrative disengagement from the West Bank. The PLO started getting more involved in the territories' affairs.

Overturning Achievements in the Field to Political Attainments, August–November 1988

The thrust of the uprising shifted to the political arena. Two problems arose. The first was disunity among the political groups over a number of issues: Arafat's declarations and new policy, the meetings between Palestinian public figures and Israeli authorities, the Shamir plan, and the dialogue with the United States. The second problem was the new economic hardships following the collapse of the Jordanian dinar and the sharp decline in the power of the Israeli shekel. Controlled escalation of the level and extent of events is visible now, too. Commemorative days of national and religious character became dates for violent activities and riots. On November 15, 1988, in the Nineteenth Conference of the National Palestinian Council, the PLO announced the "Palestinian Independence Declaration."

Institutionalization of Violent Activity and Passive Resistance—1989

In addition, acceleration of the political activity became visible. In May, Israel announced a new initiative to solve the dispute. The struggle between the "external" PLO and the apparatuses of "interior" PLO on controlling the regulation of the uprising became aggravated.

Stagnation versus Escalation—1990

The political stagnation and feelings of frustration among the Palestinians led to deeper involvement of the fundamental Islamic bodies in the uprising. On October 8, riots occurred in the Temple Mount in Jerusalem. Other terrorist acts were also registered in this year.

A Year of Turn—1991

The Gulf War and the Palestinian support of Iraq in the war led to the beginning of the political process that gradually brought to an end the Intifada. On October 30 the Madrid Conference was opened.

Just as important as the spontaneous extension of the rioting was the Palestinian perception of its meaning: They saw the Intifada not as expressing individual grievances, but those of all the individuals and localities together, a collective uprising. The events soon were consciously compared to the revolt of 1936–1939. Its fighters were not professional guerrillas, but "children of the stone," faces veiled by *kafiyas* or masks, standing ready to defy Israeli soldiers. Countless poems glorified the new hero—making the important jump from a child to a *shahid,* or martyr.

Martyrdom became the concept that constructed the acts of the "children of the stone" into a legend. The family of a martyr was accorded special honor, and posters of him were carried at demonstrations and hung on walls. The PLO financially supported the martyr's family. While the popular imagination was fixed on individual, youthful heroism—indeed, often the stone throwing of groups of *shabab*—existing youth organizations, such as the *shabiba,* and numerous new other youth groups, stood behind the uprising's more institutionalized "strike forces."

While the "shock troops" of the Intifada were represented by a young, masked face, the new local leadership was represented by the anonymous leaflets distributed in public, itself a way to shroud its true face. Two camps—the national and the religious—conducted the widespread activity and struck deep roots within the local population during the Intifada. Both camps were involved in writing leaflets as means for directing events on the ground and instructing the population. There were four major bodies behind the wording of the leaflets, that is to say, behind the Intifada: the Unified National Command (UNC), the Islamic Resistance Movement (known as the Hamas), the left-wing Palestinian factions, and the Islamic Jihad.

The UNC was a coalition of supporters of Fatah, the Democratic Front, the Popular Front, and the Communist Party. Territory-wide leaflets appeared by the end of December on behalf of the UNC. There were leaflets that carried the signature of the Unified National Command of the Uprising in the Occupied Territories, later accompanied by the signature of the PLO. The close interrelationship between the UNC and the PLO was given explicit expression in the lead-in to the UNC's leaflets. Each such communiqué opened with the same declaration: "No voice can overcome the voice of the Palestinian people—the people of the PLO."

The left-wing organizations, although affiliating themselves with the UNC, published separate leaflets. By doing so, they could emphasize their sheer presence in the field. In addition they could demonstrate ideological and organizational independence by stressing their differences with Fatah on key issues, particularly on relations with Jordan and on a political settlement.

The other major body, the Hamas, was an umbrella organization for activists of the Muslim Brothers movement in Gaza and for the body by the name *al-Mujamma al-Islami* (the "Muslim Association"). The Islamic Jihad, whose orientation is also religious, operated separately from Hamas and put out its own leaflets. Its independent activity was motivated by a profound disagreement with both the Muslim Brothers and *al-Mujamma al-Islami* on how to advance the creation of an Islamic state in Palestine. The Jihad maintained organizational ties with Fatah, though it avoided affiliating itself with the UNC. Its cooperation with Fatah appeared to be motivated by logistic considerations—to smooth its activity in the uprising. The interrelation of the four bodies, both ideologically and organization-ally, enabled an intensive level of activity to be maintained and ensured a high level of obedience by the population to the directives contained in the leaflets.

But the Intifada was much more than that; it was the creation of social, cultural and educational institutions, and efforts aimed at economic self-support. The Intifada created the seeds of a new Palestinian civil society. As the time passed, the Intifada took on a life of its own, and people tried to make themselves as indepen-dent from the occupation as possible.

THE GOALS OF THE INTIFADA

The different groups active in the Intifada had two overriding common goals: to undermine the authority of Israeli rule in the occupied territories by means of a civil revolt that would force Israel to withdraw from these areas and to establish a Palestinian state. Through a steady coordination of activities via the PLO in Tunisia, the Intifada actually became a practical framework for a feasibility of a Palestinian state.

Hamas and the UNC were at loggerheads about the character of a Palestinian state and consequently differed over their attitude toward a political settlement with Israel. Hamas aspired to establish an Islamic state in all of Palestine (west side of Jordan River). In August 1988 Hamas issued its charter, which declared that the soil of Palestine was a Muslim trust. Hamas saw itself as a link in the chain of *jihad* ("effort"), which is a continuous holy war against Israel. Its emphatic claim to all of Palestine found frequent expression in its leaflets. Leaflet No. 28 (August 18, 1988), for example, declared an "Islamic Palestine from the [Mediterranean] Sea to the [Jordan] River."

In Hamas eyes, the Muslim's right to all of Palestine leaves no opening for a dia-logue or a political settlement with Israel. Its leaflets exemplify this approach: "Land for peace . . . this is no more than a mirage, a deceit" (March 4, 1988). "Let any hand be cut off that signs [away] a grain of sand in Palestine in favor of the enemies of God" (March 13, 1988).

A different picture emerged from the leaflets of the UNC, which served as a mouthpiece for the national camp. The UNC perceived the conflict with Israel more in secular-political terms than religious ones. The Palestinian society would be healed through "self-determination and the establishment of an independent state with Arab Jerusalem as its eternal capital" (Leaflet No. 28, August 18, 1988), rather than by imposing the kingdom of Islam on the Palestinian world.

The second goal of the Intifada shared by the UNC and the Hamas was to cause a civil revolt in the territories. On this issue the two groups shared a common approach. This was reflected in their nearly identical directives to the Palestinian public abut its role in the uprising.

The population was called upon to cooperate in both violent and nonviolent actions. The former included throwing stones and incendiary bombs, erection of barricades, burning tires, wielding knives and axes, clashing with the Israeli forces, and attacking collaborators. To ensure that these operations were carried out, the

UNC made use of "shock squads" *(al-firaq al-dariba)*. These units had the task of ensuring that the required actions, both violent and nonviolent, were implemented. A detailed description of their activity appeared in one of the leaflets:

The United National Command salutes the shock squads for their active role against the occupation forces, their agents, and departments. . . . They are called on to strike with an iron fist . . . and are requested to block roads on general strike days and to allow only doctors' vehicles to pass. They should write national-unity slogans [on walls]. . . . They should raise flags, organize demonstrations, burn tires and throw stones and Molotov cocktails. (UNC's leaflet No. 22, July 21, 1988)

The directives on severing ties with Israel included not working in Israel, not working in Jewish settlements in the occupied territories, boycotting Israeli products, resigning from the service of the Israeli Civil Administration, developing a home-based economy, and setting up and expanding popular committees on education, information, guard duty, and agriculture.

Directives regarding civil disobedience included nonpayment of taxes and fines, staging partial commercial strikes, and holding general strikes on specified days, activities to enhance solidarity, such as day-long strikes of solidarity with prisoners and with families of victims, and memorial days to commemorate traumatic events from the past, such as the civil war in Jordan in September 1970.

CONCLUSIONS

It is impossible to understand the Intifada without following the tangential circles in which the lives of Israelis and Palestinians moved during twenty years of Israeli rule. The critical circles were demography, economy, and education received by the young generation. It was the convergence of the three factors, primarily during the latter part of the 1970s, that fostered a climate of political radicalism among Palestinian youth; and it was Israeli policy in the 1980s—which sought to purge the local Palestinian leadership of PLO supporters—that accelerated a process whereby the radical mood was transformed into militant action.

The groups that were behind the uprising believed that violence was a necessity—extreme action served as an outlet for the younger generation's ideological fervor and political frustrations. The demographic weight of the younger Palestinians, their level of education and political awareness, together with the organizational frameworks at their disposal, made them leading instigators in the uprising. Moreover, as the violence grew and claimed more casualties on the Palestinian side, the Intifada's political gains increased accordingly. The daily skirmishes between the population and Israeli troops, widely covered in the media, thrust the Palestinian problem and the PLO back into international consciousness. Public personalities, politicians, and the press in countries friendly to Israel were sharply criticizing Israeli policy, and governments and international organizations condemned the methods employed to suppress the uprising.

The surging violence also deeply affected Israel and its society. Many Israelis perceived the occupation as morally indefensible, socially deleterious, economically ruinous, and politically and militarily harmful. Israel's political leadership faced mounting pressure from broad segments of the public to stop trying to quell the uprising by force and to propose political solutions that would put a stop to the bloodshed.

In short, it was the Palestinians' growing awareness of the vital role played by violence in propelling the Intifada and in producing political gains that accounted for the significant increase in the violent directives in UNC leaflets, which were distributed regularly, and the consistently high level of violent directives in the Hamas leaflets.

However, the Intifada's real capacity for endurance depended on the Palestinians' economic stamina. In the absence of self-sustaining economic capability, dependence on Israel had become a way of life. Under these circumstances, excessive pressure to sever contact with Israel was ineffective. To obey the calls of the Intifada would mean economic hardship for tens of thousands of laborers who earned their living in Israel and a huge loss of revenue for many local merchants and factory owners who maintained commercial ties with Israeli firms. A severe economic crisis within these sectors could also weaken the influence of the UNC and Hamas. Thus the inability or unwillingness of merchants, factory owners, and workers to break off economic ties with Israel forced both the UNC and Hamas to adapt themselves to the circumstances.

The Intifada's strength has come from its ability to forge a sense of mutual dependence and partnership between the middle class and the radical youth; between the merchants, businessmen, doctors, lawyers, and other members of white-collar sector, on the one hand, and the "rolling stones" generation on the other. This young generation existed before the outbreak of the Intifada. But the conditions conducive to its cooperation with the middle class could not materialize as long as a prominent urban leadership held power and was able to cooperate simultaneously with Israel, Jordan, and the PLO. Thanks to this political cooperation, the local leadership could shield the middle class from radical pressures exerted by the young guard.

The cooperation between the youngsters and the merchants and the rest of the middle class accounts for the fury of the outburst but not for its duration. The merchants and the businessmen lost money and complained; so did the Civil Administration employees who had to resign. Their interests were not identical with the interests of the youngsters who were fired by national fervor and a passion for self-sacrifice. The solidarity between the middle-class groups and the younger generation came as a result of the ability of the UNC and Hamas to reduce the danger of a split by using organizational tools, economic means, and symbolic rewards.

Israel's failure to suppress the Intifada resulted from its inability to come up with a quick and effective response to the coercion and persuasion mechanisms wielded on the Palestinian population in the West Bank and Gaza by the groups behind the uprising. Israel's difficulties in this sphere have diverse causes: political constraints, domestic differences, legal limitations, and moral considerations that guided the nation's political and military levels. These factors continued to dictate the nature of Israeli activity and, in turn, this activity rendered it difficult for Israel to prevent those behind the Intifada from continuing to gain the obedience and compliance of the population. Thus, political dialogue became an unavoidable option.

The way to negotiations with the Palestinians and the PLO was open, beginning with the Madrid Conference in October 1991, and ending with the Israel/Palestine agreements, which were conceived in 1993 after extensive secret meetings between the two parties, and the Declaration of Principles signed in Oslo. This was followed by "Oslo II," signed in Washington on September 28, 1995, by the prime minister of Israel, Yitzhak Rabin, and chairman of the PLO, Yasser Arafat. It was, in many ways, a new approach to peace negotiation and it has had a profound impact on the Middle East. But the effects of the "Oslo process" in terms of creative peace have been meager. Five years later, the "*al-Aqsa* Intifada" erupted.

BIBLIOGRAPHY

Benvenisti, Meron, *Fatal Embrace: Intifada, the Gulf War, the Peace Process* (Hebrew), Jerusalem: Keter, 1992.

Gilbar, Gad, and Susser, Asher (eds.), *At the Core of the Conflict: The Intifada* (Hebrew), Tel Aviv: Tel Aviv University, 1992.

Hilterman, Joost R., *Behind the Intifada: Labor and Women's Movements in the Occupied Territories,* Princeton, NJ: Princeton University Press, 1991.

Hunter, F. Robert, *The Palestinian Uprising: A War by Other Means,* Berkeley: University of California Press, 1991.

Mishal, Shaul, and Aharoni, Reuben, *Speaking Stones: Communiques from the Intifada Underground,* Syracuse: Syracuse University Press, 1994.

Shalev, Aryeh, *The Intifada: Causes and Effects* (Hebrew), Tel Aviv: Papyrus Publishing House, Tel Aviv University, 1990.

Sheef, Zeev, and Ya'ari, Ehud, *Intifada* (Hebrew), Tel Aviv and Jerusalem: Schocken Publishing House, 1990.

Swirski, Shlomo, and Pappe, Ilan (eds.), *The Intifada: An Inside View* (Hebrew), Tel Aviv: Mifras Books, 1992.

12

"Ebb and Flow" versus "The al-Aqsu Intifadah": The Israeli-Palestinian Conflict, 2000–2003

Shaul Shay

"EBB AND FLOW," EVENTS PRECEDING OPERATION "DEFENSIVE SHIELD" (SEPTEMBER 2000–APRIL 2002)

On September 28, 2000, Knesset member Ariel Sharon visited Jerusalem's Temple Mount. Owing to its sensitivity, the visit was coordinated with the Palestinian Authority and the heads of the Waqf in Jerusalem. These steps were taken in order to ensure that peace would be kept during the visit. In spite of their promise to maintain order, violent clashes took place between Arab protesters (among them Israeli Arab members of Knesset) and security forces accompanying the visit.

The next day (September 29), following worship on the Temple Mount tens of thousands of incited worshippers erupted in a frenzy of violence. Six Palestinians were killed in the ensuing riots and dozens were wounded. This violent eruption marked the opening of the *al-Aqsu* Intifadah, or the events of "ebb and flow," as coined by the IDF.

Ariel Sharon's visit and the spontaneous violent outburst that it provoked were exploited by the Palestinian Authority and facilitated a strategic turnaround, that is, a return to the use of violence and armed struggle, while planting the blame squarely on Israel's shoulders.

This strategic decision adopted by Arafat, probably at the conclusion of the Camp David summit, was implemented already in the beginning of the year 2000 with an array of intensive preparations towards the conflict that included the generality of the Palestinian Authority's security apparatus. Thus, Arafat was able to ignite Judea and Samaria as well as the Gaza Strip in a very short time. Despite the fact that the Palestinians prepared themselves in advance for this armed confrontation, it was presented to the world as a popular insurrection (an *Intifadah* in Arabic) for propagandistic purposes. This enabled the Palestinian side to adopt the underdog strategy, namely to blame Israel for the instigation of violence against a civilian population demanding independence rather than presenting it as an armed struggle between the Palestinian Authority and the Israeli security forces.

The violence expanded like fire in a fallow field all over Judea and Samaria and the Gaza Strip, and in the beginning was mainly characterized by severe riots, placement of explosives, and shooting (until the end of 2000). The events took place mostly in Judea and Samaria and Gaza, but also in Jerusalem and on the Israeli side of the "green line." In contrast with the violence following the Oslo Agreement, initiated by extremist Islamic terror organizations, the *al-Aqsu* Intifadah was initiated by the Palestinian Authority and the Fatah—Tanzim organizations under the leadership of Marwan Barguti—with the blessing of the Chairman of the Palestinian Authority, who denied the involvement of the Tanzim and the Palestinian security apparatus in these incidents.

The violence escalated in 2001 and in the beginning of 2002 in frequency and scope. There was more infiltration across the "green line," and the number of casualties among civilians and security forces grew steadily.

In early 2002 suicide attacks became frequent and a high body count became the main feature of the attacks. The number of casualties among civilians (as compared to casualties among security forces) increased, and feelings of uncertainty, insecurity, and frustration prevailed among Israel's civilian population. Attack followed attack, bombing followed bombing, the "Tanzim" becoming an active and dominant part in their initiation; and the number of terror alerts increased immeasurably.

In an attempt to deal with the situation, the security forces and the Israeli police allocated extensive military and police forces and civilians were called upon to exercise vigilance. Success was only partial, however, and despite the large investment in security the suicide attacks became more and more frequent.

Along with the escalation of violence in 2000 and 2001 many political solutions were suggested with the purpose of achieving a degree of quiet and a cease-fire, mainly through American mediation. At first it was President Clinton who aspired to conclude his term in office with the achievement of a cease-fire and/or an agreement between the Israelis and the Palestinians. On December 20, 2000, Clinton presented his plan for an agreement between the sides (the Clinton plan), but it remained unimplemented as of January 20, 2001.

Following his election, President George Bush joined the efforts, and acceded to Egyptian President Hosni Mubarak's request to become more involved in the search for a solution to the conflict. Bush sent the head of the Central Intelligence Agency (CIA) George Tenet, General Anthony Ziny, and Secretary of State Colin Powell to the region to function as mediators and offer compromise—proposals acceptable to both sides. The initiatives led by President Bush were aimed also to serve American interests, that is, maintaining stability in the region after the September 11 attack and the expected campaign against Iraq.

Successive attempts to terminate the conflict were put into motion: beginning with UN Secretary General Koffi Anan, followed by the European Union's peace plan, the Egyptian-Jordanian initiative, and the Saudi initiative.

At first, Israel showed restraint and attempted to moderate its military reactions, so that the political efforts to achieve a solution acceptable both to Israel and to the Palestinians would have a chance. Military operations were confined to retaliation and at this stage the offensive initiative was rarely taken. When the violence and the attacks persisted the Israelis responded by "taking care of" imminent threats and implemented a policy of "focused preemption"—the elimination of wanted terrorists directly involved in the planning and execution of terrorist operations (this policy was first implemented on November 9, 2000 when Hassin Abiath was killed in Bethlehem by a helicopter missile aimed at his car).

The IDF's retaliation policy included the bombardment of objectives in areas under Palestinian control, but avoided collateral damage as much as possible, that is, the injury or death of civilians. This modus operandi was meant to show the Palestinian Authority the error of its ways and bring about a change in their policy. Other steps taken were sieges and closures of Palestinian cities in order to prevent any terrorist infiltration. On February 6, 2001, general elections were held in Israel: The elected Prime Minister Ariel Sharon formed a unity government, with Simon Peres as foreign minister and Binyamin Ben Eliezer as defense minister.

The newly established government showed restraint and forbearance in face of the continuing terror attacks, and persevered in its policy of focused preemption and political dialogue, but this was ineffectual. The IDF was requested by the government to reenter "Area A" in order to bring an end to the attacks against the Jewish population.

On April 16, 2001, the IDF reentered Area A for the first time since Oslo, and occupied positions in Beith Hanun in the Gaza Strip after mortar shells fell on the town of Sderot. Following an extensive air, sea, and land operation the IDF occupied other positions in Area A, but soon withdrew because of the American pressure and Washington's condemnation of the operation.

In May 2001, the Mitchell Committee report was published (based upon the understandings of the Sharem Summit in October 2000). The report outlined ways in which regional stability could be achieved. Israel accepted the committee's recommendations and the prime minister instructed the IDF to act in accordance and to respect the cease-fire "except in cases of direct threats." Yasser Arafat, on the other hand, refused to declare a cease-fire, and accepted the renewal of security coordination meetings only.

In June 2001, George Tenet, the head of the CIA arrived in the region as the representative of President Bush, and attempted to create a formula both sides would accept to be used as a basic negotiation plan when a cease-fire was achieved.

The Israeli government decided, after much hesitation, to accept the Tenet plan and the prime minister announced a cease-fire, committing to it on paper. Yasser Arafat, after heavy pressure, also signed the document and on June 13 the Palestinians and the Israelis committed to a cease-fire. On June 22, 2001, the Palestinian Authority violated the agreement and announced the resumption of attacks against settlers.

As result of the sharp increase in the number of attacks (mainly suicide bombings) and the high body count, the IDF issued, as of August 6, more flexible orders for the opening of fire and reoccupied the positions it had held prior to the Tenet understandings.

On August 27, 2001, in response to the constant gun and mortar fire aimed at the Gilo neighborhood in Jerusalem, the IDF entered the village of Beit Jala. On August 30, 2001, however, the IDF withdrew from Beit Jala after the signature of a cease-fire agreement, limited to Beit Jala, approved by Peres and Arafat, but the terror attacks persisted.

THE SEPTEMBER 11 ATTACKS ON THE UNITED STATES AND THEIR IMPLICATIONS VIS-À-VIS THE ISRAELI-PALESTINIAN CONFLICT

The September 11 attacks, which caused the death of some 3,000 people in the United States, brought about a forceful response on the part of American legislators and the immediate (although temporary) cessation of Palestinian attacks.

The Palestinian Authority declared (as of September 11, 2001) a cease-fire, condemned the attacks in the United States, and promptly acted to prevent any expression of Palestinian solidarity or identification with Bin Laden, who was behind the attacks in the United States.

A short time after the September 11 attacks, seventeen Palestinian groups condemned "[any] attacks directed against innocent civilians." The signatories, who identified themselves as the "National and Islamic Palestinian Forces," included armed organizations directly responsible for attacks against civilians both in Israel and in the occupied territories. These organizations did not recognize the contradiction between their condemnation of the murder of civilians in the United States and the situation in Israel and the occupied territories: "While we stress our unequivocal condemnation of terror, any definition of our legitimate struggle against the occupation of our land as such is not tolerated. We call upon the entire world to distinguish between terrorism and legitimate struggle against occupation, as is written in international conventions as well as being a basic religious tenet."

The Palestinian Authority, and perhaps other Arab countries (such as Saudi Arabia), exerted heavy pressure upon the Hamas and the Islamic Jihad organizations to cease their suicide attacks against Israel, at least within the boundaries of the "green line." They complied out of fear of the international atmosphere created after the September 11 attacks, and because suicide attacks could be defined as terrorist activity and the organizations responsible would be blacklisted by the United States. Moreover, the Palestinian Authority feared that the post-September 11 United States would allow Israel to harm the Palestinian Authority behind what was "permitted" in the past. In order to improve its international standing and create a distinction between Palestinian activities and Bin Laden-like terrorist activities, Arafat promptly declared that the Palestinian Authority stood side by side with the United States and supported its war against terror.

On September 26, 2001, a meeting took place between Arafat and Peres. In this meeting a cease-fire was agreed upon as well as a commitment to the implementation of the Mitchell recommendations and the Tenet understandings. A renewal of security coordination between the sides was also agreed upon. Immediately after the signature of the agreement, Israel began to remove its blockade of West Bank cities.

The murder of the Israeli Minister Rehavam Ze'evi (October 17, 2001) at Jerusalem's Hyatt Hotel brought the situation back to square one and Arafat's insincere commitment to fight terrorism and his unwillingness to capture wanted terrorists was demonstrated once more. IDF forces entered Jenin, Ramallah, Tul Karem, and Beit Jala, once again seeking to capture Rehavam Ze'evi's assassins.

In an attempt to halt the deterioration of the situation, Secretary of State Colin Powell sent General Zini as a special emissary to the region. The general arrived in Israel on November 26, 2001, and met the prime minister and the minister of defense as well as Palestinian Authority officials and Yasser Arafat.

Several brutal attacks took place in Israel during Zini's visit (a suicide attack in the pedestrian mall of Jerusalem on December 1, 2001, in which eleven people were killed and a suicide attack in Haifa on December 2, 2001, in which fifteen people were killed), which prompted the prime minister to declare that the Palestinian Authority "supported terror" and that the "Tanzim" and the "Fatah" were "terror organizations" (December 3, 2001). This declaration was a landmark in Israel's approach toward the Palestinian Authority as a peace partner worthy of political negotiation and a body that respects agreements.

On December 12, 2001, after Arafat promised, once again, to fight terrorism, a bus was attacked in Emmanuel, first by a roadside bomb then by gunmen. Ten civilians were killed in the attack and twenty-four were wounded. Shortly after the attack it became evident that the perpetrators were terrorists that Arafat had been requested to arrest. The prime minister informed Colin Powell that decisive resolutions were imminent. At this stage Zini's mediation was no longer useful and he returned to the United States on December 14, 2001, unsuccessful.

When it became clear that all the efforts at stabilizing the situation and achieving a cease-fire were futile, Israel was compelled to change its policy and take the offensive. On December 3, 2001, the Israeli government decided to initiate a large-scale military operation and to halt all negotiations with Arafat.

The IDF entered Ramallah and seized control of several neighborhoods in the city, including Marwan Barguti's residence. Tanks were placed near Arafat's headquarters, the Gaza Strip was divided into three parts, and the air force attacked Palestinian Authority objectives. Arafat was deemed "irrelevant" and his freedom of movement in Ramallah was restricted (he was not even allowed to leave Ramallah to attend the Christmas mass in Bethlehem, an annual tradition). The IDF operation also included the arrest of dozens of terrorist suspects, the seizure of armaments, and the destruction of terrorist's houses.

The September 11 attacks had a short-term "preventive effect" on Palestinian suicide attacks. After a short time, however, American policy became clear and the immediate targets in the American war against terrorism were defined. The Hamas and Jihad organizations resumed their operations and even increased the number of suicide attacks.

One can say that in the short term, the September 11 attacks brought about a brief cessation of suicide attacks, but in the long term the enormity of the September 11 attacks became a source of inspiration for radical Islamic elements, who now understood the strategic potency of suicide attacks as a weapon against superior forces such as the United States and Israel in the Middle East arena. The few voices among the Islamic religious authorities condemning the suicide attacks in the United States were gradually silenced and the wave of religious rulings obliging self-sacrifice in the name of Islam became the dominant message (notorious among them is Sheikh Kardawi, one of the most influential religious authorities among radical Islamists).

The first suicide attack after September 11 occurred in the beginning of October (on October 7, a suicide bomber affiliated with the Islamic Jihad blew himself up near Kibbutz Shluhot in the Beit Shean Valley). On October 17, a secular organization joined the circle of suicide bombers for the first time. A terrorist from the Popular front blew himself up by means of an explosive belt near the Karni crossing, in the Gaza Strip, injuring two Israelis. Beginning in late November 2001, the wave of suicide bombings reached a new crescendo. The attacks were not confined to the territories and took place within the "green line" and in Jerusalem as well. By the end of the year, eleven suicide attacks had taken place, five of them by the Hamas organization. December 15 marked the first time that a Fatah member attempted a suicide attack. The attempted attack took place at an IDF roadblock in Judea and Samaria (33 Israelis were killed in the attacks and 257 were wounded).

On December 16, 2001, in order to improve his image and to placate Israel, Arafat called upon the Palestinian Authority and the terrorist organizations to respect the cease-fire. Two days later (December 18), however, in a speech given in Ramallah, he issued a call to continue in the struggle for Jerusalem and praised the suicide bombers. This ambivalent approach was characteristic of Arafat from the beginning of the disturbances until that point—on one hand he expressed willingness to respect the cease-fire and on the other hand to support terror, but from that point onward his public declarations became more vehement and extreme, up to his call to commit suicide attacks and his expressed willingness to become a "Shahid" (a martyr). His support of terrorism was not confined to declarations of support. His direct involvement was proven when on January 4, 2002, the Israeli navy captured the *Karin A,* a ship loaded with a huge cargo of weaponry destined for the Palestinian Authority. It became evident that the chairman of the Palestinian Authority was personally involved in the acquisition of the ship and the transfer of the armaments to the Palestinian Authority.

In spite of the violence, efforts at resolutions and contacts between Israel and the Palestinian Authority persisted, with the support and participation of Peres and Arafat's advisor, Abu 'alah, the goal of which was to formulate a memorandum that would assist the sides to find a solution to the situation.

March 2002 was the most difficult month. The suicide attacks took place almost daily, the number of casualties was very high, and the pictures transmitted in the media were horrific. Feelings of frustration and insecurity among civilians prevailed. After the suicide attacks of March 2, 2002, in Jerusalem, and on March 3, 2002, near a roadblock in the vicinity of Ofrah in which ten people were killed, the state-security cabinet authorized the exertion of continuous military pressure upon Palestinian Authority areas.

On March 7, 2002, President Bush decided to send General Zini to the region once again and the prime minister consented (to the American request) to waive his demand of seven days of quiet as a condition for the opening of negotiations (using the Mitchell outline).

On March 14, 2002, Anthony Zini arrived in the region and helped renew security coordination meetings. Sharon gave his consent to the additional American request to halt the IDF actions in the territories and after a Security Committee meeting convened under Zini's patronage, the IDF began to withdraw from Area A. The attacks, however, did not cease, instead they became more frequent. As mentioned, March 2002 was the bloodiest month since the outbreak of hostilities and a record number of suicide attacks took place.

On March 20, 2002, a suicide bomber attacked a bus en route from Tel Aviv to Nazareth and killed seven people. On March 21, another suicide attack took place, this time in the center of Jerusalem; three people were killed. On March 27, 2002, Passover eve, a suicide bomber blew himself up in the "Park" Hotel in Netanya while the hotel guests were seating themselves for the ritual "Seder" meal. The attack claimed twenty-nine lives and many were wounded. On March 28—at the conclusion of the first day of Passover—a terrorist penetrated the Alon Moreh settlement and killed four members of a family.

Following this chain of attacks, the government convened on the night of March 28–29, and decided that Israel could not continue to exercise restraint and that it had an obligation to do everything in its power to secure its citizens, and thus the government decided to initiate "Operation Defensive Shield" and instructed the IDF to act.

Yasser Arafat's declaration after the attack on the "Park" Hotel regarding his willingness to announce a cease-fire was not heeded, since his previous declarations in similar situations were never implemented in practice.

FROM THE INITIATION OF OPERATION DEFENSIVE SHIELD UNTIL SEPTEMBER 2002

The goals of Operation Defensive Shield, decided upon by the Israeli government on the night of March 28–29, 2002, after the serious escalation of Palestinian terror, were twofold. The operation was meant to deal the Palestinian terror infrastructure a telling blow and to isolate and restrict the freedom of movement of the Palestinian leader who had been previously deemed by the Israeli government as "irrelevant" (he was granted this dubious title on December 13, following the attack on the bus in Emmanuel).

Since the outbreak of the Intifadah on September 28, 2000, Israel's policy had been one of restraint and self-control, so as to allow American political maneuvers and mediation efforts a good chance to succeed. Thus far, Israel responded positively to the American initiatives and accepted the recommendations of Mitchell and Tenet. The military operations had been limited and of a retaliatory nature, and the political-security cabinet had abstained from ordering operations of wider scope.

As time passed and the attacks persisted and became more frequent, more violent, and more deadly it became evident that political maneuvers were not bearing fruit. The government decided, therefore, to retaliate more heavily and granted the IDF a mandate to alter the character of its operations and to initiate offensive action. The American government openly criticized the Israeli moves, which in their eyes were discordant with their regional interests, and exerted pressure upon the prime minister to grant Arafat more opportunities to destroy the terrorist infrastructures.

As mentioned, the United States exerted heavy pressure upon Israel during the IDF implementation of Operation Defensive Shield, and called upon the Israelis to conclude the operation. In a public statement President Bush demanded that Israel withdraw its military forces from the Palestinian cities.

In the midst of the military operation on April 11, 2002, Secretary of State Colin Powell arrived in the region seeking to halt hostilities and achieve a cease-fire. The day Secretary of State Powell met Sharon (April 12) a suicide bomber blew himself up in Machaneh Yehuda (Jerusalem's open market), killing seven and wounding seventy-one. In his subsequent meeting with Colin Powell on April 13, Arafat refused to meet the two conditions placed upon him by the American secretary of state—a commitment to a cease-fire and the extradition of the late Minister Ze'evi murderers entrenched in his blockaded "Muqta'ah."

On April 17, 2002, Powell concluded his mission, unable to achieve a cease-fire, and returned to the United States to report to President Bush.

The failure of Powell's mission and the beginning of the IDF's withdrawal from West Bank cities brought about a change in the American position towards Israel, and President Bush praised Israeli actions, calling Prime Minister Sharon a "leader of peace." Bush said that Israel had heeded the American request that they withdraw from the territories and that he understood the need to maintain a military presence in Ramallah and Bethlehem. Other factors contributing to this reversal were the September 11 attacks, which essentially changed the American attitude towards terrorism, and the capture of the *Karin A* on January 3, 2002, which directly implicated the Palestinian Authority in terrorist activity. Arafat continued to dig his heels in and refused to discuss the issue of a cease-fire while Israel maintained a military presence in the territories.

On April 25, 2002, Prime Minister Sharon announced the conclusion of the first stage of Operation Defensive Shield and on the same day the IDF evacuated all its forces from Nablus and parts of Ramallah; Arafat's headquarters, however, remained under siege.

The two outstanding issues were the siege on Arafat's headquarters until the extradition of Minister Ze'evi murderers and the armed terrorists entrenched in the Church of the Nativity. International mediators attempted to find solutions acceptable to both sides.

On May 1, 2002, an agreement was reached regarding the fugitives entrenched in Arafat's headquarters and they were transferred to Jericho, where they were imprisoned under American and British surveillance. This resulted in the removal of the siege on Arafat's headquarters and the Israeli minister of defense decided upon a renewal of security coordination meetings.

The Nativity Church crisis was resolved on May 10, 2002, thanks to the mediation efforts of European Union foreign ministers. The negotiations were long and difficult since the deportation process was lengthy and a long time passed until countries willing to accept the terrorists into their territory were found. Twenty-six men were transferred to the Gaza Strip and thirteen more were deported to Cyprus and later dispersed around the globe—in Italy, Spain, Austria, Greece, Luxemburg, and Canada. All others were released.

Operation Defensive Shield and later Operation "Determined Path" marked a watershed in the history of the current Israeli-Palestinian conflict. The wave of terror attacks that swept Israel in March 2002 obliged the State of Israel to change its policy concerning Palestinian terror. Operation Defensive Shield was the largest military operation undertaken by the IDF since the Lebanese Peace of the Galilee war. The operation required a partial deployment of reserves and an unprecedented number of forces helped reconquer the Palestinian cities in Judea and Samaria as well as the rural regions. During the operation, some 250 Palestinians were killed, 600 were wounded, and 5,000 were arrested. Huge quantities of weaponry were confiscated, laboratories for the manufacture of explosives, Kasam missiles, and mortars were uncovered, and the infrastructure of terrorist organizations was destroyed.

Thirty IDF soldiers were killed and 128 were wounded in the fighting. The outcome of Operation Defensive Shield and to a greater degree Operation Determined Path, was the virtually complete freedom of action in the area of Judea and Samaria, which dramatically improved the IDF's ability to frustrate attacks. This in turn resulted in a sharp decrease in the number of attacks in general, and of suicide attacks in particular, in comparison with the period prior to Operation Defensive Shield. It seems that the operation proved to the Palestinians the extent of Israel's determination and the endurance of Israeli society in the face of adversity. This operation also opened a debate in Palestinian society as to the benefits of an armed struggle and for the first time, Arafat's "path" was openly criticized. The operation and the military actions that followed it isolated Arafat, weakened his prestige, and jumpstarted the process of reformation and change in the Palestinian governmental apparatus.

On May 5, 2002, after the conclusion of the Operation Defensive Shield, Prime Minister Sharon met with President Bush once again in order to formulate a joint plan. Sources in the prime minister's entourage said, after the meeting, that "The President and the Prime Minister are in complete agreement regarding the unsuitability of the Palestinian Authority—in its present composition—as a peace partner."

This visit anticipated President Bush's June 24 speech, in which he presented his "credo" for the solution to the Israeli-Palestinian conflict. Discussed at this meeting was the idea of an international conference, which had been proposed subsequent to the previous meeting of the leaders. Sharon viewed this idea as a catalyst facilitating the political process but not as an alternative to direct negotiations between Israelis and Palestinians. The leaders also discussed the issue of reformation in the Palestinian Authority.

During Prime Minister Sharon's visit in the United States, another suicide attack took place in Rishon Le Tzion, in which fifteen people died and fifty were wounded. The attack cut the visit short and the prime minister returned to Israel and summoned his political-security cabinet. In this meeting the defense minister's recommendations for military action in the Gaza Strip were approved, the target of the operation would be primarily the Hamas, since it was the Hamas leadership that was behind the attack in Rishon Le Tzion. The IDF began calling up reservists, but then the operation was frozen following American pressure and because of the way the operation was publicized. The call-up of reserve forces was halted and the operation was postponed.

At the beginning of June 2002 President Bush invited Prime Minister Sharon to the United States once again, this time to discuss a new political initiative.

In his meetings with the President and American law makers in June 2002, the prime minister presented to the leaders of the American legislature his plan for a long-term interim accord during which a Palestinian State would be established without final borders. The American government considered his plan as a possible basis for a future agreement.

After the suicide attack at the Megido junction (June 5, 2002), in which seventeen people were killed and forty-two people were wounded, the IDF initiated operation "Road Ruler," and put the Muqata'ah (in Ramallah) under siege once again, destroying parts of the building with explosives.

President Bush's reaction to the IDF's renewed siege of the Muqata'ah differed from past sieges and blockades, and he saw it as a defensive measure and declared: "Israel is entitled to defend itself." President Bush repeated this statement several times, after the suicide attack in Jerusalem on June 18, 2002, in which twenty-two people were killed and seventy-three people were wounded, and after another attack on June 19, 2002, in which seven people were killed and thirty-seven were wounded at the Giva Ha Tzarfatit junction in Jerusalem.

Following these attacks the IDF initiated Operation "Determined Manner" (June 19, 2002)—a long-term operation since this time Israel was planning to remain in Area A for a significant period of time. This type of operation was necessary as it had become clear that the closures and sieges of Palestinian cities were insufficient and did not prevent the departure of suicide bombers towards Israel. The IDF received the permission from the political-security cabinet to act in the Palestinian cities as required.

On June 24, 2002, President Bush delivered a speech (postponed several times because of the attacks on Israel) and expressed an unambiguous and sharp turn-around in the American position regarding the conflict and ways of solution. In his speech the President presented his political plan for the resolution of the Israeli-Palestinian conflict, emphasizing the importance of changing the Palestinian government and electing a new leadership. He called upon the Palestinian public to act towards a regime change, stipulating that this change was a precondition for America supporting the establishment of a Palestinian State and for peace.

In his speech he delineated the American plan, the centerpiece of which was the establishment of an independent Palestinian State after a comprehensive reformation of Palestinian government and Palestinian institutions. The implementation of this plan would fall mainly upon the Palestinians. The president specified a number of steps that the Palestinians would have to take in order to achieve independence.

President Bush's speech was received with great satisfaction in Israel and governmental sources confirmed that the president saw eye to eye with Israel regarding solutions to the Israeli-Palestinian conflict. Among Palestinians the reactions to the speech were uncomplimentary and they claimed that speech was clearly "pro-Israeli."

President Mubarakh described the speech as "balanced but with many points in need of clarification." The Jordanian government declared that the speech was the "beginning of the end of the Israeli-Arab conflict." Two days later (on June 26, 2002) at the G8 Summit of Industrialized Countries in Canada, President Bush called upon the participating countries to support his position and to bring about a change in Palestinian leadership.

After criticism began to be heard regarding the American involvement in internal Palestinian affairs, Secretary of State Colin Powell published a clarification in the media and said that the United States would not try to impose a specific leader upon the Palestinian people, but would not support the Palestinian position so long as the current leadership remained in power. The result of the president's speech was a temporary rift in the relationship between the United States and the Palestinian Authority.

On July 15, 2002, Defense Minister Binyamin Ben Eliezer met President Mubarakh in Alexandria, and presented the Egyptian president with his plan for advancing the peace process which he called: "Gaza First." According to this plan Israel would take steps to restore normality in Gaza in return for the cessation of terror. He also said that if this plan succeeded, it would be implemented in additional Palestinian cities. The minister of defense got the impression that the Egyptian president saw the initiative in a favorable light and he promised to consider Egyptian assistance in training the Palestinian security apparatuses and supervising their unification.

As proof, President Mubarakh held a phone conversation on this matter with Prime Minister Sharon, and the latter authorized the defense minister to present his plan to the Palestinians and to forward its implementation.

The next day (July 16, 2002) a shooting attack took place in Emmanuel in which nine people were killed, which resulted in the cancellation of the meeting scheduled between the political teams who were supposed to renew negotiation that very day.

On July 31, 2002, a cafeteria was blown up at the Hebrew University in Jerusalem. Arafat did not condemn the attack but claimed that "it was necessary to exercise caution because of the delicate situation in which the Palestinian people find themselves vis-à-vis the international community."

In spite of the two suicide attacks (on August 4 and 5 at the Miron junction and at the Um el Fahem junction) Defense Minister Ben Eliezer met with the Palestinian minister of interior, Abdel Razek el Hyhia, and they discussed the plan, the security reforms, and ways to resume security coordination between Israel and the Palestinian Authority.

On August 7 the security meetings between the Palestinians and the Israelis resumed, in the face of repeated declarations from senior American officials claiming "there is no chance of an agreement between Israel and the Palestinians with the present leadership."

On August 18, 2002, following deliberations with the Palestinians and the addition of Bethlehem to Ben Eliezer's plan, the implementation of the plan"Gaza and Bethlehem First"—was agreed upon.

According to this agreement Israel allowed gun-toting Palestinian policemen into the relevant cities (namely Gaza and Bethlehem), and permitted the transfer of troops whose purpose it was to impose (their) authority on Gaza and Bethlehem. Israel also promised to do its utmost to alleviate the distress of the Palestinian population. As per agreement, the IDF withdrew from Bethlehem (on August 19, 2002) and tightened the closure on the city.

The feeling that political military achievements were feasible without resorting to violence fortified the moderate elements within the Palestinian Authority and thus Palestinian Minister of Interior Abdel Razek el Hyhia stated that "the Intifadah's strategy should be altered and the struggle should continue in accordance with international standards of legitimacy."

On September 2, 2002, Palestinan Minister of Interior Abdel Razek El Hyhia said once more that the path of violence must be abandoned and suggested civil disobedience instead. During this period the IDF continued to implement its policy of "focused preemption," the detention of wanted people, and its search for explosives and weapons.

On July 23, 2002, in accordance with its "focused preemption" policy, the IDF killed Tzalah Sh'hade, the commander of the military arm of the Hamas in the Gaza Strip. The house where Sh'hade was staying was bombed by the Israeli air force and 15 Palestinians were killed and 120 were wounded. The operation was condemned by international officials such as the UN Secretary General and the European Union; President Bush's reaction, however, was more moderate: "The president expresses his sorrow for the loss of innocent lives and Israel should consider the consequences of its actions." The Arab League convened, following the event, and called upon the Security Council not to be satisfied with a condemnation but to adopt practical steps and to bring the "war criminals" to justice.

On July 29, 2002, the Palestinian Leadership headed by Arafat met in Ramallah and called upon the Security Council to adopt a binding resolution that would bring about a cease-fire, and an Israeli withdrawal to the September 28, 2000, lines. They also suggested that international observers be sent to the region.

The Palestinian Legislative Council gathered on September 9, 2002. In his speech to the Council, Arafat called for an end to the attacks against innocent civilians, since they functioned as an excuse for Israel to escalate its military operations against the Palestinian people. The spokesman for the American State Department, Richard Baucher, praised Arafat's message reservedly, and said that such statements had been heard in the past and that the United States was still looking for a new Palestinian Authority leadership.

The suicide attack on a Tel Aviv bus (September 9, 2002) set the IDF in motion once again, and it initiated Operation "a Matter of Time." Arafat's bureau came under siege once again, parts of the Muqata'ah in Ramallah that were still standing were destroyed, and Israel demanded the extradition of the terrorists hidden within. Once more a curfew was imposed on West Bank cities.

This operation brought no results of consequence. The character of the operation and its timing were inopportune and both the European Union and the United States, which was occupied with its preparations for the war in Iraq, exerted pressure upon Israel.

The Security Council passed a resolution calling upon Israel to lift the siege it was maintaining on the Muqata'ah in Ramallah. The United States abstained from voting on the measure but did not impose a veto as on previous occasions, in order to emphasize its discontent over Israel's operation. President Bush said: "The IDF operation does not help the development or the establishment of the required institutions for the founding of the Palestinian State." In an explicit message to the prime minister delivered by the American ambassador, Bush said: "Put an end to the siege on Arafat as soon as possible and do not interfere with the Iraqi issue."

The United States clarified that Israel's operation in the Muqata'ah interfered with its efforts to form an international coalition for the Iraqi operation and therefore Israel had to put an end to the siege and withdraw its forces without finding a solution for the terrorists entrenched in Arafat's headquarters.

On September 30, 2002, the IDF withdrew from the Muqata'ah and Arafat triumphantly left his besieged headquarters, allowing some of the terrorists hiding there to go free. The United States was satisfied when the siege on the Muqata'ah ended and the Palestinian public saw the withdrawal as a victory. The operation strengthened Arafat's position and brought back some of the Palestinian public's support.

THE PALESTINIAN AUTHORITY REFORMS

Already on January 28, 2002, following the capture of the *Karin A* and the presentation of substantive proof to the American administration regarding the Palestinian Authority's direct involvement in the planning and execution of attacks, President Bush said that he did not regard Arafat as a partner in the war against terrorism. "When the weapons ship arrived it caused me great disappointment, I thought that he would help us in the fight against terrorism."

The United States was not the only country to express disappointment regarding Arafat—Egypt, Jordan, and Saudi Arabia, interested in being regarded by the Western world as countries nonsupportive of terrorism, began to signal Arafat that he should intensify his war efforts against terrorist acts and their perpetrators. King Abdullah of Jordan even expressed his dissatisfaction publicly and during a visit to the United States, stated: "I am disappointed with Arafat."

Joining the ranks of the disappointed were European Union countries, which until then had been sympathetic of Arafat's moves and had openly supported the immediate establishment of a Palestinian State.

Documents captured during Operation Defensive Shield clearly testifying to the complicity of the Palestinian Authority in terror and economic corruption added to the overall disappointment in Arafat and his leadership. A direct by-product of this disappointment was the beginning of the reformation of the Palestinian Authority's governmental apparatus, a tumultuous process that would be subject to many ups and downs.

On May 6, 2002, at the meeting between Prime Minister Sharon and President Bush, ideas for a structural reform of the Palestinian Authority were presented. The Americans spoke of the creation of a "pseudogovernment," that is, the establishment of a temporary government that would govern the Palestinian Authority until new elections were held and a new constitution was ratified. The Americans expressed their satisfaction at the unprecedented statements in support of the democratization of the Palestinian governmental apparatus. In their conversation, Sharon said to Bush that Israel must not be involved in the reformation process not even outwardly, so that the success of the process would be facilitated. President Bush noted that it was important to integrate the European Union in the reformation process, because the Europeans were the main contributors and financiers of the Palestinian Authority.

The coordination of the president's and the prime minister's position, during Sharon's visit to Washington in May 2002, as well as the persisting suicide attacks against Israel, were another sign of the sharp turn in the American position regarding Arafat. This was also expressed in the President's June 24 speech, in which he conditioned American support for the establishment of a Palestinian State with the replacement of Arafat and the implementation of reforms that would lead to new governmental norms in the political, economic, and security apparatuses of the Palestinian authority.

Following President Bush's speech, Arafat felt that his hold on the reins of power was loosening and that he could not avoid the adoption of concrete steps that would bring about changes in the Palestinian Authority's institutions. Therefore, he announced his intention to hold elections for the Legislative Council and the presidency in January 2003, and for local government no later than March 2003.

On June 9, 2002, Arafat formed a new interim government, and Yasser Abed Rabu, the minister of propaganda, summoned a press conference. Abed Rabu explained that the principles guiding the composition of the government were reformation, transparency, rehabilitation because of the damage caused by the Israeli army, and a cut in government expenses. According to Abed Rabu, twelve ministers were dismissed and seven were moved to different ministries. The numbers of ministers was cut from thirty-one to twenty-one and five new ministers were appointed. The new appointees were Salem Fiad, who had previously headed the World Monetary Fund delegation in the territories, to the Finance Ministry; General Abed el Razek el Hi'hia to the Ministry of Interior—his responsibilities included directing the Palestinian security apparatuses; Dr. Ghazan el Khatib, a lecturer at the University of Bir Zeit, to the Ministry of Labor; Dr. Naim Abu el Hummus to the Ministry of Education; and Ibrahim Durma to the Ministry of Justice. The appointment of Fiad as minister of finance was in conformity with American criteria and Legislative Council demands. Fiad was a professional whose job would be to uproot unorthodox financial norms prevalent in the Palestinian Authority.

On June 26, 2002, the new Palestinian cabinet, which had begun its term on June 12, presented the "100-day plan." The plan had been formulated by a ministerial committee headed by the minister of propaganda and culture, Abed Rabu, and was described in detail at a press conference by the minister in charge of local authority, Saib Arikat. Arikat emphasized that the plan had begun to take shape before President Bush delivered his speech, and was in accordance with Palestinian interests and not a response to external pressure. The plan called upon the Palestinian cabinet to begin implementing the principle of separation of powers immediately, as well as other reformative steps.

This move was proof that the demand for the reformation and democratization of the Palestinian Authority governmental apparatus did not originate solely from the outside, but was an internal Palestinian desire, that until then had not been heard in public.

During July 2002, Arafat continued his implementation of the reforms. He dismissed some of the authority's elite and appointed Muhammad Dahlan, the head of preventive security in Gaza, to be the Palestinian Authority's national security advisor and assigned him the task of rehabilitating the Palestinian security apparatuses in the territories.

Senior officers in the IDF were aware of the changes taking place within the Palestinian Authority and saw it as proof that their political and military policies were correct. The exiting chief of staff, Shaul Mofaz, said: "A change has begun in the Palestinian Authority, part of which is a weakening of Arafat's status who is regarded as irrelevant to the solution of the conflict both in the international community as well as among Arabs." Another statement in the same vein was made on August 10, 2002, by the exiting head of Central Command, General Yitzhak Ethan: "The Palestinians are going through a major upheaval, because of operation 'Defensive Shield' and other IDF actions. An underground debate is going on. The majority of the participants in this debate do not dare express their opinion publicly—as of yet, but most of them understand that they have lost the campaign against Israel."

On July 17, 2002, the ministers of the "Quartet" (the foreign ministers of the United States, Europe, Russia, and the UN) convened and discussed the establishment of an international "task force" that would assist the Palestinians in the implementation of the reforms. Contrary to the American position, that is, the imperative of finding a replacement for Arafat in order to facilitate the advance towards a Palestinian State, the Quartet saw Arafat as the legitimate leader until elections were held and a new leader was elected and expressed willingness to negotiate with him. At the same time, they agreed with the objectives formulated by Bush in his June 24 speech—to fight terrorism, the establishment of a Palestinian State within three years, and the alleviation of the harsh living conditions in the territories.

On July 21, 2002, the American administration published the revised Tenet plan for the reformation of the Palestinian Authority's security apparatuses. The plan was based upon three principles:

1. The unification of Palestinian security forces under the authority of two or three organizations, the operation of which would be governed by a unified civil authority, and the transfer of authority to this unified security apparatus in places the IDF withdraws from.

2. The exclusion of individuals involved in terrorist activities from service in the security apparatus and the recruitment of new forces with Egyptian and American aid. The security forces would be cut off from any control of the financial sector. A team headed by Americans would supervise the implementation of the initial stages of the plan.

3. According to the American plan, following the implementation of security and economic reforms, preparations for general elections would begin. A Palestinian prime minister would be appointed, subordinate to Arafat, and if peace and quiet prevailed, direct negotiations between Palestinians and Israelis regarding the establishment of the temporary Palestinian State would be initiated.

On August 8, 2002, the Fatah movement called upon Arafat to appoint Abu Mazen as prime minister, a call that Arafat rejected saying that he would appoint a prime minister only when the occupation ended and an independent Palestinian State was established. (On June 6 Arafat rejected a Legislative Council proposal to hold a vote of confidence.) On August 9, 2002, Arafat said in an interview with the media that American, Jordanian, and Egyptian security officers would supervise the reformation of Palestinian security forces and train the recruits. This declaration marked the essential acceptance of the Tenet plan for the reformation of the Palestinian security apparatus published by the Americans on July 21, 2002.

The Palestinian organizations gathered in order to formulate an inclusive political platform, specifying national goals and the means by which these goals were to be achieved and called for the democratization of the governmental apparatus. On August 14 Arafat authorized the establishment of "a Palestinian investment fund" as another step in the implementation of the economic reform.

The "task force" composed of representatives from the countries who had contributed to the teams supervising the implementation of the Palestinian Authority reforms met in Paris on August 23 with Palestinian representatives and were favorably impressed by the progress made in the implementation of the reforms in the economic sphere.

In spite of these measures, seen as positive steps towards the implementation of the reforms, the Palestinian cabinet resigned on September 11, 2002, after it became clear that the majority of Legislative Council members intended to support the "no confidence" vote.

Arafat was charged with the formation of a new cabinet within two weeks, which would function as an interim cabinet, because of the Presidential Order signed by Arafat on September 10 calling for elections for the presidency and the Legislative Council on January 20. On September 15, senior security officials arrived from Egypt and Jordan and convened in Jericho in order to begin the formation and instruction of the new Palestinian security force in accordance with the reformation plan.

THE ESTABLISHMENT OF THE NEW PALESTINIAN GOVERNMENT

Following the resignation of the Palestinian cabinet in September 2002, Arafat was charged with the formation of a new government. Internal and external pressure was exerted on Arafat to make far-reaching changes in his government, the main demand being the removal of officials suspected of corruption or the illegitimate use of the Authority's funds for their personal purposes. Arafat was supposed to have inaugurated his government in September 2002, but the IDF's operation in the Muqata'ah was a convenient excuse to postpone the formation of a new cabinet.

On October 1, 2002, the Fatah's Central Committee decided to postpone the nomination of the prime minister, hoping to focus the pressure on Israel and the United States rather than Arafat and thus relieve his political distress. At the conclusion of the meeting on October 2, 2002, a resolution was adopted extending Arafat's deadline by three weeks.

In the background, the media was abuzz with conjectures and commentary regarding the identity of the prime minister Arafat would nominate. One of the candidates mentioned most often was the richly experienced Abu Mazen, who had negotiated with the Israelis in the past.

The United States continued to insist that part of Arafat's wide-reaching authorities be transferred to the future Palestinian leadership, and that if this condition was not met the Americans would consider their reformation demands unfulfilled. On October 9, Arafat attacked this American involvement and suggested that they pressure Israel to fully implement the cease-fire. On October 29, the Palestinian cabinet was presented to the Palestinian Legislative Council. It did not differ in essence from its predecessor, but in spite of this the council approved its composition. The new government did not fundamentally change its policies and the promised reforms were not implemented.

A Palestinian prime minister was not appointed and Arafat's authority remained as it was. The new government's composition changed somewhat, but it was a cosmetic change and not a fundamental one.

THE FORMULATION OF A NEW AMERICAN PLAN: "THE ROAD MAP"

In early October 2002, the American administration had already begun to formulate a new political plan for the resolution of the Israeli-Palestinian issue as an extension of Bush's June 24 speech.

On October 1, the PLO representative in Washington, Hassan Abdul el Rahman, said that administration representatives had informed him of the arrival of American Undersecretary of State William Burns to the region in order to present the plan to the Israelis and Palestinians.

Prime Minister Sharon left Israel on October 15 for a visit to Washington. On the morrow, President Bush presented Sharon with the new American plan for the resolution of the Israeli-Palestinian conflict, which from then on was called the "Road Map."

THE ROAD MAP INCLUDES THREE MAIN STAGES

The first stage or the "Emergency stage" was supposed to be implemented until mid-2003. Its focus was calming the situation, ending the violence, and implementing the promised reformation of the Palestinian Authority, including a partial reduction of Arafat's authority and especially the reformation of the Palestinian security apparatus. Israel would implement parallel humanitarian steps, it would remove roadblocks, discontinue sieges, and would not impose curfews on the cities.

If deemed successful and after a cessation of violence, Israel would withdraw IDF forces and redeploy to positions previously occupied on September 28, 2000.

The second stage would be implemented by the end of 2003 and would include Palestinian Authority elections and afterwards an international conference that would lead to the establishment of an independent Palestinian State with temporary borders and international guarantees.

The third stage would be implemented by the end of 2005. This stage would include permanent status negotiations and the achievement of an agreement. The Egyptian and Jordanian ambassadors would be returned to Tel Aviv and other confidence-building measures would be adopted by the Arab world. The process would be completed by the end of 2005, or the beginning of 2006 at the latest.

On October 26, 2002, William Burns, the American envoy to the Middle East, met with Foreign Minister Simon Peres in Israel. Peres told the guest that "The road map had political potential" but added that Israel had reservations regarding security issues. Israel demanded that the Palestinians be compelled to take significant steps in the war against terror from the beginning. Israel also opposed the Quartet's jurisdiction to decide when and whether to proceed from one stage to the next. The following day the American envoy met with Prime Minister Sharon who commented on the American plan, and demanded once again that the Palestinians fight terrorism from the outset.

On October 24, William Burns held several meetings with senior representatives of the Palestinian Authority as part of his effort to formulate a final version of the "Road Map." The Palestinians claimed that the American plan seemed to be a serious one but that several reservations needed to be included in their official response to the American initiative. The Palestinians claimed that a rigid timetable should be imposed in order to ensure Israeli compliance. In their opinion Israel would have a hard time meeting the plan's requirements and its fulfillment must be ensured. Arafat said that the American plan was "positive." There was opposition to the plan, however, among his newly elected ministers (see previous discussion) who claimed that the temporary state mentioned in the plan was confined to Areas A and B and that its area would be no greater than 50 percent of the territory conquered by Israel in 1967. Another claim voiced by the opposition was that the plan did not mention the immediate halt of settlement activity.

In spite of the Palestinian reservations, Arafat stated (November 12, 2002) that the Palestinian Authority accepted the "Road Map" on principle but "was still discussing the issue with other Arab countries and would soon deliver their official position."

The next day the Palestinian delegation met with David Satterfield in order to discuss the "Road Map." During the meeting the Palestinian delegation presented its reservations to the plan and made the following demands:

- A clear definition as to when settlement activity would cease

- A timetable for the establishment of a Palestinian State

- The reopening of Palestinian Institutions in Jerusalem, closed by Israel

At the conclusion of the meeting, Saib Arikath said that the sides had agreed that the United States would present the final draft of the "Road Map" to the Quartet in mid-December 2002. This contradicted a statement made by Israeli officials in Jerusalem who had said that the prime minister's request to freeze the "Road Map" until after the Israeli elections and the formation of a new government was accepted.

On November 11, 2002, the prime minister held a special meeting to discuss Israel's position regarding the "Road Map." The prime minister had reservations concerning major portions of the draft, but at the same time thought that Israel must address these issues unobtrusively and try not to create a political crisis. The prime minister's decision, therefore, was to ask the Americans if Israel could postpone the delivery of their response. This marked the prime minister's acceptance of Foreign Minister Netanyahu's proposal that the implementation or nonimplementation of the "Road Map" be dealt with after the war in Iraq. It also echoed Defense Minister Mofaz's serious reservations.

On November 12, 2002, the American administration consented to the prime minister's request to put the "Road Map" on hold until after the elections and the formation of a new government. The Palestinians and the Europeans were not appreciative. Following United States' acceptance of the delay, the presentation of the new version of the plan with the Palestinian and Israeli comments, as well as those of the Quartet, was postponed from December 2002 to March 2003. (The plan was not presented in March either, due to the American involvement in the Iraqi war).

The schedule of the revised version of the plan was formulated in November 2002. By May 2003, the plan called for a cessation of terrorist activities and other forms of violence, normalization of Palestinian life, and the establishment of Palestinian institutions. Israel would withdraw from Palestinian territory and the pre-Intifadah status quo would be reinstated, as well as security cooperation, as per the Tenet plan. Construction in the settlements would be frozen, as per the Mitchell plan.

From July to December 2003 the "Interim stage" would be implemented. This would include the establishment of a Palestinian State with temporary borders and a new constitution. An international conference headed by the Quartet would be convened "after consultation with both sides" (in the original version both sides had to agree to the conference). After the conference Israeli-Palestinian negotiations would begin regarding the establishment of a Palestinian State with temporary borders. After the State's establishment, the members of the Quartet would strive for the international recognition of the Palestinian State and its acceptance as a member of the UN (this paragraph remains controversial).

In 2004 and 2005, the "Road Map" would reach its final and permanent stage. The revised version formulated in November 2002 stipulates that the objective of the agreement was to end the Israeli-Palestinian conflict. At the beginning of 2004 a second international conference would be convened, the Palestinian State would be declared with the blessing of the international community, and permanent status negotiations would commence.

The revised version of the "Road Map" contains a "Jerusalem clause" not found in the original October draft, which stipulates "that negotiations regarding Jerusalem's final status would take the political and religious concerns of both sides into account and would protect the religious interests of Jews, Christians, and Moslems worldwide."

Since the initiation of Operation Defensive Shield, Palestinian voices began to be heard against suicide bombings, for although suicide bombings were a highly lethal weapon, they severely damaged the Palestinians' image in the West, and the IDF's harsh response to the attacks such as curfews and sieges made it impossible to lead a normal life. These first signs of criticism were expressed at the Fatah's general convention in November 2002.

At the beginning of the discussions concerning the American "Road Map," the Palestinians wished to create the impression of cooperation with the United States, which compelled the Palestinian Authority to accommodate American pressure regarding the achievement of a cease-fire. It was evident that in this atmosphere suicide attacks made the process difficult, increased international criticism against Palestinians, and was harmful to them. The heads of the Hamas, however, did not feel committed to the road map nor to the efforts to achieve a cease-fire, and made a declaration to this effect on November 11, 2002, saying that they would not put an end to the suicide attacks and that they considered this tactic the best way to fight Israel.

Talks between representatives of the Fatah and Hamas organizations in Cairo under Egyptian patronage concluded on November 13, 2002, and among other issues, they discussed their differences of opinion regarding suicide attacks. Egypt participated in the discussions as a mediator, aiming to be the one to successfully hammer out an agreement between the organizations. On November 14, 2002, Omar Suliman, the head of the Egyptian intelligence, visited Israel and updated Prime Minister Sharon regarding efforts to achieve an agreement.

The statements published at the end of the talks between the organizations were inconsistent and ambiguous. The official statement to the media was as follows:

- It was decided to use every mean possible to halt the belligerence of the occupying forces.
- Resistance and political struggle were a natural and legitimate right of the Palestinian People.
- An atmosphere propitious for the realization of Palestinian hopes regarding the establishment of an independent state must be sought.

On November 19, 2002, the media reported that elements within the Arab world threatened to discontinue their support, if the Hamas and the Islamic Jihad organizations did not stop their suicide attacks against Israeli targets. A senior Hamas official, Abed el Aziz el Rantisi, responded to these threats by saying that suicide attacks must be increased rather than decreased since they were evidently politically potent. According to Rantisi, the Labor Party's prime ministerial candidate, Amram Mitzna's statement regarding the need to withdraw from the territories was a testimony to the effectiveness of suicide attacks.

A suicide attack in Jerusalem on November 12, 2002, sharpened the internal Palestinian debate concerning the need to achieve an understanding between the Fatah and Hamas organizations regarding their modus operandi vis-à-vis Israel. On November 26, 2002, Abu Mazen called for a halt to suicide attacks, which he said provided Israel with an excuse to continue occupying more Palestinian territory. "I have always been against the use of weapons," said Abu Mazen. "In my opinion it was a mistake to use weapons during the Intifadah, and to perpetrate attacks in Israel since they provide Israel with an excuse to conquer the Gaza Strip. I am not against the use of stones and other nonviolent means."

The dismantling of the Unity government in Israel, the formation of an interim government, and the decision to hold elections (on January 28, 2003), as well as the American preparations for the war in Iraq, brought about a temporary freeze in discussions concerning the "Road Map." The conclusion of the American campaign in Iraq in April 2003 led to the renewal of diplomatic efforts in the Middle East, and the "Road Map" once again became a subject of discussion.

As part of the reformation plan to which the Palestinian Authority had agreed to and after a difficult power struggle with Arafat, a new government headed by Abu Mazen was formed on April 25, 2003.

The establishment of the new Palestinian government and the renewal of political dialogue with Israel on the foundations of the "Road Map" encountered serious opposition in the form of a terrorist campaign initiated by Palestinian terror organizations whose goal was the torpedoing of the process.

Between May 18–20 2003, five suicide attacks took place in which twelve people died and more than seventy were wounded (one suicide attack in Hebron, two attacks in Jerusalem, one in the Gaza Strip, and one in an Afula Mall). Besides the suicide attacks, terrorist organizations increased their shooting of Kassam missiles toward Sderot and other towns in the western Negev, obliging the IDF to engage the terrorist organizations in the Beit Hanun area in order to prevent the shooting of missiles. In the beginning of June 2003, President Bush met with Israeli Prime Minister Sharon and Palestinian Prime Minister Abu Mazen in order to "jump start" the political process. The three made statements regarding their genuine commitment to move towards an agreement. Abu Mazen brokered a cease-fire agreement (also known as the "Hudna") with the various Palestinian factions—an agreement that was meant to give his government a chance to calm the situation. In the beginning of July 2003, Israel transferred security responsibilities in Bethlehem to the Palestinian security apparatus as a first step towards returning the territory to the Palestinians. The IDF withdrew from areas it controlled in the Gaza Strip and even released Palestinian prisoners who had been held in Israel as a gesture of goodwill, meant to bolster Abu Mazen.

The cease-fire, however, was not genuine. The terror organizations used the temporary lull to upgrade their weapons and to recruit more suicide bombers. Israel restrained itself at this time, even after the suicide attacks in Rosh Ha-ayin and Ariel, and focused its operations against "ticking bombs" in an attempt to give Abu Mazen an opportunity to gain a measure of control. The suicide attack on a Jerusalem bus in mid-August compelled Israel to take matters into its own hands, the IDF resumed full-force operations in Palestinian cities, and the policy of focused preemption was reinstated, specifically against Hamas leaders in Gaza.

The "Hudna" collapsed, Abu Mazen quit his job in the beginning of September, and Abu Ala was appointed in his place. The newly appointed prime minister formed a government in October, and is attempting to achieve a new "Hudna" with the various Palestinian factions as these lines are being written.

It is still too soon to determine the fate of the new Palestinian government or the fate of the American "Road Map." It is quite clear, however, that the Israeli-Palestinian conflict is far from ending and that the Palestinian government, to the extent that it is interested in moving the political process forward, will be obliged to face the complex confrontation with radical elements who'd like to continue their armed struggle.

Index

About the Editor
and Contributors

Reuven Aharoni is a teaching Fellow at Haifa University. He is the author (together with Shaul Mishal) of *Speaking Stones—Communiqués from the Intifada,* Albany, New York, 1994. Among his publications in Hebrew are *Leaning Masts: Ships of Jewish Illegal Immigration* and *Arms after World War II,* Ramat Efal, 1998, and (with Yitzhak Reiter) *The Political Life of the Arabs in Israel,* Beit Berl, 1993.

Mordechai Bar-On is currently a Senior Research Fellow at Yad Itzhak Ben-Zvi Institute in Jerusalem. Formerly he was a Senior Fellow both at the U.S. Institute of Peace in Washington, D.C., and the Ben-Gurion Center in Sdeh Boker. A one-time member of Knesset and Chief Education Officer of the IDF, he is the author of six books and numerous articles (mostly in Hebrew). His English publications include *The Gates of Gaza: Israel's Road to Suez and Back, 1955–1957,* New York, 1994, and *In Pursuit of Peace: A History of the Israeli Peace Movement,* Washington, D.C., 1996.

Yigal Eyal is a lecturer at the IDF's Staff and Command College and the Tactical Command College, both attached to the Hebrew University in Jerusalem. He is an expert in strategy, military history, and limited warfare (guerrilla, terror, and insurgency). Previously he held senior command posts in the IDF and was head of its Historical Division. He wrote a number of studies for internal use in the IDF as well as his book, *The First Intifada,* Tel Aviv, 1998 (in Hebrew).

Yoav Gelber is professor of History at Haifa University and head of the Herzl Institute for the Research of Zionist History. He is a prolific writer. Among his publications are *Jewish-Transjordan Relations 1921–1948,* London, 1997, and *Palestine*

1948, Brighton, Sussex, 2001. His Hebrew books of special note are: *The Service of Israeli Jews in the British Army during World War II, Jerusalem 1984,* and *The History of the Jewish Intelligence Services in Palestine 1920–1948,* Tel Aviv 2000.

Ami Gluska had been Aide-de-Camp, private secretary, and spokesman for two of Israel's Presidents: Yitzhak Navon and Chaim Herzog. He later held a senior diplomatic position in the negotiation with the Palestinians and was a senior policy advisor for the Ministry of Public Security and speech writer for Premiers Shimon Peres and Ehud Barak. His Ph.D. thesis at the Hebrew University, "Israel's Military Command and Political Leadership in Face of the Security Problem, 1963–1967," is shortly due for publication.

Shimon Golan is a senior researcher in the History Department of the IDF, specializing in decision-making processes on the strategic level of recent wars. He has written *Allegiance in the Struggle: The Activism in the Labour Movement and in the Dissenting Jewish Clandestine Military Movements 1945–1946,* Efal, 1988 (in Hebrew); and *Hot Border, Cold War: Israel's Security Policy 1949–1953,* Tel Aviv, 2000 (in Hebrew).

Motti Golani is chairman of the Department of Israeli Studies at Haifa University. Among his books are: *Zion in Zionism: The Zionist Policy on the Question of Jerusalem, 1937–1949,* Tel Aviv, 1992 (in Hebrew); *Israel in Search of War: The Sinai Campaign 1955–1956,* Brighton, UK, 1998; *La Guerre du Sinai 1955–1956,* Paris, 2000; *Wars Don't Just Happen: Force, Choice and Responsibility,* Tel Aviv, 2002 (in Hebrew).

Benny Michelsohn, who was once head of the IDF's History Department, is currently a senior consultant on Intelligence and Operations with Wales Ltd. He is an occasional guest lecturer at the Academy of the Ministry of Defence of Japan. He had served for twenty-five years in the IDF as an armor commander and later as a senior intelligence officer. He has published four books and numerous articles in Hebrew, mostly on military history, strategy, and current security affairs.

Michael Oren is a senior fellow at the Shalem Center in Jerusalem. He studied at Princeton and Columbia and had been a fellow at the Ben Gurion Center in Sdeh Boker. He is the author of numerous works on "Great Power" diplomacy and the Arab-Israeli conflict. His most recent book: *Six Days of War: June 1967 and The Making of Modern Middle East,* Oxford, 2003, was rated by the *New York Times* as a best-seller. It secured the Los Angeles Times Prize and the National Jewish Book Award.

Dan Schueftan is a Senior Fellow at the National Security Studies Center of the University of Haifa. He teaches at the political science department of Haifa University and at the Israel Defense Forces National Security College and IDF Command and Staff College. He has published extensively on contemporary Middle Eastern history, with emphasis on Arab-Israeli relations, Inter-Arab politics, and American policy in the Middle East. His books include: *A Jordanian Option—Israel, Jordan and the Palestinians* (1986); *Attrition: Egypt's Post War Political Strategy 1967–1970* (1989); and *Disengagement—Israel and the Palestinian Entity* (1999).

Shaul Shay is head of the Military History Department of the IDF and a Senior Research Fellow at the Policy Institute for Counter Terrorism (ICT). He had in the past served for many years as a senior officer in the IDF's Intelligence Services. Dr. Shay is the author and editor of seven books and numerous articles, such as *The Endless Jihad: The Mugahidin, the Taliban and Bin Laden,* Herzeliya, 2002, and *The Globalization of Terror: The Challenge of Al Qaida and the Response of the International Community,* New Brunswick, 2003.

David Tal is a lecturer in the Department of History at Tel Aviv University. He is the author of *War in Palestine: Strategy and Diplomacy,* London, 2004, and *The Conception of Israel's Security Problems 1949–1956,* Beer Sheva, 1998 (in Hebrew).

Eyal Zisser is an associate professor in the Department of Middle Eastern and African Studies and Senior Research Fellow at the Moshe Dayan Center for Middle Eastern Studies, both at Tel Aviv University. He is the author of *Lebanon: The Challenge of Independence,* London, 1999, and *Asad's Legacy: Syria in Transition,* New York, 2000.